AP COMPARATIVE GOVERNMENT AND POLITICS:

AN ESSENTIAL COURSEBOOK

EIGHTH EDITION

by Ethel Wood

WoodYard Publications

AP Comparative Government and Politics: An Essential Coursebook, Eighth Edition

Published by
WoodYard Publications
285 Main Street
Germantown, NY 12526
Ph. 610-207-1366
Fax 610-372-8401
ejw@woodyardpublications.com

http://woodyardpublications.com

ISBN 978-1-7321410-2-5

TABLE OF CONTENTS

Why Comparative Government and Politics?

I taught social studies classes for many years, mostly at Princeton High School in Princeton, New Jersey. Like most social studies teachers, my experience included classes in United States history and government. I have also published review books, textbooks, readers, and web materials that have required me to do extensive research in various types of American studies. Needless to say, I believe that an education in these areas is incredibly important for high school students, and every secondary curriculum should include them. So why is comparative government and politics particularly significant?

The 21st century has taught us that we cannot ignore the world around us. Happenings around the globe now directly impact our lives, and social studies teachers and students around the country face the challenge of interpreting complex, puzzling events. The AP comparative course focuses on government and politics in other countries and provides a theoretical framework to compare political systems around the world. It is my hope that this book will help students to grasp something of the political complexities of our global environment, and gain some understanding of both commonalities and differences among modern political systems. In today's world, we cannot afford not to know.

Ethel Wood
Germantown, NY
August 2018

Other Books by Ethel Wood

American Government: A Complete Coursebook

AP European History: An Essential Coursebook, 1st, 2nd, and 3rd editions

AP Human Geography: A Study Guide, 1st, 2nd, 3rd, and 4th editions

AP United States History: An Essential Coursebook, 1st, 2nd, and 3rd editions

AP World History: An Essential Coursebook, 1st, 2nd, 3rd, and 4th editions

The Immigrants: An Historical Reader

Introduction to Sociology

Multiple Choice and Free-Response Questions in Preparation for the AP United States Government and Politics Examination, editions 1-7

Multiple Choice and Free-Response Questions in Preparation for the AP World History Examination, editions 1 and 2

Teacher's Guide - AP Comparative Government and Politics, College Board

The Presidency: An Historical Reader

PREFACE: THE COMPARATIVE GOVERNMENT AND POLITICS EXAMINATION

The AP Comparative Government and Politics Examination administered by the College Board in May lasts for two hours and 25 minutes and consists of the following parts:

- 55 multiple-choice questions (45 minutes allowed; 50% of AP grade)

- a 100-minute free response section consisting of 8 questions (50% of AP grade)

The multiple-choice questions cover all the topics listed below, and test knowledge of comparative theory, methods, and government and politics in Britain, Russia, China, Mexico, Iran, and Nigeria. On the exam, the College Board no longer subtracts one-fourth of the number of questions answered incorrectly from the number of questions answered correctly to come up with your score. Since there is no penalty for guessing, it is advisable to answer all questions the best that you can.

The free-response questions are of three types:

- Definition and description (25% of free-response grade) – Students provide brief definitions or descriptions of five concepts or terms, briefly explaining their significance. Students may have to provide an example of the definition or description in one or more of the six core countries.

- Conceptual analysis (one question; 25% of free-response grade) – Students must use major concepts from comparative politics, explain important relationships, or discuss the causes and implications of politics and policy.

- Country context (two questions; 50% of free-response grade; each question 25%) – These questions focus on specific countries, and require students to use core concepts to analyze one country or compare two countries.

The recommended total time for definition and description terms is 30 minutes; for the conceptual analysis question, 30 minutes; and for each of the two country context questions, 20 minutes. However, there are no time divisions among the free-response questions. Instead, a total of 100 minutes is allotted to answer all of them.

Generally, multiple-choice questions are distributed fairly evenly among the six countries. In addition, many questions are not country-specific, but instead test knowledge of the major concepts. According to the College Board, the topics of the multiple choice questions are distributed as follows:

Introduction (methods, purpose of comparisons)............................5%

Sovereignty, Authority, and Power..20%

Political Institutions...35%

Citizens, Society, and State..15%

Political and Economic Change...15%

Public Policy...10%

This newly revised 8th Edition of *AP Comparative Government and Politics: An Essential Coursebook* is designed to help you prepare for the exam by giving you a sound footing in comparative concepts as well as country-specific information about the six core countries. The book is divided into three parts:

- **Part One** – Introduction to Comparative Government and Politics: A Conceptual Approach

- **Part Two** – Country Cases: Advanced Democracies (Great Britain), Communist and Post-Communist Regimes (Russia and China), and Less-Developed and Newly-Developing Countries (Mexico, Iran, and Nigeria)

- **Part Three** – Practice Examinations: Two complete practice exams, each with 55 multiple-choice questions and 8 free-response questions

Your best preparation for the exam is to know your stuff. The questions do require reading and writing skills, but the surer you are of the material, the more likely you are to answer the questions correctly. This book provides the concepts and information, as well as plenty of practice questions that will prepare you for the exam. The most important things are that you learn something about comparative government and politics, and that you learn to love it, too!

PART ONE:
CONCEPTS FOR COMPARISONS

**CHAPTER ONE:
INTRODUCTION TO COMPARATIVE
GOVERNMENT AND POLITICS:
A CONCEPTUAL APPROACH**

Comparative government and politics provides an introduction to the wide, diverse world of governments and political practices that exist in modern times. Although the course focuses on specific countries, it also emphasizes an understanding of conceptual tools and methods that form a framework for comparing almost any governments that exist today. Additionally, it requires students to go beyond individual political systems to consider international forces that affect all people in the world, often in very different ways. Six countries form the core of the course: Great Britain, Russia, China, Mexico, Iran, and Nigeria. The countries are chosen to reflect regional variations, but more importantly, to illustrate how important concepts operate both similarly and differently in different types of political systems: "advanced" democracies, communist and post-communist countries, and newly-industrialized and less-developed nations. This book includes review materials for all six countries.

Goals for the course include:

- Gaining an understanding of major comparative political concepts, themes, and trends

- Knowing important facts about government and politics in Great Britain, Russia, China, Mexico, Iran, and Nigeria

- Identifying patterns of political processes and behavior and analyzing their political and economic consequences

- Comparing and contrasting political institutions and processes across countries

- Analyzing and interpreting basic data for comparing political systems

WHAT IS COMPARATIVE GOVERNMENT AND POLITICS?

Most people understand that the term **government** is a reference to the leadership and institutions that make policy decisions for a country. However, what exactly is **politics?** Politics is basically all about power. Who has the power to make the decisions? How did power-holders get power? What challenges do leaders face from others – both inside and outside the country's borders – in keeping power? So, as we look at different countries, we are not only concerned about the ins and outs of how the government works; we will also look at how power is gained, managed, challenged, and maintained.

College-level courses in comparative government and politics vary in style and organization, but they all cover topics that enable meaningful comparisons across countries. These topics are introduced in the pages that follow, and will be addressed in greater depth when each of the countries is covered separately.

The topics are:

- The Comparative Method

- Sovereignty, Authority, and Power

- Political and Economic Change

- Citizens, Society, and the State

- Political Institutions

- Public Policy

TOPIC ONE: THE COMPARATIVE METHOD

Political scientists sometimes argue about exactly what countries should be studied and how they should be compared. One approach is to emphasize **empirical data** based on factual statements and statistics, and another is to focus on **normative** issues that require value judgments. For example, the first approach might compare statistics that reflect economic development of a group of countries, including information about Gross National Product, per capita income, and amounts of imports and exports. The second approach builds on those facts to focus instead on whether or not the statistics bode well or ill for the countries. Empiricists might claim that it is not the role of political scientists to make such judgments, and their critics would reply that the empirical approach alone leads to meaningless data collection. The approaches give us different but equally important tools for analyzing and comparing political systems.

As with research in any social science, comparative government and politics relies on scientific methods to objectively and logically evaluate data. After reviewing earlier research, scholars formulate a **hypothesis**, a speculative statement about the relationship between two or more factors known as **variables.** Variables are measurable traits or characteristics that change under different conditions. For example, the poverty level in a country may change over time. One question that a comparative researcher might ask is, "Why are poverty rates higher in one country than in others?" In seeking to answer this question, the researcher want to identify which variable or variables may contribute to high levels of poverty. In other words, the researcher is trying to discover **causation** – the idea that one (or more) variable causes or influences another. So a credible hypothesis might be that higher poverty levels are caused by lower levels of formal education. In this hypothesis, one variable (the poverty level) is called the **dependent variable** because it is caused or influenced by another variable (the level of formal education), which is called the **independent variable.** A **correlation** exists when a change in one variable coincides with a change in the other. Correlations are an indication that causality *may* be present; they do not necessarily indicate causation. Comparative researchers seek to identify the causal link between variables by collecting and analyzing data.

How do we go about comparing countries? The model most frequently used until the early 1990s was the **three-world approach,** largely based on cold war politics. The three worlds were 1) the United States and its allies; 2) the Soviet Union and its allies; and 3) **"third world"** nations that did not fit into the first two categories and were economically underdeveloped and deprived. Even though the

TOPICS IN COMPARATIVE GOVERNMENT: VARIABLES, CAUSATION, AND CORRELATION

Variables – measurable traits that change under different conditions.

Causation – the idea that one variable (the independent variable) causes another (the dependent variable)

INDEPENDENT VARIABLE	➡	DEPENDENT VARIABLE

Correlation exists when a change in one variable accompanies a change in another.

Soviet Union collapsed in 1991, this approach is still taken today by many comparative textbooks, whose comparisons are based on democracy vs. authoritarianism and communism vs. capitalism. Even though this method is still valid, newer types of comparisons between countries are reflected in the following three trends:

- **The impact of informal politics** – Governments have formal positions and structures that may be seen on an organizational chart, but these formal elements are not all that there is to political systems. For example, in formal terms Great Britain is led by a prime minister and has a House of Lords and a House of Commons. In comparison, the United States has a president, a Senate, and a House of Representatives. You may directly compare the responsibilities and typical activities of each position or structure in Britain to its counterpart in the United States. However, you gain a deeper understanding of both political systems if you connect **civil society** – the way ~~OUTSIDE gov~~ that citizens organize and define themselves and their interests – to the ways that the formal government operates. **Informal politics** takes into consideration not only the ways that politicians operate outside their formal powers, but also the impact that beliefs, values, and actions of ordinary citizens have on policy-making.

- **The importance of political change** – One reason that the three-world approach has become more problematic in recent years is that the nature of world politics has changed. Since 1991, the world no longer is dominated by two superpowers, and that fact has had consequences that have reverberated in many areas that no one could have predicted. However, it creates an opportunity to compare the impact of change on many different countries.

- **The integration of political and economic systems** – Even though we may theoretically separate government and politics from the economy, the two are often intertwined almost inextricably. For example, communism and capitalism are theoretically economic systems, but how do you truly separate them from government and politics? Attitudes and behavior of citizens are affected in many ways by economic inefficiency, economic inequality, and economic decision making. If citizens turn to the government for solutions to economic problems and government does not respond, they may revolt, or take other actions that demand attention from the political elite.

Keeping these trends in mind, in this book we will study countries in three different groups that are in some ways similar in their political and economic institutions and practices. These groups are:

- **"Advanced" democracies** – These countries have well established democratic governments and a high level of economic development. Of the six core countries that we study in this course, Great Britain represents this group.

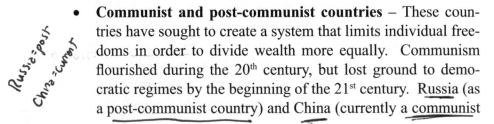

- **Communist and post-communist countries** – These countries have sought to create a system that limits individual freedoms in order to divide wealth more equally. Communism flourished during the 20th century, but lost ground to democratic regimes by the beginning of the 21st century. Russia (as a post-communist country) and China (currently a communist country) represent this group in our study of comparative government and politics.

- **Less-developed and newly-industrializing countries** – We will divide the countries traditionally referred to as the "Third World" into two groups, still very diverse within the categories. The newly-industrializing countries are experiencing rapid economic growth, and also have shown a tendency toward democratization and political and social stability. Mexico and Iran represent this group, although, as you will see, Iran has many characteristics that make it difficult to categorize as one or the other. Less-developed countries lack significant economic development, and they also tend to have authoritarian governments. Nigeria represents this group, although it has shown some signs of democratization in very recent years.

Important concepts that enable meaningful comparisons among countries are introduced in this chapter, and will be addressed with each of the individual countries separately. However, it is important to remember that the main point of comparative government and politics is to use the categories to compare among countries. For example, never take the approach of "Here's Britain," "Here's Russia," without noting what similarities and differences exist between the two countries.

TOPIC TWO: SOVEREIGNTY, AUTHORITY, AND POWER

We commonly speak about powerful individuals, but in today's world, power is territorially organized into **states,** or countries, that control what happens within their borders. What exactly is a state? German scholar Max Weber defined state as the organization that maintains a monopoly of violence over a territory. In other words, the state defines who can and cannot use weapons and force, and it sets the rules as to how violence is used. States often sponsor armies, navies, and/or air forces that legitimately use power and sometimes violence, but individual citizens are very restricted in their use of force. States also include **institutions**: stable, long-lasting organizations that help to turn political ideas into policy. Common examples of institutions are bureaucracies, legislatures, judicial systems, and political parties. These institutions make states themselves long-lasting, and often help

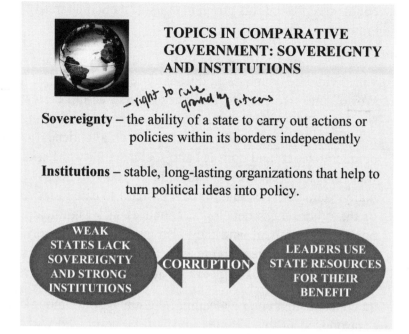

TOPICS IN COMPARATIVE GOVERNMENT: SOVEREIGNTY AND INSTITUTIONS

— right to rule granted by citizens

Sovereignty – the ability of a state to carry out actions or policies within its borders independently

Institutions – stable, long-lasting organizations that help to turn political ideas into policy.

> WEAK STATES LACK SOVEREIGNTY AND STRONG INSTITUTIONS ◀ CORRUPTION ▶ LEADERS USE STATE RESOURCES FOR THEIR BENEFIT

them to endure even when leaders change. By their very nature, states exercise **sovereignty,** the ability to carry out actions or policies within their borders independently from interference either from the inside or the outside.

A state that is unable to exercise sovereignty lacks autonomy, and because it is not independent, it may be exploited by leaders and/or organizations that see the state as a resource to use for their own ends. Frequently, the result is a high level of corruption. The problem is particularly prevalent in newly-industrializing and less-developed countries, largely because their governments lack autonomy. For example, military rulers in Nigeria stole vast amounts of money from the state during the 1990s, making it one of the most corrupt countries in the world. Today Nigeria's tremendous revenues from oil largely evaporate before they reach ordinary citizens, providing evidence that corruption is still a major issue in Nigeria.

States, Nations, and Regimes

States do much more than keep order in society. Many have important institutions that promote general welfare – such as health, safe transportation, and effective communication systems – and economic stability. The concept of state is closely related to a **nation,** a group of people bound together by a common political identity. **Nationalism** is the sense of belonging and identity that distinguishes one nation from another. Nationalism is often translated as patriotism, or the resulting pride and loyalty that individuals feel toward their nations. For more than 200 years now, national borders ideally have been drawn along the lines of group identity. For example, people within one area think of themselves as "French," and people in another area think of themselves as "English." Even though individual differences exist within nations, the nation has provided the overriding identity for most of its citizens. However, the concept has always been problematic – as when "Armenians" live inside the borders of a country called "Azerbaijan." Especially now that globalization and fragmentation provide counter trends, the nature of nationalism and its impact on policymaking are clearly changing.

Variations of the Nation State

A **binational** or **multinational state** is one that contains more than one nation. The former Soviet Union is a good example of a multinational state. It was divided into fifteen "soviet republics" that were based on nationality, such as the Ukraine, Kazakhstan, Estonia, Latvia, and Lithuania. When the country fell apart in 1991, it fell along ethnic boundaries into independent nation-states. Today Russia (one of the former soviet republics) remains in itself a large multinational state that governs many ethnic groups. Just as ethnic pressures challenged the sovereignty of the Soviet government, the Russian government has faced "breakaway movements" – such as in Chechnya – that have threatened Russian stability. Minority ethnic groups may feel so strongly about their separate identities that they demand their independence. **Stateless nations** are a people without a state. In the Middle East the Kurds are a nation of some 20 million people divided among six states and dominant in none. Kurdish nationalism has survived over the centuries, and has played an important role in the politics that followed the reconfiguration of Iraq after the Iraqi War that began in 2003.

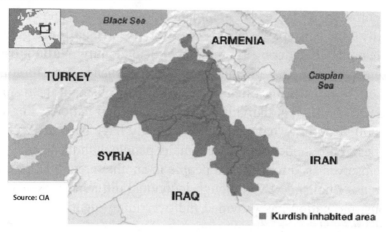

A Stateless Nation. The Kurds have had a national identity for many centuries, but they have never had a state. Instead, 20 million Kurds are spread in an area that crosses the formal borders of six countries: Turkey, Syria, Iraq, Iran, Armenia, and Azerbaijan.

Core Areas

Most of the early nation-states grew over time from **core areas**, expanding outward along their frontiers. Their growth generally stopped when they bumped up against other nation-states, causing them to define boundaries. Today most European countries still have roughly the same core areas as long ago, and many countries in other parts of the world also have well-defined core areas. They may be identified on a map by examining population distributions and transportation networks. As you travel away from the core area, into the state's **periphery** (outlying areas), towns get smaller, factories fewer, and open land more common. Clear examples of core areas are the Paris Basin in France and Japan's Kanto Plain, centered on the city of Tokyo. States with more than one core area – **multicore states** – may be problematic, especially if the areas are ethnically diverse, such as in Nigeria. Nigeria's northern core is primarily Muslim and its southern core is Christian, and the areas pull the country in different directions. To compensate for this tendency for the country to separate, the capital city was moved from Lagos (in the South) to Abuja, near the geographic center of the state.

A multicore character is not always problematic for a country. For example, the United States still has a primary core area that runs along its northeastern coastline from Washington D.C. to Boston. A secondary core area exists on the West Coast that runs from San Diego in the south to San Francisco in the north. Arguably, other core areas have developed around Chicago and other Midwestern cities, and Atlanta in the South. Despite the multiple core areas, regional differences do not threaten the existence of the state, as they do in Nigeria.

The rules that a state sets and follows in exerting its power are referred to collectively as a **regime.** Regimes endure beyond individual governments and leaders. We refer to a regime when a country's institutions and practices carry over across time, even though leaders and particular issues change. Regimes may be compared by using these two categories: democracies and authoritarian systems.

Democracies

Regime change: Democracy → Author.
↳ NEED change of institutions + process

This type of regime bases its authority on the will of the people. Democracies may be **indirect,** with elected officials representing the people, or they may be **direct**, when individuals have immediate say over many decisions that the government makes. Most democracies are indirect, mainly because large populations make it almost impossible for individuals to have a great deal of direct influence on how they are governed. Democratic governments typically have three major branches: executives, legislatures, and judicial courts. Some democracies are **parliamentary systems** – where citizens vote for legislative representatives, who in turn select the leaders of the executive branch. Others are **presidential systems** – where citizens vote for legislative representatives as well as for executive branch leaders, and the two branches function with separation of powers. Democratic governments vary in the degree to which they regulate/control the economy, but businesses, corporations, and/or companies generally operate somewhat independently from the government.

parliament - elect legislature → pick executive

- **Parliamentary systems** – In this type of democracy, the principle of **parliamentary sovereignty** governs the decision-making process. Theoretically, the legislature makes the laws, controls finances, appoints and dismisses the prime minister and the cabinet (the other ministers), and debates public issues. In reality, however, strong party discipline within the legislature develops over time, so that the cabinet initiates legislation and makes policy. The majority party in the legislature almost always votes for the bills proposed by its leadership (the prime minister and cabinet members). Even though the opposition party or parties are given time to criticize, the legislature eventually supports decisions made by the executive branch. Because the prime minister and cabinet are also the leaders of the majority party in the legislature, no separation of powers exists between the executive and legislative branches. Instead, the two branches are fused together. Also typical of the parliamentary system is a separation in the executive branch between a **head of state** (a role that symbolizes the power and nature of the regime) and a **head of government** (a role that deals with the everyday tasks of running the government). For example, in Great Britain, the queen is the head of state who seldom formulates and executes policy, and the prime minister is the head of government who directs the country's decision-making process in his or her position as leader of the majority party in parliament.

- **Presidential systems** – In this type of democracy, the roles of head of state and head of government are given to one person – the president. This central figure is directly elected by the people and serves as the chief executive within a system of **checks and balances** between the legislative and executive (and sometimes judicial) branches. The **separation of powers** between branches ensures that they share power and that one branch does not come to dominate the others. As a result, power is diffused and the policymaking process is sometimes slowed down because one branch may question decisions that another branch makes. In order for presidential systems to truly diffuse power, each branch must have an independent base of authority recognized and respected by politicians and the public. The United States is a presidential system, as are Nigeria and Mexico. As we will see, an important question is whether or not the branches have truly independent bases of authority in Mexico and Nigeria.

TOPICS IN COMPARATIVE GOVERNMENT: REGIME TYPE – DEMOCRACY

Parliamentary System	Presidential System
Principle of parliamentary sovereignty – Legislature makes laws, controls finances, appoints and dismisses prime minister. **No separation of powers** – Prime minister and cabinet are leaders of the majority party in the legislature. **Separation in the executive branch exists** between a head of state and a head of government.	**Roles of head of state and head of government** are combined (president). President is **directly elected** by voters. A system of **checks and balances** and **separation of powers** exists between branches of the government. **"Gridlock"** is a common problem.

Some countries combine elements of the presidential and parliamentary systems, as is illustrated in Russia's 1993 Constitution. Although Russia is a questionable democracy, the Constitution clearly provides for a **semi-presidential system** where a prime minister coexists with a president who is directly elected by the people and who holds a significant degree of power. Until recently, the Russian president has had a disproportionate amount of power, but the prime minister's position became much more important when Vladimir Putin, after serving two terms as president, took the position in 2008. Since Putin was elected president again in 2012 and 2018, the presidency has regained its previous power. In other semi-presidential systems – such as France and India – the amount of power held by each executive is quite different.

Authoritarian Regimes

In this type of regime, decisions are made by political **elites** – those who hold political power – without much input from citizens. These regimes may be ruled by a single dictator, an hereditary monarch, a small group of aristocrats, or a single political party. The economy is generally tightly controlled by the political elite. Some authoritarian regimes are based on **communism**, a theory developed in the 19th century by Karl Marx and altered in the early 20th century by V. I. Lenin and Mao Zedong. In these regimes, the communist party controls everything from the government to the economy to social life. Other authoritarian regimes practice **corporatism** – an arrangement in which government officials interact with people/groups outside the government before they set policy. These outside contacts are generally business and labor leaders, or they may be heads of huge **patron-client systems** that provide reciprocal favors and services to their supporters.

Common characteristics of authoritarian regimes include:

- A small group of elites exercising power over the state

- Citizens with little or no input into selection of leaders and government decisions

- No constitutional responsibility of leaders to the public

- Restriction of civil rights and civil liberties

Authoritarianism and Totalitarianism

A common misconception about authoritarian regimes is that they are not legitimate governments. If the people accept the authority of the leaders, and other countries recognize the regime's right to rule, authoritarian regimes may be said to be legitimate.

Many people think of authoritarianism and **totalitarianism** as the same thing, but the term "totalitarian" has many more negative connotations, and is almost always used to describe a particularly repressive, often detested, regime. For example, during the Cold War era, westerners often referred to the Soviet Union as a "totalitarian regime." However, authoritarian systems are not necessarily totalitarian in nature. Unlike totalitarian regimes, authoritarian governments do not necessarily seek to control and transform all aspects of the political and economic systems of the society. Totalitarian regimes generally have a strong ideological goal (like communism) that many authoritarian systems lack, and authoritarian governments do not necessarily use violence as a technique for destroying any obstacles to their governance.

Military Rule

One form of nondemocratic rule is **military rule**, especially prevalent today in Latin America, Africa, and parts of Asia. In states where legitimacy and stability are in question, and especially when violence is threatened, the military may intervene directly in politics, since it often is the only organization that can resolve the chaos. Military rule usually begins with a **coup d'état**, a forced takeover of the government. The coup may or may not have widespread support among the people. Once they take control, military leaders often restrict civil rights and liberties, and, in the name of order, keep political parties from forming and elections from taking place. Military rule usually lacks a specific ideology, and the leaders often have no charismatic or traditional source of authority, so they join forces with the state bureaucracy to form an authoritarian regime. Military rule may precede democracy, as occurred in South Korea and Taiwan during the 1990s, or it may create more instability as one coup d'état follows another, reinforcing a weak, vulnerable state.

Corporatism in Authoritarian and Democratic Systems

Modern corporatism is a system in which business, labor, and/or other interest groups bargain with the state over economic policy. In its earliest form corporatism emerged as a way that authoritarian regimes tried to control the public by creating or recognizing organizations to represent the interests of the public. This practice makes the government appear to be less authoritarian, but in reality the practice eliminates any input from groups not sanctioned or created by the state. Only a handful of groups have the right to speak for the public, effectively silencing the majority of citizens in political affairs. Often non-sanctioned groups are banned altogether. For example, in Mexico's one-party system that existed for most of the 20th century, oil wells and refineries were placed under the control of state-run PEMEX, and many private oil businesses were forced out of the country. Corporatism gives the public a limited influence in the policy-making process, but the interest groups are funded and managed by the state. Most

Mexico example of corporatism
⌐ PEMEX 20th cent.

people would rather have a state-sanctioned organization than none at all, so many participate willingly with the hope that the state will meet their needs.

A less structured means of **co-optation**, or the means a regime uses to get support from citizens, is **patron-clientelism**, a system in which the state provides specific benefits or favors to a single person or small group in return for public support. Unlike corporatism, clientelism relies on individual patronage rather than organizations that serve a large group of people. Responsibilities and obligations are based on a hierarchy between elites and citizens. We will see example of clientelism in China, Russia, Mexico, and Nigeria.

More recently, corporatist practices have emerged in democratic regimes as well. In democracies corporatism usually comes into play as the state considers economic policy planning and regulation. In some cases, such as in Scandinavian countries, many major social and economic policies are crafted through negotiations between the representatives of interests and the government agencies. In democracies that have nationalized industries, the directors are state officials who are advised by councils elected by the major interest groups involved. In democracies that do not nationalize industries, many regulatory decisions are made through direct cooperation between government agencies and interests. *compete for influence*

A basic principle of democracy is **pluralism,** a situation in which power is split among many groups that compete for the chance to influence the government's decision making. This competition is an important way that citizens may express their needs to the government, and in a democracy, the government will react to citizens' input. **Democratic corporatism** is different from pluralism in two ways:

1) In democratic pluralism, the formation of interest groups is spontaneous; in democratic corporatism, interest representation is institutionalized through recognition by the state. New groups can only form if the state allows it.

2) In democratic pluralism, the dialogue between interest groups and the state is voluntary and the groups remain autonomous; in democratic corporatism, organizations develop institution-

alized and legally binding links with the state agencies, so that the groups become semi-public agencies, acting on behalf of the state. As a result, groups and individuals lose their freedoms.

Just how much corporatism a democracy will allow before it becomes an authoritarian state is a question of much debate. For example, in the United States, the National Recovery Act of 1934 was judged by the Supreme Court to be unconstitutional, largely because it gave the government too much say in private industries' hiring and production decisions. In more recent years, U.S. government agencies have been criticized for hiring people from private interest groups to fill regulatory positions, allegedly giving special interests control of policy and destroying the ability of the government to guard the public interest. In the 1970s, labor unions in Great Britain were often accused of strong-arming public officials, including the prime minister, into passing labor-friendly policies into law. In all of these cases, the entangling of government and private interests has been criticized for undermining the principle of diffusion of power basic to a democracy.

The Democracy Index

In 2007, *The Economist* Intelligence Unit began publishing a "**Democracy Index**", in which the organization ranks countries around the globe in terms of their democratic practices. The index is based on five categories: electoral process and pluralism, civil liberties, the functioning of government, political participation, and political culture.

Democracy Index 2017, by Regime Type

	# of countries	% of countries	% of world population
Full democracies	19	11.4	4.5
Flawed democracies	57	34.1	44.8
Hybrid regimes	39	23.4	16.7
Authoritarian regimes	52	31.1	34.0

Source: Economist Intelligence Unit, 2018

democracy is a relatively new concept not seen in many regions yet

Countries are categorized into four types of regimes: full democracies, flawed democracies, hybrid regimes, and authoritarian regimes. Of the core countries, the United Kingdom is categorized as a full democracy; Mexico as a flawed democracy; and Nigeria, Russia, China, and Iran as authoritarian regimes.

Legitimacy

Who has political power? Who has the authority to rule? Different countries answer these questions in different ways, but they all answer them in one way or another. Countries that have no clear answers often suffer from lack of political **legitimacy** – or the right to rule, as determined by their own citizens.

Legitimacy may be secured in a number of ways, using sources such as social compacts, constitutions, and ideologies. According to political philosopher Max Weber, legitimacy may be categorized into three basic forms:

- **Traditional legitimacy** rests upon the belief that tradition should determine who should rule and how. For example, if a particular family has had power for hundreds of years, the current ruling members of that family are legitimate rulers because it has always been so. Traditional legitimacy often involves important myths and legends, such as the idea that an ancestor was actually born a god or performed some fantastic feat like pulling a sword out of a stone. Rituals and ceremonies all help to reinforce traditional legitimacy. Most monarchies are based on traditional legitimacy, and their authority is symbolized through crowns, thrones, scepters, and/or robes of a particular color or design. Traditional legitimacy may also be shaped by religion, so that political practices remind people of deep-seated ancient beliefs. For example, the Inca believed that their chief ruler, called the Inca, was a deity descended from the sun, and his status as a god-king was reflected in his elaborate dress, with fine textiles woven just for him. Although the belief in a god-ruler is not generally accepted in the modern world, many leaders in the Middle East today base authority on their ability to interpret *sharia* (traditional religious) law.

- **Charismatic legitimacy** is based on the dynamic personality of an individual leader or a small group. Charisma is an almost indefinable set of qualities that make people want to follow a leader, sometimes to the point that they are willing to give their lives for him or her. For example, Napoleon Bonaparte was a charismatic leader who rose in France during a time when the traditional legitimacy of the monarchy had been shattered. By force of personality and military talent, Napoleon seized control of France and very nearly conquered most of Europe. However, Napoleon also represents the vulnerability of charismatic legitimacy. Once he was defeated, his legitimacy dissolved, and the nation was thrown back into chaos. Charismatic legitimacy is notoriously short-lived because it usually does not survive its founder. A modern example of a charismatic leader was Hugo Chavez, president of Venezuela, who led the country from 1999 until his death in 2013. Chavez so dominated Venezuelan politics with the force of his personality that the country descended into chaos that has continued through the present.

- **Rational-legal legitimacy** is based neither on tradition nor on the force of a single personality, but rather on a system of well-established laws and procedures. This type of legitimacy, then, is highly institutionalized, or anchored by strong institutions (such as legislatures, executives, and/or judiciaries) that carry over through generations of individual leaders. People obey leaders because they believe in the rules that brought them to office, and because they accept the concept of a continuous state that binds them together as a nation. Rational-legal legitimacy is often based on the acceptance of the rule of law that supersedes the actions and statements of individual rulers. The rule may take two forms: 1) **common law** based on tradition, past practices, and legal precedents set by the courts through interpretations of statutes, legal legislation, and past rulings; and 2) **code law** based on a comprehensive system of written rules (codes) of law divided into commercial, civil, and criminal codes. Common law is English in origin and is found in Britain, the United States, and other countries with a strong English influence. Code law is predominant in Europe and countries influenced by the French, German, or Spanish systems. Countries in the comparative government course that have code law systems are China, Mexico, and Russia.

Most modern states today are based on rational-legal legitimacy, although that does not mean that traditional and charismatic legitimacy are not still important. Instead, they tend to exist within the rules of rational-legal legitimacy. For example, charismatic leaders such as Martin Luther King have captured the imagination of the public and have had a tremendous impact on political, social, and economic developments. Likewise, modern democracies, such as Britain and Norway, still maintain the traditional legitimacy of monarchies to add stability and credibility to their political systems.

Many factors contribute to legitimacy in the modern state. In a democracy, the legitimacy of leaders is based on fair, competitive elections and open political participation by citizens. As a result, if the electoral process is compromised, the legitimacy of leadership is likely to be questioned as well. For example, the controversial counting of votes in Florida in the U.S. presidential election of 2000 was a crisis for the country largely because the basic fairness of the electoral process (an important source of legitimacy) was questioned. Factors that encourage legitimacy in both democratic and authoritarian regimes are:

- **Economic well-being** – Citizens tend to credit their government with economic prosperity, and they often blame government for economic hardships, so political legitimacy is reinforced by economic well-being.

- **Historical tradition/longevity** – If a government has been in place for a long time, citizens and other countries are more likely to view it as legitimate.

- **Charismatic leadership** – As Max Weber said, charisma is a powerful factor in establishing legitimacy, whether the country is democratic or totalitarian.

- **Nationalism/shared political culture** – If citizens identify strongly with their nation, not just the state, they are usually more accepting of the legitimacy of the government.

- **Satisfaction with the government's performance/responsiveness** – Chances are that the government is a legitimate one if citizens receive benefits from the government, if the government wins wars, and/or if citizens are protected from violence and crime.

Political Culture and Political Ideologies

Historical evolution of political traditions shapes a country's concept of who has the authority to rule as well as its definition of legitimate political power. This evolution may be gradual or forced, long or relatively brief, and the importance of tradition varies from country to country. **Political culture** refers to the collection of political beliefs, values, practices, and institutions that the government is based on. For example, if a society values individualism, the government will generally reflect this value in the way that it is structured and in the way that it operates. If the government does not reflect basic political values of a people, it will have difficulty remaining viable.

Political culture may be analyzed in terms of **social capital**, or the amount of reciprocity and trust that exists among citizens, and between citizens and the state. Societies with low amounts of social capital may be more inclined toward authoritarian and anti-individual governments, and societies with more social capital may be inclined toward democracy. Some argue that Islam and/or Confucianism are incompatible with democracy because they emphasize subservience and respect for differing statuses in life. As the argument goes, social capital is not valued within such traditions. Critics of social capital theory say that it relies too heavily on stereotypes, and that it ignores the fact that democracy has flourished in traditional societies, such as India, South Africa, and Turkey.

Types of Political Culture

The number and depth of disagreements among citizens within a society form the basis for categorizing political cultures into two types: consensual and conflictual.

- **Consensual political culture** – Although citizens may disagree on some political processes and policies, they tend generally to agree on how decisions are made, what issues should be addressed, and how problems should be solved. For example, citizens agree that elections should be held to select leaders, and they accept the election winners as their leaders. Once the leaders take charge, the problems they address are considered by most people to be appropriate for government to handle. By and large, a **consensual political culture** accepts both the legitimacy of the regime and solutions to major problems.

- **Conflictual political culture** – Citizens in a **conflictual political culture** are sharply divided, often on both the legitimacy of the regime and its solutions to major problems. For example, if citizens disagree on something as basic as capitalism vs. communism, conflict almost certainly will be difficult to avoid. Or if religious differences are so pronounced that followers of one religion do not accept an elected leader from another religion, these differences strike at the heart of legitimacy, and threaten to topple the regime. When a country is deeply divided in political beliefs and values over a long period of time, political subcultures may develop, and the divisions become so imbedded that the government finds it difficult to rule effectively.

No matter how we categorize political cultures, they are constantly changing, so that over time, conflictual political cultures may become consensual, and vice versa. However, political values and beliefs tend to endure, and no political system may be analyzed accurately without taking into consideration the political culture that has shaped it. So when the Russian president dictates a major change of policy, the Chinese government enforces economic development of rural lands, the British prime minister endures another round of derision, or Mexican citizens take a liking to a leftist leader, you may be sure that political culture is a force behind the stories in the news.

Political Ideologies

Political culture also shapes political ideologies that a nation's citizens hold. **Political ideologies** are sets of political values held by individuals regarding the basic goals of government and politics. Examples of political ideologies are:

- **Liberalism** places emphasis on <u>individual political and eco-nomic freedom</u>. Do not confuse liberalism as an ideology with its stereotype within the U.S. political system. As a broad ideology, liberalism is part of the political culture of many modern democracies, including the United States. Liberals seek to <u>maximize freedom for all people</u>, including free speech, freedom of religion, and freedom of association. Liberals also believe that citizens have the right to disagree with state decisions and act to change the decisions of their leaders. For example, in recent years many U.S. citizens openly expressed their disagreements with the Trump administration concerning immigration and homeland security issues. The U.S. political culture supports the belief that government leaders should allow and even listen to such criticisms. Public opinion generally has some political impact in liberal democracies, such as the U.S. and Britain.

- **Communism**, in contrast to liberalism, generally values <u>equality over freedom</u>. Whereas liberal democracies value the ideal of equal opportunity, they usually tolerate a great deal of inequality, especially within the economy. Communism rejects the idea that personal freedom will ensure prosperity for the majority. Instead, it holds that an inevitable result of the competition for scarce resources is that a small group will eventually come to control both the government and the economy. For communists, liberal democracies are created by the rich to protect the rights and property of the rich. To eliminate the inequalities and exploitation, communists advocate the takeover of all resources by the state that in turn insures that true economic equality exists for the community as a whole. As a result, private ownership of property is abolished. Individual liberties must give way to the needs of society as a whole, creating what communists believe to be a true democracy.

- **Socialism** shares the value of equality with communism but is also influenced by the liberal value of freedom. Unlike communists, <u>socialists accept and promote private ownership and free market principles</u>. However, in contrast to liberals, socialists believe that the state has a <u>strong role to play in regulating</u>

the economy or even owning key industries within it, and providing benefits to the public in order to ensure some measure of equality. Socialism is a much stronger ideology in Europe than it is in the United States, although both socialism and liberalism have shaped these areas of the world.

- **Fascism** is often confused with communism because they both devalue the idea of individual freedom. However, the similarity between the two ideologies ends there. Unlike communism, fascism permits the continued private ownership of property, at least by elites. Fascism also rejects the value of equality, and accepts the idea that people and groups exist in degrees of inferiority and superiority. Fascists believe that the state has the right and the responsibility to mold the society and economy and to eliminate obstacles (including people) that might weaken them. The powerful authoritarian state is the engine that makes superiority possible. The classic example is of course Nazi Germany. No strictly fascist regimes currently exist, but fascism still is an influential ideology in many parts of the world.

- **Religions** have always been an important source of group identity and continue to be in the modern world. Many advanced democracies, such as the United States, have established principles of separation of church and state, but even in those countries, religion often serves as a basis for interest groups and voluntary associations within the civil society. Even though some European countries, such as Great Britain, have an official state religion, their societies are largely secularized, so that religious leaders are usually not the same people as political leaders. However, the British monarch is still formally the head of the Anglican Church, as well as head of state for the country. In our six countries we will see religion playing very different roles in all of them – from China, whose government recently squelched the Falon Gong religious movement, to Iran, which bases its entire political system on Shia Islam. In Nigeria, religious law (*sharia*) is an important basis of legitimacy in the Muslim north but not in the Christian south.

TOPIC THREE: POLITICAL AND ECONOMIC CHANGE

Comparativists are interested not only in the causes and forms of change, but also in the various impacts that it has on the policymaking process. Profound political and economic changes have characterized the 20th and early 21st centuries, and governments and politics in all of the six core countries of the AP Comparative Government and Politics course illustrate this overall trend toward change. More often than not, political and economic changes occur together and influence one another. If one occurs without the other, tensions are created that have serious consequences. For example, rapid economic changes in China have strongly pressured the government to institute political changes. So far, the authoritarian government has resisted those changes, a situation that leaves us with the question of what adjustments authoritarian governments must make if they are to guide market economies.

Types of Change

Change occurs in many ways, but it may be categorized into three types:

- **Reform** is a type of change that does not advocate the overthrow of basic institutions. Instead, reformers want to change some of the methods that political and economic leaders use to reach goals that the society generally accepts. For example, reformers may want to change business practices in order to preserve real competition in a capitalist country, or they may want the government to become more proactive in preserving the natural environment. In neither case do the reformers advocate the overthrow of basic economic or political institutions.

- **Revolution,** in contrast to reform, implies change at a more basic level, and involves either a major revision or an overthrow of existing institutions. A revolution usually impacts more than one area of life. For example, the Industrial Revolution first altered the economies of Europe from feudalism to capitalism, but eventually changed political systems, transportation, communication, literature, and social classes. Likewise, the French and American Revolutions were directed at the political systems, but they significantly changed the economies and societal practices of both countries, and spread their influence throughout the globe.

- **Coup d'état** generally represent the most limited of the three types of change. Literally "blows to the state," they replace the leadership of a country with new leaders. Typically coups occur in countries where government institutions are weak and leaders have taken control by force. The leaders are challenged by others who use force to depose them. Often coups are carried out by the military, but the new leaders are always vulnerable to being overthrown by yet another coup.

Attitudes Toward Change

The types of change that take place are usually strongly influenced by the attitudes of those that promote them. Attitudes toward change include:

- **Radicalism** is a belief that rapid, dramatic changes need to be made in the existing society, often including the political system. Radicals usually think that the current system cannot be saved and must be overturned and replaced with something better. For example, radicalism prevailed in Russia in 1917 when the old tsarist regime was replaced by the communist U.S.S.R. Radicals are often the leaders of revolutions.

- **Liberalism** supports reform and gradual change rather than revolution. Do not confuse a liberal attitude toward change with liberalism as a political ideology. The two may or may not accompany one another. Liberals generally do not think that the political and/or economic systems are permanently broken, but they do believe that they need to be repaired or improved. They may support the notion that eventual transformation needs to take place, but they almost always believe that gradual change is best.

- **Conservatism** is much less supportive of change in general than are radicalism and liberalism. Conservatives tend to see change as disruptive, and they emphasize the fact that it sometimes brings unforeseen outcomes. They consider the state and the regime to be very important sources of law and order that might be threatened by making significant changes in the way that they operate. Legitimacy itself might be undermined, as well as the basic values and beliefs of the society.

- **Reactionary beliefs** go further to protect against change than do conservative beliefs. Reactionaries are similar to conservatives in that they oppose both revolution and reform, but they differ in that reactionaries also find the status quo unacceptable. Instead, they want to turn back the clock to an earlier era, and reinstate political, social, and economic institutions that once existed. Reactionaries have one thing in common with radicals: both groups are more willing to use violence to reach their goals than are liberals or conservatives.

Three Trends

In comparing political systems, it is important to take notice of overall patterns of development that affect everyone in the contemporary world. Two of these trends – democratization and the move toward market economies – indicate growing commonalities among nations, and the third represents fragmentation – the revival of ethnic or cultural politics.

Democratization

Even though democracy takes many different forms, more and more nations are turning toward some form of popular government. One broad, essential requirement for democracy is the existence of **competitive elections** that are regular, free, and fair. In other words, the election offers a real possibility that the incumbent government may be defeated. By this standard, a number of modern states that call themselves "democracies" fall into a gray area that is neither clearly democratic nor clearly undemocratic. Examples are Russia, Nigeria, and Indonesia. In contrast, **liberal democracies** display other democratic characteristics beyond having competitive elections:

- **Civil liberties**, such as freedom of belief, speech, and assembly

- **Rule of law** that provides for equal treatment of citizens and due process

- **Neutrality of the judiciary** and other checks on the abuse of power

- **Open civil society** that allows citizens to lead private lives and mass media to operate independently from government

- **Civilian control of the military** that restricts the likelihood of the military seizing control of the government

Liberal democracies may also be called **substantive democracies** where citizens have access to multiple sources of information. Whereas no country is a perfect substantive democracy, some have progressed further than others. Countries that have democratic procedures in place but have significant restrictions on them are referred to

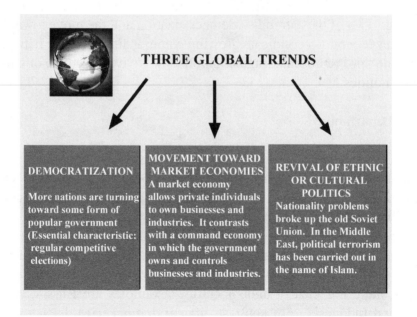

THREE GLOBAL TRENDS

DEMOCRATIZATION	MOVEMENT TOWARD MARKET ECONOMIES	REVIVAL OF ETHNIC OR CULTURAL POLITICS
More nations are turning toward some form of popular government (Essential characteristic: regular competitive elections)	A market economy allows private individuals to own businesses and industries. It contrasts with a command economy in which the government owns and controls businesses and industries.	Nationality problems broke up the old Soviet Union. In the Middle East, political terrorism has been carried out in the name of Islam.

as **illiberal democracies,** or **procedural democracies**. For example, the rule of law may be in place, but it may not be consistently followed by those who have political power. Presidents in illiberal systems often hold a disproportionate share of power, and the legislatures are less able to check executive power. Another typical characteristic of illiberal democracies is that political parties and interest groups are restricted so that elections lack true competitiveness. The presence of a procedural democracy is a necessary condition for the development of substantive democracy, but many procedural democracies do not qualify as substantive democracies because they are missing the other necessary characteristics. In fact, theorists G. Bingham Powell, Jr. and Eleanor N. Powell do not consider procedural democracies to be democratic at all, but instead view them as forms of "electoral authoritarianism."

Huntington's "Three Waves" of Democratization

According to political scientist Samuel Huntington, the modern world is now in a **"third wave" of democratization** that began during the 1970s. The "first wave" developed gradually over time; the "second wave" occurred after the Allied victory in World War II, and continued until the early 1960s. This second wave was characterized by de-colonization around the globe. The third wave is characterized by the defeat of dictatorial or totalitarian rulers in South America, Eastern Europe, and some parts of Africa. The recent political turnover in Mexico may be interpreted as part of this "third wave" of democratization.

Why has democratization occurred? According to Huntington, some factors are:

- The **loss of legitimacy** by both right and left wing authoritarian regimes

- The **expansion of an urban middle class** in developing countries

- A new emphasis on **"human rights"** by the United States and the European Union

- The **"snowball" effect** has been important: when one country in a region becomes democratic, it influences others to do so. An example is Poland's influence on other nations of eastern Europe during the 1980s.

One of the greatest obstacles to democratization is poverty because it blocks citizen participation in government. Huntington gauges democratic stability by this standard: democracy may be declared when a country has had at least two successive peaceful turnovers of power.

Democratic Consolidation

An authoritarian regime may transition to a democracy as a result of a "trigger event," such as an economic crisis or a military defeat. Political discontent is generally fueled if the crisis is preceded by a period of relative improvement in the standard of living, a condition called the **"revolution of rising expectations."** The changes demanded may not necessarily be democratic. Democratization begins when these conditions are accompanied by a willingness on the part of the ruling elite to accept power-sharing arrangements, as well as a readiness on the part of the people to participate in the process and lend it their active support. This process is called **democratic consolidation**, which creates a stable political system that is supported by all parts of the society. In a consolidated democracy, all institutions and many people participate, so that democracy penetrates political parties, the judiciary, and the bureaucracy. The military, too, cooperates with political leaders and subordinates its will to the democratically-based government. A state that progresses from procedural democracy to substantive democracy through democratic consolidation is said to experience **political liberalization,** which eventually leads other states to recognize it as a liberal democracy.

Movement toward **Economic Liberalism** and Market Economies

A second trend of the 20th and early 21st centuries is a movement toward economic liberalism and market economies. Political scientists disagree about the relationship between democratization and marketization. Does one cause the other, or is the relationship between the two spurious? Many countries have experienced both, but two of the country cases for the comparative government course offer contradictory evidence. Mexico has moved steadily toward a market economy since the 1980s, and democratization appears to have followed, starting in the late 1980s. On the other hand, China has been moving toward capitalism since the late 1970s without any clear sign of democratization.

Political and Economic Liberalism

The ideology of liberalism has its roots in 19th century Europe, where its proponents supported both political and economic freedoms, and so gave rise to the belief that political liberalism goes hand in hand with economic liberalism. Most liberals were **bourgeoisie** – middle-class professionals or businessmen – who wanted their views to be represented in government and their economic goals to be unhampered by government interference. They valued political freedoms – such as freedoms of religion, press, and assembly – and the rule of law, and they also wanted economic freedoms, such as the right to own private property. They advocated free trade with low or no tariffs so as to allow individual economic opportunities to blossom. These values clashed with those of radicals, who emphasized equality more than liberty and generally believed that liberals tolerated too much inequality within their societies.

Command and Market Economies

The 19th century radicals who advocated equality more than liberty included Karl Marx, whose communist theories became the basis for 20th century communist countries, including the U.S.S.R. and China. In order to achieve more equality – at least in theory – these countries relied on a **command economy**, in which the government owned almost all industrial enterprises and retail sales outlets. The economies were managed by a party-dominated state planning committee, which produced detailed blueprints for economic production and distribution, often in the form of five-year plans. Central planning supported economic growth in many cases – especially in the Soviet Union – but by the 1980s, most communist countries found themselves in deep economic trouble. A major problem was that economic growth of major industries had not translated into higher living standards for citizens.

Many political economists today declare that the economic competition between capitalism and socialism that dominated the 20th century is now a part of the past. The old **command economies**, with socialist principles of centralized planning, quota-setting, and state ownership, are fading from existence, except in combination with market economies. It appears as if most societies are drifting toward market economies based on private ownership of property and little inference from government regulation. This process of limiting the power of the state over private property and market forces is commonly referred to as **economic liberalization**. The issue now seems to be what type of **market economy** will be most successful: one that allows for significant control from the central government – a "**mixed economy**" – or one that does not – a pure market economy. For example, modern Germany has a "social market economy" that is team-oriented and emphasizes cooperation between management and organized labor. In contrast, the United States economy tends to be more individualistic and opposed to government control.

Two factors that have promoted the movement toward market economies are:

1) **Belief that government is too big** – Command economies require an active, centralized government that gets heavily involved in economic issues. Anti-big government movements began in the 1980s in the United States and many western European nations, where economies had experienced serious problems of inefficiency and stagnation. Margaret Thatcher in Britain and Ronald Reagan in the United States rode to power on waves of public support for reducing the scale of government.

2) **Lack of success of command economies** – The collapse of the Soviet Union is the best example of a command economy failure that reverberated around the world. This failure was accompanied by changes among the eastern European satellite states from command to market economies. Meanwhile, another big command economy – China – has been slowly infusing capitalism into its system since its near collapse in the

1970s. Today China is a "socialist market economy" that is fueled by ever-growing doses of capitalism.

Marketization is the term that describes the state's re-creation of a market in which property, labor, goods, and services can all function in a competitive environment to determine their value. **Privatization** is the transfer of state-owned property to private ownership. One important disadvantage of a free-market economy is that it inevitably goes through cycles of prosperity and scarcity. Recessions, small market downturns, or even depressions – big downturns – happen, but the market corrects itself eventually as supply and demand adjust to correct levels. However, a market downturn may be devastating, as it was during the 1930s when the world went into global depression. This disadvantage of market economies has led many countries to conclude that a "mixed economy" is the best solution, with the government playing a more active role than it does with a market economy, but a less active role than with a command economy.

All economies fall somewhere on the continuum between command and market systems, as illustrated on the graph below. For example, the United States is mostly a market economy, but competition and profit are regulated by the government, so it has some characteristics of a mixed economy. On the other end of the continuum is the former Soviet Union, where the government controlled the economy and allowed virtually no private ownership. Countries may move along the continuum over time. A good example is China, which has moved steadily away from a command economy toward a market economy since 1979.

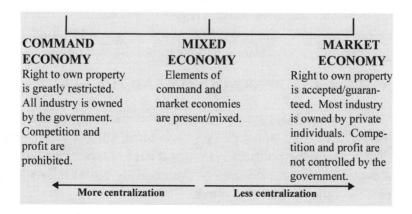

COMMAND ECONOMY	MIXED ECONOMY	MARKET ECONOMY
Right to own property is greatly restricted. All industry is owned by the government. Competition and profit are prohibited.	Elements of command and market economies are present/mixed.	Right to own property is accepted/guaranteed. Most industry is owned by private individuals. Competition and profit are not controlled by the government.

← **More centralization**　　**Less centralization** →

Revival of Ethnic or Cultural Politics

Until recently, few political scientists predicted that **fragmentation** – divisions based on ethnic or cultural identity – would become increasingly important in world politics. A few years ago **nationalism** – identities based on nationhood – seemed to be declining in favor of increasing globalization. However, nationality questions almost certainly derailed Mikhail Gorbachev's attempts to resuscitate the Soviet Union, and national identities remain strong in most parts of the world. Perhaps most dramatically, the **politicization of religion** has dominated world politics of the early 21st century. Many Westerners have been caught off guard by this turn of events, especially in the United States, where separation of church and state has been a basic political principle since the founding of the country. In the Middle East, political terrorism has been carried out in the name of Islam, and some people believe that many modern international tensions are caused by conflicts between Muslims and Christians.

Samuel Huntington has argued that our most important and dangerous future conflicts will be based on clashes of civilizations, not on socioeconomic or even ideological differences. He divides the world into several different cultural areas that may already be poised to threaten world peace: the West, the Orthodox world (Russia), Islamic countries, Latin American, Africa, the Hindu world, the Confucian world, the Buddhist world, and Japan. Some political scientists criticize Huntington by saying that he distorts cultural divisions and that he underestimates the importance of cultural conflicts within nations. In either case – a world divided into cultural regions or a world organized into multicultural nations – the revival of ethnic or cultural politics tends to emphasize differences among nations rather than commonalities.

TOPIC FOUR: CITIZENS, SOCIETY AND THE STATE

Government and politics are only parts of the many facets of a complex society. Religion, ethnic groups, race, social and economic classes all interact with the political system and have a tremendous impact on policymaking. These divisions – theoretically out of the realm of politics – are called **social cleavages**.

- **Bases of social cleavages** – What mix of social classes, ethnic and racial groups, religions, and languages does a country have? How deep are these cleavages, and to what degree do they separate people from one another (form **social boundaries**)? Which of these cleavages appear to have the most significant impact on the political system?

- **Cleavages and political institutions** – How are cleavages expressed in the political system? For example, is political party membership based on cleavages? Do political elites usually come from one group or another? Do these cleavages block some groups from fully participating in government?

Comparing Citizen/State Relationships

Governments connect to their citizens in a variety of ways. We may successfully compare government-citizen relationships by categorizing, and in turn noting differences and similarities among categories. For example, citizens within democracies generally relate to their governments differently than do citizens that are governed by authoritarian rulers. Or, different countries may be compared by using the following categories:

- **Attitudes and beliefs of citizens** – Do citizens trust their government? Do they believe that the government cares about what they think? Do citizens feel that government affects their lives in significant ways? One important measure of connections between citizens and their government is **political efficacy**, or a citizen's capacity to understand and influence political events. If citizens have a high level of political efficacy, they believe that the government takes their input seriously and cares about what they have to say. They also believe in their own abilities to understand political issues and to participate in solving problems. If citizens lack political efficacy, they may not believe that it is important to vote, or they may try to ignore the government's efforts to enforce laws.

SOCIAL CLEAVAGES

Social class – Even though class awareness has declined in industrial and post-industrial societies, it is still an important basis of cleavages. For example, traditionally in Great Britain, middle-class voters have supported the Conservative Party and working-class voters have supported the Labour Party. These differences have declined significantly in recent elections. In less developed countries class tensions may appear between landless peasants and property owners. In India, vestiges of the old caste system (now illegal) have slowed India's movement toward a democratic political system.

Ethnic cleavages – In the early 20th century, ethnic cleavages are clearly the most divisive and explosive social cleavages in countries at all levels of development. Ethnic clashes are the cause of several full-scale civil wars in the former Yugoslavia, some of the former U.S.S.R. republics, and African countries such as Liberia, Rwanda, and Angola. Ethnic cleavages are based on different cultural identities, including religion and language, and are important considerations in evaluating the political systems of all six country cases in the AP Comparative course.

Religious cleavages – Religious differences are often closely intertwined with ethnicity. For example, the conflict in Northern Ireland has a strong religious dimension, with the Irish nationalists being strong Catholics and the loyalists strong Protestants. However, religious differences may also exist among people of similar ethnic backgrounds. For example, some have argued that a basic cleavage exists in the United States between fundamentalist and non-fundamentalist Christians.

Regional cleavages – In many modern states, differing political values and attitudes characterize people living in different geographic regions. These populations compete for government resources such as money, jobs, and development projects. Regional differences are often linked to varying degrees of economic development. For example, regional conflicts in Nigeria coming in large part from economic inequalities resulted in the secession of Biafra and a tragic civil war.

Coinciding and cross-cutting cleavages – When every dispute aligns the same groups against each other, **coinciding cleavages** are likely to be explosive. **Cross-cuting cleavages** divide society into many potential groups that may conflict on one issue but cooperate on another. These tend to keep social conflict to more moderate levels.

- **Political socialization** – How do citizens learn about politics in their country? Do electronic and print media shape their learning? Does the government put forth effort to politically educate their citizens? If so, how much of their effort might you call "propaganda"? How do children learn about politics? At any specific time, a person's political beliefs are a combination of many feelings and attitudes, including both general and specific identifications. At the deepest level, people identify with their nation, ethnic or class groups, and religions. At a middle level, people develop attitudes toward politics and the ways that government operates. On a narrower level, people have immediate views of current events, or political topics that the media, family, friends, or schools may call to their attention.

- **Types of political participation** – In authoritarian governments, most citizens contact government through **subject activities** that involve obedience. Such activities are obeying laws, following military orders, and paying taxes. In democracies, citizens may play a more active part in the political process. The most common type of participation is voting, but citizens may also work for political candidates, attend political meetings or rallies, contribute money to campaigns, and join political clubs or parties.

- **Voting behavior** – Do citizens in the country participate in regular elections? If so, are the elections truly competitive? If not, what is the purpose of the elections? What citizens are eligible to vote, and how many actually vote? Do politicians pay attention to elections, and do elections affect policymaking?

- **Factors that influence political beliefs and behaviors** – Consider the important cleavages in the country. Do they make a difference in citizens' political beliefs and behaviors? For example, do the lower classes vote for one political party or the other? Are women's beliefs and behaviors different from those of men? Are younger people as likely to vote as older people are? Do people in rural areas participate in government?

COMPARATIVE VOTER TURNOUT
SELECTED PRESIDENTIAL ELECTIONS 2016-2018

Country	Date of Election	Voter Turnout
Russia	March 18, 2018	67.5%
France	April 23, 2017	76%
Mexico	July 1, 2018	63%
Venezuela	May 20, 2018	45%
United States	November 8, 2016	59.7%
South Korea	May 9 2017	77%
Turkey	June 24, 2018	82%
Colombia	June 17, 2018	52%
Egypt	March 26, 2018	38%

Comparative Voter Turnout. Voter turnout may be compared across countries, as shown in the chart of recent presidential elections above. The chart does not explain why some voter rates are lower than others, but a little research will yield some hypotheses. For example, the 2017 election in France was of high interest because of the strong challenge from the National Front, an extreme rightist party.

Source: Election Guide, www.electionguide.org,

- **Level of transparency** – A transparent government is one that operates openly by keeping citizens informed about government operations and political issues and by responding to citizens' questions and advice. In a 2009 memo to the heads of executive departments and agencies, U.S. President Barack Obama asserted, "Government should be transparent. Transparency promotes accountability and provides information for citizens about what their Government is doing...My Administration will take appropriate action, consistent with law and policy, to disclose information rapidly in forms that the public can readily find and use." This ideal does not have to be limited to democracies, but low levels of transparency are often found in authoritarian governments, and corruption also tends to be lower in countries where government activities are relatively transparent.

Social Movements

Social movements refer to organized collective activities that aim to bring about or resist fundamental change in an existing group or society. Social movements try to influence political leaders to make policy decisions that support their goals. Members of social movements often step outside traditional channels for bringing about social change, and they usually take stands on issues that push others in mainstream society to reconsider their positions. For example, early leaders in the women's suffrage movement in Great Britain and the United States were considered to be radicals, but their goals were eventually recognized and accomplished. The modern civil rights movement in the United States consisted of collective action that influenced state, local, and national governments to support racial equality. The African National Congress (ANC), a political organization that sought to overthrow the state-supported system of apartheid in South Africa, eventually pushed the government to lift the decades-old ban and release ANC leader Nelson Mandela from prison. The success of social movements varies from case to case, but even if they fail, they often influence political opinion.

Civil Society

Civil society refers to voluntary organizations outside of the state that help people define and advance their own interests. Civil society is usually strong in liberal democracies where individual freedoms are valued and protected. The organizations that compose it may represent class, religious, or ethnic interests, or they may cross them, creating strong bonds among people that exist outside of government control. Political scientists are interested in civil society since it helps to define the people's relationship to and role in politics and community affairs. Groups in civil society may be inherently apolitical, but they serve as a cornerstone of liberty by allowing people to articulate and promote what is important to them. In many ways, civil society checks the power of the state and helps to prevent the **tyranny of the majority**, i.e., the tendency in democracies to allow majority rule to neglect the rights and liberties of minorities. Advocacy groups, social networks, and the media all may exist within the civil society, and if they are strong enough, they may place considerable pressure on the state to bring about reform.

By the early 21ˢᵗ century, a global civil society has emerged, with human rights and environmental groups providing international pressures that have a significant effect on government-citizen relations. Some argue that a global **cosmopolitanism** – a universal political order that draws its identity and values from everywhere – is emerging. This global civil society can take shape in **nongovernmental organizations (NGOs)** or more informally through people that find common interests with others that live in far corners of the globe. Nongovernmental organizations are national and international groups, independent of any state, that pursue policy objectives and foster public participation. Examples are Doctors without Borders and Amnesty International. Societal globalization, then, may change the definition of who are "us" and who are "them", and reshape a world that formerly defined reality in nationalistic terms.

By their very nature, authoritarian states do not encourage civil society, and they often feel that their power is threatened by it. Civil society does not necessarily disappear under authoritarian rule, as is illustrated by the survival of the Russian Orthodox Church and social reform movements in eastern Europe during decades of communist rule. Generally, civil society is weak in most less-developed and newly-industrializing countries. Individuals tend to be divided by ethnic, religious, economic, or social boundaries, and do not identify with groups beyond their immediate surroundings that might help them articulate their interests to the government. One step in the development of civil society is civic education, in which communities learn their democratic rights and how to use those rights to give meaningful input to political institutions. One positive sign in less developed countries is the growing involvement of women in NGOs that deal with a variety of health, gender, environmental, and poverty issues.

TOPIC FIVE: POLITICAL INSTITUTIONS

An important part of studying comparative government and politics is developing an understanding of **political institutions**, which are structures of a political system that carry out the work of governing. Some governments have much more elaborate structures than others, but these structures often have similarities across cultures. However, just because you see the same type of institution in two different countries, don't assume that they serve the same functions for the political system. For example, a legislature in one country may have a great deal more power than a comparable structure in another country. Only by studying the way that the structures operate and the functions they fill will you be able to compare them accurately. Common structures that exist in most countries are legislatures, executives, judicial systems, bureaucracies, and armies.

Levels of Government

Every state has multiple levels of authority, though the geographic distribution of power varies widely. A **unitary system** is one that concentrates all policymaking powers in one central geographic place, and the central government is responsible for most policy areas. A **confederal system** spreads the power among many sub-units (such as states), and has a weak central government. A **federal system** divides the power between the central government and sub-units, and regional bodies have significant powers, such as taxation, lawmaking, and keeping order. Federalism is sometimes criticized for inefficiency, since power is dispersed among many local authorities whose policies may sometimes conflict.

All political systems fall on a continuum from the most concentrated amount of power to the least. Unitary governments may be placed close to one end, according to the degree of concentration; confederal governments are placed toward the other end; and federal governments fall in between. Most countries have unitary systems, although of the six core countries, Britain is devolving some power to regional governments and Russia, Mexico, and Nigeria have federalist structures. In recent years, state governments in Mexico have gained some autonomy from the central government so that a real dispersal of power appears to have taken place.

International Organizations and Globalization

All political systems exist within an environment that is affected by other governments, but more and more they are affected by international organizations that go beyond national boundaries. Some have more international and/or regional contacts than others, but most countries in the world today must cope with influences from their outside interactions with others. These organizations reflect a trend toward

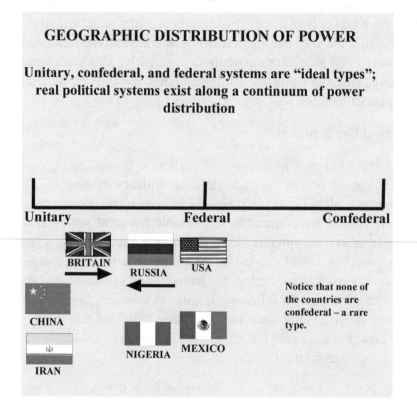

GEOGRAPHIC DISTRIBUTION OF POWER

Unitary, confederal, and federal systems are "ideal types"; real political systems exist along a continuum of power distribution

Unitary   **Federal**   **Confederal**

BRITAIN

RUSSIA   USA

Notice that none of the countries are confederal – a rare type.

CHINA

NIGERIA   MEXICO

IRAN

Geographic Distribution of Power in Seven Countries. Above is a representation of the geographic distribution of power in seven countries: the six core countries of AP Comparative Government and Politics and the United States. Just as we might disagree about the actual balance of power between state and national government in the United States, we might also disagree about exactly where to place the other six countries. Nigeria and Russia in particular are difficult to place because although they have federalist structures, a great deal of power in both countries rests in the central executive.

integration, a process that encourages states to pool their sovereignty in order to gain political, economic, and social clout. Pooling of sovereignty creates a **supranational organization** that transcends the authority of the nation-state. Integration binds states together with common policies and shared rules. In the 20th century, many national governments established relationships with regional organizations – such as NATO, the European Union, NAFTA, and OPEC – and with international organizations, such as the United Nations. Most international organizations currently do not challenge national sovereignty, although the European Union illustrates a supranational organization with a great deal of authority over its member-states.

These international organizations reflect the phenomenon of globalization – an integration of social, environmental, economic, and cultural activities of nations that has resulted from increasing international contacts. Political globalization is a countertrend to the organization of political power by states, and it complicates the ability of states to maintain sovereignty since it binds them to international organizations that take responsibility for tasks that national governments normally conduct. Globalization has changed the nature of comparative politics, largely because it breaks down the distinction between international relations and domestic politics, making many aspects of domestic politics subject to global forces. Likewise, it also internationalizes domestic issues and events. Economic globalization intensifies international trade, tying markets, producers, and labor together in increasingly extensive and intensive new ways. Economic globalization also integrates capital and financial markets around the world so that banking, credit, stocks, and **foreign direct investments** (purchase of assets in a country by a foreign firm) are increasingly interrelated.

Because globalization deepens and widens international connections, local events, even small ones, can have ripple effects throughout the world. Perhaps most apparent is the effect of technology and its ability to ignore national boundaries. The internet allows news from every corner of the globe to rapidly spread to other areas, so that what happens in one place affects other parts of the world. On the other hand, many political scientists point out a counter-trend – **fragmentation** – a tendency for people to base their loyalty on ethnicity, language, religion, or cultural identity. Regional international organizations may be seen as evidence of fragmentation because they divide the world into super blocs that often compete with one another. Although globalization and fragmentation appear to be opposite concepts, they both transcend political boundaries between individual countries.

Modern Challenges to the Nation-State Configuration

Nation-states have always had their challenges, both internal and external, but today new international forces are at work that have led some to believe that the nation-state political configuration itself may be changing. Is it possible that large regional organizations, such as the European Union, will replace the smaller state units as basic organizational models? Or will international organizations, such as the United Nations, come to have true governing power over the nation-states? If so, then the very nature of sovereignty may be changing, especially if nation-states of the future have to abide by the rules of **international organizations** (cooperating groups of nations that operate on either a regional or international level) for all major decisions and rules.

INTERNATIONAL ORGANIZATIONS: GLOBALIZATION OR FRAGMENTATION?

GLOBALIZATION	FRAGMENTATION
FORCES THAT TIE THE PEOPLE OF THE WORLD TOGETHER; THE INTEGRATION OF SOCIAL, ENVIRONMENTAL, ECONOMIC, AND CULTURAL ACTIVITIES OF NATIONS	FORCES THAT TEAR PEOPLE OF THE WORLD APART; LOYALTIES BASED ON ETHNICITY, LANGUAGE, RELIGION, OR CULTURAL IDENTITY

Centripetal vs. Centrifugal Forces

A recurring set of forces affects all nation-states: **centripetal forces** that unify them, and **centrifugal forces** that tend to fragment them.

- **Centripetal forces** bind together the people of a state, giving it strength. One of the most powerful centripetal forces is **nationalism**, or identities based on nationhood. It encourages allegiance to a single country, and it promotes loyalty and commitment. Such emotions encourage people to obey the law and accept the country's overall ideologies. States promote nationalism in a number of ways, including the use of symbols, such as flags, rituals, and holidays that remind citizens of what the country stands for. Even when a society is highly heterogeneous, symbols are powerful tools for creating national unity. Institutions, such as schools, the armed forces, and religion, may also serve as centripetal forces. Schools are expected to instill the society's beliefs, values, and behaviors in the young, teach the nation's language, and encourage students to identify with the nation. Fast and efficient transportation and communications systems also tend to unify nations. National broadcasting companies usually take on the point of view of the nation, even if they broadcast internationally. Transportation systems make it easier for people to travel to other parts of the country, and give the government the ability to reach all of its citizens.

- **Centrifugal forces** oppose centripetal forces. They destabilize the government and encourage the country to fall apart. A country that is not well-organized or governed stands to lose the loyalty of its citizens, and weak institutions can fail to provide the cohesive support that the government needs. Strong institutions may also challenge the government for the loyalty of the people. For example, when the U.S.S.R. was created in 1917, its leaders grounded the new country in the ideology of communism. To strengthen the state, they forbid the practice of the traditional religion, Russian Orthodoxy. Although church membership dropped dramatically, the religious institution never disappeared, and when the U.S.S.R. dissolved, the church reappeared and is regaining its strength today. The church was a centrifugal force that discouraged loyalty to the communist state. Nationalism, too, can be a destabilizing force, especially if different ethnic groups within the country have more loyalty to their ethnicity than to the state and its government. These loyalties may lead to **separatist movements** in which nationalities within a country may demand independence. Such movements served as centrifugal forces for the Soviet Union as various nationalities – such as Lithuanians, Ukrainians, Latvians, Georgians, and Armenians – challenged the government for their independence. Other examples are the Basques of Northern Spain, who have different customs (and language) from others in the country, and the Tamils in Sri Lanka, who have waged years of guerrilla warfare to defend what they see as majority threats to their culture, rights, and property. Characteristics that encourage separatist movements are a peripheral location and the existence of social and economic inequality. One reaction states have had to centrifugal force is **devolution**, or the tendency to decentralize decision making to regional governments. Britain has devolved power to the Scottish and Welsh parliaments in an effort to keep peace with Scotland and Wales. As a result, Britain's unitary government has taken some significant strides toward federalism, although London is still the geographic center of decision-making for the country.

Devolution: Ethnic, Economic, and Spatial Forces

Devolution of government powers to sub-governments is usually a reaction to centrifugal forces – those that divide and destabilize. Devolutionary forces can emerge in all kinds of states, old and new, mature and newly created. We may divide these forces into three basic types:

1) **Ethnic forces** – An **ethnic group** shares a well-developed sense of belonging to the same culture. That identity is based on a unique mixture of language, religion, and customs. If a state contains strong ethnic groups with identities that differ from those of the majority, it can threaten the territorial integrity of the state itself. **Ethnonationalism** – the tendency for an ethnic group to see itself as a distinct nation with a right to autonomy or independence – is a fundamental centrifugal force promoting devolution. The threat is usually stronger if the group is clustered in particular spaces within the nation-state. For example, most French Canadians live in the province of Quebec, creating a large base for an independence movement. If ethnically French people were scattered evenly over the country, their sense of identity would be diluted, and the devolutionary force would most likely be weaker. Devolutionary forces in Britain – centered in Wales, Scotland, and Northern Ireland – have not been strong enough to destabilize the country, although violence in Northern Ireland has certainly destabilized the region. Ethnic forces broke up the nation-state of Yugoslavia during the 1990s, devolving it into separate states of Slovenia, Croatia, Bosnia, Macedonia, and Serbia-Montenegro.

2) **Economic forces** – Economic inequalities may also destabilize a nation-state, particularly if the inequalities are regional. For example, Italy is split between north and south by the "Ancona Line", an invisible line extending from Rome to the Adriatic coast at Ancona. The north is far more prosperous than the south, with the north clearly part of the European core area, and the south a part of the periphery. The north is industrialized, and the south is rural. These economic differences inspired the formation of the Northern League, which advocated an independent state called Padania that would shed the north of the "economic drag" it considered the south to be. The movement failed, but it did encourage the Italian government

to devolve power to regional governments, moving it toward a more federal system. A similar economic force is at work in Catalonia in northern Spain, with Catalonians only about 17% of Spain's population, but accountable for 40% of all Spanish industrial exports.

3) **Spatial forces** – Spatially, devolutionary events most often occur on the margins of the state. Distance, remoteness, and peripheral location promote devolution, especially if water, desert, or mountains separate the areas from the center of power

Economic Devolutionary Forces in Italy and Spain. Geographically, southern Italy and most of Spain lie outside the European core, creating economic devolutionary forces within the two nation-states. In Spain, the Catalonians in the north are connected to the core, but the bulk of Spain is not. In Italy the core extends its reach over the northern half of the country, creating centrifugal tensions between north and south.

and from neighboring nations that may support separatist objectives. For example, the United States claims Puerto Rico as a territory, and has offered it recognition as a state. However, Puerto Ricans have consistently voted down the offer of statehood, and a small but vocal pro-independence movement has advocated complete separation from the U.S. The movement is encouraged by spatial forces – Puerto Rico is an island in the Caribbean, close to other islands that have their independence.

Executives

The executive office carries out the laws and policies of a state. In many countries the executive is split into two distinct roles: **the head of state** and **the head of government.** The head of state is a role that symbolizes and represents the people, both nationally and internationally, and may or may not have any real policymaking power. The head of government deals with the everyday tasks of running the state, and usually directs the activities of other members of the executive branch. The distinction is clearly seen in a country such as Britain, where formerly powerful monarchs reigned over their subjects, but left others (such as prime ministers) in charge of actually running the country. Today Britain still has a monarch that is head of state, but the real power rests with the prime minister, who is head of government. Likewise, the Japanese emperor still symbolically represents the nation, but the prime minister runs the government. In the United States, both roles are combined into one position – the president. However, in other countries, such as Italy and Germany, the president is the head of state with weak powers, and the prime minister is the head of government. In still others, such as Russia and France, the president is head of state with strong powers, and the prime minister is the head of government with subordinate powers, although the relationship in Russia has changed, depending on whether Vladimir Putin was president or prime minister.

Functions of the Chief Executive

Usually the chief executive is the most important person in the policymaking process, initiating new policies and playing an important role in their adoption. In presidential systems, the president usually has

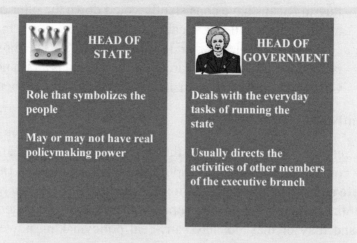

GOVERNMENT INSTITUTIONS: EXECUTIVES

HEAD OF STATE

Role that symbolizes the people

May or may not have real policymaking power

HEAD OF GOVERNMENT

Deals with the everyday tasks of running the state

Usually directs the activities of other members of the executive branch

the power to veto legislation, while the executive in a parliamentary system usually does not have that authority. The political executive also oversees policy implementation and can hold other officials in the executive branch accountable for their performance. The central decisions in a foreign policy crisis are generally made by the chief executive.

The Cabinet

In parliamentary systems, the cabinet is the most important collective decision-making body. Its ministers head all the major departments into which the executive branch is divided, and the cabinet is led by the prime minister, or "first among equals." The ministers are also leaders of the majority party in parliament, or if the country has a multi-party system with no clear majority party, a **cabinet coalition** will form, where several parties join forces and are represented in different cabinet posts. A common problem of cabinet coalitions is that they tend to be unstable, especially if they result from a fragmented legislature. In presidential systems, the president chooses the cabinet members from almost any area of political life, and his appointments may have to be approved by the legislature, as with the U.S. Senate. Because the cabinet members are not necessarily party leaders or members of the legislature, they often have more independence from the president than ministers do from the prime minister. However, the president usually has the power to remove them from office, so they can't stray too far from the president's wishes.

Bureaucracies

Bureaucracies consist of agencies that implement government policy. They usually are a part of the executive branch of government. Their size has generally increased over the course of the 20th and early 21st centuries, partly due to government efforts to improve the health, security, and welfare of their populations.

German political philosopher Max Weber created the classic conception of bureaucracy as a well-organized, complex machine that is a "rational" way for a modern society to organize its business. He did not see bureaucracies as necessary evils, but as inevitable organizational responses to a changing society.

According to Weber, a bureaucracy has several basic characteristics:

- **Hierarchical authority structure** – The chain of command is hierarchical; the top bureaucrat has ultimate control, and authority flows from the top down.

- **Task specialization** – A clear division of labor means that every individual has a specialized job.

- **Extensive rules** – All people in the organization follow clearly written, well-established formal rules.

- **Clear goals** – All people in the organization strive toward a clearly defined set of goals.

- **The merit principle** – Merit-based hiring and promotion requires that no jobs be granted to friends or family unless they are the best qualified.

- **Impersonality** – Job performance is judged by productivity, or how much work the individual gets done.

Bureaucracies have acquired great significance in most contemporary societies and often represent an important source of stability for states.

Bureaucracies in Democracies

Max Weber formulated these characteristics of bureaucracies with European democracies in mind. He was less than enthusiastic about their growing importance largely because of the alienation that he believed they created among workers. A modern issue has to do with the **discretionary power** given to bureaucrats – the power to make small decisions in implementing legislative and executive decisions. These small decisions arguably add up to significant policymaking influence, but democratic beliefs require decisions to be made by elected officials, not by appointed bureaucrats. Yet the bureaucracy is often an important source of stability in a democracy, since the elected officials may be swept out of office and replaced by new people with little political experience. The bureaucrats stay on through the changes in elected leadership positions, and as a result, they provide continuity in the policymaking process.

Bureaucracies in Authoritarian Regimes

Bureaucracies in authoritarian regimes differ from those in democracies in that the head of government exercises almost complete control over their activities. For example, Soviet leader Joseph Stalin placed his own personal supporters (members of the communist party) in control of bureaucratic agencies, such as the secret police and the network of political commissars who served as watchdogs over the military. These bureaucracies not only managed the economy but directly controlled vast resources, including human labor, and the number of prisoners in labor camps under secret police administration increased dramatically under Stalin's rule. Executive power over the bureaucracy was questioned in the 19th century in the United States, when presidents had a great deal of control over government jobs under the **patronage system**, in which political supporters received jobs in return for their assistance in getting the president elected. However, this system was reformed after President James Garfield was assassinated by a disgruntled supporter, and was gradually replaced by a merit-based system meant to curtail the president's patronage powers. As a result, bureaucratic appointments came to abide by more democratic, less authoritarian rules.

Other examples of bureaucratic-authoritarian regimes developed in Brazil, Argentina, Chile, and Uruguay during the 1960s and 1970s. In these Latin American countries a military regime formed a ruling coalition that included military officers and civilian bureaucrats, or **technocrats**. The coalition seized control of the government and determined which other groups were allowed to participate. The authoritarian leaders were seen as modernizers seeking to improve their countries' economic power in the world economy. They controlled the state partly in the name of efficiency – democratic input into the government was seen as an obstacle in the modernization process, and so the governments in these countries have often been oppressive.

Common Characteristics of Bureaucracies

All bureaucracies, whether they are democratic or authoritarian, tend to have many features in common:

- **Non-elected positions** – Bureaucrats are appointed, usually salaried, and are not elected by the public.

- **Impersonal, efficient structures** – Bureaucracies tend to be impersonal because they are goal oriented and have little concern for personal feelings. Bureaucracies are meant to be efficient in accomplishing their goals.

- **Formal qualifications for jobs** – Although authoritarian leaders may appoint whoever they want to government positions, they must at least factor in formal qualifications (education, experience) in making their appointments. Otherwise, the bureaucracy cannot fulfill its goals of efficiency and competent administration. Most democracies have institutionalized formal qualifications as prerequisites for appointments to the bureaucracy.

COMPARATIVE BUREAUCRACIES

Bureaucracies consist of agencies that implement government policy, but their functions generally depend on whether they exist in a democracy or an authoritarian regime.

Bureaucracies in Democracies	Bureaucracies in Authoritarian Regimes
Bureaucrats usually have **discretionary power,** which allows them to make small decisions that influence policy.	The head of government exercises almost complete control over bureaucratic activities.
Bureaucrats are usually appointed, not elected, so they often serve as a source of stability when elected officials are voted out of office.	Bureaucrats are more likely to receive their jobs through **patronage** (loyalty or favors to the leaders) than merit, although patronage exists in democratic systems as well.

- **Hierarchical organization** – Most bureaucracies are hierarchical, top-down organizations in which higher officials give orders to lower officials. Everyone in the hierarchy has a boss, except for the person at the very top.

- **Red tape/inefficiency** – Despite their common goal of efficiency, large bureaucracies seem to stumble under their own weight. Once the bureaucracy reaches a certain size and complexity, the orderly flow of business appears to break down, so that one hand doesn't appear to know what the other is doing.

Legislatures

The legislature is the branch of government charged with making laws. Formal approval for laws is usually required for major public policies, although in authoritarian states, legislatures are generally dominated by the chief executive. Today more than 80% of the countries belonging to the United Nations have legislatures, suggesting that a government that includes a representative popular component increases its legitimacy.

Bicameralism

Legislatures may be **bicameral**, with two houses, or **unicameral**, with only one. The most usual form is bicameral, and may be traced to Britain's House of Lords and House of Commons. Despite the fact that one house is referred to as "upper" and the other as "lower," the upper house does not necessarily have more power than the lower house. In the United States, it is debatable which house is more powerful than the other, and in Britain and Russia, the upper house has very little power.

Why do most countries have a bicameral legislature? If the country practices federalism, where power is shared between a central and subunit governments, bicameralism allows for one house (usually the upper chamber) to represent regional governments and local interests. Seats in the other chamber are usually determined by population, and so the body (usually the lower house) serves as a direct democratic link to the voters. Bicameralism may also counterbalance disproportionate power in the hands of any region. For example, in the United States, populous states such as California, New York, and Texas have large numbers of representatives in the lower house, so the voices of citizens in those states are stronger than those in more sparsely populated states. However, that large-state advantage is counterbalanced in the Senate, where all states are equally represented by two senators each. Even in a unitary state where all power is centralized in one place, bicameralism may serve to disperse power by requiring both houses to approve legislation. Some scholars view the upper house as a "cooling off" mechanism to slow down impulsive actions of the "hotheaded" lower house that is directly elected by the people.

Memberships in the legislature may be determined in different ways, with many houses being elected directly by voters. However, others are selected by government officials, or their membership may be determined by political parties. The six core countries offer a variety of contrasting methods for determining legislative memberships.

Functions of Legislatures

Assembly members formulate, debate, and vote on political policies. They often control the country's budget in terms of both fund-raising and spending. Some assemblies may appoint important officials in the executive and judicial branches, and some (such as the British House of Lords until 2009) have served as courts of appeal. They may also play a major role in **elite recruitment**, i.e., identifying future leaders of the government, and they may hold hearings regarding behaviors of public officials.

Regarding policymaking, legislatures in different countries hold varying degrees of power. For example, the U.S. Congress plays a very active role in the formulation and enactment of legislation. In contrast, the National People's Congress of the People's Republic of China is primarily a rubber-stamp organization for policies made by the leadership of the Chinese Communist Party.

Judiciaries

The judiciary's role in the political system varies considerably from one country to another. All states have some form of legal structure, and the role of the judiciary is rarely limited to routinely adjudicating civil and criminal cases. Courts in authoritarian systems generally have little or no independence, and their decisions are controlled by the chief executive. Court systems that decide the guilt or innocence of lawbreakers go back to the days of medieval England, but **constitutional courts** that serve to defend democratic principles of a country against infringement by both private citizens and the government are a much more recent phenomenon. The constitutional court is the highest judicial body that rules on the constitutionality of laws and other government actions.

In some states the judiciary is relatively independent of the political authorities in the executive and legislative branches. It may even have the authority to impose restrictions on what political leaders do. **Judicial review**, the mechanism that allows courts to review laws and executive actions for their constitutionality, was well established in the United States during the 19th century, but it has developed over the past decades in other democracies. The growth of judicial power over the past century has been spurred in part by the desire to protect human rights. Some have criticized the acceptance of the constitutional court in liberal democracies today, saying that the judges are not directly elected, so they do not represent the direct will of the people. Despite these developments, the judiciary is still a relatively weak branch in most of the six core countries of the Comparative Government and Politics course, but it takes a different form in each of them.

Linkage Institutions

In many countries we may identify groups that connect the government to its citizens, such as political parties, interest groups, and print and electronic media. Appropriately, these groups are called **linkage institutions.** Their size and development depends partly on the size of the population, and partly on the scope of government activity. The larger the population and the more complex the government's policy-making activities, the more likely the country is to have well developed linkage institutions.

Parties

The array of political parties operating in a particular country and the nature of the relationships among them is called a party system. Political parties perform many functions in democracies. First, they help bring different people and ideas together to establish the means by which the majority can rule. Second, they provide labels for candidates that help citizens decide how to vote. Third, they hold politicians accountable to the electorate and other political elites. Most democracies have multi-party systems, with the two-party system in the United States being a more unusual arrangement. Communist states have one-party systems that dominate the governments, but non-communist countries have also had one-party systems. An example is Mexico during most of the 20th century when it was dominated by PRI.

The **two-party system** is a rarity, occurring in only about 15 countries in the world today. The United States has had two major political parties – the Republicans and the Democrats – throughout most of its history. Although minor parties do exist, historically those two parties have had the only reasonable chance to win national elections. The most important single reason for the existence of a two-party system is the plurality electoral system. Most European countries today have **multi-party systems**. They usually arise in countries with strong parliamentary systems, particularly those that use a proportional representation method for elections.

Electoral Systems and Elections

Electoral systems are the rules that decide how votes are cast, counted, and translated into seats in a legislature. All democracies divide their populations by electoral boundaries, but they use many different arrangements. The United States, India, and Great Britain use a system called **first-past-the-post**, in which they divide their constituencies into **single-member districts** in which candidates compete for a single representative's seat. It is also called the **plurality system**, or the **winner-take-all system**, because the winner does not need a majority to win, but simply must get more votes than anyone else.   In contrast, many countries use **proportional representation** that creates **multi-member districts** in which more than one legislative seat is contested in each district. Under proportional representation, voters cast their ballots for a party rather than for a candidate, and the percentage of votes a party receives determines how many seats the party will gain in the legislature. South Africa and Italy use a system based solely on proportional representation, and many countries, including Germany, Mexico, and Russia (until 2007), have used a **mixed system** that combines first-past-the-post and proportional representation. For example, in Mexico, 300 of the 500 members of the Chamber of Deputies (the lower house) are elected through the winner-take-all system from single-member districts, and 200 members are selected by proportional representation.

Plurality systems encourage large, broad-based parties because no matter how many people run in a district, the person with the largest number of votes wins. This encourages parties to become larger, spreading their "umbrellas" to embrace more voters. Parties without big groups of voters supporting them have little hope of winning, and often even have a hard time getting their candidates listed on the ballot. In contrast, the proportional representation electoral system encourages multiple parties because they have a good chance of getting some of their candidates elected. This system allows minor parties to form coalitions to create a majority vote so that legislation can be passed.

Democracies also vary in the types of elections that they hold. A basic distinction between a presidential and parliamentary system is that the president is directly elected by the people to the position, and the prime minister is elected as a member of the legislature. The prime minister becomes head of government because (s)he is the leader of his or her party or coalition.

In general, these types of elections are found in democracies:

- **Election of public officials** – The number of elected officials varies widely, with thousands of officials elected in the United States, and far fewer in most other democracies. However, even in a unitary state, many local and regional officials are directly elected. Legislators are often directly elected, both on the regional and national levels. Now citizens of many European countries also elect representatives to the European Union's Parliament. Lower houses are more likely to be directly elected than upper houses, with a variety of techniques used for the latter.

- **Referendum** – Besides elections to choose public officials, many countries also have the option of allowing public votes on particular policy issues. A ballot called by the government on a policy issue is called a **referendum**. Such votes allow the public to make direct decisions about policy itself. Referenda exist only on the state and local level in the United States and Canada, but many other countries have used them nationally. The French and Russian presidents have the power to call referenda, and they have sometimes had important political consequences. For example, when a referendum proposed by French President Charles De Gaulle failed, he resigned his office in reaction to the snub by the voters. In Russia, the Constitution of 1993 was presented as a referendum for approval by the voters. In Britain, devolution of powers to the Scottish and Welsh parliaments was put before the voters in those regions in the form of referenda. In 2018, British voters supported Brexit, withdrawing Britain's membership in the European Union.

ELECTORAL SYSTEMS

PLURALITY SYSTEM	PROPORTIONAL REPRESENTATION	MIXED SYSTEM
Individual candidate run in single-member districts.	Voting is arranged in multimember districts.	Voting is arranged in combination of multi-member and single-member districts.
↓	↓	↓
Voters cast votes for individual candidates.	Voters cast votes for parties.	Voters cast votes for individuals and parties.
↓	↓	↓
Candidate with more votes than other candidates wins the seat.	Seats are divided among parties on the basis of percentage of overall vote.	Some seats are filled by winners in plurality races; others are filled by party.
↓	↓	↓
One result is a two (or few) party system.	Proportional representation generally results in a multi-party system.	A mixed system results in an in-between number of parties.

The European Constitution failed because it was voted down in referenda in the Netherlands and France. A variation of a referendum is a **plebiscite**, or a ballot to consult public opinion in a nonbinding way.

- **Initiative** – Whereas referenda are called by the government, an **initiative** is a vote on a policy that is initiated by the people. Although less common than the referendum, the initiative must propose an issue for a nationwide vote and its organizers must collect a certain number of supporting signatures from the public. The government is then obliged to schedule a vote.

Interest Groups

Interest groups are organizations of like-minded people whose main political goal is to influence and shape public policy. In liberal democracies, interest groups that are independent from the government are usually an important force in the maintenance of a strong civil society. Groups may be based on almost any type of common interest – occupation, labor, business interests, agriculture, community action, ethnic identities, or advocacy for a cause. Groups may be formally organized on a national level, or they may work almost exclusively on the local level. Interest groups often have nonpolitical goals, too. For example, a business group might organize to promote the growth of its products by directly advertising them to the public. Most interest groups have a political side, too, that focuses on influencing the decisions that governments make.

Differences between Parties and Interest Groups

Parties and interest groups have a great deal in common because they represent political points of view of various people who want to influence policymaking. However, some significant differences still exist. Parties influence government primarily through the electoral process. Although they serve many purposes, parties always run candidates for public office. Interest groups often support candidates, but they do not run their own slate of candidates. Another important difference is that parties generate and support a broad spectrum of policies; interest groups support one or a few related policies. In a multi-party system, however, parties with a narrow base of interests tend to appear. For example, a number of "green parties" have appeared in many European party systems that have a particular interest in environmental issues.

The Strength of Interest Groups

An important factor in assessing how important interest groups are in setting public policy is to determine the degree of autonomy they have from the government. To exercise influence on public policy, groups need to be able to independently decide what their goals are and what methods they will use to achieve them.

In authoritarian states, groups have almost no independence. For example, in China, only government-endorsed groups may exist. Groups in communist China have often been agents to extend the party's influence beyond its own membership to shape the views of its citizens. The government cracks down on unrecognized groups, such as the religious organization, Falon Gong, so that they are either forced underground or out of existence. Political scientist Frank Wilson refers to interest groups in this type of system as **"transmission belts"** that convey to their members the views of the party elite.

At the other extreme are the interest groups in many western industrial democracies. These groups guard their independence by selecting their own leaders and raising their own funds. These autonomous groups compete with each other and with government for influence over state policies in a pattern called **interest group pluralism.** Working from outside the formal governmental structures, rival groups use a variety of tactics to pressure government to make policies that favor their interests.

In between these two extreme patterns is **corporatism**, where fewer groups compete than under pluralism, with usually one for each interest sector, such as labor, agriculture, and management. The group's

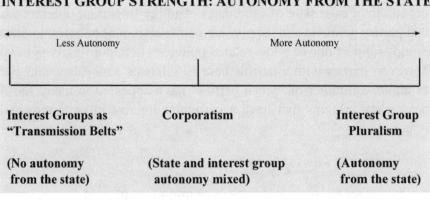

INTEREST GROUP STRENGTH: AUTONOMY FROM THE STATE

Less Autonomy — More Autonomy

Interest Groups as "Transmission Belts"	**Corporatism**	**Interest Group Pluralism**
(No autonomy from the state)	**(State and interest group autonomy mixed)**	**(Autonomy from the state)**

monopoly over its sector is officially approved by the state and some-times protected by the state. There are two forms of corporatism: **state corporatism**, where the state determines which groups are brought in; and **societal corporatism** (or **neocorporatism**), where interest groups take the lead and dominate the state.

Political Elites and Political Recruitment

All countries have **political elites,** or leaders who have a dispropor-tionate share of policy-making power. In democracies, these people are selected by competitive elections, but they still may be readily identified as political elites. Every country must establish a method of elite **recruitment**, or ways to identify and select people for future leadership positions. Also, countries must be concerned about leader-ship **succession**, which is the process that determines the procedure for replacing leaders when they resign, die, or are no longer effective.

TOPIC SIX: PUBLIC POLICY

All political systems set policy, whether by legislative vote, execu-tive decision, judicial rulings, or a combination of the three. In many countries interest groups and political parties also play large roles in policymaking. Policy is generally directed toward addressing issues and solving problems. Many issues are similar in almost all countries, such as the need to improve or stabilize the economy or to provide for a common defense against internal and external threats. However, governments differ in the approaches they take to various issues, as well as the importance they place on solving particular problems.

Common policy issues include:

- **Economic performance** – Governments are often concerned with economic health/problems within their borders. Most also participate in international trade, so their economies are deeply affected by their imports and exports. The six core countries provide a variety of approaches that states may take, and they experience an assortment of consequences of both good and poor economic performances. Economic performance may be measured in any number of ways including 1) **Gross Domes-tic Product (GDP)** – all the goods and services produced by a country's economy in a given year, excluding income citizens and groups earn outside the country; 2) **Gross National Product (GNP)** – like GDP, but also includes income citizens earned outside the country; 3) **GNP per capita** – divides the GNP by the population of the country; 4) **Purchasing Power Parity (PPP)** – a figure like GNP, except that it takes into consideration what people can buy using their income in the local economy.

- **Social welfare** – Citizens' social welfare needs include health, employment, family assistance, and education. States provide different levels of support in each area, and they display many different attitudes toward government responsibility for social welfare. Some measures of social welfare are literacy rates, distribution of income, life expectancy, and education levels. Two commonly used measures of social welfare are: 1) the **Gini Index**, a mathematical formula that measures the amount of economic inequality in a society; and 2) the **Human Development Index (HDI)** that measures the well-being of a country's people by factoring in adult literacy, life expectancy, and educational enrollment, as well as GDP.

- **Civil liberties, political rights, and political freedoms** – Civil liberties refer to promotion of freedom, whereas civil rights usually refer to the promotion of equality. Although the two concepts overlap, the protection of political rights usually implies that the government should be proactive in promoting them. In addition to differences in how much proactive government support is advisable, liberal democracies also vary in terms of which civil liberties should be preserved. All liberal democracies uphold the rights of free speech and association, but they vary in terms of rights to assemble and/or criticize the government. The constitutions of many liberal democracies guarantee civil liberties and rights, and most communist, post-communist, developing, and less developed countries pay lip service to them. **Freedom House**, an organization that studies democracy around the world, ranks countries on a 1 to 7 freedom scale, with countries given a 1 being the most free

THE GINI INDEX FOR SELECTED COUNTRIES*

Norway	.268
Canada	.34
United Kingdom	.34
Russia	.377
Iran	.388
United States	.41
China	.422
Nigeria	.43
Mexico	.482
South Africa	.634

*A low Gini coefficient indicates more equal income or wealth distribution, while a high Gini coefficient indicates unequal income or wealth distribution. "0" corresponds to perfect equality (everyone has the same income), and "1" corresponds to complete inequality (one person has all the income; everyone else has zero income).

Source: World Bank

and those given a 7 being the least free. A number of post-communist countries have made significant strides in this area in recent years, but many others remain highly authoritarian.

- **Environment** – Many modern democratic states take a big interest in protecting the environment. European countries in particular have had a surge of interest expressed through the formation of "green" parties that focus on the environment.

Environmental groups have also promoted the development of a global civil society by operating across national borders. For example, environmental groups in the western democracies assist environmental groups in developing nations by providing advice and resources to address the issues facing their countries. National groups meet at international conferences and network via the internet to address environmental issues on a global level.

TABLE OF COMPARATIVE INDEXES

INDEX	CHINA	IRAN	MEXICO	NIGERIA	RUSSIA	BRITAIN
GDP (in trillions)	17,62	1.334	2,141	1.049	3.565	2.549
PPP per capita	12,900	17,100	17,900	6,000	24,800	39,500
HDI	.719	.749	.750	.504	.778	.892

Note: GDP and PPP per capita are converted and compared to U.S. dollars

Sources: International Monetary Fund (2012), CIA World Factbook, 2013, Human Development Report, United Nations, 2013

COMPARATIVE INDEXES

A common way countries can be compared is with statistical data. Some of these measures are familiar ones, because they are often cited in news stories, journals, and textbooks. They are often presented as if they are an authoritative description of a country's economy and society. However, these statistics are estimates, compiled by statistical bureaus of each country's government, as well as by international agencies such as the United Nations and the World Bank. Here are some of the statistical indicators most commonly used by those who study comparative government:

Gross Domestic Product (GDP) is an economic indicator that compiles data on all forms of wealth produced within a country, including all goods (agricultural crops, for example, or industrial products such as cars) and services (such as banking, education, and even haircuts). GDP is calculated by each nation, but there are standards of accuracy established by the international organizations that use them.

GDP per capita is an economic measure that takes the total value of a country's GDP and divides it by the country's population. This can reveal more information than straightforward GDP numbers. Two countries with fairly similar GDPs, for example, might lead one to think they have similar standards of living. However, when measured against each other using GDP per capita, the country with a greater population will have a lower GDP than the other.

Purchasing Power Parity (PPP) per capita adjusts for relative costs of living in various countries and converts different economies into a single currency, usually the U.S. dollar. GDP can be deceiving, since the same amount of money will buy more in some countries than others. PPP per capita attempts to estimate the buying power of income in each country by comparing costs of basic commodities, such as housing and food, using prices in the U.S. as a benchmark.

Human Development Index (HDI) measures a country's standard of living., First developed by the United Nations in 1991. HDI combines population statistics of years of schooling, adult literacy, life expectancy, and income levels. The index scale is from 0 to 1; countries scoring over .8 are considered to have high levels of human development, those under .5 are low.

IMPORTANT TERMS AND CONCEPTS

advanced democracies
authoritarian regime
bicameral, unicameral legislatures
bureaucratic authoritarian regimes
bureaucracy
cabinet coalition
causation
checks and balances
civil liberties
civil society
coinciding/crosscutting cleavages
command economies
common law/code law
communism
competitive elections
confederal system
conflictual political culture
consensual political culture
conservatism
constitutional courts
co-optation
corporatism
correlation
cosmopolitanism
coup d'état
democratic consolidation
democratic corporatism
direct democracy
economic liberalization
electoral systems
elites
empirical data
fascism
federal system
first-past-the-post (plurality, winner-take-all)
foreign direct investment

fragmentation
Freedom House ratings
Gini Index
globalization (economic and political)
GDP, GNP, GNP per capita
government
head of government
head of state
hypothesis
illiberal democracies
independent variable/dependent variable
indications of democratization
indirect democracy
informal politics
initiative
institutions, institutionalized
integration
interest group pluralism
judicial review
legitimacy (traditional, charismatic, rational-legal)
liberal democracies
liberalism as a political ideology
liberalism as an approach to economic and political change
linkage institutions
market economies
marketization
military rule
mixed economies
mixed electoral system
multi-member districts, single-member districts
multi-party system
nation
nationalism
normative questions
parliamentary system
party system
patronage
patron-client system

plebiscite
pluralism
political culture
political efficacy
political elites
political frameworks
political ideologies
political liberalization
political rights
political socialization
politicization of religion
presidential system
privatization
procedural democracy
proportional representation
purchase power parity (PPP)
radicalism
reactionary beliefs
recruitment of elites
referendum
reform
regime
revolution
revolution of rising expectations
rule of law
Samuel Huntington's "clash of civilizations"
semi-presidential system
separation of powers
social boundaries
social capital
social cleavages
social movements
socialism
societal corporatism (neo-corporatism)
sovereignty
state
state corporatism
subject activities

substantive democracy
succession
technocrats
"third wave" of democratization
third world
three-world approach
totalitarianism
"transmission belt"
transparency
two-party system
tyranny of the majority
unitary systems

Questions for Concepts for Comparison

Multiple-choice Questions:

1. Which of the following is a normative statement?

A) The presidents of Mexico and Russia are both directly elected by the people.
B) The head of government in Iran is the president.
C) The Chinese judicial system would serve the country better if it were more independent.
D) The European Union expanded rapidly during the first few years of the 21st century.
E) Iran's head of state is not directly elected by Iran's citizens.

2. "Falling oil prices have had a serious negative impact on Russia's economy."

In the statement above, falling oil prices may be identified as a(n)

A) independent variable
B) correlation
C) causation
D) dependent variable
E) hypothesis

3. A system in which citizens vote for legislative representatives, who in turn select the leaders of the executive branch is called a

A) corporatist system
B) presidential system
C) parliamentary system
D) unitary system
E) confederal system

4. The process that a nation uses to identify and select people for future political leadership positions is called

A) leadership succession
B) political socialization
C) patronage
D) competitive selection
E) recruitment of elites

5.Which of the following is most similar to a procedural democracy?

A) an illiberal democracy
B) a substantive democracy
C) an advanced democracy
D) a consolidated democracy
E) a market-based democracy

6. Which of the following types of states allow sub-governments to exercise power separate from the central government?

A) unitary systems only
B) confederal systems only
C) unitary, federal, and confederal systems
D) federal and confederal systems only
E) unitary and federal systems only

7. An important difference between a head of state and a head of government is that a head of government

A) symbolizes the people
B) deals with the everyday tasks of running the state
C) has no power to direct the activities of the legislature
D) does not have real policymaking power
E) is not directly elected by the people

8. In a federalist bicameral political system, the upper house of the legislature often provides

A) representation to regional interests
B) a direct tie to popular interests
C) better representation to high population areas
D) representation for titled nobility and inherited wealth
E) support for the policies of the chief executive officer

9. If a state's boundaries do not closely follow the outline of a group bonded by a common political identity, the state is not consistent with

A) its sovereignty
B) its core area
C) devolutionary forces
D) its size
E) the nation

10. Which of the following is most likely to be a centrifugal force that negatively affects a nation-state?

A) use of symbols to create cohesiveness
B) strong religious values
C) extensive transportation systems
D) strong separatist movements
E) schools that instill the society's beliefs

11. Which of the following is the best example of a regime?

A) a strong president that successfully imposes his will on the people
B) a hereditary monarch that has been passed down through several generations of a family
C) a newly established democratic government that has not yet experienced its first election
D) a dictator that has recently overthrown the previous ruler and has estabished a strong military organization
E) a society that has little use of government

12. Which of the following is NOT an advantage of a bicameral legislature?

A) One house may be determined by population, the other by regions.
B) The policymaking process is usually more efficient and less time-consuming.
C) Bicameralism may counterbalance disproportionate power in the hands of any region.
D) Bicameralism disperses power and keeps one body from becoming too powerful.
E) Bicameralism may guard against hasty or impulsive legislation.

13. A political system in which the state provides specific benefits or favors to a single person or small group in return for public support is called

A) patron-clientelism
B) democratic corporatism
C) pluralism
D) traditionalism
E) totalitarianism

14. Common law differs from code law in that it is based more on

A) written laws
B) tradition and past practices
C) the wishes of the chief executive
D) the wishes of the legislature
E) judicial review

15. Which of the following ideological groups would be MOST likely to advocate the elimination of inequality by the state taking over all resources to insure that true economic equality exists for the community as a whole?

A) liberals
B) socialists
C) communists
D) fascists
E) Islamists

16. Which of the following is the most direct measure of social welfare?

A) GNP
B) GNP per capital
C) PPP
D) Freedom House rankings
E) HDI

17. Which of the following changes is MOST likely to impact more than one area of life?

A) social reform
B) political reform
C) a military coup d'état
D) a revolution
E) a economic depression

18. Which of the following democratic characteristics is an illiberal democracy MOST likely to display?

A) guarantee of some civil liberties and rights
B) rule of law
C) regularly scheduled elections
D) an open civil society
E) neutrality of the judiciary

19. The anti-big government movements that began in the U.S. and western Europe in the 1980s promoted the 20th century trend toward

A) democratization
B) nationalization of industry
C) fascism
D) market economies
E) fragmentation

20. The most common type of political participation in most countries is

A) voting in local elections
B) protesting
C) supporting candidates for office
D) contacting government representatives concerning problems
E) voting in national elections

21. Civil society is usually strongest in

A) liberal democracies
B) illiberal democracies
C) authoritarian states
D) less-developed countries
E) Latin American countries

22. Which of the following countries clearly combines the roles of head of state and head of government into one political position?

A) Great Britain
B) The United States
C) Japan
D) France
E) Germany

23. In a mixed electoral system, some seats in the legislature are filled by winners in the plurality race, and others are filled by

A) the political party
B) a coalition of interest groups
C) the head of the national government
D) heads of sub-governments
E) referenda

24. Which of the following is a likely outcome when a country has a plurality electoral system?

A) a two (or few) party system
B) low voter turnouts
C) a parliamentary system
D) separation of powers
E) corporatism

(Questions 25 and 26 are based on the following chart):

Democracy Index 2017, by Regime Type

	No. of countries	% of countries	% of world population
Full democracies	19	11.4	4.5
Flawed democra-cies	57	34.1	44.8
Hybrid regimes	39	23.4	16.7
Authoritar-ian regimes	52	31.1	34.0

25. According to the chart, more than half the world's population lives in countries that are

A) either full democracies or flawed democracies
B) full democracies
C) flawed democracies
D) either hybrid regimes or authoritarian regimes
E) authoritarian regimes

26. Which of the following core countries is not categorized by the Democracy Index 2017 as an authoritarian regime?

A) China
B) Mexico
C) Iran
D) Nigeria
E) Russia

27. If a government's citizens and other nations recognize its authority to rule, then that government almost certainly has

A) democratic consolidation
B) a stable economy
C) a high level of legitimacy
D) integration
E) strong linkage institutions

28. Which of the following is NOT an example of a linkage institution?

A) a political party
B) an interest group
C) a newspaper
D) a television network
E) a local government agency

29. Which of the following is the best definition of a political culture?

A) the formal structure of the government and the relationship between central government and sub-governments
B) the historical evolution of political traditions that shape the current government's policy actions
C) the right to rule, as determined by the citizens of a country
D) the collection of political beliefs, values, practices, and institutions that the government is based on
E) the interaction between the government and the economy

30. Modern-day experiments with the transfer of some important powers from central governments to sub-governments encourage the process of

(A) fragmentation
(B) devolution
(C) privatization
(D) democratization
(E) separatism

Conceptual Analysis Question: (30 minutes)

Economic systems may be categorized as command economies, market economies, and mixed economies.

A) Explain two differences between command and market economies.
B) Identify and explain two factors that have promoted the movement away from command economies toward market economies since the mid-20th century.
C) Explain one reason why a government might choose to maintain a mixed economy.

PART TWO:

COUNTRY CASES

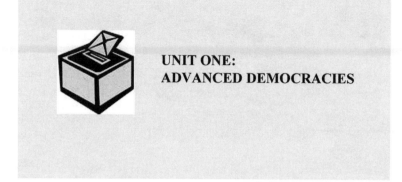

**UNIT ONE:
ADVANCED DEMOCRACIES**

During the era of the Cold War, most political science scholars categorized countries of the world according to the "Three Worlds" approach. The First World included the United States and its allies; the Second World included the U.S.S.R. and its allies; and the Third World included all countries that could not be assigned to either camp. Today, with the Cold War over and the world encompassed by forces of globalization and fragmentation, we will use these three categories to more effectively compare political systems: advanced democracies, communist and post-communist countries, and developing/less-developed countries. In this section of the book, we will consider advanced democracies.

What do we mean by the term, "advanced democracies"? The term applies to countries that have a long history of democracy that has stabilized as the established form of government. We may consider these countries according to two dimensions: political type and level of economic development.

POLITICAL DIMENSIONS

Politically, advanced democracies exemplify many facets of democracy, not just the characteristic of holding regular and fair elections. Other qualities of advanced democracies are:

- **Civil liberties**, such as freedom of belief, speech, and assembly

- **Rule of law** that provides for equal treatment of citizens and due process

- **Neutrality of the judiciary** and other checks on the abuse of power

- **Open civil society** that allows citizens to lead private lives and mass media to operate independently from government

- **Civilian control of the military** that restricts the likelihood of the military seizing control of the government

Advanced democracies generally have a high degree of legitimacy, partly because their systems have been in place for a long time. Another source of legitimacy is a large amount of **social capital,** or reciprocity and trust that exists among citizens, and between citizens and the state. All advanced democracies guarantee participation, competition, and liberty, but they differ in the methods that they use. For example, some have proportional representation electoral systems; others have plurality systems; and still others combine the two systems. Participation rates vary considerably, too. The uses of referenda and initiatives differ greatly across these countries; most advanced democracies use them, although the United States, Japan, Canada, and Germany do not allow such votes on the national level. In most of the countries, it is the responsibility of the state to ensure that all eligible voters are automatically registered to vote. However, in the United States and France, the responsibility to register rests with the individual. In several Scandinavian countries, citizenship is not required for voting; anyone who is a permanent resident may vote. In Australia, Argentina, Uruguay, and Belgium, voting is mandatory.

ECONOMIC DIMENSIONS

In thinking about the values that form the political culture of advanced democracies, they may be described as reflecting **post-modernism.** **Modernism** is a set of values that comes along with industrialization. Values of modernism include secularism (an emphasis on non-religious aspects of life), rationalism (reasoning), materialism (valuing concrete objects and possessions), technology, bureaucracy, and an emphasis on freedom rather than collective equality. In other words,

POLITICAL SYSTEMS IN ADVANCED DEMOCRACIES

PARLIAMENTARY	SEMI-PRESIDENTIAL	PRESIDENTIAL
Australia	Austria	The United States
Belgium	Finland	
Canada	France	
Denmark	Portugal	
Germany		
Israel		
Italy		
Japan		
Netherlands		
New Zealand		
Norway		
Spain		
Sweden		
Great Britain		

Parliamentary, Semi-Presidential and Presidential Systems. As the chart demonstrates, most advanced democracies have a parliamentary system. Although the United States is the only advanced democracy with a presidential system, other countries – such as Mexico and Nigeria – also have it.

industrialization encouraged making money and gaining economic success. Advanced democracies, such as Britain and the United States, experienced this transformation during the 19th century. Others were later, but all advanced democracies have also experienced post-modernism, a set of values that emphasizes quality of life over concern for material gain. Some examples of post-modern values are the preservation of the environment and the promotion of health care and education. These values accompany the economic changes of **post-industrialism**, in which the majority of people are employed in the **service (tertiary) sector**, including such industries as technology, health care, business and legal services, finance, and education. These contrast to the most common type of job created earlier by industrialization, the **industrial (secondary) sector**, which employs people to create tangible goods, such as cars, clothing, or machinery. The **agricultural (primary) sector** of post modern societies is very small since mechanized farming (first developed during the industrial era) allows only a few farmers to produce enough food to feed all the workers in the industry and service sectors.

The sector percentages for some advanced democracies look something like this:

EMPLOYMENT BY ECONOMIC SECTOR IN ADVANCED DEMOCRACIES			
	Services	Industry	Agriculture
United States	79.1%	20.3%	.7%
Canada	76%	19%	2%
Japan	70.9%	26.2%	2.9%
Britain	83.5%	15.2%	1.3%
France	77.9%	20.1%	2%
Germany	74.3%	24.2%	1.4%

Source: *CIA Factbook*, 2006-2017 estimates, as percentage of employment by sector

We may also refer to advanced democracies as liberal democracies, which value individual freedoms in both economic and political realms. Many advanced democracies, but not all, established democratic political systems many years ago, and now operate under stable governments that have long followed democratic traditions.

Many countries in Europe are among the most stable democracies in the modern world. Although their political systems operate in a variety of ways, they share common characteristics that allow effective comparison of both similarities and differences The citizens of each country are diverse, and they actively participate in political affairs. In the AP Comparative Government and Politics course, Britain represents this group. Britain has a well-organized, competitive party system and interest groups, as well as a representative form of government.

INTERNATIONAL ORGANIZATIONS: THE EUROPEAN UNION AND NAFTA

One of the most important developments of the past few decades in Europe has been the slow but steady march toward integration of the continent's countries. After World War II the most obvious need was to rebuild the infrastructures of countries devastated by the conflict. As the Cold War set in, the "Iron Curtain" separated western and eastern Europe based on economic and political differences, with countries in the east dominated by communism. Still, the urge to integrate, first economically and eventually politically, continued throughout the century. By the early 21st century, the European Union had emerged as a strong **supranational organization** that encourages cooperation among nations and promises to redefine the meaning of national sovereignty. Old nationalist impulses currently threaten to weaken or even dissolve the Union, but so far, the supranational organization has held together.

The North American Free Trade Agreement (NAFTA) is an international organization that binds the United States, Canada, and Mexico. Created in 1995 mainly as a free trade area, NAFTA has much narrower integration goals than the EU, and its member-states still retain their sovereignty. Unlike the EU, no common currency has been adopted for North American countries, and no parliament or court systems have been set up.

In the first part of this section, the political system of Britain will be discussed, and students should note that the outline of concepts in Chapter One is followed throughout. The second part of this section is a brief review of the development and current status of international organizations, with a focus on the European Union, a major force that has shaped policymaking in Britain and other European countries.

IMPORTANT TERMS AND CONCEPTS

modernism
post-modernism
post-industrialism
sectors of the economy (agriculture, industry, service)
supranational organization

CHAPTER TWO: GOVERNMENT AND POLITICS IN BRITAIN

GREAT BRITAIN OR LITTLE ENGLAND?

Britain clearly has had one of the most influential and powerful political systems in world history. It was the first country in Europe to develop a limited monarchy, which was achieved gradually so as to maintain stability. Modern democratic institutions and modern industrialization have their roots in English soil, and English influence spread all over the world during the 18th and 19th centuries throughout a far-flung empire. At the beginning of the 20th century, Britain was undoubtedly the most powerful country in the world, so truly the name "Great Britain" applies to its many accomplishments.

Yet many British subjects refer to their homeland affectionately as "Little England." Perhaps there is something of the "David and Goliath" appeal – the little island that miraculously conquered the world. At any rate, the two names aptly define Britain's dilemma in the early years of the 21st century. As a precursor in the development of modern democracy, industrialization, and imperialism, it is now a model in the art of growing old gracefully. Britain has lost much of its empire and has slipped out of the front rank of the economies of western Europe, and yet the country is still a major player in world politics.

Many other nations watch as Britain helps define the meaning of progress. However, it is not unilateral – onward ever, backward never. Instead, Britain is adjusting to its new reality as one European country among many, and yet the nation's influence remains strong. Many believe that regeneration is in the making – politically, economically, and socially – despite the challenges presented by the recent global economic recession.

SOVEREIGNTY, AUTHORITY, AND POWER

Great Britain has the oldest democratic tradition of any country in the world, and as a result, has many sources of authority and power that provide stability and legitimacy. This section is divided into three parts:

- Social compacts and constitutionalism

- Historical evolution of national political traditions

- Political culture

Social Compacts and Constitutionalism

The legitimacy of Britain's government has developed gradually, so that today tradition is a primary source of stability. Like so many other advanced democracies in Europe, **traditional legitimacy** for many years was based on the belief that an hereditary ruling family had the right to rule. Although the tradition includes a monarchy, the limitation of the king's power began early, until the power of Parliament gradually eclipsed that of the king by the end of the 17th century. Today most British citizens accept democracy as a basic component of their government. With the notable exception of Protestant/Catholic conflicts in Northern Ireland, most British citizens accept a church/state relationship in which the church does not challenge the authority of the government.

Ironically, the country that influenced the development of so many other modern democracies has never had a written constitution as such. Instead, the "constitution" has evolved over time, with important documents, common law, and customs combining to form what is often called the **"Constitution of the Crown."**

CHANGE OVER TIME: KEY FEATURES IN THE DEVELOPMENT OF CONSTITUTIONALISM IN BRITAIN

By the end of the 17th century, Britain's political system was clearly based on **rational-legal authority** – a system of well-established laws and procedures. Despite Britain's beginnings centuries before in the traditional legitimacy of an hereditary monarch, the country had gradually developed a "Constitution of the Crown" through many important documents and legal principles, including these:

- **Magna Carta** – In 1215 King John signed this document, agreeing to consult nobles before he made important political decisions, especially those regarding taxes. Magna Carta, then, forms the basis of limited government that placed restrictions on the power of monarchs.
  – NOT for citizens

- **The Bill of Rights** – This document lists rights retained by Parliament, not by individual citizens. William and Mary signed this document in 1688, giving important policymaking power to Parliament, including the power of the purse.

- **Common law** – This legal system is based on local customs and precedent rather than formal legal codes. It developed gradually in Britain, and today is found in Great Britain, the United States, and other countries with a strong English influence. Common law allows the decisions that public officials and courts make to set precedents for later actions and decisions, eventually forming a comprehensive set of principles for governance.

Historical Evolution of National Political Traditions

The British political system is influenced by many traditions from the country's long history. Britain's political culture has developed for the most part gradually and consensually, although not totally without conflict. However, many current political conflicts result from unresolved issues that rose from the dramatic changes brought by the Industrial Revolution in the late 18th and 19th centuries. The evolution of British political traditions may be analyzed in these historical categories:

- **The shaping of the monarchy** – The British monarchy has been in place for many centuries and has survived many transformations. Britain established a limited monarchy as early as the 13th century when nobles forced King John to sign the Magna Carta. During the English Civil War of the 1640s, the monarch, Charles I, was beheaded, but the monarchy was brought back later in the 17th century with powers seriously restricted by Parliament. Today, the monarchy has no decision-making power but plays an important symbolic role in British society.

- **The ascendancy of Parliament** – The English Civil War was a conflict between the supporters of the king, Charles I, and those of Parliament (the Roundheads). Parliament won, the king was executed, and the Roundhead leader, Oliver Cromwell, took over the country. However, the "Protectorate" that followed was short-lived, and the monarchy was restored when Parliament brought Charles II, the beheaded king's son, to the throne. Succeeding kings did not always respect the power of Parliament, but the balance of power was decided by the Glorious Revolution of 1688. This bloodless revolution established the constitutional monarchy when William and Mary agreed to written restrictions on their power by signing the Bill of Rights. Parliament and its ministers continued to gain strength as the monarchy lost power through succeeding kings. The authority of the king's prime minister was firmly established during the 18th century by Robert Walpole, minister to Kings George I and George II.

- **Challenges of the Industrial Revolution** – During the 18th century, two very important economic influences – colonial mercantilism and the Industrial Revolution – established England as a major economic power. The results radically changed traditional English society and its economic basis in the feudal relationship between lord and peasant. The brisk trade with colonies all over the world and the manufacture of goods created unprecedented wealth held by a new class of merchants and businessmen. The lives of peasants were transformed as they left rural areas, moved to cities, and went to work in factories.

Merchants, businessmen, and workers all demanded that the political system respond by including them in decision making. The 19th century reforms reflected their successes.

- **Colonialism** – During the era from about 1750 to 1914, the forces of nationalism and industrialization made it possible for European nations to build global empires that stretched across the continents. The famous statement, "The sun never sets on the British Empire", describes the huge network of control that Britain was able to establish during the 19th century, making it among the most powerful empires in all of world history. Nationalism enabled the government to rally citizens' support for overseas expansion. Industrialization allowed the British to produce goods to sell in foreign markets, and it encouraged them to look for raw materials not available at home. Claiming lands far away increased the country's ability to create wealth and assert power. Industrialization also made communications and transportation so much more efficient that it became possible to link lands together across the globe under one imperial banner. Just as Britain's democratization was gradual, so too was the erosion of the British Empire. It began with the loss of the American colonies in the late 18th century, although Britain actually gained in stature and wealth during the 19th century, with expansion in Asia and Africa.

- **Britain in the 20th and early 21st centuries** – At the dawn of the 20th century, Britain was the greatest imperialist nation in the world. By the early 21st century, its power had been diminished by two world wars, serious economic problems of the 1970s, and the rising power of the United States. After World War II, Britain developed a strong welfare state, which was curtailed during the 1980s by a wave of "**Thatcherism**", a conservative, capitalist backlash led by Prime Minister Margaret Thatcher. In more recent years, Labour Prime Minister Tony Blair charted a course toward what he called "A Third Way", but Blair's political fortunes waned when he supported the U.S.-led war in Iraq. His successor, Gordon Brown, lost the election of 2010, when no party won a majority in Parliament, forcing a coalition government between the Conservatives and Liberal Democrats. Modern Britain, then, is adjusting to a new level of world power, and is trying to find the right balance between the benefits of the welfare state and the trend toward greater reliance on a market economy.

Political Culture

"This fortress built by Nature for herself,
Against infection and the hand of war,
This happy breed of men, this little world,
This precious stone set in the silver sea,
Which serves it in the office of a wall,
Or as a moat defensive to a house,
Against the envy of less happier lands;
This blessed plot, this earth, this realm, this England."

Richard II
William Shakespeare

This famous quote tells us a great deal about the political culture of Great Britain. It reflects a large amount of **nationalism**, or pride in being English. It also reflects **insularity**, or the feeling of separation from the continent of Europe. In modern times, insularity has caused Britain to have a cautious attitude toward participation in the European Union. When most of the EU members accepted the euro as a common currency in January 2002, Britain refused, and instead kept the English pound. In 2016, British citizens voted in a referendum to leave the EU. However, despite Shakespeare's joy in this "fortress" state, his country has been far from isolated and has spread its influence around the world.

Other characteristics of the political culture include:

- *Noblesse oblige* **and social class** – Although the influence of social class on political attitudes is not as strong as it has been in the past, a very important tradition in British politics is *noblesse oblige*, the duty of the upper classes to take responsibility for the welfare of the lower classes. The custom dates to feudal times when lords protected their serfs and land in return for labor. Today, *noblesse oblige* is reflected in the general willingness of the British to accept a "**welfare state**," including the National Health Service. The welfare state gained support in many other European nations in the period after World War II, with a common acceptance of the government's responsibility to provide public benefits, such as education, health care, and transportation. However, during the 1980s, Margaret Thatcher's government brought Britain's acceptance of the welfare state into question by cutting social services significantly. *Noblesse oblige* also supported the building of Britain's colonial empire as the country extended its paternalism to overseas possessions.

- **Multi-nationalism** – Although Britain has a relatively large amount of **cultural homogeneity**, its boundaries include England, Scotland, Wales, and Northern Ireland, all of which have been different nations in the past, but are united under one government today. Although English is a common language, it is spoken with different dialects, and religious differences between Catholics and Protestants in Northern Ireland remain a major source of conflict today. These national identities are still strong today, and they greatly impact the way that the political system functions.

The legitimacy of the British government is evidenced by the willingness of the English people to obey the law. Britain's police force is smaller than that of most other advanced democracies, and crimes tend to be based on individual violence, and not on strikes against the state, such as assassinations. Until relatively recently, the only notable exception was Northern Ireland, where many crimes have been carried out with the political objective of overturning an elected government. In more recent years, Britain has experienced terrorist acts as part of the larger wave of terrorism that has swept over many advanced democracies in the post-9/11 world.

POLITICAL AND ECONOMIC CHANGE

Political change in Britain has always been characterized by its gradual nature. **Gradualism** in turn established strong traditions. This process helps to explain the transition in policymaking power from the

BRITAIN: THE INFLUENCES OF GEOGRAPHY

England's geographic features have shaped its political culture through the years. Important features include:

- **An island** – Britain is far enough away from mainland Europe for protection as long as it has had a good navy. Yet the island is close enough to the mainland to allow interaction.
- **Small size** – As a result, its resources are limited. This geographical fact shaped its efforts to colonize other lands and become an imperial power.
- **A short supply of fertile soil, short growing season** – Britain's ability to feed its population is limited as a result.
- **Temperate climate, but cold, chilly, and rainy** – Britain's population density is one of the highest in the world, but it is considerably lower in northern areas.
- **No major geographical barriers** – No large mountains, deserts, or raging rivers hamper transportation/communication within the country.

king to Parliament. That transition may be traced to the days shortly after William the Conqueror defeated Harold II at the Battle of Hastings in 1066. In order to ensure his claims to English lands, William (a Norman) gathered support from the nobility by promising to consult them before he taxed them. This arrangement led to a gradual acceptance of a "House of Lords", and as commercialism created towns and a new middle class, eventually the establishment of a "House of Commons". Both were created through evolution, not revolution. Of course, there are important "marker events" that demonstrate the growing power of Parliament – the signing of the Magna Carta, the English Civil War, and the Glorious Revolution – but the process was gradual and set strong traditions as it developed.

Despite the overall pattern of gradualism, Britain's political system has had to adjust to internal economic changes, as well as international crises. Some sources of change have been the Industrial Revolution, imperialistic aspirations, the two world wars of the 20th century, and the economic crises of the 1970s and 2008. These events have had significant consequences for Britain's political system.

Adjusting to the Industrial Revolution

The Industrial Revolution that began in England during the late 18th century created two new social classes that were not accommodated under the parliamentary system: a business middle class and laborers. At first, Parliament resisted including them, thinking that it might lead to disaster, perhaps even a revolution like the one that France had in 1789. However, the tradition of gradualism guided the decision to incorporate the new elements into the political system. The decision is a reflection of *noblesse oblige,* an extension of elite obligations to the rest of the population. Starting in 1832, the franchise gradually broadened:

Extension of Voting Rights and Work and Welfare Reforms

- **Great Reform Act of 1832** – About 300,000 more men gained the right to vote, and the House of Commons gained more power in relation to the House of Lords.

- **Reform Act of 1867** – The electorate reached 3,000,000, as many working-class people were given the right to vote.

- **Representation of the People Act of 1884** – The electorate was further expanded so that the majority of the voters were working class.

- **Women's suffrage** – In 1918, another Representation of the People Act enfranchised all males and women over the age of 30 who already had the right to vote in local elections. 8,400,000 women were enfranchised. By 1928, all women 21 and over were allowed to vote.

The gradual inclusion of the people in the political process meant that Marxism did not take root as it did in many other European countries, where the middle and lower classes had few political rights.

During the 19th century, labor unions formed to protect workers' rights on the job. By the end of the 19th century, some basic provisions were made for social services. For example, in 1870, mandatory elementary education was put into law. From 1906 until 1914, laws were enacted providing for old age pensions.

Political Effects of the Extension of Rights to the "Common Man"

The balance of power between the House of Commons and the House of Lords changed slowly but surely, as the new commercial elites became Members of Parliament. By 1911, the House of Lords was left with only one significant power – to delay legislation. The House of Commons was clearly the dominant legislative house by the early 20th century. By then political party membership was determined largely by class lines. The **Labour Party** was created in 1906 to represent the rights of the newly-enfranchised working man, and the Conservative Party drew most of its members from middle-class merchants and businessmen.

With the enfranchisement of the working class, a demand for welfare measures put pressure on the political system to change. Reform measures were passed by Parliament, including legislation for public education, housing, jobs, and medical care. These demands supported the creation of a new party – Labour. By the end of World War I, Labour had pushed the Liberals into third party status where they have remained ever since. Labour was never Marxist, but it combined militant trade unionism with intellectual social democracy to create a pragmatic, gradualist ideology that sought to level class differences in Britain. The **Trade Union Council** emerged as a coalition of trade unions that became a major force in British politics. The British labor movement has always been tough and especially resentful of being treated like inferiors. That militancy carries through to today, although it was softened in recent years by party leaders Neil Kinnock, John Smith, Tony Blair, Gordon Brown, and Ed Miliband. Many believe that the selection of left-leaning Jeremy Corbyn as the Labour Party leader in 2015 indicates a redirection of the party back to its roots.

Reacting to the Loss of Its Status as an Imperialist Power

In contrast to World War I, when physical destruction was limited to the front lines around the trenches on the Continent, the nature of warfare during World War II brought much more widespread damage to Britain. German bombing raids decimated roads, bridges, public buildings, and homes, and Britain had many war debts. Although the economic aid by the United States-sponsored Marshall Plan eventually aided economic recovery in Britain, an important price that the country paid was the loss of many of its colonies in Africa and Asia. In most cases, Britain helped the colonies to prepare for independence, and as a result retained economic and political bonds to them, which contributed to Britain's eventual economic recovery. However, because other European powers were also letting their colonies go because they could no longer afford to maintain them, World War II marks the collapse of the old imperialist order and the beginning of the global hegemony of the United States and the Soviet Union. Britain, then, had to adjust to its new place in world politics, and since then, has had to balance its relationship with the United States against a history-ridden relationship with the European continent. This new reality has shaped British foreign policy through to the present.

Collective Consensus

Britain joined the allied forces during World War II under the leadership of Winston Churchill. Churchill emphasized the importance of putting class conflicts aside for the duration of the war. Although he gained the Prime Minister's post as leader of the Conservative Party, he headed an all-party coalition government with ministers from both major parties. The primary objective was to win the war. After the war was over, the spirit of **collective consensus** continued until well into the 1960s, with both Labour and Conservative Parties supporting the development of a modern welfare system. Before the war was over, both parties accepted the **Beveridge Report**, which provided for a social insurance program that made all citizens eligible for health, unemployment, pension, and other benefits. One goal of the Beveridge Report was to guarantee a subsistence income to every British citizen. In 1948, the **National Health Service** was created under the leadership of the Labour Party. Even when Conservatives regained control in 1950, the reforms were not repealed. Although the electorate was divided largely by social class, with 70% of working class voting Labour and even larger percentages of middle class voting Conservative, both parties shared a broad consensus on the necessity of the welfare state. As a result, the foundations were laid for a **mixed economy**, with the government directing the economy and nationalizing major industries without giving up basic principles of capitalism, such as private ownership of property.

Challenges to the Collective Consensus since 1970

During the late 20th and early 21st centuries, Britain has experienced considerable economic and political turmoil. The era began with a serious decline in the economy, followed by a growing divide between the Labour and Conservative Parties. Labour took a sharp turn to the left, endorsing a socialist economy and serving as a mouthpiece for labor union demands. The Conservatives answered with a sharp turn to the right, advocating denationalization of industries and support for a pure market economy. During the 1990s, both parties moderated their stances, and the economy showed some signs of recovery.

Economic Crises of the 1970s

The collective consensus began to break apart with social and economic problems beginning in the late 1960s. Britain's economic problems included declining industrial production and international influence, which were exaggerated by the loss of colonies and the shrinking of the old empire. The impact of **OPEC** (Organization for Petroleum Exporting Countries) was devastating. The quadrupling of oil prices and the embargo by oil-producing countries caused recession, high unemployment rates, a drop in the GNP, and inflation.

The economic problems led labor unions to demand higher wages, and crippling strikes – such as the coal strike of 1972-73 – plagued the nation. The Labour Party lost membership, and many voters turned to the Liberals, the Conservatives, or the various nationalist parties. Many middle-class voters reacted against Labour, and the Conservatives selected Margaret Thatcher as their leader. Her very conservative stance on political and economic issues was appealing enough to sweep the Conservatives to power in 1979.

Thatcherism

Margaret Thatcher blamed the weakened economy on the socialist policies set in place by the government after World War II. Her policies were further influenced by a distinct turn toward leftist politics by the Labour Party that gave a great deal of power to labor unions. In response, she privatized business and industry, cut back on social welfare programs, strengthened national defense, got tough with labor unions, and returned to market force controls on the economy. Her policies reflect the influence of **neoliberalism**, a term that describes the revival of classic liberal values (p. 33) that support low levels of government regulation, taxation, and social expenditures as well as the protection of individual property rights. She was prime minister for eleven years. Her supporters believed her to be the capable and firm **"Iron Lady"**, but her critics felt that her policies made economic problems worse and that her personality further divided the country. Thatcher resigned from office in 1990 when other Conservative Party leaders challenged her authority. Despite the controversial nature of her leadership, her policies redirected Britain's path to the welfare state, and although her successors moderated her stances, privatization and downsizing of government have remained important trends in policymaking.

The Third Way and the "Big Society"

After the jolts of the economic crisis of the 1970s and Margaret Thatcher's firm redirection of the political system to the right, moderation again became characteristic of political change in Britain. Thatcher's hand-picked successor, **John Major**, at first followed her policies, but later abolished the poll tax, reconciled with the European Union, and slowed social cutbacks and privatization. The Conservative Party retained the majority in the 1993 parliamentary elections, but only by a very slim margin. Then, in 1997, Labour's gradual return to the center was rewarded with the election of **Tony Blair**, who promised to create a "New Labour" Party and rule in a **"third way"** – a centrist alternative to the old Labour Party on the left and the Conservative Party on the right. Tony Blair's popularity slipped sharply after he supported the United States in the Iraq War in 2003. By sending troops and publicly committing his support to U.S. President George Bush, he not only alienated other European leaders, but much of the British public as well. In 2007, Blair stepped down from his post to be replaced by long-time cabinet member **Gordon Brown**, who despite his attempts to step out from the shadow of his controversial predecessor, had a great deal of trouble convincing the British public to remain loyal to the Labour Party. The economic recession of 2008 hit Britain particularly hard, making it even more difficult for Brown to maintain control of the government.

By the election of 2010, the "third way" was in trouble, and challenges to Labour control of government were abundant. Although Labour went down to defeat, the Conservatives could not muster a majority, and so a coalition government was formed between the Conservatives and Liberal Democrats. The new prime minister, **David Cameron,** initiated his vision of a "**Big Society**," one that is energized by grassroots volunteers and private organizations, no longer harnessed by "big government." In 2015, the Conservative Party regained its majority in the House of Commons, as both the Labour Party and the Liberal Democratic Party lost a significant number of seats. However, after the Brexit vote in 2016, Cameron was forced to resign, and **Theresa May** was appointed as prime minister. May called a snap election in 2017, in which the Conservative Party again lost its majority.

CITIZENS, SOCIETY, AND THE STATE

In many ways, Britain is a homogeneous culture. English is spoken by virtually all British citizens, and only about 13% of the United Kingdom's 64 million people are ethnic minorities. For much of British history, the major **social cleavages** that shape the way the political system worked were based on multi-national identities, social class distinctions, and the Protestant/Catholic split in Northern Ireland. In recent years a major cleavage has developed based on race and ethnicity, with tensions regarding Muslim minorities increasing, as evidenced in race riots in May 2001 in the northern town of Oldham, and similar disturbances in Burnley, Leeds, and Bradford a few weeks later. In more recent years, terrorist activities have deepened the divisions, a situation that many advanced democracies of Europe and North America now face.

Multi-National Identities

The "United Kingdom" evolved from four different nations: England, Wales, Scotland, and part of Ireland. England consists of the southern 2/3 of the island, and until the 16th century, did not rule any of the other lands. By the 18th century, England ruled the entire island, and became known as "Great Britain." In the early 20th century, Northern Ireland was added, creating the "United Kingdom." These old kingdoms still have strong national identities that greatly impact the British political system.

- **England** – The largest region of Great Britain is England, which also contains the majority of the population. Throughout most of the history of the British Isles, the English have dominated other nationalities, and they still have a disproportionate share of political power. Today the challenge is to integrate the nationalities into the country as a whole, but at the same time allow them to keep their old identities.

- **Wales** – west of England – became subject to the English king in the 16th century, and has remained so till the present. Modern Welsh pride is reflected in the flag – the **Plaid Cymru** – and in the fact that the language is still alive and currently being taught in some Welsh schools. Even though Wales accepted English authority long ago, some resentment remains, as well as some feelings of being exploited by their richer neighbors.

- **Scotland** – For many years the Scots resisted British rule, and existed as a separate country until the early 1600s. Ironically, Scotland was not joined to England through conquest, but through intermarriage of the royalty. When Queen Elizabeth I died without an heir in 1603, the English throne went to her nephew James I, who also happened to be king of Scotland. A century later both countries agreed to a single Parliament in London. However, Scots still have a strong national identity, and tend to think of themselves as being very different from the English. The Scots too have their own national flag, and the Scottish Parliament has recently been revived. In 2015, a vote for Scottish Independence was narrowly defeated.

- **Northern Ireland** – England and Ireland have a long history of arguing about religion. After Oliver Cromwell won the English Civil War in the mid 17th century, he tried to impose Protestantism on staunchly Catholic Ireland to no avail. English claims to Irish lands were settled shortly after World War I ended, when Ireland was granted **home rule**, with the exception of its northeast corner, where Protestants outnumbered Catholics by about 60% to 40%. Home rule came largely because of pressure from the **Irish Republican Army (the IRA)**, who used guerrilla warfare tactics to convince the British to allow Irish independence. Finally, in 1949, the bulk of Ireland became a totally independent country, and Northern Ireland has remained under British rule, but not without a great deal of conflict between Protestants and Catholics.

The British Settlement with Ireland, 1922. In December 1922, after intense guerilla warfare in Ireland, the Irish parliament sitting in Dublin proclaimed the existence of the Irish Free State, a self-governing dominion which included all of Ireland except the six northern counties of Ulster, where Protestants outnumbered Catholics by about 60% to 40%. These counties formed Northern Ireland, which still sends representatives to the British Parliament.

Social Class Distinctions

Distinctions between rich and poor have always been important in Britain, with the most important distinction today being between working and middle-class people. The two classes are not easily divided by income, but psychologically and subjectively, the gulf between them is still wide. German sociologist Ralf Dahrendorf explains the divide in terms of **solidarity**, particularly among the working class. The point is that keeping the old job and living in the old neighborhood – the sense of family and friends – is more important than individual success.

British social classes have traditionally been reinforced by the education system. "**Public schools**" were originally intended to train boys for "public life" in the military, civil service, or politics. They are expensive, and they have educated young people to continue after their parents as members of the ruling elite. A large number of Britain's elite have gone to "public" boarding schools such as Eton, Harrow, Rugby, St. Paul's, and Winchester. Middle-class students commonly attend private grammar schools, where students wear uniforms but do not reside. The percentage of British seventeen-year-olds that are still in school is lower than in many other industrialized democracies. However, the leaving age for compulsory education was raised from 16 to 18 by the Education and Skills Act of 2008. The change took effect in 2013 for 16-year-olds and 2015 for 17-year-olds.

The most important portal to the elite classes is through Oxford and Cambridge Universities, or **Oxbridge.** Nearly half of all Conservative Members of Parliament went to Oxbridge, as have about one quarter of all Labour MPs. Percentages in cabinet positions are even higher, and prime ministers almost always graduate from one or the other school. Since World War II, more scholarships have been available to Oxbridge, so that more working and middle-class youths may attend the elite schools. Also, the number of other universities has grown, so that higher education is more widespread than before. However, this trend was recently challenged, since Parliament raised the maximum level of tuition to English universities from $5,400 to $14,500 in 2012, making higher education less accessible to many students.

Ethnic Minorities

According to the 2011 census, about 13% of the British population is of non-European origins, with most coming from countries that were formerly British colonies. However, most members of the minority ethnic population grew rapidly, increasing from about 7% in the 2001 census. The main groups are:

- black/African/Caribbean/black British 3%

- Asian/Asian British: Indian 2.3%,

- Asian/Asian British: Pakistani 1.9%,

- mixed 2%,

- other 3.7%

Because of tight immigration restrictions in the past, most ethnic minorities are young, with about half of the population under the age of 25. Percentages of minorities have grown despite the restrictions that were placed on further immigration during the Thatcher administration of the 1980s. The Labour government kept the restrictions in place, and the Conservative-Liberal Democrat coalition government pledged to halve net immigration, which was about 200,000 people in 2010. Since it could not curb arrivals from the European Union, that meant a cutback on non-Europeans.

The British have often been accused of adjusting poorly to their ethnic population. Reports abound of unequal treatment by the police and physical and verbal harassment by citizens. The May 2001 race riots in several cities increased tensions, and new fears of strife have been stoked by post 9/11 world politics. Widespread rioting in the summer of 2011 was triggered when a young black man was killed by the police, leading to accusations of racial bias. Today there is some evidence that whites are leaving London to settle in surrounding suburban areas, resulting in a higher percentage of minority population living in London. Despite this segregation, the mixed-race population appears to be increasing, with the census of 2001 offering for the first time in British history a category for mixed-race people.

Muslim Minorities

Terrorist attacks, successful and attempted, have occurred in Britain over the past few years, with a major attack in 2005, schemes foiled by the government in the summer of 2006, and car-bombings in 2007. Other advanced democracies have suffered attacks and plots as well. Of course, the United States was attacked on September 11ᵗʰ, 2001, and the Madrid bombings in 2004 were Europe's most lethal terrorist incidents. In Canada 17 people were arrested in June 2007 on suspicion of scheming to blow up buildings.

In recent years, concern about radicalized British Muslims has increased as some have joined extremist groups, such as the Islamic State in Iraq and Syria (ISIS). The British government estimates that 500 or more British men and women have gone to fight for militant groups in Iraq and Syria. The 2014 beheading of American journalist James Foley drew renewed attention to the dangers posed by radicalized young British Muslims, and the government turned to anti-extremist imams for help to prevent their followers from adopting radical views.

Although many European countries face these problems, Britain's risk for home-grown terrorist attacks may be greater than many other countries. Several problems for Britain are:

- **Distinct minority/majority cleavages** – Muslims have an identity of being a minority distinct from a well-established majority, such as the English in Britain, the French in France, and the Germans in Germany. In contrast, many people in the United States are immigrants, and the "majority" ethnicity of white Americans in many U.S. cities has already become a minority. With so many different ethnic and racial identities, the majority identity in the United States is not as clear-cut as it is in most European countries.

- **Social class differences of Muslims** – In the United States, many Muslims tend to be relatively well-off, while many British Muslims are disaffected and unemployed. Many British Muslims are the children of illiterate workers who entered as cheap industrial labor, and their childhood experiences have not endeared them to British culture.

- **Pakistani Muslims** – Many Muslims in the rest of Europe came from Turkey and Africa, but the largest group of British Muslims comes from Pakistan. Since Osama bin Laden and his companions were found in Pakistan, some scholars think that a higher percentage of British Muslims are linked to al-Qaeda than are Muslims in other countries.

- **Lack of integration of minorities** – Polls suggest that alienation of minorities in Britain may be higher than it is in other countries because the national culture has not absorbed the groups into mainstream culture. This problem is apparent in France as well, where girls are not permitted to wear head scarves at school. In Britain they may attend classes in full *hijab*, but many minorities still feel as if they are treated as second-class citizens.

Immigrants from Eastern Europe and the Middle East

Another major change in British demographics is an influx of about one million immigrants from the eight central and eastern European countries that joined the European Union in 2004. Poles, who have made up about two-thirds of the newcomers, are now the largest group of foreign nationals in Britain, up from 13th place in 2004. The main draw has been better job opportunities in Britain than in eastern Europe, but the recession in 2008 led many newcomers to return home since the British job market withered. However, since the job market has been even worse in eastern Europe, at least some of the new workers stayed in Britain. Many are migrant workers who pick crops in rural areas or fill other low-paying jobs that British workers shun, although with unemployment rates going up, the potential for labor conflict is real. By 2012, more than 130,000 immigrants from Romania and Bulgaria were living in Britain, and the numbers of immigrants coming from these two countries is continuing to grow.

In 2015, as the civil war in Syria intensified, refugees poured out of the country and into Europe. The exodus created a crisis in Europe, and the British reaction was criticized by many. Britain did not accept quotas set by the European Union, but instead came up with a separate policy. In September 2015, the prime minister announced the government's decision to accept 20,000 refugees from camps neighboring Syria, but none who have already travelled to Europe, sparking intense debate about the appropriate response to the refugee crisis. According to Prime Minister Cameron, the refugee crisis "complicated" the issue of whether or not Britain would remain in the European Union.

Political Beliefs and Values

In the early 1960s political scientists Gabriel Almond and Sidney Verba wrote that the **"civic culture"** (political culture) in Britain was characterized by trust, deference to authority and competence, pragmatism, and harmony. The economic crisis of the 1970s and the continuing conflicts regarding Northern Ireland challenged this view of citizenship in Britain, as have fears of terrorism in recent years. However, the overall characteristics seem to still be in place today.

British citizens reflect what Almond and Verba saw as good qualities for democratic participation: high percentages of people that vote in elections, acceptance of authority, tolerance for different points of view, and acceptance of the rules of the game. However, social and economic changes during the 1970s altered these characteristics so that today British citizens are less supportive of the collective consensus and more inclined to values associated with a free market economy. Many observers believe that the **"politics of protest"** – or the tendency to disagree openly and sometimes violently with the government – have become increasingly acceptable. The rioting in 2011 confirmed this analysis, although the reasons for the riots are far from clear.

Some manifestations of changing political beliefs and values include:

- **Decreasing support for labor unions** – British labor unions have strong roots in the Industrial Revolution, and class solidarity supports union membership. However, when unions staged crippling strikes during the 1970s, public opinion turned against them, as people began to view unions as "bullies" to both the government and the general population. Margaret Thatcher's tough stance against the unions intensified strife between unions and the Conservative government.

- **Increased violence regarding Northern Ireland** – The issues surrounding British claims to Northern Ireland intensified during the early 1970s after British troops killed thirteen Catholics in a "bloody Sunday" incident in January 1972. The IRA and Protestant paramilitaries stepped up their campaigns of violence. Although in recent years the groups have consented to negotiate with the government, the threat of violent eruptions remains strong today.

- **Thatcherism** – The Conservative Party controlled British government from 1979 until 1997. Although later modified by Prime Minister John Major, Margaret Thatcher's "revolution" toward a free market economy certainly affected political attitudes. She rejected collectivism and its emphasis on the redistribution of resources from rich to poor and government responsibility for full employment. Thatcherism fostered entrepreneurial values of individualism and competition over the solidarity of social classes and the tradition of *noblesse oblige.*

- **New Labour** – Despite the radical changes of the 1970s and 1980s, Britain has not deserted its traditional political culture. **Tony Blair** led a Labour Party that loosened its ties to labor unions, and a new "Good Friday" Agreement on Northern Ireland was reached in 1998. Thatcherism has been incorporated into political attitudes, but in the early 21st century, both parties are more inclined toward a middle path, or "**third way.**" The coalition government formed in 2010, at first criticized as unworkable, also encouraged compromise, although significant differences of opinion existed among cabinet members. The election of 2015 left the Labour Party much weakened, and the choice of left-leaning Jeremy Corbyn as the party leader may represent a move away from the "third way."

- **Protests over the Iraq War** – Not only did ordinary citizens vocally protest Britain's involvement in the Iraq War, many political leaders openly criticized it as well. In a political system where party loyalty is valued above all, many Labour MPs (Members of Parliament) withdrew their support for Blair's policy in Iraq. Their resistance to the party leadership extended to the cabinet, with several party leaders resigning their posts, despite the strong tradition of collective consensus. The ill will spread into domestic affairs as well, so that Blair had little choice but to resign from office in June 2007.

Voting Behavior

As in most other European countries, a relatively high percentage of qualified British voters go to the polls. Although there was a notable decline in recent elections (66% voted in 2015 and 68.6% voted in 2017) more than 70% of eligible citizens normally vote in parliamentary elections. Today voters have less party loyalty than they once did, but voting behavior is still clearly tied to social class and region.

- **Social class** – Until World War II, voting in Britain largely followed class lines. The working class supported the Labour Party, and the middle class voted Conservative. However, today the lines of distinction are blurred, partly because the society and the parties themselves have changed. For example, some middle-class people who grew up in working-class homes still vote the way their parents did. On the other hand, many in the working classes have been attracted to the Conservative platform to cut taxes and keep immigrants out. In recent years, both parties have come back to the center from the extreme views of the 1970s and 1980s, as reflected in Labour leader Tony Blair's program to provide a "third way," or a centrist alternative. However, the Labour victories of 1997, 2001 and 2005 showed that the party was strongest among people who feel disadvantaged: the Scots, the Welsh, and the poor. In the post-Blair years, the distinctions between Labour and Conservative Parties have continued to blur, leaving room for other parties, particularly the Liberal Democrats, to compete for votes in all social classes.

- **Regional factors** – The Labour Party usually does well in urban and industrial areas and in Scotland and Wales. However, in 2015, Labour lost seats to the Scottish National Party, with SNP picking up 56 of the 59 seats in Scotland. In 2017, the SNP lost seats, winning only 35, but still enough to give the party a voice in Parliament. The industrial cities of the north – around Liverpool, Manchester, and Newcastle, and in Yorkshire – almost always support the Labour candidates, as do people that vote in central London. The areas where Conservatives usually win are mostly in England, especially in rural and suburban areas. These voting patterns are tied to social class, but they also reflect urban vs. rural values.

POLITICAL INSTITUTIONS

Strong political traditions and institutions that have been in place for hundreds of years guide Britain's stable democratic regime. The monarch still rules as head of state, but the prime minister and the cabinet form the policymaking center. The system is **parliamentary**, which means that the prime minister and cabinet ministers are actually members of the legislature. In this section, we will explore the parts of the British political system and the ways that they interact to make policy.

Linkage Institutions

Linkage institutions play a very important role in British government and politics. Political parties, interest groups, and print and electronic media have long connected the government to British citizens. The British government's policymaking activities are complex, and its linkage institutions are well developed.

Political Parties

Britain's political parties began to form in the 18th century, and their organization and functions have shaped the development of many other party systems (including the United States) through the years. At first they were simply **caucuses**, or meetings of people from the same area or of like mind. Only in the 19th century did a two-party system emerge with roots in the electorate. The labels "**Whig**" and "**Tory**" first appeared under Charles II, with the Tories supporting the king and the Whigs opposing. Both were derisive names: Whigs were Scottish bandits; Tories, Irish bandits. The Whigs eventually became the Liberal Party and the Tories (still a nickname today) the Conservatives. The Labour Party emerged in the early 20th century in response to new voter demands created by the Industrial Revolution.

Today the two major political parties are **Labour** and **Conservative**, but several other significant parties are represented in Parliament. Historically, Britain has had strong third parties that significantly affect election results. For example, in the 1980s, the **Liberal Democratic Alliance Party** garnered as much as 26% of the popular vote, but because of Britain's single-member plurality election system (one member per district who only has to get more votes than anyone else, not a majority), it never claimed more than 62 seats in the House of Commons. The House of Commons is dominated by the two largest parties, but three or four-way elections for MPs are usual. The 2010 parliamentary elections resulted in an unusual, but not unprecedented, **hung parliament**, in which no party gained a majority and a coalition government formed. The Conservative Party recaptured the majority in the 2015 elections, winning 330 seats, but lost it again in 2017, winning only 317 seats.

The Labour Party

The largest party on the left is the Labour Party. It controlled the British government between 1997, when **Tony Blair** became prime minister, and 2010, when Labour ceded power to a coalition government. The party began in 1906 as an alliance of trade unions and socialist groups that were strengthened by the expansion of rights for the working class during the 19th century. Traditionally, labor unions have provided most party funds, although Blair loosened the union ties and sought to broaden the base of party membership.

The early history of the party was defined partially by the controversial "**Clause 4**" that called for nationalization of the "**commanding heights**" of British industry. The growing moderation of the party was reflected by the removal of the clause from the Labour Party Constitution in the early 1990s. The shift in policies toward the center became apparent shortly after **Neil Kinnock** became the party leader in the early 1980s, and continued under leaders **John Smith** (1993-

1994), **Tony Blair** (1994-2007), **Gordon Brown** (2007-2010), and **Ed Miliband** (2010 to 2015). After Labour's serious losses in 2015, Miliband resigned, and many believe that the new leader, **Jeremy Corbyn**, has reversed the party's move toward moderation.

Labour's 1992 loss in an election that they were widely predicted to win almost certainly was a turning point in its development. Its failure to capture the majority led to the resignation of Neil Kinnock as party leader, and the appointment of John Smith, a moderate Scotsman who the party hoped would solidify support from Scottish nationalist groups. Smith died suddenly in 1994, and was replaced by Tony Blair, a young leader who did not come from union ranks. Instead, he was an Oxford educated barrister-turned-politician who hoped to bring more intellectuals and middle-class people into the party. Labour won the elections of 1997, 2001, and 2005, and tried to redefine itself as a moderate party with support from many different types of voters. Even though the party won the 2005 election, its margin of victory was much smaller than before, contributing to Blair's resignation as party leader in 2007.

Labour's prospects for the future continued to fall after Britons in the local elections across England in June 2009 gave the party only 23% of the vote, its worst showing ever and well behind the opposition Conservatives' 38%. In the elections for the European Parliament on the same day, Labour won less than 16% of the vote. Labour lost the election of 2010, and Gordon Brown resigned, leaving the party leadership to **Ed Miliband**, whose political preferences were left of center. As the coalition government formed between the Conservatives and Liberal Democrats, the Labour Party was left to struggle to regain voter support. The party's losses in the election of 2015 reinforced its waning influence. However, it gained seats in the election of 2017, reviving its prospects once more.

The Conservative Party

The Conservative Party dominated British politics between World War II and 1997, holding the majority in Parliament for all but sixteen years during that period. The Conservative Party is the main party on the right, but it has prospered partly because it traditionally has been a pragmatic, rather than an ideological party. Although the party supported a market-controlled economy, privatization, and fewer social welfare programs during the 1980s under the leadership of Margaret Thatcher, the Conservatives moved back toward the center under Prime Minister John Major (1990-1997).

The party is characterized by *noblesse oblige*, and its power is centered in London. The organization of the party is usually viewed as elitist, with the MPs choosing the party leadership. No formal rules for choosing their leader existed until recently, but now the leadership must submit to annual leadership elections. This new process proved to be problematic for Margaret Thatcher in 1990, when she was challenged strongly in the election and virtually forced to resign.

After Labour seized control of the government in 1997, the Conservative Party was weakened by deep divisions between two groups:

- **The traditional wing (one-nation Tories)** values *noblesse oblige* and wants the country ruled by an elite that takes everybody's interests into account before making decisions. This wing generally supports Britain's membership in the European Union.

- **The Thatcherite wing** of strict conservatives wants to roll back government controls and move to a full free market. The members of this wing are often referred to as **Euroskeptics** because they see the EU's move toward European integration as a threat to British sovereignty.

Until 2016, the party leader and prime minister was **David Cameron**, who won the position in December 2005. Cameron's youth and debating ability, as well as Tony Blair's vulnerability as Labour leader, revived the Conservative Party's hope of recapturing the majority. During 2006 and early 2007 the party established a lead in opinion polls, but with Blair's resignation and the rise of **Gordon Brown** to the prime minister's post, Labour regained its lead in major polls during the summer of 2007. However, with Brown's growing unpopularity during 2008, the Conservatives again gained support and were well positioned for the election in 2010. Cameron was generally more of a "one-nation"

Tory, and at first he distanced himself from the Thatcherite wing, but by 2009 his words were more conciliatory as he hoped to unite his party for victory in the election of 2010. When his party won a plurality, but not a majority of seats, Cameron became prime minister of a coalition government formed with the Liberal Democrats, with **Nick Clegg** – the Liberal Democrat leader – serving as deputy prime minister. The party regained its majority in 2015, extending Cameron's leadership until 2016, when he was forced to resign after the Brexit referendum passed. He was replaced by Theresa May, who called a snap election in 2017, in which the Conservative Party once again lost its majority.

**COMPARISON:
LABOUR AND CONSERVATIVE
PARTIES IN BRITAIN**

LABOUR PARTY	CONSERVATIVE PARTY
Main party on the left; began as an alliance of trade unions and socialist groups; have moved toward the center since the 1990s; was the majority party from 1997 until 2010; generally more supportive of EU membership	Main party on the right; split between the traditional wing (*noblesse oblige*) and "Thatcherites" who want to roll back government controls and move to a full free market; tend to see EU as threat to British sovereignty

The Liberal Democrats

Two parties – the Liberals and the Social Democrats – formed an alliance in the 1983 and 1987 elections, and formally merged in 1989, establishing the Liberal Democratic Party. The goal was to establish a strong party in the middle as a compromise to the politics of the two major parties: Thatcher's extremely conservative leadership and

Labour's leftist views and strategies. The party won an impressive 26% of the votes in 1983, but because of the single member district **plurality voting system** (see the section on Elections, p. 127) in Britain, it only won 23 seats (3.5%). Liberal Democrats have campaigned for **proportional representation**, which would give them an equal percentage of the MP seats, and for a **Bill of Rights** modeled after the first ten amendments of the U.S. Constitution.

The party's strength declined in the early 1990s as both the Conservative and Labour Parties moved to the center of political opinion, and in the 1992 election the party picked up only about 17% of the total votes cast. The party held on, though, partly due to the popularity of its leader, Paddy Ashdown, and to some strong stands on the environment, health, and education. Ashdown retired in 1999, and was replaced by a Scottish MP, Charles Kennedy, and the Liberal Democrats picked up seven seats in the 2001 election. The party also benefited from public disillusionment with the Blair government's support for the war in Iraq when it picked up 11 more MPs in the election of 2005. In December 2007, party leadership passed to Nick Clegg, who criticized the Labour government for its erosion of individual civil liberties, a stand that the party has long supported. However, the party still remains tremendously underrepresented in Parliament, considering their relative popularity at the polls. After the 2005 elections, the Liberal Democrats had 62 MPs (out of 646), even though they won more than 22% of the vote. In 2010, the party won 23% of the vote, but only managed to capture 57 seats in the House of Commons. However, since no party won a majority, the Conservative leader, David Cameron, invited the Liberal Democrats to help form a coalition government, and Nick Clegg became deputy prime minister.

The formation of the coalition was controversial among long-time supporters of the party, with some criticizing Clegg for supporting the center-right policies of the Conservative Party. The coalition showed signs of stress, since the two parties took increasingly different positions on issues such as Britain's role in Europe – with Liberal Democrats generally being more supportive of the EU – and on reform of Britain's unelected upper house of parliament. The Liberal Democrats' poor showing in the election of 2015 forced Clegg's resignation, leaving the party seriously weakened. The current leader is Tim Farron.

Other Parties

Britain has many smaller parties including nationalist groups in Wales, Scotland, and Northern Ireland. **Plaid Cymru** in Wales and the **Scottish National Party** in Scotland both won seats in the House of Commons during the 1970s, and they have managed to virtually shut the Conservative Party out in the elections in their regions since the late 1990s. The parties' fortunes were strengthened after Labour's return to power in 1997, when the Blair leadership created regional assemblies for Scotland and Wales. However, Labour has been strong in the two regions, and the two parties combined won only nine seats in the House of Commons in 2010. The Scottish National Party surged in popularity in 2015, winning 56 of Scotland's 59 seats in Commons, largely at the expense of the Labour Party. However, in 2017, the SNP won only 35 seats. The Plaid Cymru currently has 11 of 60 seats in the Welsh Assembly, and the Scottish National Party has 64 of 129 seats in the Scottish Parliament. Northern Ireland has always been dominated by regional parties, including **Sinn Fein** (the political arm of the IRA) and the **Democratic Unionist Party**, led by Protestant clergymen. Together they captured 12 parliamentary seats in 2015. In 2017, Sinn Fein won 4 seats, and the DUP won 8 seats.

Two parties on the far right benefitted from the growing criticism of the Labour government before the 2010 election: the **British National Party,** and the **UK Independence Party.** The British National Party formed in 1982, but has never been represented in Parliament. Historically the BNP has been overtly anti-Semitic, but in recent years it has focused on ousting Muslims from Britain. During the 2010 General Election, the BNP received 1.9% of the vote and failed to win any seats. All three mainstream political parties in the UK openly condemn the BNP. The UK Independence Party has focused more on its opposition to British membership in the European Union. In the 2009 European elections, the BNP won two seats in the European Parliament, representing the first time that the party ever won in a national poll. The UKIP, which had previously held twelve seats in the European Parliament, picked up an extra seat, giving it a total of 13 (finally settling to 11 due to defections), which tied the number of seats that the Labour Party won. In the 2010 UK general election, the party polled 3.1% of the vote (up 0.9%). Despite being the fourth largest party in terms of vote share, UKIP failed to win any seats. In 2015, the party only won one seat in Parliament, but it picked up 12.6% of the vote, reflecting its growing popularity. In 2017, UKIP's share of the votes was reduced to 1.8% of the vote, causing it to lose its only seat.

Elections

The only national officials that British voters select are members of Parliament. The prime minister is not elected as prime minister but as an MP from a single electoral district, averaging about 65,000 registered voters. Elections must be held every five years, but traditionally, the prime minister could call them earlier. Officially, elections occur after the Crown dissolves Parliament, but that always happens because the prime minister requests it. The power to call elections has always been very important, because the prime minister – as head of the majority party – always calls them when (s)he thinks that the majority party has the best chance of winning.

The **Fixed-term Parliaments Act of 2011** altered these traditions by introducing fixed-term elections to Parliament. Under the provisions of the Act, parliamentary elections must be held every five years, beginning in 2015. Fixed-term Parliaments, where general elections ordinarily take place in accordance with a schedule set far in advance, were part of the Conservative–Liberal Democrat coalition agreement that was produced after the 2010 general election. The act limits the prime minister's power to call elections, except in the case of a vote of no confidence. An early election might also be called if 2/3 of the MPs vote to do so.

The Plurality Electoral System

As in the United States, British parliamentary elections are "winner-take-all," with no runoff elections. Within this single-member plurality system, each party selects a candidate to run for each district post, although minor parties don't always run candidates in all districts. The person that wins the most votes gets the position, even if (s)he does not receive the majority of votes in the district. The British nickname for this system is "first-past-the-post" (like a race horse). Since MPs do not have to live in the districts that they represent, each party decides who runs in each district. So party leaders run from safe districts where the party almost always wins. Political neophytes are selected to run in districts that a party knows it will lose. They are usually happy to just make a good showing by receiving more votes than the party usually gets.

The "winner-take-all" system often exaggerates the size of the victory of the largest party and reduces the influence of minor parties. This system is the main reason that the Liberal Democrats have not been able to get a good representation in Parliament. Regional parties tend to fare better. For example, the Scottish National Party generally has a good chance of picking up districts in Scotland, as it did in 2015 and 2017. However, Parliament still remains a two-party show, even though many other parties may get a sizeable number of votes. For example, in the election of 2005, the Labour party received 35.3% of the vote (not a majority), but they received 356 out of 646 seats (i.e., a majority). Likewise, in 2015, UKIP won 12.6% of the vote but only won one seat in Parliament.

In 2010, Liberal Democrats garnered 23% of the popular vote, but only won 57 of 650 seats in the House of Commons. This situation inspired Nick Clegg, the Liberal Democrat leader and deputy prime minister, to call for a referendum in May 2011, on an **alternate vote (AV)**, which would have allowed voters to rank candidates on the ballot in order of preference. If after a first round no candidate had more than 50% of the votes, cast, the votes of the least popular candidate would be redistributed, following the second preferences indicated by supporters of that eliminated candidate. Rounds of redistribution continue until someone crosses the 50% line. Along with the Liberal Democrats, the Labour leader Ed Miliband supported the AV, but Conservatives and many Labour MPs opposed it. The referendum went down to decisive defeat, so national elections in Britain continue to follow the first-past-the-post model. The 2017 election – called by Prime Minister Theresa May – was supposed to solidify the Conservative Party's majority. However, since the party lost enough seats to lose the majority, the move backfired, weakening her authority, insteadof increasing her majority in Parliament.

 **BRITISH GENERAL ELECTION, 2017**

650 Seats Total

Leader	Theresa May	Jeremy Corbyn	Tim Farron
Party	Conservative	Labour	Liberal Democrat
Seats won	317	262	12
Seat change	-13	+30	+4
Popular vote	13,636,684	12,878,460	2, 371,910
Percentage	42.4%	40%	7.4%

The Effects of First-past-the-post Voting. Even though the Conserative Party won only 42.4% of the vote, it captured just under a majority of the seats in the House of Commons. The Liberal Democratic Party won 7.4% of the vote, but only won 12 seats because its supporters were spread out over the country. In contrast, the Scottish Nationalist Party won only 3% of the vote, but because ts votes were concentrated in Scottish district, the party won 35 seats.

Elections for Regional Governments

Some signs of change in the electoral system have emerged in very recent years. For example, in the **Good Friday Agreement** of April 1998, Britain agreed to give Northern Ireland a regional government in which all parties would be represented on a proportional basis. In other words, the religion-based parties would each have a percentage of representatives that matched the percentage of the total vote each received. According to later agreements with Scotland and Wales, their regional parliaments also are based on **proportional representation**. As a result, both bodies have often not had a clear majority party. However, the largest party in the Welsh Assembly after the election of 2011 was Labour, with 30 of 60 members. In the Welsh Assembly, the Plaid Cymru won 11 seats, and the Conservatives won 14. After the Scottish election of 2011, the Scottish National Party had 68 of

129 total members, with Labour at 37 and Conservatives at 15. Other changes have occurred on the local level, with the mayor of London now elected directly for the first time ever.

U.S. vs. British Elections*

United States	Britain
Parties are less powerful.	Party determines who runs where.
Members must live in districts.	Members usually don't live in their districts.
Party leaders run in their respectivie districts.	Party leaders run in "safe districts."
Individual votes for four officials on the national level.	Individual votes for only one official on the national level.
Between 30 and 60 percent of the eligible voters actually vote (more in recent elections)	About 70 percent of the eligible voters actually vote (less in 2001, 2005, 2010, 2015, and 2017).
Elections are by first-past-the-, post single-member districts; almost no minor parties get representation.	Elections are by first-past-the-post, single-member districts; minor parties get some representation, but less than if they had proportional representation (regional elections in Ireland, Scotland and Wales use proportional representation).

*Note: The Comparative AP Exam does not require knowledge of U.S. government, but this chart is intended to help students understand British elections.

European Parliament Elections

Britain has participated in the elections to the European Parliament, which is the directly elected parliamentary institution of the European Union. The elections are held every five years by people of the EU's member-states. In 2014, 73 members were elected from Britain using proportional representation, with 19 seats going to the Conservatives, 24 to the UK Independence Party, and 20 to Labour. Most notable was the drop in support for Conservative Party candidates, with the UK Independence Party actually garnering more votes than any other party. The Scottish Nationalists won 2 seats, and the Liberal Democrats secured only 1 seat. With Britain's impending withdrawal from the EU, it will lose its votes in the European Parliament.

Campaign Financing

British campaigns for public office are much shorter and less expensive than those in the United States. However, in 2006 both major political parties were under police investigation for campaign financing. The two areas of investigation were the use of peerages (seats in the House of Lords) and the disclosure of non-commercial loans. In the first, parties were investigated for breaking a parliamentary act of 1925 that prohibited the offering of peerages in return for money. Secondly, parties were suspected of breaking a 2000 law, which requires parties to disclose the benefits they derive from personal loans. In question were secret loans from wealthy well-wishers. The investigation increased the pressure on Tony Blair to step down as Labour leader.

Interest Groups

Like most other advanced democracies, Britain has well-established interest groups that demonstrate **interest group pluralism** (pp. 71-72) with relatively autonomous groups competing with one another for influence in policymaking. British politics are also characterized by **neocorporatism**, in which interest groups take the lead and sometimes dominate the state. Perhaps the greatest influence of British interest groups comes through **quangos** (quasi-autonomous nongovernmental organizations), or policy advisory boards appointed by the government. Using a neocorporatist model, quangos, together with government officials develop public policy, working in different policy areas. Some simply advise on policy while others deliver public services. Quangos weakened while Margaret Thatcher was prime minister, and their numbers have declined even more during recent years. In recent years, a number of quangos have been abolished under Conservative plans to reduce the overall budget deficit. However, about a thousand still remain.

Not surprisingly, the most influential interest groups have been those linked to class and industrial interests. Between 1945 and 1979, business interests and trade unions fiercely competed for influence over the policymaking process. The powerful **Trade Unions Congress (TUC)**, which represents a coalition of unions, had a great deal of clout because the government often consulted them on important decisions. While no comparable single group represents business interests, they too had an open door to inner government circles. For example, in 1976, Chancellor of the Exchequer Denis Healy negotiated with TUC and **the Confederation of Business Industries** (CBI) to limit TUC's wage demands in exchange for 3% reduction in income tax rates. All of this changed when Margaret Thatcher took control in 1979. Thatcher wanted to reduce the power of interest groups in general, and she slammed the door shut on TUC. As labor unions lost public support, they also lost political sway, and the Labour Party loosened its ties to unions and began to broaden its voter base. Since Thatcher left in 1990, interest groups have regained power, but the government has partnered not only with unions, but with businesses as well.

The Role of the Media

Not surprisingly, British newspapers reflect social class divisions. They are sharply divided between quality news and comment that appeals to the middle and upper classes, and mass circulation tabloids that carry sensational news. Radio and television came to life during the collective consensus era, so originally they were monopolized by the **British Broadcasting Corporation (BBC)**. The BBC sought to educate citizens, and it was usually respectful of government officials. Commercial television was introduced in the 1950s, and now there are five stations that compete, as well as cable. A variety of radio stations also exist. Despite the competition from private companies, the government strictly regulates the BBC and the commercial stations. For example, no advertisements may be sold to politicians, parties, or political causes.

BBC and Government Relations

The BBC had a significant clash with the Blair government in 2003 over support for the war in Iraq. BBC reporter Andrew Gilligan wrote that a government statement that Iraqi forces could deploy weapons of mass destruction within 45 minutes was based on false intelligence that officials knew was unreliable. The conflict grew into a crisis when weapons inspector Michael Kelly (the alleged source of the "false intelligence") committed suicide. Tony Blair appointed appeals judge Lord Hutton to investigate the death, and the judge ended the crisis when he exonerated the Blair government in early 2004 and criticized the BBC for its reporting. The report prompted the chairman of the BBC board of governors to resign, an action that signaled an almost unprecedented embarrassment for the network.

Despite this disagreement, the Labour government continued to support the BBC with a license fee levied on any household in Britain with a television that receives broadcasts. This fee has allowed the BBC to maintain its large presence on television and the internet and to support BBC Worldwide, the corporation's commercial arm. The Conservatives have been critical of raising the license fee, and they have advocated for a more transparent BBC, with full audits and expenditures published online.

Media Scandal of 2011

An investigation into phone-hacking practices of major British tabloids led to the closing of one of Rupert Murdock's most influential newspapers, *The News of the World*, in the summer of 2011. When it was discovered that the paper's employees hacked the cell phone of a murdered 13-year-old, the scandal snowballed as it became apparent that phone hacking was a common practice among the tabloids. Even though David Cameron called for an investigation, his own credibility was questioned, since his former media chief, Andy Coulson, who had been an editor for the Murdock paper, was questioned and arrested by the police. The scandal escalated to include London's Metropolitan Police, who were charged with failing for years to fully investigate phone-hacking at *The News of the World*.

Gender Pay Gap at the BBC

In the summer of 2018, it was revealed that female news presenters at the BBC earned significantly less than their male counterparts, especially those in high-paying jobs. Whereas pay for men and women was fairly equal for lower-paying jobs, the gap for the top positions was quite signficant. The differences were made public in accordance with a new law that requires all major employers to publish data on the pay gap between their male and female employees. This pattern reflects the common practice of bidding up salaries for television stars, and for many reasons, women often do not do well with this process.

THE INSTITUTIONS OF NATIONAL GOVERNMENT

Just like most other countries of the world today, the British government has three branches of government and a bureaucracy. Furthermore, the legislature is divided into two houses, a model that the British invented, and is now widely copied. However, their system is **parliamentary**, and the interactions among the branches are very different from those in a **presidential system,** such as in the United States. In a parliamentary system, the executive branch is fused with the legislative branch because the prime minister and the cabinet are actually the leaders of parliament. As a result, separation of powers – a major principle of American government – does not exist. Also, the judicial branch lacks the power of judicial review, so it has no role in interpreting the "Constitution of the Crown".

Britain is a **unitary state** with political authority centralized in London. Decisions made by the central government – both laws passed by Parliament and regulations prepared by the bureaucrats in Whitehall – are binding on all public agencies.

The Cabinet and the Prime Minister

The cabinet consists of the prime minister and ministers, each of which heads a major bureaucracy of the government. Unlike the U.S. cabinet, the British cabinet members are party leaders from Parliament chosen by the prime minister. The **collective cabinet** is the center of policymaking in the British political system, and the prime minister has the responsibility of shaping decisions into policy. The cabinet does not vote, and all members publicly support the prime minister's decisions. In other words, as the leaders of the majority party elected by the people, they take **"collective responsibility"** for making policy

COMPARATIVE EXECUTIVES*

PRIME MINISTER OF BRITAIN	PRESIDENT OF THE U.S.
Serves only as long as he/she remains leader of the majority party/coalition	Elected every four years by an electoral college based on popular election
Elected as a member of Parliament	Elected as president
Has an excellent chance of getting his/her programs past Parliament	Has an excellent chance of ending up in gridlock with Congress
Cabinet members are always MPs and leaders of the majority party/coalition	Cabinet members usually not from Congress (although they may be)
Cabinet members not experts in policy areas; rely on bureaucracy to provide expertise	Expertise in policy areas one criteria for appointment to cabinet; members head vast bureaucracies

*Note: The Comparative AP Exam does not require knowledge of U.S. government, but this chart is intended to help students understand the British executive.

for the country. The unity of the cabinet is extremely important for the stability of the government. The prime minister is the "**first among equals**", but (s)he stands at the apex of the **unitary government**. Despite many recent changes, political authority in Britain is still centralized in the London-based government. The prime minister is not directly elected by the people, but is a member of Parliament and the leader of the majority party. In 2010, no majority party emerged from the election, so a coalition government formed with David Cameron, the Conservative leader, as prime minister, and Nick Clegg, the Liberal Democrat leader, as deputy prime minister. Since the system is designed to work with a clear majority party, the coalition cabinet had to incorporate the points of view of both parties in the coalition, and Labour and minor parties were left as the "loyal opposition." After the Conservative Party regained the majority in 2015, the system returned to normal, but the party again lost the majority in the election of 2017.

The prime minister

- speaks legitimately for all members of Parliament
- chooses cabinet ministers and important subordinate posts
- makes decisions in the cabinet, with the agreement of the ministers
- campaigns for and represents the party in parliamentary elections

Parliament

Although British government consists of three branches, little separation of powers exists between the cabinet and parliament. Like most other parliamentary systems, the executive and legislative branches are fused, largely because the leaders of the majority party in Parliament are also the cabinet members.

The House of Commons

Even though Britain has multiple political parties, the House of Commons is based on the assumption that one party will get the majority number of seats, and another will serve as the "opposition." One way to look at it is that Britain has a multi-party system at the polls, but a two-party system in the House of Commons. Whichever party wins a plurality at the polls becomes the majority party, and the second party becomes the **"loyal opposition"**.

Set-up of the House of Commons

The House of Commons is set up with long benches facing one another with a table in between that is by tradition two-sword-lengths wide. The prime minister – who is elected as an MP like all the rest – sits on the front bench of the majority side in the middle. He or she becomes prime minister because the members of the majority party have made that selection. The majority party members may vote to change their leader, and the prime minister will change as a result. Right across from the prime minister sits the leader of the "opposition" party, whose members sit on benches facing the majority party. Between them is the table. Cabinet members sit on the front rows on the majority side, and the **"shadow cabinet"** faces them on the opposition side. On the back benches sit less influential MPs – the "**back-benchers**" – and MPs from other political parties sit on the opposition side, but at the end, far away from the table.

Debate

The "**government**", then, consists of the MPs on the first rows of the majority party side, and they are the most important policymakers as long as they hold power. Debate in the House is usually quite spirited, especially once a week during **Question Time**. During the hour the prime minister and his cabinet must defend themselves against attack from the opposition, and sometimes from members of their own party. The **speaker of the house** presides over the debates. Unlike the

House of Commons. The chamber is small enough that it is crowded when all MPs are present. The majority party faces the opposition parties, with the prime minister sitting in front by the table with the leader of the opposition directly across – two sword lengths away.

speaker in the U.S. House of Representatives, the speaker is supposed to be objective and often is not a member of the majority party. The speaker's job is to allow all to speak, but not to let things get out of hand. (S)he often has to gavel MPs down that get too rowdy.

One reason that debate can be so intense is that the floor of Parliament is the place where MPs gain attention from others, possibly casting themselves as future leaders. Also, the opposition is seen as the "check" on the majority party, since checks and balances between branches do not exist.

Party Discipline

Because the majority party in essence is the government, party discipline is very important. If party members do not support their leadership, the government may fall into crisis because it lacks legitimacy. Above all, the majority party wants to avoid losing a "**vote of no confidence**", a vote on a key issue. If the issue is not supported, the cabinet by tradition must resign immediately, and elections for new MPs must be held as soon as possible. This drastic measure is usually avoided by settling policy differences within the majority party membership. If a party loses a vote of no confidence, all MPs lose their jobs, so there is plenty of motivation to vote the party line. A vote of no confidence occurred in early 2005, when the Labour government's Higher Education Bill squeaked by with an approval vote of 316 to 311. The bill proposed raising university fees, a measure criticized by not only the opposition, but also by some outspoken Labour MPs. The vote narrowly allowed Blair's government to continue to control Commons. The policymaking power of the House is very limited since many government decisions are ratified by the cabinet and never go to Parliament.

Since the 1970s, backbenchers have been less deferential to the party leadership than in the past. A backbencher rebellion against John Major's EU policy weakened the prime minister significantly. Tony Blair faced a major rebellion of Labour backbenchers on key votes in February and March 2003 regarding the use of force in Iraq. After the disastrous 2009 local and European elections, many Labour MPs called for Gordon Brown's resignation, and five cabinet members resigned. In an effort to shore up his support, Brown reshuffled his cabinet, giving choice positions to key people in the government, and breaking the momentum of the cabinet meltdown that threatened to force him out. The near-collapse of the government came on the heels of the exposure of a widespread parliamentary expenses scandal, in which Parliament members charged thousands of pounds' worth of expenses to the taxpayers. The scandal questioned the very nature of **parliamentary sovereignty** (the principle that Parliament's decisions are final), and the government had a great deal to do to restore its image with the public.

Parliament has some substantial powers because its members

- debate and refine potential legislation

- are the only ones who may become party leaders and ultimately may head the government.

- scrutinize the administration of laws

- keep communication lines open between voters and ministers

The House of Lords

Britain is no exception to the rule in its bicameral legislative structure. However, many of the benefits of bicameralism (including the dispersing of power between two houses) do not operate because the House of Lords has so little power. The House of Lords is the only hereditary parliamentary house in existence today, and although historically it was the original parliament, today it has minimal influence. The House of Commons established supremacy during the 17th century, and Lords gradually declined in authority. Since the turn of the 20th century, the only remaining powers are to delay legislation, and to debate technicalities of proposed bills. Lords may add amendments to legislation, but the House of Commons may delete their changes by a simple majority vote. Until 2009, the chamber also included five law lords, who served as Britain's highest court of appeals, but they could never rule acts of Parliament unconstitutional.

Until 1999 about one-half of the members of Lords were **hereditary peers**, who hold seats that have been passed down through family ties over the centuries. The remaining were **life peers**, people appointed to nonhereditary positions as a result of distinguished service to Britain. In 1999 the Labour government took seats away from most of the hereditary peers, so that today only 92 hereditary seats remain among 567 life peers. In late 2001, the government announced plans for a new upper house with about 550 mostly appointed members, but with no hereditary posts. In March 2007 the House of Commons voted, in principle, in favor of replacing the Lords with an elected chamber, either 100% elected or 80% elected, 20% appointed.). However, the House of Lords, feeling threatened by the idea of dismantlement, rejected this proposal and voted for an entirely appointed House of Lords. In 2008 Jack Straw, a top cabinet member, introduced a "white paper" (an announcement of government policy) that proposed to replace the House of Lords with an 80-100% elected chamber, with one third being elected at each general election, for a term of 12 to 15 years. The current system continues, despite the ongoing debate.

One criticism of the British parliamentary system is that the lack of separation between the prime minister and the legislature creates a dangerous concentration of power, since both are controlled by the same party. Supporters of the parliamentary system praise its efficiency, since it does not experience the crippling "gridlock" found between Congress and the president in the United States.

The Bureaucracy

Britain has hundreds of thousands of civil servants who administer laws and deliver public services. Most civil servants do clerical work and other routine work of a large bureaucracy. However, a few hundred higher civil servants directly advise ministers and oversee work of the departments. They actually coordinate and implement the policies that cabinet members set.

The British bureaucracy is a stable and powerful force in the political system. Top-level bureaucrats almost always make a career of government service, and most are experts in their areas. Because the ministers are party leaders chosen by the prime minister, they understand a great deal about British politics, but they generally are not experts in particular policy areas. In contrast, the top bureaucrats usually stay with their particular departments, and the ministers rely on their expertise. As a result, the top civil servants often have a great deal of input into policymaking, including **discretionary power** to make many decisions in implementing legislative and executive decisions. The minister has a powerful position in the cabinet, but (s)he relies heavily on the advice of the bureaucrats. Bureaucrats almost never run for public office and are usually not active in party politics. Therefore, as cabinets come and go, the bureaucrats stay and fulfill an important role in government.

The Judiciary

English ideas about justice have shaped those of many other modern democracies. For example, the concept of trial by jury goes back to the time of Henry II in the 13th century. Britain has had a judicial branch for centuries, but ironically, the modern judiciary has much more limited powers than those in the United States, France, and Germany. In Britain, the principle of **parliamentary sovereignty** (Parliament's decisions are final) has limited the development of judicial review (the courts' ability to decide whether or not actions, laws, and other court decisions are unconstitutional). British courts can only determine whether government decisions violate the common law or previous acts of Parliament. Even then, the courts tend to rule narrowly because they defer to the authority of Parliament. By tradition, the courts may not impose their rulings on Parliament, the prime minister, or the cabinet.

The British legal system based on **common law** contrasts to the stricter **code law** (see p. 29) practiced in the rest of Europe. Code law is much less focused on precedent and interpretation than common law. British courts, like those in most other advanced democracies, do make distinctions between original and appellate jurisdiction. District Courts hear cases that may be appealed to the High Courts, which until 2009 were in turn appealed to the highest court in the land – the **law lords**. They were actually members of the House of Lords who were designated as the highest judicial authority in Great Britain to settle disputes from lower courts.

In 2009, a **Supreme Court** was created to replace the law lords as the highest judicial authority in the United Kingdom. The court consists of a president and eleven justices appointed by a panel of lawyers. Its chief function is to serve as the final court of appeal on points of law in cases across the country, although Scotland maintains a separate legal system. The British Supreme Court has much more limited powers than its counterpart in the United States. It can nullify government actions if they are judged to exceed powers granted by an Act of Parliament, but it cannot declare an Act of Parliament unconstitutional. Parliament remains the supreme authority under the principle of parliamentary sovereignty.

In general, judges have the reputation of being independent, impartial, and neutral. Few have been MPs, and almost none are active in party politics. Judges are appointed on "good behavior," but they are expected to retire when they reach the age of 75. Most judges are educated in public schools and at Oxford and Cambridge, and their positions are prestigious.

Despite the limited policymaking power of the judiciary, Britain's membership in the European Union gave judges a new responsibility that promised to become even more important in the future. Since Britain has been bound by EU treaties and laws, it has been the judges' responsibility to interpret them and determine whether or not EU laws conflict with parliamentary statutes. With the Brexit decision in 2016, this responsibility is subject to the terms of British withdrawal from the European Union.

PUBLIC POLICY AND CURRENT ISSUES

Many serious issues confront the British political system today. Some of the most important are:

- **The evolving relationship between government and the economy**
- **Transparency in government**
- **Relationships with the European Union**
- **Terrorism and cohesion**
- **Relationships with the U.S.**
- **Devolution and constitutional reform**

The Evolving Relationship between Government and the Economy

The historical basis for Britain's political economy is **liberalism**, the philosophy that emphasizes political and economic freedoms for the individual and the market. Yet liberalism in Great Britain has been reshaped over the years, particularly in recent decades. The recession that began in late 2007 deepened the economic issues that preoccupy the government, as unemployment rates went up and business earnings decreased. The state-owned Bank of England, which is the central bank for all of Britain, responded to the economic crisis in September 2008 by cutting interest rates and by buying government bonds and corporate debt. The Bank has kept interest rates low since then, but Britain's economy was slow to recover until 2013, when GDP began to grow and unemployment rates began going down.

Since the end of World War II, the British government has redefined its relationship with the economy several times. Until the 1970s, the **collective consensus** philosophy was based on social democratic values that support a great deal of government control of the economy, including the nationalization of many major industries. The approach taken is called **Keynesianism** (after British economist John Maynard Keynes), in which the government took action to secure full employment, expand social services, maintain a steady rate of growth, and keep prices stable. Then, Margaret Thatcher reversed this trend by emphasizing **neoliberalism**, a revival of the old political and economic philosophy of liberalism that had guided Britain in earlier years. Thatcher's policies moved toward a free market economy and denationalization of industries. Since then, the government has tried to establish a middle way, but the best balance between state control and the free market is a matter of great dispute.

During the Blair years (1997-2007) the prime minister teamed with Gordon Brown, the chancellor of the exchequer (treasury), to craft the direction of the political economy. By 2001 the Blair-Brown team had succeeded in bringing Britain's **"misery index"** (inflation plus unemployment) down to a new low. While holding income tax rates steady, the government still managed to fund a variety of welfare programs, including those intended to improve living standards and job opportunities for the poor. However, with the recession that began in late 2007, economic growth stagnated, and the new coalition government faced growing deficits. As GDP growth slowed significantly, the government looked for ways to cut the budget, putting a particular squeeze on public sector spending, such as health care and education. In response, David Cameron advocated his **"Big Society"**, a vision of Britain's future that emphasizes greater roles for private companies, charities and employee-owned cooperatives: groups funded by the state, but embedded in society. Cameron's argument was that the British state had become too big, impersonal and monolithic, and he wanted to devolve more power to local councils and individual citizens.

Austerity Programs

The Liberal Democrats generally shared Cameron's vision, but the coalition suffered criticism for its drastic reductions in public spending. In 2010, the government introduced an **austerity program**, a series of reductions in public spending, intended to cut welfare and other public institutions. One example is the government plan to shift college tuition costs from the state to students by raising the maximum fees English universities can charge. In 2010, Parliament voted to increase the maximum from $5,400 to $14,500 by 2012, an action that sparked angry protest demonstrations from students. Most universities appear to be setting tuitions at the maximum level, leaving Cameron's government open to further criticism. Although austerity programs were meant to end in 2016, in 2014, the Treasury extended the austerity period until at least 2018.

Protests to the government's austerity plans have grown louder as the economy has improved, with many people concerned about welfare cuts that have reduced social security benefits. Disability rights groups have argued that budget cuts disproportionately affect disabled people. Critics point out that the use of food banks has increased as benefit claimants feel the pinch of government cuts.

Health Care Issues

The attempt to balance the budget is illustrated by debates over what to do with the National Health Service (NHS). Many support it, saying that the British population is much healthier than it used to be, and that the British working class has especially benefited. However, the system is challenged by the aging population, a general trend in most mature democracies today. Others criticize the service for the increasing expense to the government and for a long wait lists for medical treatment. Private medical care is becoming more common, but many Britons want to keep the NHS, especially if it can be reformed. The NHS and education were "ringfenced" and protected from the austerity program's spending cuts, but the high cost of health care is still controversial.

In 2012, after much debate, Parliament passed the Health and Social Care Act. At its heart are plans for a radical restructuring of the health service, which gives general practitioners control of much of the NHS's annual budget, cuts the number of health bodies, and introduces more competition into services, all with the intention of reducing administrative costs, something the government says is essential if the health service is to cope with the ever-rising cost of caring for an aging population, and new, expensive medicines and treatments.

Transparency in Government

The British government has long had a solid reputation for its transparency, so the parliamentary scandal that broke in the spring of 2009 was surprising to many people around the globe. The *Daily Telegraph* reported first on expense reports from Labour ministers, then on Labour backbenchers, and finally on Conservative and Liberal Democrat MPs. The reports revealed huge amounts of personal expenses charged to the government, ranging from small, everyday purchases to thousands of pounds' worth of home improvements. One particularly controversial type of spending was categorized as the "second-homes allowance" for MPs who maintain homes in both London and their constituencies. Some MPs were getting reimbursements for improvements to both of their homes, and others were spending money on their homes just before they re-classified them as main residences, even though both practices were against the rules for the second-homes allowance. The depth of the damage to Parliament's image was reflected by the resignation of Michael Martin, the House of Commons speaker, who claimed thousands of pounds for a chauffeur-driven car that drove him about his Glasgow constituency, one of Britain's poorest.

The British public reacted strongly against these exposures, causing the leadership to apologize for the entire Parliament and promise that colleagues would pay back unjustified claims. Brown called for an end to the functioning of Parliament as "a gentlemen's club" that makes its own rules on members' benefits. Other reforms demanded wider changes that would make Parliament and the government more accountable to the people. Some suggestions included reducing the number of MPs, parliamentary committees with real powers of oversight and investigation, and primary elections to select parliamentary candidates. This scandal caused British citizens, already beleaguered by recession, to lose trust in their government.

Even before the scandal, an April 2009 YouGov poll showed very low political efficacy rates among Britons, with a third of the respondents indicating that they trusted no politician to tell the truth. Of course, the fact that the scandals have been exposed indicates that the transparency level is still high, since an independent press may freely criticize the government. The coalition government elected in 2010 made increased transparency a priority, with the prime minister's office announcing in late 2010 the launching of a new website (www.number10.gov.uk) whose purpose it was to provide users with information abut government activities and policies. The website features detailed information about ministers' schedules and access to videos of the prime minister's statements and questions in Parliament.

Relations with the European Union/Brexit

British insularity has always meant that the country tends to keep its allies at arm's length. The British government did not enter the Common Market (a precursor to the European Union) when it was established in 1957. When Britain finally decided to enter in the early 1960s, its membership was vetoed twice by French President Charles De Gaulle. Finally, in 1978, Britain joined the Common Market, but the Thatcher government was opposed to rapid integration of European markets, and she was adamantly opposed to the adoption of the euro in place of the pound. Under Prime Minister John Major, Britain signed the Maastricht Treaty that created the European Union, and under Labour's Tony Blair, the government was still more favorable. When the Labour government first took power, it openly advocated adoption of the euro and further integration with the EU. However, once in power, Labour backed away from its initial commitment, although during the 2005 campaign Blair promised future referenda on the new EU constitution and the euro. Since Blair's time in office, the EU constitution has been abandoned, but Britain's membership in the EU has remained controversial, with the Conservative Party openly split over EU matters.

Gordon Brown was much less vocal in his support for strong ties with the EU than Tony Blair was, and David Cameron was caught between the conflicting wings of the Conservative Party, which could not agree on Britain's role in the EU. Meanwhile, many British citizens expressed their disapproval of the EU in the 2015 elections by supporting UKIP candidates, who received about 12.6% of the total vote. In 2013, bowing to pressure from Euroskeptics in his party, David Cameron promised a renegotiation of the U.K.'s membership of the EU, followed by a popular vote on whether to stay in the bloc, if his party won the 2015 general election outright, which it did. Cameron reiterated the party's commitment to hold an "in-out" referendum on Britain's membership of the European Union, following negotiations with EU leaders.

Official groups formed to campaign on both sides of the issue, including Britain Stronger in Europe advocating remaining, and Vote Leave supporting leaving. The referendum was held on June 23, 2016, with the question "Should the United Kingdom remain a member of the European Union or leave the European Union?" Those who supported Brexit drew on British nationalism, as well as resentment toward economic competition from Eastern European immigrants. Those who opposed Brexit emphasized the importance of cooperating with countries on the continent, especially where the economy is concerned.

The results startled many people, but they reflected Britain's age-old insularity in regards to the European continent. The vote was very close – 51.89% in favor of leaving the EU (Brexit), and 48.11% in favor of remaining. 72.21% of registered voters actually voted. Since Cameron supported remaining, he resigned as prime minister and was replaced by the then home secretary, **Theresa May**.

Since the referendum, the government has been in negotiations with the EU, with the scheduled departure set for March 2019, with a "transition" period that will last until December 21, 2020. The debate has centered on the nature of the break, with May advocating a continuing trading partnership with the EU, but hardliners – such as Foreign Secretary **Boris Johnson** – arguing for a clean break. Brexit reflects the ongoing redefinition between the nation-state system of sovereignty and the role that international organizations play in world politics. In the summer of 2018, after Johnson and two other cabinet members resigned from May's cabinet amid disagreements over Brexit terms, some – including former Prime Minister Tony Blair – advocated a second referendum on Brexit.

Terrorism and Violence

Tony Blair aptly described changes in the nature of terrorism in Britain in an essay published in *The Economist* at the end of his tenure:

> "Over ten years I have watched this [terrorism] grow. (If you had told me a decade ago that I would be tackling terrorism, I would have readily understood, but thought you meant Irish Republican terrorism.)"

The meaning of terrorism certainly changed after four British Muslim suicide bombers attacked the London transit system in July 2005, killing 52 people. Two other major terrorist plots were uncovered in 2006, and in 2007 several car bombs exploded – one outside a London nightclub, one near Trafalgar Square in London, and one in the Glasgow airport. Within four days of the car bombs, the main players had been arrested. The government is now earmarking extra money for security, a mosque watchdog is in operation, and the M15 (British security service) is keeping track of many suspected terrorists.

In his first press conference as prime minister, Gordon Brown reacted to the 2007 attacks by affirming his government's commitment to nonviolence, and expressed his distaste for the "extreme message of those who practice violence and would maim and murder citizens on British soil." Shortly afterward, the government began a pilot curriculum to be taught in some Muslim religious classes that emphasizes nonviolence among British Muslims. The program has been criticized for singling out young Muslims for civics lessons, and the British government is still struggling with how to isolate the extremist Muslim minority from the moderate majority. One of the thorniest issues of all is maintaining a cohesive society, despite the demographic changes of recent years.

Torn between the task of narrowing the social, economic and cultural gap between Muslims – especially in poor urban areas of northern Britain – and the rest of society – and simply fighting terrorism, the government believes that it must at least do the latter. Probing and preempting attacks by Muslim extremists occupies about 75% of the energy of the British security services, who have had a fair amount of success in uncovering terrorist plots before the last minute, according to a report in *The Economist* in February 2009. The riots that broke out across Britain in the summer of 2011 also increased anxiety over maintaining law and order, even as Britons struggled to understand why the rioting occurred. Recent budget cuts have made it more difficult for the police to do their job, and security pressures were strong as London hosted the Olympics in 2012. Tensions increased after G4S, a company hired by the government to provide security during the games failed to fulfill its contract. However, the army deployed troops to make up the shortfall, and the games passed without notable security scares.

Relationship with the United States

When Tony Blair became prime minister of the United Kingdom in 1997, he took on a very ambitious agenda. Domestically, he wanted to sustain economic prosperity and increase social equality, as well as reinforce traditional British national identity and political institutions. Internationally, he sought to develop a new relationship with Europe in which the United Kingdom would play a central and self-confident role, and yet maintain a special relationship with the United States that had been in place since World War II.

Blair's efforts seemed to succeed until the Iraq crisis drove Washington in the opposite direction from Paris and Berlin. France and Germany were outspoken in their criticism of the U.S. invasion of Iraq and of Britain's support for the war under Blair's watch. The crisis challenged the cornerstone of Tony Blair's vision that the United Kingdom could act as a bridge across the Atlantic. It damaged Britain's relationship with France and raised questions about the wisdom of its special relationship with the United States. It caused dissent within the Labour leadership and seriously undermined Blair's popular support, a situation that resulted in the party losing many seats in the House of Commons in the election of 2005, and eventually led to Blair's resignation in 2007.

After the election of American president, Barack Obama, in November 2008, the direction of U.S./British relations was positive. The global economic crisis required Obama and Brown, and then Cameron, to work together to address the problems. During Obama's state visit to Britain in 2011, both leaders referred to their "essential relationship," and the two countries ave been crucial allies in building coalitions to deal with international crises. However, British budget cuts have seriously impacted the country's defense capabilities, so that the country's ability to provide real international military support has been in question. With the election of Donald Trump as U.S. president in 2016, his "Make America Great Again" campaign has challenged the traditional partnership between the two countries, with Trump questioning the world order of alliances among democratic leaders put in place after World War II.

Devolution and Constitutional Reform

The British government is still a **unitary** one, with the most authority emanating from London. However, continuing desire by the Scottish and Welsh for their independence and the problems with Northern Ireland have led to the development and implementation of the policy of **devolution**, or turning over of some political powers to regional governments. Even before Margaret Thatcher delayed the process when she took office in 1979, the Labour party supported devolution. However, a 1977 referendum to create Scottish and Welsh assemblies failed. In 1999, though, referenda in both regions passed, and each now has its own regional assembly, which has powers of taxation, education, and economic planning.

Northern Ireland

In the 1998 Good Friday Agreement, a parliament was set up for Northern Ireland as well, although London shut down its activities after violence broke out in 2002. The Northern Ireland Assembly remained suspended for almost five years, not reopening until May 2007. A new challenge was presented to the Assembly in early 2009, when two British soldiers and a police constable were killed and dissident republican terrorists claimed responsibility for both killings. These first murders of members of the security forces since 1998 brought thousands out in peaceful protest rallies across Northern Ireland. Some observers found hope in the response by political leaders of Sinn Fein, the Democratic Union Party, and the English boss of the Northern Ireland police, who appeared and were photographed standing shoulder-to-shoulder outside the Northern Ireland Assembly. Just how much these new parliaments will affect London's authority is yet to be seen. Devolution has also included the creation of the office of mayor and a general assembly for London, giving the city more independence from the central government.

In the summer of 2018, a small republican dissident group, calling itself the "New IRA", sponsored some terrorist acts, including lobbing petrol bombs, in Derry-Londonderry. This group aims to resurrect the IRA's campaign of violence, but so far, the attacks have not spread, and an anti-violence rally was held to protest the violence, and the Sinn Fein leader, Mary Lou McDonald, condemned the group's actions.

Scottish Independence

In recent years, the movement for Scottish independence has gained momentum, coming up for a vote in a referendum in September 2014. The Scottish Parliament set the arrangements for the referendum in November 2013, when it passed the Scottish Independence Referendum Act, following an agreement between the Scottish and the UK governments. The campaign was intense, with both sides presenting heated arguments for their points of view. The question was "Should Scotland be an independent country?" The "No" side won with 55.3% of the voters, while 44.7% voting "Yes." The voter turnout of 84.6% was much higher than for any election or referendum in the United Kingdom in recent memory. Although the campaign for independence failed, it has many supporters, and most believe that the issue remains a viable one, especially since many Scots – including the Scottish Independence Party – opposed Brexit.

Some critics have argued that devolution should be only one step toward modernizing the political system. Other reforms under consideration include a written Bill of Rights for individual citizens, a written constitution, freedom of information, and a new electoral system.

One crucial reform – proportional representation – was rejected by British voters in 2011, but its supporters are still numerous. Whatever reforms are made, Britain still retains a strong attachment to its many traditions, and the government's long lists of accomplishments are not all in the past. As the nation redefines both external and internal political relationships, Britain still serves as a role model for the development of democratic traditions in the modern world.

IMPORTANT TERMS AND CONCEPTS

alternate voting (AV)
austerity program
backbenchers
Beveridge Report
Blair, Tony
Brexit
British Broadcasting Corporation
British National Party
Brown, Gordon
Cameron, David
caucuses
"civic culture"
Clause 4
Clegg, Nick
coalition government
collective consensus
collective responsibility
Confederation of Business Industries
Conservative Party
"Constitution of the Crown"
cultural heterogeneity
Democratic Unionist Party
devolution
the English Bill of Rights
Euroskeptics
"first-past-the-post" voting system
Fixed-term Parliaments Act of 2011
the Glorious Revolution
the "government"

gradualism

hereditary peers

home rule

hung parliament

insularity

Irish Republican Army

"Iron Lady"

Keynesianism

Labour Party

law lords

Liberal Democratic Alliance

liberalism

life peers

limited government

"loyal opposition"

Magna Carta

Miliband, Ed

"misery index"

mixed economy

multi-nationalism

neo-corporatism

neo-liberalism

noblesse oblige

OPEC

Oxbridge

parliamentary system

Plaid Cymru

plurality voting system

politics of protest

proportional representation

quangos

Question Time

rational-legal legitimacy

referendum

safe districts

Scottish Independence Movement

Scottish National Party

"shadow cabinet"

Sinn Fein
solidarity
Speaker of the House
Thatcherism
the third way
Tories
Trade Union Congress
traditional leadership
UK Independence Party
unitary government
"vote of no confidence"
welfare state
Whigs

Questions for Advanced Democracies and Britain

1. An important difference between modernism and post-modernism is that post-modernism puts more emphasis on

A) secularism
B) preservation of the environment
C) rationalism
D) technology
E) individual freedom

2. A major goal of both the European Union and NAFTA is the establishment of

A) a common currency
B) a free trade system
C) tightened restrictions for border crossings
D) rule of law that applies equally to all member-states
E) common agricultural regulations

3. Which of the following is NOT a necessary characteristic of advanced democracies?

A) civil liberties
B) neutrality of the judiciary
C) private ownership of property
D) rule of law
E) open civil society

4. Important documents that legitimize Britain's rational-legal authority are

A) the written Constitution, Magna Carta, and common law
B) the written Constitution, the Bill of Right and Magna Carta
C) common law, the Beveridge Report, and the Bill of Right
D) common law, the Bill of Right, and Magna Carta
E) the Beveridge Report, the Constitution of the Crown, and the Bill of Right

5. An important demographic change in Britain in recent years that puts pressure on the National Health Service is the

A) aging of the population
B) decrease in the birth rate
C) large number of people who are emigrating from Britain
D) increase in the death rate
E) increase in the fertility rate

6. Which of the following is an accurate description of the influence of social class on voting in modern Britain?

A) The working class strongly supports the Labour Party, and the middle class strongly supports the Conservative Party.
B) British voters have few loyalties to political parties, so social class has no consistent influence on voting behavior.
C) Social class is not as important an influence on voter loyalties and opinions as is age.
D) Social class is still a strong influence on voter choices in England, but it has little impact on voters in Scotland, Wales, and Northern Ireland.
E) The working class tends to support Labour and the middle class tends to support the Conservatives, but the lines of distinction have blurred in recent years.

7. In which of the following areas would British voters be MOST likely to vote for Conservative Party candidates?

A) cities of the industrial mid-section
B) Scotland
C) Wales
D) central London
E) rural England

8. This British political party generally supports a market controlled economy, privatization of industry, and fewer social welfare programs. They also attract supporters who are "Euroskeptics." Who are they?

A) Labour Party
B) Liberal Democratic Party
C) Conservative Party
D) UK Independence Party
E) Scottish Nationalist Party

9. This poltical party has received as much as 26% of the popular vote in modern British elections, but it has neverclaimed more than 62 seats in te House of Commons. Which political party is it?

A) British National Party
B) UK Independence Party
C) Liberal Democratic Party
D) Scottish Nationalist Party
E) Plaid Cymru

10. The concept of "collective responsibility" is most relevant to the policymaking practice of the British

A) House of Commons
B) House of Lords
C) bureaucracy
D) Conservative Party
E) cabinet

11. Which of the following is the best description of the responsibilities of the British speaker of the House?

A) the speaker is the leader of the "loyal opposition"
B) the speaker is the leader of the majority party
C) the speaker serves as a liaison with the Queen
D) the speaker coordinates legislative activities and process with the House of Lords
E) the speaker objectively presides over debates in the House of Commons

12. All of the following are powers of the British House of Commons EXCEPT:

A) debating and refining potential legislation
B) serving as a source of all current and future ministers
C) holding the prime minister and cabinet accountable for policymaking practices
D) initiating policy and legislation
E) keeping communication lines open between voters and ministers

13. Which of the following is the BEST description of the role the British bureaucracy plays in the political system?

A) It is a major source for recruitment of new cabinet members.
B) Most are in tune with the legislative process because they have held seats either in the House of Commons or the House of Lords.
C) Top level bureaucrats serve as a major source of stability because they make a career of government service.
D) Although bureaucrats don't often run for public office, they are often leaders of political parties.
E) Bureaucrats only carry out decisions made by the cabinet and have little policy making power.

14. The involvement of quangos in the British policymaking process provides supportive evidence of the influence of

A) interest group puralism
B) neo-corporatism
C) state corporatism
D) interest groups as "transmission belts"
E) economic liberalization

15. The electoral system that is used for the British House of Commons is

A) proportional representation
B) a mixed system
C) patron-client system
D) a hybrid presidential-parliamentary system
E) a plurality system

16. Which of the following is NOT a power held by the British prime minister?

A) to call for parliamentary elections
B) to disband the House of Lords
C) to choose cabinet ministers and important subordinate posts
D) to make decisions in the cabinet, with the agreement of the ministers
E) to campaign for and represent the party in parliamentary elections

17. The concept of "home rule" is most associated with the British political policy of

A) devolution
B) integration with the European Union
C) geographic concentration of power in London
D) insularity
E) support for U.S. policy in Iraq

18. Which of the following is the BEST description of Britain's ethnic and racial minority population?

A) Most of Britain's minority population comes from Sub-Saharan Africa.
B) Britain's minority population is small and very stable in numbers.
C) Britain's minorities live primarily in rural areas.
D) Britain's minority population is relatively small, but it is growing rapidly.
E) Britain's ethnic and racial minorities have intermarried freely with the native population.

19. Oxbridge serves the British political system as an important source for

A) recruitment of political elites
B) Labour Party financial support
C) propaganda ideas to garner popular support for controversial government programs
D) interest group activity and coordination
E) educating foreigners about British politics

20. Which of the following political figures is most likely to be a policy expert in a particular policymaking field?

A) a member of Parliament
B) a peer in the House of Lords
C) the prime minister
D) the cabinet member that heads the department that deals with the policy topic
E) a top-level bureaucrat in the department that deals with the policy topic

21. The British parliamentary system is most fundamentally characterized by

A) clear separation of powers between the legislative and executive branches
B) very little separation of powers between the cabinet and parliament
C) a strong judicial branch with powers of judicial review
D) a bureaucracy that strictly follows orders from the cabinet
E) local governments that have a great deal of sovereign powers separate from the central government

22. What is the main purpose of the weekly Question Time in the House of Commons?

A) to allow the prime minister to ask for opinions on proposed legislation
B) to hold the prime minister and cabinet accountable for their actions
C) to debrief the Queen regarding important events of the week
D) to give backbenchers an opportunity to speak their mind regarding proposed policies
E) to inform the opposition party of decisions made by the majority party

23. Which of the following principles of governance has been MOST directly responsible for blocking the development of judicial review in Britain?

A) fusion of church and state
B) multi-nationalism
C) plurality voting system
D) *noblesse oblige*
E) parliamentary sovereignty

24. Which of the following parties are most supportive of rightist political and economic policies?

A) the UK Independence Party
B) Labour Party
C) Democratic Unionist Party
D) Scottish National Party
E) Sinn Fein

25. In British politics, the most significant "check" on the prime minister and cabinet is the

A) House of Commons
B) House of Lords
C) loyal opposition
D) bureaucracy
E) Supreme Court

26. Which of the following issues was addressed directly by the Good Friday Agreement of 1998?

A) socialism v. market economic
B) integration of the British economy with the EU
C) devolution of power to the Scottish Parliament
D) devolution of power to a Northern Ireland Parliament
E) the role of the Anglican Church in shaping political policies

27. Wales, Scotland, and Northern Ireland have different political traditions, but what do they all have in common?

A) The government of Ireland at one time ruled all of them.
B) All have been independent countries at some time in the past.
C) All are currently part of the United Kingdom, but London has devolved some powers to their regional governments.
D) None have been granted representation in the House of Commons in London, although all have demanded it.
E) They all were at one time part of the United Kingdom, but today they are independent nations.

28. Which of the following accurately describes a recent trend in the House of Commons?

A) Question Time has become less confrontational.
B) Backbenchers have become less deferential to the party leadership.
C) Representation from regional parties has increased.
D) The threat of a vote of confidence no longer is taken seriously.
E) Criticism from the House of Lords is more likely to shape decisions made by the House of Commons.

29. Which of the following is the best overall description for political and economic change over time in the British political system?

A) Britain's history is marked with many violent revolutions and radical changes.
B) Britain's history is remarkably stable, and the country has changed very little in the last 200 years.
C) Britain has experienced a few coup d'états, but has not been characterized by change through reform or revolution.
D) Britain's change has mainly been gradual, with significant social reforms along the way.
E) Britain has been subjected to dramatic, violent political change, but its economic changes have been gradual.

30. Which political body is most clearly the center of policymaking power in British government?

A) the cabinet
B) the House of Commons
C) the House of Lords
D) the High Court
E) the bureaucracy

Country-Context Question (20 minutes):

An important characteristic of British political culture is insularity.

A) Explain the concept of insularity, and describe geographical reasons why insularity historically has characterized British political culture.

B) Explain two ways that insularity has long defined the British relationship with the European Union.

C) Explain one way that insularity has shaped the problems that Britain has had in defining the terms of Brexit since 2016.

CHAPTER THREE:
THE EUROPEAN UNION
AND OTHER INTERNATIONAL
ORGANIZATIONS

As we have seen, one major trend in Britain is **devolution,** or the process of decentralizing the unitary state to share policymaking power with regional governments. Yet all the countries of Europe, including Britain, are deeply affected by a countertrend – **integration.** Integration is a process that encourages states to pool their sovereignty in order to gain political, economic, and social clout. Integration binds states together with common policies and shared rules. The **supranational organization** that integrates the states of Europe is called the European Union.

INTERNATIONAL ORGANIZATIONS

International organizations have been around for some time now, but their nature is changing, with some real implications for the sovereignty of individual nation-states. Several countries formed the Concert of Europe in the early 19th century in an effort to restore balance of power after the fall of Napoleon Bonaparte. It was a voluntary agreement, and it did not prevent the outbreak of several limited wars. However, many scholars believe that the effort to balance power that the agreement sparked was at least partly responsible for the relative peace among quarrelsome European neighbors until World War I began in 1914. That war stimulated another more global effort to form a lasting international organization, and resulted in the creation of the League of Nations, whose fate was doomed with the outbreak of World War II in 1939. Even before the United States joined the war, U.S. President Franklin Roosevelt and British Prime Minister Winston Churchill agreed to try again when the war ended. In this spirit the United Nations was formed in 1945.

The United Nations

Only 49 nation-states signed the original charter of the United Nations in 1945, but because many new nations have been created since then, the membership of the U.N. has grown to 193 by 2018. It has lasted for 70 years, and its membership makes it a truly global organization. Membership in the U.N. is voluntary, but it has some limited powers to force its members to abide by the organization's peacekeeping principles. As a result, it plays an important role in geopolitics, and changes the dynamics of international relationships from the previous almost exclusive focus on nation-states as individual actors on the world stage. The U.N. encourages collective action, but it alters the nature of national sovereignty only in limited ways.

An important power of the U.N. is that its members can vote to establish a peacekeeping force in a "hotspot" and request states to contribute military forces. The body responsible for making this decision is the **Security Council**, and any one of its five permanent members (the U.S., Britain, France, China, and Russia) may veto a proposed peacekeeping action. During the era of the Cold War, the Security Council was often in gridlock because the U.S. and Russia almost always disagreed. Today that gridlock is broken, but it is still difficult for all five countries to agree on a single course of action. Peacekeeping forces have been sent to calm warring forces in Eastern Europe, the Middle East, and Sub-Saharan Africa. U.N. forces are supposed to remain neutral, and they usually have restrictions on their rights to use weapons against either side in a dispute. Despite its limitations, the United Nations is a forum where most of the states of the world can meet and vote on issues without resorting to war.

The U.N. is an umbrella organization that includes many sub-organizations that promote the general welfare of the world's citizens and monitor and aid world trade and other economic activities. These efforts are funded by membership dues, and represent an extension of international cooperation into areas other than peacekeeping. Examples of such organizations are the World Bank, the International Court of Justice, and UNESCO (an economic and social council).

Other Worldwide Organizations

The United Nations continues to function as a major peacekeeping organization, although its authority is limited and its challenges are many. The organization's goals have broadened over the years, and other worldwide organizations have appeared in more recent years. Two other important international organizations of the late 20th and early 21st centuries include:

- **The World Trade Organization** – Established in 1995, the WTO is an organization of member-states that have agreed to rules of world trade among nations. It is responsible for negotiating and implementing new trade agreements; it serves as a forum for settling trade disputes; and it supervises members to be sure that they follow the rules that the organization sets. Most of the world's trading nations belong to the WTO, with Russia joining the organization in 2012. The WTO oversees about 60 different agreements which have the status of international legal texts that bind its 159 members. The process of becoming a WTO member is unique to each applicant country, and the terms of membership are dependent upon the country's stage of economic development and current trade regime. The process takes about five years, but it can last longer if the country's economic status is questionable or if political issues make it objectionable. For example, China was denied WTO status for many years because of questions about human rights abuses, but its growing economic prowess finally influenced member-states to approve it.

- **The World Bank** – Although the World Bank was created in 1944 to aid countries in rebuilding after World War II, its focus today is on loaning money to low and middle-income countries at modest interest rates. The Bank's goals are to eliminate poverty in these countries and to support economic development through investment in projects that build businesses, improve transportation and communications, provide jobs, and eliminate corruption in government. The Bank has also supported health initiatives – such as vaccination programs for disease and research to combat AIDS – and efforts to reduce greenhouse gases that contribute to global warming. One of the strongest criticisms of the World Bank has been the way in which it is governed. While the World Bank represents 186 countries, a small number of economically powerful countries choose the leadership and senior management of the World Bank, and so critics say that their interests dominate the bank.

Regional Organizations

During the Cold War era, regional military alliances appeared, and countries joined based on their affiliation either with the United States or Russia. The North Atlantic Treaty Organization (NATO) formed in the late 1940s with 14 European members, the United States, and Canada. An opposing alliance – the Warsaw Pact – began in 1955 and was composed of the Soviet Union and six eastern European countries. Together the two organizations were designed to maintain a bipolar balance of power in Europe. The Warsaw Pact disbanded with the breakup of the Soviet Union, and NATO expanded to include many of its former members. Other regional organizations include the Organization of American States (OAS), created to promote social, cultural, political, and economic links among member states; the Arab League, which was founded to promote the interests and sovereignty of countries in the Middle East; and the Organization for African Unity (OAU), that has promoted the elimination of minority white-ruled governments in southern Africa. The number of regional international organizations has grown steadily over the past 70 years or so, but the one that has integrated states the most successfully so far is the European Union.

THE EUROPEAN UNION

Europe's history is one of diverse national identities. Its wars have encompassed the continent as first its kingdoms, and then its countries, fought over religion, power, land, and trade. Perhaps most dramatically, its conflicts erupted in two devastating world wars during the 20th century. Shortly after World War II ended, European leaders decided on a new direction – cooperation among nations – that led to the creation of the European Union, a supranational organization that has not supplanted nationalism, but has altered its members' policymaking practices substantially.

A Brief History

The organization began in an effort to revitalize a war-torn Europe after World War II ended. The most immediate need was to repair the nations' broken economies, so the initial goals were almost completely economic in intent. In 1949 the Council of Europe was formed, and although it had little power, it provided an opportunity for national leaders to meet. The following year an international authority was formed to coordinate the coal and steel industries, both damaged heavily during the war. Later evolutions of the new organization included:

- **The EEC** (European Economic Community) – The Treaty of Rome established the EEC – informally named the "**Common Market**" – in 1957. Its most important provisions called for the elimination of all bilateral tariffs between European nations, and the creation of new ones that applied to all.

- **The EC** (European Community) – Established in 1965, the EC expanded the organization's functions beyond economics. One major concern other than tariffs and customs was a unified approach to the peaceful use of atomic energy. However, the development of the EC was limited by disagreements as to how much power it should be given, with many nations concerned that their national sovereignty would be weakened. The urge toward integration was given a boost by the collapse of Soviet dominance in eastern Europe in the late 1980s. With new democracies emerging, their transitions from communism to capitalism demanded guidance from an international regional power.

- **The EU** (European Union) – The 1991 **Maastricht Treaty** created the modern organization, and gave it authority in new areas, including monetary policy, foreign affairs, national security, transportation, the environment, justice, and tourism. An important goal was to coordinate economic policies, particularly through a common currency (the **euro)** to replace the national currencies of the member-states, such as the French franc and the German mark; and a common **European Central Bank**, with enormous supranational authority to influence the economic policies of the member-states. The treaty established the **three pillars**, or spheres of authority:

1. Trade and other economic matters, including economic and monetary union into a single currency, and the creation of the European Central Bank

2. Justice and home affairs, including policy governing asylum, border crossing, immigration, and judicial cooperation on crime and terrorism

3. Common foreign and security policy, including joint positions and actions, and common defense policy

Membership

Ongoing expansion is a major characteristic of the European Union, with a total membership of 28 countries as of 2015. The European Union began with six members in 1957: Belgium, France, Germany, Italy, Luxembourg, and the Netherlands. Denmark, Great Britain, and Ireland joined in the early 1970s; Greece in 1981; Portugal and Spain in 1986; and Austria, Finland, and Sweden in 1995. Ten countries joined on May 2, 2004: Cyprus (Greek part), the Czech Republic, Estonia, Hungary, Latvia, Lithuania, Malta, Poland, Slovakia and Slovenia. Bulgaria and Romania joined on January 1, 2007. Enthusiasm for further growth has waned in recent years, as questions of economic and political stability of newer members has threatened to break the union apart. Even so, Croatia was admitted for membership in June 2013.

Several countries are currently under consideration as candidates for membership, including Macedonia and Turkey. Turkey is controversial for many reasons, including its relatively low Gross Domestic Product per capita of about 12,000 euro, considerably less than the EU average. Turkey also has been questioned because of its history of authoritarian governments. Turkey's candidacy also brings up the question of whether or not it is actually a European country since most of the country is technically in Asia. A deeper issue is the largely Muslim population of Turkey. If the EU is mainly an economic organization,

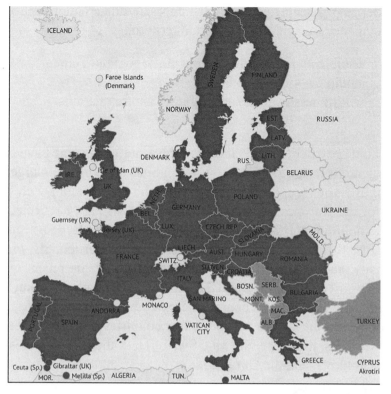

The European Union. Ongoing expansion is a major characteristic of the European Union, with a total membership of 28 countries as of 2018.

then it shouldn't matter that all Turkey's religious leanings are quite different from those of current members, whose populations are overwhelmingly Christian. However, if the EU fulfills its other pillars (justice and home affairs, and common foreign and security policy), some fear that religious differences could hinder the integration process.

Even though the political and economic muscle of so many countries united is considerable, this rapid integration presents many difficult issues for the EU. First, organizational issues abound. Structures that work for six countries do not necessarily operate smoothly for 28. Second, the expansion brings in many former communist countries whose economies were relatively weak by the early 21st century. Older member-states worry that immigrants from the east will flood their labor markets and strain their economies. EU supporters believe that these problems will be overshadowed by the benefits of common markets, currencies, political policies, and defense.

In order to be accepted for membership, candidate nations must provide evidence to meet three important criteria:

- a stable and functioning democratic regime
- a market-oriented economy
- willingness to accept all EU laws and regulations

The rapid growth of the EU has brought about what some have called **enlargement fatigue**. Polls show a decline in support for enlargement among EU voters, and many believe that the French and Dutch rejections of the European Constitution (see p. 179) partly reflected dissatisfaction over the 2004 enlargement. Also, many EU governments have lost their enthusiasm for further growth, particularly France, Germany, and Austria. The economic benefits of the recent expansions are still questionable, and the concerns surrounding Turkey have cooled some support. Of course, there is a limited amount of growth potential remaining because only a few countries of the continent are non-members, including Norway, Switzerland, the Balkan states, Belarus, Moldova, and the Ukraine.

Organization

The European Union is composed of four major bodies: The Commission, the Council of Ministers, the European Court of Justice, and the European Parliament.

- **The Commission** – This body currently has 28 members, one from each member state of the EU, supported by a bureaucracy of several thousand European civil servants. Each Commissioner takes responsibility for a particular area of policy, and heads a department called a Directorate General. The Commission is headed by a president, currently Jose Manuel Durao Barroso of Portugal. Although their home governments nominate them, commissioners swear an oath of allegiance to the EU and are not supposed to take directions from their national governments. The Commission forms a permanent executive that supervises the work of the EU, much in the way that a national cabinet operates.

- **The Council of Ministers** – Whereas the Commission acts cooperatively as the director of EU activities, the Council demonstrates the continuing power of the states. The Council consists of foreign ministers, finance ministers, the president of France, and all the prime ministers of the other members. They hold frequent meetings – some for only one type of minister – and the heads of state meet every six months as the **European Council**. The Council is central to the EU's legislative process. Until 2009, the president of the Council rotated every six months, but the Lisbon Treaty made the position permanent and full-time, with a 2½ year term of office, renewable once. The first president appointed under these conditions was Herman Van Rompuy of Belgium, who was reappointed in 2012. In 2014, Donald Tusk, the former Polish prime minister, became the second president under the new rules. The Commission may initiate legislation, but its proposals don't become law until they have been passed by the Council. Each country is assigned a number of votes in proportion to its share of population.

- **The European Parliament** – Contrary to the implications of its name, the European Parliament historically has not had a great deal of legislative power. However, since 1979 its members (MEPs) have been directly elected by the people of their respective countries, so they do have some independence from their national governments. Parliament may propose amendments to legislation, and it may reject proposals from the Council outright. However, the Council may override a rejection by a unanimous vote. EU citizens vote directly for representatives to the EP every five years. Apportionment of representatives is not strictly based on population, and smaller member-states have disproportionately greater representation than larger ones. The meetings of the EP are held in Strasbourg, although committees meet in Brussels. The Lisbon Treaty enhanced the power of the EP significantly, since new rules govern its relationship with the European Council.

- **The European Court of Justice** – The ECJ is the supreme court of the European Union, and it has the power of judicial review. It meets in Luxembourg, where it interprets European law, and its decisions may limit national sovereignty. For example, the ECJ ruled against Italy's policy of jailing illegal migrants who do not obey expulsion orders. In 2011, it decided that insurance companies in Britain were not allowed to charge women drivers (less of an accident risk) a lower premium than men. As such, the ECJ is more powerful than most national judicial systems of the EU's member-states. It has a broad jurisdiction, and hears cases that rule on disagreements among the Commissioners, the Council of Ministers, and the members of parliament. It also may settle disputes among member nations, private companies, and individuals. The ECJ consists of 28 judges, with each one nominated by a different member state. Cases are decided by a simple majority.

ORGANIZATION OF THE EUROPEAN UNION

The Commission

Initiates new programs; does not take directions from national governments

Council of Ministers
Demonstrates the continuing power of the states; heads of governments meet every 6 months as the European Council

European Parliament

Directly elected by people; smaller member-states have disproportionately greater representation; growing power

European Court of Justice

Supreme Court of the EU; has power of judicial review; settles disputes among member-states

Policymaking Power

Although the European Union has made only rudimentary policy in many areas – such as defense and social policy – it clearly sets strong policies in other areas that previously were controlled by the individual countries. Three areas of active policymaking are:

- **Creating and maintaining a single internal market** – By and large, the EU has removed most of the old tariffs and other barriers to trade among its members. For example, trucking goods across national borders is much easier today than it was before the EU was created. Also, most professional licenses, such as those for doctors and beauticians, are accepted in all member states. An exception is that lawyers' licenses are only good in the country that issues them. So policy differences still exist among the nations, but the single market has greatly affected both European governments and their citizens. More options are available to shoppers and consumers now that goods are freely transported across national borders.

- **Union of monetary policy** – The EU has made remarkable strides in its ability to set European **monetary policy,** the control of the money supply. Today the euro has replaced many of the old national currencies, which are well on their way to being phased out. Also, the power to set basic interest rates and other fiscal policies is being passed from national banks and governments to the **European Monetary Union** and its new central bank. Today, in most of the member countries, the euro is accepted as a common currency both in banking and for everyday business transactions. Most of the newer members are in the process of changing their currencies to the euro, but two exceptions to the rule are Britain and Sweden, which still refuse to give up their national currencies in favor of a common European currency. The economic recession that began in late 2007 was a challenge for the viability of the euro, but so far there has been no strong movement to abandon it. For most of the newer members, the recession made conversion to the euro even more important, since their national currencies are generally not as stable as the euro. The recession also put pressure on the economic coordination capabilities of the EU. Most of the stimulus money generated in Europe after the worldwide monetary crisis in September 2008 came from individual member-states. In November 2008 the European Commission set out proposals for a Europe-wide fiscal stimulus, but it had no authority to compel member-states to contribute, so it had to serve mainly a coordinating role. What followed was disagreement among member-states over how or whether to use the stimulus money, illustrating the reluctance that governments have in ceding control over their own revenues.

- **Common agricultural policy** – Implementation of policy in this area has generally been less successful than others, but the EU has put in place significant new agricultural programs, with almost half of the organization's budget going to this policy. One goal has been to modernize inefficient farms so that they might compete in the common market. In order to meet this goal, the EU established **farm subsidies**, guarantees of selling goods at high prices. The subsidies have proved very expensive and have yet to improve farm efficiency in any measurable way. Recent reforms of the system have transferred subsidies away from price supports for specific crops and toward direct payments to farmers. A growing chunk of the money goes to rural-development projects, not farming as such.

By the late 1990s, the European Union began to lay the groundwork for future policies in these areas:

- **Common defense** – European integration began with economic policy, so EU defense policy is much less well developed than those for trade and common currency. However, the Maastricht Treaty made foreign and defense policy one of the three "pillars" of the EU, so some defense policies have been put in place. In 1999, the European Council placed **crisis management** tasks at the core of the development of common security and defense of EU members. Crises were defined as humanitarian, rescue, and peacemaking tasks. The Council set as a goal that the EU should be able to deploy up to 60,000 troops within sixty days that could be sustained for at least one year. The agreement left troop commitment and deployment up to the member-states, and, as a result, did not create a European army.

- **Justice and Home Affairs** – The 1997 **Treaty of Amsterdam** set major policy initiatives for judicial affairs. The aim was to establish within a few years the **free movement** of European Union citizens and non-EU nationals throughout the Union. Free movement has involved setting policy regarding visas, asylum, and immigration. Additionally, the Treaty of Amsterdam helped to define cooperation among national police forces and judicial authorities in combating crime. Although member nations may support an EU structure in areas of justice, freedom, and security, they are not compelled to participate. In these areas, Britain, Ireland, and Denmark restrict their participation to only a few select provisions.

- **Terrorism** – The EU has become very concerned about terrorism since the September 11, 2001 attacks on the World Trade Towers and the Pentagon in the United States. More recent bombings have rocked transportation systems in Spain (2004) and Britain (2005), reminding Europeans that terrorists have almost certainly taken advantage of the increasing ease of travel across country borders created by integration of nations. Beginning in April 2004, United States and European Union officials held a series of policy dialogues on border and transportation security that focused on better addressing common security concerns and identifying areas where U.S.-EU cooperation and coordination might be enhanced.

The European Constitution and the Lisbon Treaty

On October 29, 2004, European heads of government signed a treaty establishing a **European Constitution.** The intention of the Constitution was to replace the overlapping sets of treaties that govern member-states' interactions, and to streamline decision-making as the organization had grown to 27 states by then. The Constitution went through the process of ratification by member-states, and was scheduled to go into effect on November 1, 2006. However, in mid-2005, French and Dutch voters rejected the treaty in separate referenda, prompting other countries, including Britain, to postpone their ratification procedures. In December 2007, in an effort to salvage the goals of the Constitution, the heads of state or government of the then-27 member-states signed the **Lisbon Treaty**, a document that attempted to consolidate previous treaties that were still in force. Some important provisions of the treaty are:

- **A strengthening role for the European Parliament** – The treaty gives the Parliament new powers over EU legislation that place it on an equal footing with the European Council, gaining new rights in farm subsidy policies, border controls, asylum, and integration. Members of the European Parliament (MEPs) also have more say over the EU Budget, bowing to national government in only a handful of areas like tax and foreign policy.

- **A greater involvement of national parliaments** – National parliaments have more opportunities to be involved in the work of the EU, particularly through a new mechanism that ensures that the Union only acts where results can be better achieved at EU level. The aim is to enhance democracy and increase legitimacy in the functioning of the Union.

- **Clarification of the relationship between member-states and the EU** – The treaty created a system called "categorization of competencies" that more clearly delineates the realms of responsibility of the EU in contrast to the initiatives best left up to the national governments.

- **Withdrawal from the Union** – For the first time, the possibility for a member-state to withdraw from the EU was recognized.

- **The creation of a permanent president of the EU** – Before the treaty was signed, the presidency of the European Council rotated every six months and it was usually filled by the top executive of one of the member-states, and so the position has a limited amount of power. The Lisbon Treaty made that position permanent and full-time, and provides for a 2 ½ year term of office, renewable once.

- **Introduction of a Charter of Fundamental Rights** – The Charter promotes individual civil, political, economic, and social rights for European citizens.

The negative reactions in France and the Netherlands to the European Constitution reflected a growing resistance to integration, especially as the European Union membership continues to grow. Many fear that the power shift from national to supranational institutions will result in a **democratic deficit**, the loss of direct control of political decisions by the people. The European Parliament is the only directly elected body, and it is the weakest of the major EU bodies. The EU, then, is perceived by many as lacking accountability to citizens in member-states. The provisions of the Lisbon Treaty were meant to address these concerns, but it too was rejected by a popular referendum, this time in Ireland in June 2008. However, the treaty was eventually ratified by all the member-states, and it went into effect in December 2009.

The post-World War II visionaries who first conceived of a European Union saw not only an economically united Europe, but one with close political cooperation as well. So far, the European Union has shown little movement toward political integration, although the Maastricht Treaty of 1991 did include it within the "three pillars", or spheres of authority. More cooperation in foreign and national security policy is still on the EU's agenda, but economic integration remains the focus today.

Economic Issues

The European Union has long been defined by a tension between **economic liberalism** that favors open, free markets, and an economic nationalism that seeks to protect national economic interests from the uncertainty of free markets. The older, more established EU members tend to reflect the latter policy orientation, while the newer, less economically stable members often favor economic liberalism. Supranationalism encourages economic integration but the proper balance with national interests is often a controversial topic. The **sovereign**

debt crisis that began with the near-collapse of the Greek economy in 2010 illustrates this tough issue, and the arguments that have erupted since then strike at the heart of this old tension.

Austerity Programs

In reaction to the sovereign debt crisis, many European countries put **austerity programs** in place. These programs were designed to reduce budget deficits by cuts in spending and tax increases, and they quickly became controversial as unemployment rates increased and GDPs stagnated. Countries that put austerity programs in place include Germany, the Czech Republic, Britain, Italy, Greece, Ireland, Portugal, Romania, and Spain. In many places, the programs sparked protests, especially as government welfare programs were cut. Austerity programs became quite controversial as economists debated their effectiveness in solving the debt crisis.

The Greek Crisis

It was no surprise that the debt crisis began in Greece, which failed to join the euro area when it was set up in 1999 because it did not meet the economic or fiscal criteria for membership. Revisions to its budget figures showed that it probably shouldn't have been allowed in when it did join in 2001. After the international banking crisis of 2008, concern for "sovereign debts" (debts of individual EU countries) increased, especially for those with high debt-to-GNP ratios. Attention focused first on Greece, and in May 2010, the eurozone countries and International Monetary Fund agreed to a large loan to Greece, conditional on the implementation of harsh austerity measures. The Greek bailout was followed by a rescue package for Ireland in November and another for Portugal in May 2011.

During the summer of 2015, Greece once again could not meet its credit obligations, and the Greek prime minister, Alexis Tsipras, staged a showdown with Greece's creditors — the other nations that use the euro, the European Central Bank, and the International Monetary Fund. Mr. Tsipras balked at further austerity measures, and sponsored a referendum in which Greek voters strongly supported him. However, the prime minister finally gave in and accepted a new package of budget cuts, tax increases and other economic policy changes in return for an additional 86 billion euros, or \$97.2 billion, in aid necessary to reopen Greece's banks and avert default on its loans.

Bailouts and Economic Restructuring

These bailouts have been controversial, with some arguing that they are essential for keeping the economic health of the entire EU region, but others complaining that it is unfair to expect taxpayers in healthier countries to pay for the economic woes of less stable members. The bailouts are particularly unpopular in Germany, where one poll showed that a majority of the public thinks that the rescue of Greece was a mistake. As talk of a second bailout for Greece materialized in mid-2011, there was strong resistance in Germany to further assistance to the Greek economy. At summit meetings in 2011, European political leaders discussed the possibility of "**restructuring**" the economies of Greece, Ireland, and Portugal. **Economic structural adjustment** would mean that at least part of the debt would be forgiven. Supporters of restructuring claim that it is the only way to allow the weakened countries to recover; critics believe that restructuring makes the stronger countries pay for the weaker ones, a process that they claim weakens the entire continent. The crisis seriously questions the economic stability of the euro and the European banking system, and so the solutions that European leaders find will almost certainly influence the future development of the EU.

The sovereign debt crisis has impacted the economies of almost all European countries, not just those with the most fragile economies. The countries that adopted the euro were supposed to adhere to strict spending standards to prevent their debt from getting too big. They agreed to a debt target of 60 percent of their economic output. Some did, but others could finance their deficit spending at relatively low interest rates as long as Europe's economy remained healthy. However, when the financial crisis erupted, the economies shrank and their debts ballooned. Investors began to lose faith in the ability of those countries to repay their debts. By 2012, not even the strongest economies in Europe met the target. Germany's ratio of gross government debt to gross domestic product was 79%, but other countries had much higher ratios, such as Greece, with a ratio of 153%.

Migration Issues

Migration has long been an issue for EU member-states, but the rising number of refugees seeking asylum in Europe reached a crisis level in 2015. Most were fleeing war-ridden states, especially Syria, Afghanistan, and Eritrea. The crisis drew attention in April 2015, when five boats carrying almost two thousand migrants to Europe sank in the Mediterranean Sea, leaving more than 1,200 people dead. The European Union has struggled to cope with the crisis, with EU member-states receiving about 395,000 new asylum applications during the first half of 2015. In September 2015, EU interior ministers approved a plan to relocate 120,000 asylum seekers over two years from Italy, Greece, and Hungary to all other EU countries (except Denmark, Ireland, and Britain). These mandatory migrant quotes quickly became controversial, with the Czech Republic, Hungary, Romania, and Slovakia voting against them. Britain agreed to accept 20,000 migrants over five years, but only those coming from states outside Europe.

The Impact of Brexit

One of the most important challenges to the European Union in recent times was the 2016 referendum in Britain that endorsed the country's withdrawal from membership in the EU. The impact of the decision on Britain is an important consideration, but the impact on the supranational organization and its future is also likely to be significant. Without Britain, does the EU lose some of its importance as a trading bloc? Does Britain's withdrawal portend the withdrawal of other member states? What will be the terms of Britain's withdrawal, and what implications will those terms have for other member states? The answers to these questions will shape the future of the European Union and will also influence the fate of other international organizations as well.

Does Brexit represent a clash between nationalism and internationalism that will disrupt world politics? Does the European Union represent the trend toward globalization in the world? Or is it a better example of fragmentation? Perhaps the EU is forging the way toward global connections, particularly in terms of trade and economic cooperation. On the other hand, it may be forming a bloc that invites other parts of the world to create blocs of their own, setting the stage for fragmentation and conflict among cultural areas. Only time will tell.

COMPARATIVE CAPITALISM: THE EUROPEAN AND U.S. MODELS

Whereas capitalism is the accepted economic philosophy in the United States and Europe today, two competing models had developed by the late 20th century. The U.S. model, largely shared by Britain since Thatcherism took hold in the1980s, places greater emphasis on free enterprise and the market, whereas continental western Europe has evolved a **social market economy** that is team-oriented and emphasizes cooperation between management and organized labor. The European model provides a stronger economic safety net – such as universal health care, day care for children, and generous pensions for government workers. Government-subsidized transportation systems are also characteristic of the social market economy. The two systems are based on two different attitudes toward equality, with the U.S. culture emphasizing the individual's right to compete in the marketplace and accepting any inequality that results from that competition. Many Europeans tend to view unrestricted competition more as a threat than an opportunity, since it can lead to vast inequalities. One explanation for these different views is that Europeans are more accustomed to a strong government role in society, and Americans tend to distrust their government more. Another explanation is that Americans see more possibilities for upward mobility, with each individual believing that (s)he will someday be rich, too.

IMPORTANT TERMS AND CONCEPTS

Brexit
The Commission
Common Market
The Council of Ministers
crisis management
democratic deficit
EC
economic liberalism
economic structural adjustment
EEC
enlargement fatigue

European Central Bank
European Constitution
European Council
European Court of Justice
European Parliament
European Monetary Union
EU
farm subsidies
free movement
integration
Lisbon Treaty
Maastricht Treaty
MEPs
mixed economy
monetary policy
requirements for EU membership
restructuring
social market economy
sovereign debt crisis
supranational organization
"three pillars"
Treaty of Amsterdam

EU Questions

Multiple-choice Questions

1. An organizational feature of the United Nations that has hampered united peacekeeping actions in the past is that

A) it takes too long for the General Assembly to make decisions
B) it has no body with the authority to intervene in world "hotspots"
C) any one of the Security Council's five permanent members may veto a proposed action
D) too many countries are excluded from U.N. membership to make its actions effective
E) the WTO often protests U.N. peacekeeping proposals

2. In the years after it was created in 1991, the European Union brought about the most change in Europe in regard to its

A) ability to coordinate international security
B) creation of an international judicial system
C) ability to control border crossings and immigration
D) creation of a common currency for most of its members
E) coordination of common agricultural policies

3. The European Union has its roots in post-World War II international organizations that emphasized

A) improving the economic health of European nations
B) developing international courts with jurisdiction over all European nations
C) granting asylum to refugees from both World War II and the Cold War
D) developing a common defense policy for European nations
E) regulating immigration across national borders

4. An important difference between capitalist models in the United States and continental Europe is that the European model puts more emphasis on

A) individual competition
B) limited powers of government
C) upward mobility
D) economic opportunity
E) a strong economic safety net

5. An important provision of the Maastricht Treaty was to create the

A) European Central Bank
B) Common Market
C) European Constitution
D) Lisbon Agreement
E) European Community

6. Which of the following most accurately describes current powers of the European Court of Justice?

A) The ECJ has almost no power to make decisions that limit national sovereignty.
B) The ECJ may settle disputes among member-states, but not among private companies or individuals.
C) The ECJ has the power of judicial review, and its decisions may limit national sovereignty.
D) ECJ decisions may be overridden by the Commissioners.
E) The ECJ may settle disputes between the Commissioners and the Council of Ministers, but it may not settle disputes among member-states.

7. The body of the EU that BEST demonstrates the continuing power of the nation-states is the

A) Council of Ministers
B) Commission
C) European Parliament
D) European Court of Justice
E) European Monetary Union

8. The European Parliament is the only directly elected body of the EU, and it is the weakest one. This fact may be used to argue that the EU

A) has not successfully formed a common market
B) can never replace national governments
C) will have problems integrating its newest members
D) does not have true separation of powers
E) has a democratic deficit

9. The Brexit vote was a reflection of British resistance to

A) nationalism
B) integration
C) fragmentation
D) democratization
E) market economies

10. Which of the following was the main reason that the EU abandoned the ratification process for the European Constitution?

A) Heads of government disagreed among themselves as to the best way to enforce the process.
B) National parliaments objected to the strengthening of the powers of the European Parliament.
C) The new members of the EU objected to many of the Constitution's provisions.
D) The Constitution was rejected in two separate national referenda.
E) The United States objected to changes made in trade relations.

Country-Context Question: (20 minutes)

(a) Define sovereignty. Define integration.

(b) Explain two ways in which the European Union alters the sovereignty of its member-states.

(c) Explain two ways in which integration has taken place in Europe as a result of the formation of the European Union.

**UNIT TWO:
COMMUNIST AND
POST-COMMUNIST
COUNTRIES**

Over the course of the past century, the advanced industrialized democracies (represented by Britain in this book) have become the wealthiest and most powerful countries in the world. However, these countries have been widely criticized for the degree of economic inequality that exists among their citizens, as well as the big divide in wealth and power between them and the other countries of the world. Have advanced democracies encouraged and valued freedom at the expense of equality to such a degree that we may see them as basically unjust societies? Communist countries answer this question with a resounding "Yes!" and base their governments on the belief that equality is undervalued in capitalist countries such as Britain and the United States.

During the 20th century two large countries declared themselves to be communist nations – the Soviet Union and the People's Republic of China. Together they were home to a large share of the world's population, and the economic and political influence of communism was indisputable. Today the Soviet Union has collapsed, leaving in its wake dozens of fledgling democracies, all struggling for their survival. Among major nations, only China remains under communist rule, although Cuba and North Korea are well-known communist regimes as well.

Communism has taken many forms since its birth in the mid-nineteenth century. The variations are so vast that they often appear to have little in common, although all claim to have roots in Marxism.

MARXISM

The father of communism is generally acknowledged to be Karl Marx, who first wrote about his interpretation of history and vision for the future in *The Communist Manifesto* in 1848. He saw capitalism – or the free market – as an economic system that exploited workers and increased the gap between the rich and the poor. He believed that conditions in capitalist countries would eventually become so bad that workers would join together in a revolution of the **proletariat** (workers), and overcome the **bourgeoisie**, who were owners of factories and other means of production. Marx envisioned a new world after the revolution, one in which social class would disappear because ownership of private property would be banned. According to Marx, communism encourages equality and cooperation, and without property to encourage greed and strife, governments would be unnecessary, and they would wither away.

MARXISM-LENINISM

Russia was the first country to base a political system on Marx's theory. The "revolution of the proletariat" occurred in 1917, but did not follow the steps outlined by Karl Marx. Marx believed that the revolution would first take place in industrialized, capitalist countries. Early 20th century Russia had only begun to industrialize by the late 19th century, and was far behind countries like Britain, Germany, and the United States. However, revolutionary leader **V. I. Lenin** believed that the dictatorial tsar should be overthrown, and that Russian peasants should be released from oppression. Lenin changed the nature of communism by asserting the importance of the **vanguard of the revolution** – a group of revolutionary leaders who could provoke the revolution in non-capitalist Russia. The government he established in 1917 was based on **democratic centralism**, or the "vanguard" who would lead the revolution since the people were incapable of providing leadership themselves. Democratic centralism provided for a hierarchal party structure in which leaders were elected from below. Discussion was permitted by party members until a decision was made, but "centralism" took over, and the leaders allowed no questioning of the decision after the fact. Lenin proceeded to direct industrialization and agricultural development from a centralized government, and capitalistic ventures were severely restricted in the Soviet Union.

The system that Lenin set up has been incredibly influential because all communist countries that followed based their systems on the Soviet model. Political power rests with the Communist Party, a relatively small "vanguard" organization that by its very nature allows no competing ideologies to challenge it. The legitimacy of the state rests squarely on the party as the embodiment of communist ideology. Ironically, this feature of communist systems transformed Marxism, with all of its idealistic beliefs in equality for common citizens, into authoritarianism. Communist states are often associated with the use of force, but they also rely on **co-optation**, or allocation of power throughout various political, social, and economic institutions. Recruitment of elites takes place through *nomenklatura*, the process of filling influential jobs in the state, society, or the economy with people approved and chosen by the Communist Party. *Nomenklatura* includes not only political jobs, but almost all top positions in other areas as well, such as university presidents, newspaper editors, and military officers. Party approval translates as party membership, so the easiest way for an individual to get ahead is to join the party.

Despite the authoritarian nature of communist states, it is also true that the system does allow for a certain amount of **social mobility**, or the opportunity for individuals to change their social status over the course of their lifetimes.

MAOISM AND MARKET-BASED SOCIALISM

China's version of communism began shortly after Lenin's revolution in Russia, but China's government was not controlled by communists until 1949. Almost from the beginning, China's communist leader was Mao Zedong, whose interpretation of Marxism was very different from that of the Soviet leaders. **Maoism** shares Marx's vision of equality and cooperation, but Mao believed very strongly in preserving China's peasant-based society. Although the government sometimes emphasized industrialization during Mao's long rule, by and large Mao was interested in promoting a revolutionary fervor that strengthened agriculturally-based communities.

MARXISM
(Vision of a new world without
social class or private property)

LENINISM
(Democratic centralism;
vanguard of the revolution;
industrialization)

MAOISM
(Peasant-based society,
equality, cooperation,
revolutionary fervour)

After Mao's death in 1976, Deng Xiaoping instituted **market-based socialism**, which today allows for a significant infusion of capitalism into the system. China chose a relatively gradual and smooth infusion of capitalism controlled by the government, in contrast to the internal upheavals that broke the Soviet Union apart after Mikhail Gorbachev tried to resuscitate the economy during the late 1980s. Russia's rocky road to capitalism continued during the first years of the new regime, as Boris Yeltsin tried to privatize the economy through "shock therapy".

GENDER RELATIONS IN COMMUNIST REGIMES

Marxists often see traditional gender relations – with women in subservient roles to men – as resulting from the underlying inequality encouraged by capitalist societies. Men exploit women through the family structure in much the same way that the bourgeoisie exploit the proletariat in the workplace. Communism envisions complete economic, social, and political equality between men and women. As we will see in Russia and China, this ideal was not followed in reality in any of the communist countries. However, it almost certainly increased opportunities for women, so that until the late 20th century, women in communist countries were more likely to work outside the home than women in capitalist countries.

COMMUNIST POLITICAL ECONOMY

Communist ideology led to political economies characterized by **central planning**, in which the ownership of private property and the market mechanism were replaced with the allocation of resources by the state bureaucracy. According to the basic tenets of Marxism, neither principle – ownership of private property nor the market economy – encourages equitable distribution of wealth. Countries with communist political economies have experienced these two problems:

- **Logistical difficulties** – Planning an entire economy is an extremely difficult task. The larger the economy, the more difficult the planning is and the less efficient the implementation is. In a market economy supply and demand interact spontaneously, and active management of an economy takes more work and energy.

- **Lack of worker incentives** – Capitalist countries often repeat this criticism of communist political economies. Workers have no fear of losing their jobs, and factories don't worry about going out of business, so there are few incentives for producing good quality products. In the absence of competition and incentives, innovation and efficiency disappear, and as a result, communist economies generally fall behind market economies.

In the case of the U.S.S.R., these problems were insurmountable, and they led to the dissolution of the Soviet Republics.

NEW ECONOMIC TIES

Since Russia no longer has official ties to communism and China has now integrated capitalism into its economic system, just how important theoretical communism is to either country today is in question. New directions are indicated by both countries as they establish their roles in the global marketplace. In 2001 a chief economist of Goldman Sachs first coined the term "**BRIC**" for the fast-growing economies of Brazil, Russia, India, and China. Goldman Sachs noted that the economies of the four countries are growing so fast that they might overtake the combined economies of the current richest countries of the world by 2050. In June 2009, the leaders of the BRIC countries held their first summit in Yekaterinburg, Russia, where they discussed common concerns and demanded more say in global policymaking. At the time of their meeting, the economies of Brazil, India, and China were recovering from the global monetary crisis of September 2008, but the Russian economy was still plagued by plunging oil prices. Since then they have met in various cities in the BRIC countries.

South Africa sought BRIC membership beginning in 2009 and the process for formal admission began in 2010. South Africa was officially admitted as a BRIC nation on December 24, 2010 after being invited by China and the other BRIC countries to join the group, altering the acronym to BRICS. South African President Jacob Zuma attended the BRICS summit in Sanya in April 2011 as a full member.

Both China and Russia today have authoritarian governments, although Russia (as we will see) set up democratic structures in the Constitution of 1993. Both have integrated capitalism into their economic systems, although they have taken very different paths to reach that end, and both have become important players in international markets. How these economic changes will impact their political systems is an unfolding drama, as both countries test the western assumption that capitalism and democracy go hand in hand. So far, China and Russia appear to be setting their own rules, and it is far from clear that democratic principles will be a part of their future.

In the pages that follow, we will examine in more detail the influence of communism on Russia and China. For Russia, has communism now been successfully replaced with capitalism? In China, has the system strayed so far from Marxism that it can hardly be seen as communism today?

IMPORTANT TERMS AND CONCEPTS

bourgeoisie
BRIC
central planning
The Communist Manifesto
co-optation
democratic centralism
Maoism
market-based socialism
Marxism
Marxism-Leninism
nomenklatura
proletariat
social mobility
"vanguard of the revolution"

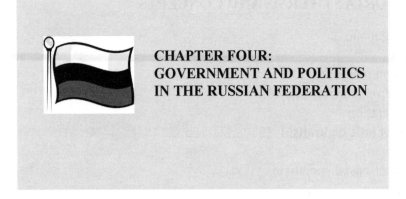

**CHAPTER FOUR:
GOVERNMENT AND POLITICS
IN THE RUSSIAN FEDERATION**

RUSSIA IN AN AGE OF DEMOCRATIZATION

Between 1945 and 1991, global politics was defined by intense competition between two superpowers: the Soviet Union and the United States. The competition encompassed almost all areas of the world and affected a broad range of economic, political, social, and cultural patterns. As a result, when the Soviet Union surprisingly and suddenly collapsed in 1991, the reverberations were heard everywhere. In the wake of its demise, the component republics broke apart, leaving the Russian Federation as the largest piece, with a population cut in half, but with a land space that allowed it to remain geographically the largest country in the world.

The first president of the Russian Federation was **Boris Yeltsin**, a former member of the Soviet Politburo who declared the end of the old Soviet-style regime. The "**shock therapy**" reforms that he advocated pointed the country in the direction of democracy and a free-market economy. Yet Yeltsin was an uneven leader, often ill or under the influence of alcohol, who reverted to authoritarian rule whenever he pleased. A small group of family members and advisers effectively took control from the weakened president, and they ran the country as an **oligarchy**, granting themselves favors and inviting economic and political corruption. However, despite this development, a new constitution was put in place in 1993, and regular, sometimes competitive elections took place in the years that followed.

A new president, **Vladimir Putin**, was elected in 2000 and 2004 without serious conflict, but many observers are still wary of the continuing influence of the oligarchy. Putin has often acted aggressively in containing the oligarchs' political and economic powers, and followed a clear path toward increasing centralization of power. As the election of 2008 approached, he followed the Constitution of 1993 by stepping down after two terms, but he announced his intention to stay on as prime minister under the new president, **Dmitri Medvedev.** Putin maintained control of the government while prime minister, and in 2012 and 2018 he successfully ran for president again. Is Putin's continuing influence in policymaking a signal that Russia is again becoming an authoritarian state and that its fling with democracy is now over?

Modern Russia, then, is a very unpredictable country. Its historic roots deeply influence every area of life, and Russia has almost no experience with democracy and a free market. Is the new structure set in place during the 1990s proof that the global trend toward democratization has influenced the Russian political system? Or perhaps it is possible that Russia is settling in as an illiberal democracy, with direct elections and other democratic structures in place, but with little hope of strengthening the democratic principles of civil liberties and rights, competitive political parties, rule of law, and an independent judiciary. However, Russia's long history of autocratic rule certainly leaves open the third possibility that democracy has little chance to survive in Russia. No one knows at this point, but Russian history and political culture leave room for all three paths. Slavic roots provide a strong tendency toward autocratic rule, but the desire to modernize and compete for world power has been apparent since the late 17th century, even though there is little evidence that current Russian leaders see democratization as a model for their country's political development. One way to categorize Russia is as a "hybrid," a system with some characteristics of a democracy, but with some strong authoritarian tendencies as well, although *The Economist's* Democracy Index (p. 27) currently categorizes Russia as an authoritarian regime.

SOVEREIGNTY, AUTHORITY, AND POWER

For most of the 20th century, public authority and political power emanated from one place: the Politburo of the Communist Party. The Politburo was a small group of men who climbed the ranks of the party through *nomenklatura*, an ordered path from local party soviets (committees) to the commanding heights of leadership. When the Soviet Union dissolved, its authority and power vanished with it, leaving in place a new government structure with questionable legitimacy. Still, the political culture and historical traditions of Russia are firmly entrenched and have shaped the genesis of the new regime, and undoubtedly will determine the nature of its future.

Legitimacy

In the earliest years of the 21st century, the legitimacy of the Russian government was at very low ebb, partly because the regime change was so recent, and partly because the change appeared to be a drastic departure from the past. However, there is growing evidence that the system has stabilized since Vladimir Putin was first elected president in 2000, and since then, Putin and Medvedev retreated from democratic practices to reestablish some of the old authoritarianism from Russia's traditional political culture.

Historically, political legitimacy has been based on strong, autocratic rule, first by centuries of **tsars**, and then by the firm dictatorship of party leaders during the 20th century. Under communist rule, **Marxism-Leninism** provided the legitimacy base for the party, with its ideology of **democratic centralism**, or rule by a few instead of the many. Although it theoretically only supplemented Marxism-Leninism, **Stalinism** in reality changed the regime to **totalitarianism**, a more complete, invasive form of strong-man rule than the tsars ever were able to implement. After Stalin, two reformers – Nikita Khrushchev and Mikhail Gorbachev – tried to loosen the party's stranglehold on power, only to facilitate the downfall of the regime.

In an attempt to reconstruct the country's power base, the **Constitution of 1993** provided for a strong president, although the power of the position is checked by popular election and by the lower house of the legislature, the **Duma**. The institution of the presidency only dates to the late 1980s, but the Duma actually existed under the tsars of the late 19th century. Yeltsin attempted to strengthen the Constitution's legitimacy by requiring a referendum by the people to endorse its acceptance. In the 1990s, the Constitution's legitimacy was seriously tested by attempted coups and intense conflict between President Yeltsin and the Duma. However, the 2000 presidential transition from Yeltsin to Putin went smoothly, an accomplishment that indicated that the Constitution is more resilient than it seemed to be during the 1990s. Under Putin's first two terms, government operations stabilized significantly, and the presidential transition from Putin to Medvedev went without incident, although Putin's retention of political power as the prime minister indicated that he continued to hold authoritarian control of the political system, as affirmed by his reelection as president in 2012 and 2018.

Historical Influences on Political Traditions

Several legacies from Russian history shape the modern political system:

- **Absolute, centralized rule** – From the beginning, Russian tsars held absolute power that they defended with brutality and force. One reason for their tyranny was geography: the Russian plain was overrun and conquered by a series of invaders, including Huns, Vikings, and Mongols. The chaos caused by these takeovers convinced Russian leaders of the importance of firm, unchallenged leadership in keeping their subjects in control. Centralized power also characterized the Communist regime of the 20th century. Many observers believe that Vladimir Putin has steered the country back to this style of leadership.

- **Extensive cultural heterogeneity** – Until the 17th century Russia was a relatively small inland culture, but even then, the numerous invasions from earlier times meant that the area was home to people of wide cultural diversity. This **cultural heterogeneity** intensified as Russia rapidly expanded its borders, until by the end of the 19th century, the empire stretched from the Baltic Sea to the Pacific Ocean. Since then, the borders of Russia have been in an almost constant state of change, so that ethnicities have been split apart, thrown together with others, and then split apart again. The name "Russian Federation" reflects this diversity, with countless "republics" and "autonomous regions" based on ethnicity, but with borders impossible to draw along ethnic lines because of the blend and locations of people. This heterogeneity has always been a special challenge to Russian rulers.

- **Slavophile v. Westernizer** – In the mid-20th century, American diplomat George Kennan identified this conflicting set of political traditions as a major source of problems for Russia. The Slavophile ("lover of Slavs") tradition has led to a pride in Slavic customs, language, religion, and history that causes Russia to resist outside influence. This tendency to value isolation was challenged first by **Tsar Peter the Great** in the late 17th and early 18th century. He used the western model to "modernize" Russia with a stronger army, a navy, an infrastructure of roads and communication, a reorganized bureaucracy, and a "**Window on the West**". The window was St. Petersburg, a city built by Peter on newly conquered lands near the Baltic Sea. His efforts to build Russia's power were followed by those of **Catherine the Great** of the late 18th century, so that by the time of her death, Russia was a powerful major empire. However, their efforts set in place a conflict, since the affection for Slavic ways did not disappear with the changes.

- **Revolutions of the 20th century** – The long, autocratic rule of the tsars suddenly and decisively came to an end in 1917 when **V. I. Lenin's Bolsheviks** seized power, and renamed the country the Union of Soviet Socialist Republics. Communist leaders replaced the tsars, and they ruled according to socialist principles, although the tendency toward absolute, centralized rule did not change. The old social classes, however, were swept away, and the new regime tried to blend elements of westernization (industrialization, economic development, and technological innovation) with those of the Slavophile (nationalism, resistance to western culture and customs). A second revolution occurred in 1991, when the U.S.S.R. dissolved, and its fifteen republics became independent nations. The Russian Federation, born in that year, is currently struggling to replace the old regime with a new one, although many of the former republics have settled into authoritarianism.

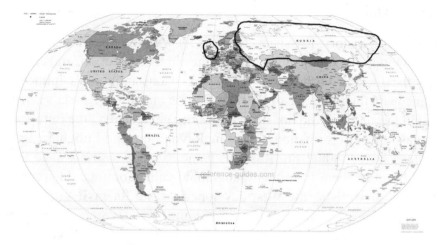

Comparative Geographic Sizes of Britain and Russia. Geographically, Britain is still "Little England," and Russia is still the largest country in the world in terms of land space, even after the breakup of the Soviet Union.

Political Culture

Russia's political culture has been shaped by its geographic setting, cultural orientation, and conflicting attitudes toward the state.

Geographic Setting

Geographically, Russia is the largest country in the world and encompasses many different ethnicities and climates. Its republics and regions border the Black Sea in the southwest, the Baltic Sea in the northwest, the Pacific to the east, the Arctic Ocean to the north, and China to the south. Its borders touch many other nations with vastly different political cultures and customs. Russia is also one of the coldest countries on earth, partly because of northern latitude, but also because so many cities are inland. Ironically for a country of its size, warm water ports are few, and its history has been shaped by the desire to conquer countries that have blocked Russian access to the sea. Russia has many natural resources, including oil, gas, and timber, but much of it is locked in frozen Siberia, and very difficult to extract. However, in recent years some of these resources have been developed, and have fueled significant economic growth.

Eastern Orthodoxy

Early in its history, Russians cast their lot with the flourishing city of Constantinople, establishing trade routes in that direction, and adopting the Eastern Orthodox religion. As Constantinople's influence waned and the influence of Western Europe increased, Russia's orientation meant that it did not share the values generated by the European Renaissance, Reformation, Scientific Revolution, and Enlightenment. Instead of individualism, Russians came to value a strong state that could protect them from their geographic vulnerabilities. In contrast to Russian **statism**, the West developed a taste for **civil society**, or spheres of privacy free from control by the state. Eastern Orthodoxy also was inextricably linked to the state, so the principle of separation of church and state never developed. Even when the Communist state forbid its citizens to practice religion, broad acceptance of government control remained.

Equality of Result (contrasted to equality of opportunity)

The Communist regime instilled in the Russian people an appreciation for equality, a value already strong in a country of peasants with similar living standards. Russian egalitarianism has survived the fall of the Soviet Union, and most Russians resent wealth and income differences. This "equality of result" is very different from western "equality of opportunity" that sees "getting ahead" as a sign of initiative, hard work, and talent. As a result, the Russian political culture is not particularly conducive to the development of capitalism.

Skepticism about Power

Despite their dependence on government initiative, Russian citizens can be surprisingly hostile toward their leadership. Mikhail Gorbachev found this out when in the late 1980s he initiated *glasnost* – a new emphasis on freedom of speech and press. As his reforms faltered, he received torrents of complaints from citizens that almost certainly contributed to the breakup of the Soviet Union. Today surveys show that citizens have little faith in the political system, although, until recently, people seemed to have more confidence in Putin than in any other individual leaders or institutions. During his first two terms as president, Putin's approval ratings remained between 70 and 80 percent and even reached almost 90 percent in 2008, but no other public officials have had comparable approval rates, including governors of regions, army generals, Duma members, or the police. According to Russia's most respected polling outfit, the Levada Institute, Putin's popularity declined after the oil bust of 2008, but since 2011, his approval rating has still remained above 60 percent. The Russian people appear to have little confidence in nongovernmental leaders, such as entrepreneurs, bankers, and media personalities.

The Importance of Nationality

Even though cultural heterogeneity has almost always been characteristic of the Russian political culture, people tend to categorize others based on their nationality, and they often discriminate against groups based on long-held stereotypes. Russians generally admire the Baltic people for their "civility" and sophistication, but they sometimes express disdain for the Muslim-Turkic people of Central Asia. In return, governments in those areas have passed laws discouraging Russians from remaining within their borders. Anti-Semitism was strong in tsarist Russia, and today some nationalists blame Jews for Russia's current problems.

POLITICAL AND ECONOMIC CHANGE

In contrast to Britain, Russia has almost always had difficulty with gradual and ordered change. Instead, its history reflects a resistance to change by reform and a tendency to descend into chaos or resort to revolution when contradictory forces meet. The most successful tsars, such as Peter the Great and Catherine the Great, understood the dangers of chaos in Russia, and often resorted to force in order to keep their power. The 19th century tsars faced the infiltration of Enlightenment ideas of democracy and individual rights, and those who tried reforms that allowed gradual inclusion of these influences failed. For example, Alexander II, who freed Russian serfs and experimented with local assemblies, was assassinated by revolutionaries in 1881. The forces that led to his assassination later blossomed into full-blown revolution, the execution of the last tsar, and the establishment of a communist regime. Likewise, the late 19th century tsars' attempts to gradually industrialize Russia were largely unsuccessful, but Joseph

RUSSIA'S CONFLICTUAL POLITICAL CULTURE

Slavic influence – customs, language, religion, and history that encourage Russia to resist outside contact.

Conflictual political culture; western reform, technology, and customs were imposed on the tsarist absolute state

Western reform initiated by Peter the Great in the late 17th century; attempt to increase Russian power and influence

Stalin's Five-Year Plans that called for rapid, abrupt economic change led to the establishment of the Soviet Union as one of two superpowers that dominated the world for a half century after the conclusion of World War II. In the late 20th century, Mikhail Gorbachev's attempts to reform the political and economic systems failed, and change again came abruptly with a failed coup d'état, and the sudden collapse of the Soviet Union.

Russia's history is characterized by three distinct time periods:

- **A long period of autocratic rule by tsars** – Tsars ruled Russia from the 14th to the early 20th century. Control of Russia was passed down through the Romanov family from the 17th century on, but transitions were often accompanied by brutality and sometimes assassination.

- **20th century rule by the Communist Party** – Communist rule began in 1917 when V.I. Lenin's Bolsheviks seized control of the government after the last tsar, Nicholas II, was deposed. The regime toppled in 1991 when a failed coup from within the government created chaos.

- **An abrupt regime change to procedural democracy and a free market in 1991** – President Boris Yeltsin put western-style reforms in place to create the Russian Federation. Since 2000, Vladimir Putin has dominated Russian government and politics, limiting democratic reforms.

The two transition periods between the major time periods were sparked by revolution and quick, dramatic change. The Slavic influence has brought some continuity to Russia's history, but in general change has rarely been evolutionary and gradual. Instead, long periods of authoritarian rule have been punctuated by protest and violence.

Tsarist Rule

The first tsars were princes of Moscow, who cooperated with their 13th century Mongol rulers, and in return for their assistance were rewarded with land and power. But when Mongol rule weakened, the princes declared themselves "tsars" in the tradition of the "Caesars" of ancient Rome. The tsars were autocratic from the beginning, and tightly controlled their lands in order to protect them from invasion and attack. The tsars also headed the **Russian Orthodox Church**, so that they were seen as both political and religious leaders. Early Russia was isolated from western Europe by its orientation to the Eastern Orthodox world, and long distances separated Russian cities from major civilizations to the south and east.

Western Influence

In the late 17th and early 18th centuries, **Tsar Peter the Great** introduced western technology and culture in an attempt to increase Russia's power and influence. From his early childhood, he was intrigued by the West, and he became the first tsar to travel to Germany, Holland, and England. There he learned about shipbuilding and other types of technology. He brought engineers, carpenters, and architects to Russia, and set the country on a course toward world power. **Catherine the Great**, who originally came from Germany, ruled Russia during the late 18th century, and managed to gain warm water access to the Black Sea, an accomplishment that had eluded Peter. Both looked to the West to help develop their country, but neither abandoned absolute rule. Catherine read widely, and was very interested in Enlightenment thought, but she checked any impulses she had to apply them to her rule. Instead, she became an **enlightened despot**, or one who rules absolutely, but with clear goals for the country in mind. Tsars after Peter and Catherine alternated between emphasizing Slavic roots and tolerating western style reform, although none of them successfully responded to the revolutionary movement growing within their country during the 19th century.

Nineteenth Century Tsars

Russia was brought into direct contact with the West when Napoleon invaded in 1812. Alexander I successfully resisted the attack, but at great cost to the empire. Western thought influenced Russian intellectuals who saw no room for western political institutions to grow under the tsars' absolutism. Their frustration erupted in the **Decembrist Revolt of 1825**, which was crushed ruthlessly by Nicholas I. By midcentury the Russian defeat in the **Crimean War** convinced many of the tsar's critics that Russian ways were indeed backward and in need of major reform. Nineteenth century tsars reacted to their demands by sending the secret police to investigate and by exiling or executing the dissenters.

Of all the 19th century tsars, the only one who seriously sponsored reform was Alexander II. However, even though he freed Russia's serfs and set up regional *zemstvos* (assemblies), the increasingly angry *intelligentsia* did not think his actions went far enough. Alexander II was assassinated in 1881 by his critics, and his son Alexander III reacted by undoing the reforms and intensifying the efforts of the secret police.

The Revolution of 1917, Lenin, and Stalin

The most immediate cause of the Revolution of 1917 was Russia's ineffectiveness in fighting the Russo-Japanese War and World War I. Tsar Nicholas II was indeed in the wrong place at the wrong time, but he also was a weak ruler who had no control over the armies. The first

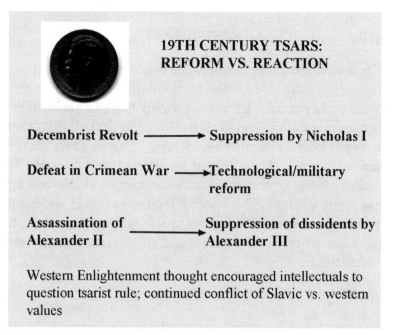

**19TH CENTURY TSARS:
REFORM VS. REACTION**

Decembrist Revolt ⟶ Suppression by Nicholas I

Defeat in Crimean War ⟶ Technological/military reform

Assassination of Alexander II ⟶ Suppression of dissidents by Alexander III

Western Enlightenment thought encouraged intellectuals to question tsarist rule; continued conflict of Slavic vs. western values

signs of the revolution were in 1905, when riots and street fighting broke out in protest to Russian losses in the war with Japan. The tsar managed to put that revolution down, but the state finally collapsed in 1917 in the midst of World War I. Russian soldiers were fighting without guns or shoes, and mass defections from the war front helped send the state into chaos.

Lenin and the Bolsheviks

By the 1890s, some of the revolutionists in Russia were **Marxists** who were in exile, along with other dissidents. However, according to Marxism, socialist revolutions would first take place not in Russia, but in capitalist countries like Germany, France, and England. At the turn of the century, Russia was still primarily an agricultural society with little industrial development. In his 1905 pamphlet *What Is To Be Done?*, **V. I. Lenin** changed the meaning of Marxism when he argued for **democratic centralism**, the idea of a "vanguard" leadership group that would lead the revolution because the people could not organize it themselves. Lenin believed that the situation in Russia was so bad that the revolution could occur even though it was a non-industrialized society. Lenin's followers came to be called the **Bolsheviks**, and they took control of the government in late 1917. In 1922, Russia was renamed the Union of Soviet Socialist Republics.

In 1918, a civil war broke out between the **White Army**, led by Russian military leaders and funded by the Allied Powers, and the **Red Army** led by Lenin. The Reds won, and in 1920, Lenin instituted his **New Economic Policy**, which allowed a great deal of private ownership to exist under a centralized leadership. The plan brought relative prosperity to farmers, but it did not promote industrialization. Would Lenin have moved on to a more socialist approach? No one knows, because Lenin died in 1924 before his plans unfolded and before he could name a successor. A power struggle followed, and Joseph Stalin, the "Man of Steel", won control and led the country to the heights of totalitarianism.

Stalinism

Stalin vastly changed Lenin's democratic centralism (also known as **Marxism-Leninism**). Stalin placed the Communist Party at the center of control, and allowed no other political parties to compete with it. Party members were carefully selected, with only about 7% of the population actually joining. Communists ran local, regional, and national governments, and leaders were identified and promoted through *nomenklatura*, or the process of party members selecting promising recruits from the lower levels. Most top government officials also belonged to the **Central Committee**, a group of party leaders who met twice a year. Above the Central Committee was the **Politburo**, the heart and soul of the Communist Party. This group of about twelve men ran the country, and their decisions were carried out by government agencies and departments. The head of the Politburo was the **general secretary**, who assumed full power as dictator of the country. Joseph Stalin was the general secretary of the Communist Party from 1927 until his death in 1953.

Collectivization and Industrialization

Stalin's economic plan for the U.S.S.R. had two parts: **collectivization and industrialization**. Stalin replaced the small private farms of the NEP with "**collective farms**" that were state run and supposedly more efficient. Private land ownership was done away with, and the farms were intended to feed workers in the cities who contributed to the industrialization of the nation. Some peasants resisted, particularly those who owned larger farms. These **kulaks** were forced to move to cities or to labor camps, and untold numbers died at the hands of government officials.

With the agricultural surplus from the farms, Stalin established his first **Five Year Plan**, which set ambitious goals for production of heavy industry, such as oil, steel, and electricity. Other plans followed, and all were carried out for individual factories by **Gosplan**, the Central State Planning Commission. Gosplan became the nerve center for the economy, determining production and distribution of virtually all goods in the Soviet Union.

Stalinism, then, is this two-pronged program of collectivization and industrialization, carried out by central planning, and executed with force and brutality.

Stalin's Foreign Policy

During the 1930s Stalin's primary focus was internal development, so his foreign policy was intended to support that goal. He advocated "socialism in one country" to emphasize his split with traditional Marxist emphasis on international revolution, and he tried to ignore the fascist threat from nearby Germany and Italy. Stalin signed a non-aggression pact with Nazi Germany in 1939, only to be attacked by Germany the following year. Russia then joined sides with the Allies for the duration of World War II, but tensions between east and west were often apparent at conferences, and as soon as the war ended, the situation escalated into the Cold War. These significant shifts in foreign policy all accommodated his main goal: the industrial development of the U.S.S.R.

The Purges

Joseph Stalin is perhaps best known for his purges: the execution of millions of citizens, including up to one million party members. He became obsessed with disloyalty in the party ranks, and he ordered the execution of his own generals and other members of the Politburo and Central Committee. Stalin held total power, and by the time of his death in 1953, some speculated that he had gone mad. His successor, **Nikita Khrushchev**, set about to reform Stalinism by loosening its totalitarian nature and publicly denouncing the purges.

Reform under Khrushchev and Gorbachev

After Stalin died in 1953, a power struggle among top Communist Party leaders resulted in the choice of Nikita Khrushchev as party secretary and premier of the U.S.S.R. In 1956 he gave his famous "**secret speech**", in which he revealed the existence of a letter written by Lenin before he died. The letter was critical of Stalin, and Khrushchev used it to denounce Stalin's rules and practices, particularly the purges that he sponsored. This denouncement led to **deStalinization**, a process that brough about reforms, such as loosening government censorship of the press, decentralization of economic decision-making, and restructuring of collective farms. In foreign policy, Khrushchev advocated "peaceful coexistence," or relaxation of tensions between the United States and the Soviet Union. He was criticized from the beginning for the suggested reforms, and his diplomatic and military failure in the Cuban Missile Crisis ensured his removal from power. Furthermore, most of his reforms did not appear to be working by the early 1960s. He was replaced by the much more conservative **Leonid Brezhnev**, who ended the reforms and tried to cope with the growing number of economic problems that were just under the surface of Soviet power.

After Brezhnev died in 1982, power fell to two short-lived successors, who were in turn replaced in 1985 by a reformer from a younger generation, **Mikhail Gorbachev**. Gorbachev was unlike any previous Soviet leader in that he not only looked and acted more "western", but he also was more open to western-style reforms than his predecessors, including Khrushchev. Gorbachev inherited far more problems than any outsider realized at the time, and many of his reforms were motivated by sheer necessity to save the country from economic disaster. His program was three-pronged:

- *Glasnost* – This term translates from the Russian as "openness"; it allowed more open discussion of political, social, and economic issues as well as open criticism of the government. Although this reform was applauded by western nations and many Russians, it caused many problems for Gorbachev. After so many years of repression, people vented hostility toward the government that encouraged open revolt, particularly among some of the republics that wanted independence from Soviet control.

- **Democratization** – Gorbachev believed that he could keep the old Soviet structure, including Communist Party control, but at the same time insert a little democracy into the system. Two such moves included the creation of 1) a new Congress of People's Deputies with directly elected representatives and 2) a new position of "President" that was selected by the Congress. However, many of the new deputies were critical of Gorbachev, increasing the level of discord within the government.

- *Perestroika* – This economic reform was Gorbachev's most radical, and also his least successful. Again, he tried to keep the old Soviet structure, and modernize from within. Most significantly, it transferred many economic powers held by the central government to private hands and the market economy. Specific reforms included authorization of some privately-owned companies, penalties for under-performing state factories, leasing of farm land outside the collective farms, price reforms, and encouragement of joint ventures with foreign companies.

None of Gorbachev's reforms were ever fully carried out because the Revolution of 1991 swept him out of office.

A Failed Coup and the Revolution of 1991

In August 1991, "conservatives" (those that wanted to abandon Gorbachev's reforms), several high-ranking Communist Party and government officials led a coup d'état that tried to remove Gorbachev from office. The leaders included the vice-president, the head of the KGB (Russian secret police), and top military advisers. The coup failed when popular protests broke out, and soldiers from the military defected rather than support their leaders. The protesters were led by **Boris Yeltsin**, the elected president of the Russian Republic and former Politburo member. Yeltsin had been removed from the Politburo a few years earlier because his radical views offended conservatives. He advocated more extreme reform measures than Gorbachev did, and he won his position as president of the Russian Republic as a result of new voting procedures put in place by Gorbachev.

MILESTONES IN RUSSIAN POLITICAL DEVELOPMENT

988 C.E. Russian Tzar Vladimir I converted to Orthodox Christianity, setting Russia on a different course of development from Western Europe.

1613 The Romanov family came to power and ruled until 1917.

1689-1725 Peter the Great ruled Russia, bringing the dynamic of "Slavophile vs. Westernizer" to Russian political development.

1762-1796 Catherine the Great, the second great Westernizer, solidified and expanded Peter's reforms, though she still ruled with an iron hand, as all Russian tsars did.

1917 The last tsar was deposed, and the Bolshevik Revolution put V.I. Lenin in control of the U.S.S.R.

1917-1921 The Russian civil war raged as many factions inside and outside Russia fought to oust Lenin from power. Lenin solidified his power in 1921.

1927-1953 Joseph Stalin ruled the U.S.S.R., reinterpreting the meaning of communism and instituting his programs of collectivization and industrialization.

1991 A coup against General Secretary Mikhail Gorbachev failed, but also instigated a process that led to the collapse of the Soviet Union.

1993 The new Russian Constitution put in place the current regime.

Gorbachev was restored to power, but the U.S.S.R. only had a few months to live. By December 1991, eleven republics had declared their independence, and eventually Gorbachev was forced to announce the end of the union, which put him out of a job. The fifteen republics went their separate ways, but Boris Yeltsin emerged as the president of the largest and most powerful republic, now renamed the Russian Federation.

The Russian Federation: 1991 to the Present

Once the Revolution of 1991 was over, Boris Yeltsin proceeded with his plans to create a western-style democracy. The old Soviet structure was destroyed, but the same problems that haunted Gorbachev were still there. The **Constitution of 1993** created a three-branch government, with a president, a prime minister, a lower legislative house called the **Duma**, and a **Constitutional Court**. Conflict erupted between Yeltsin and the Duma, and the Russian economy did not immediately respond to the "**shock therapy**" (an immediate market economy) that the government prescribed. Yeltsin also proved to be a much poorer president than he was a revolutionary leader. His frequent illnesses and alcoholism almost certainly explain the erratic behavior that led him to hire and fire prime ministers in quick succession. Yeltsin resigned in the months before the election of 2000, and Prime Minister Vladimir Putin became acting president. Although Putin supported Yeltsin's reforms, he was widely seen as a more conservative leader who many hoped would bring stability to the newly formed government. As his presidency progressed, Putin retreated significantly from the commitments that Yeltsin had made to the establishment of a democratic system. The fact that he honored the Constitution of 1993 by stepping down as president at the end of his second term is countered by his remaining on as prime minister, and most believe that he still controlled policymaking in Russia. The Constitution allowed Putin to run for president again in 2012, and his decision to run once more in 2018 solidified his hold on power for another six years.

CITIZENS, SOCIETY AND THE STATE

Russian citizens are affected by many contradictory influences from their political culture. When questioned, most say that they support the idea of a democratic government for Russia, although many do not believe that one exists today. However, they also like the idea of a strong state and powerful political leaders, characteristics that help to explain the popularity of Vladimir Putin as a political leader.

Cleavages

The Russian Federation has many societal cleavages that greatly impact policymaking, including nationality, social class, and rural/urban divisions.

Nationality

The most important single cleavage in the Russian Federation is **nationality**. Although about 80% of all citizens are Russians, the country includes sizeable numbers of Tatars, Ukrainians, Armenians, Chuvashes, Bashkis, Byelorussians, and Moldavians. These cleavages determine the organization of the country into a "federation," with "autonomous regions," republics, and provinces whose borders are based on ethnicity. Like the breakaway republics of 1991, many would like to have their independence, although most have trade benefits from the Russian government that induce them to stay within the Federation.

A notable exception is **Chechnya**, a primarily Muslim region that has fought for years for its freedom. The Russian government has had considerable difficulty keeping Chechnya a part of Russia, and the independence movement there is still very strong. In recent years, Chechens have been involved in terrorist acts, including the 2004 seizure of a school in southern Russia that resulted in gunfire and explosions that killed more than 350 people, many of them children. Almost certainly, other regions within Russia's borders are watching, and the government knows that if Chechnya is successful, other independence movements will break out in the country. In an effort to gain legitimacy for the Russian government in Chechnya, a referendum was held to vote on a new constitution for the region. The constitution was approved by the Chechen voters, even though it declared that their region was an "inseparable part" of Russia. With Putin's support, former rebel Ramzan Kadyrov became president of Chechnya in 2007, but the fighting has not stopped, with killings and kidnappings remaining quite common. Kadyrov has ruled Chechnya virtually as a separate Islamic State, with his own 20,000-strong army, his own tax system, and his own religious laws. Some have criticized Putin for allowing Kadyrov such free reign, especially since many are suspicious that Kadyrov's men have been involved in murders, kidnappings, torture and extortion.

The entire area of the Caucasus is currently restive, and Russia's invasion of Georgia in 2008 increased tensions all across the region. In the summer of 2009, a suicide bomber tried to kill the president of Ingushetia, a republic that borders Chechnya, with a Chechen group involved in the Beslan school siege taking responsibility for the attack. Explosions and bombings increased all across the Caucasus later in the summer, and suicide attacks returned after a few years of relative calm.

Russian nationalists have taken responsibility for kidnappings, beheadings and a 2006 bombing that killed 10 at a Moscow market operated mostly by immigrants. At least 37 people were killed and more than 300 injured in xenophobic attacks in 2010, according to the Sova center, a Moscow-based organization that tracks such violence. One of the most widely publicized cases came in December 2010, in the wake of a fatal shooting of an ethnic Russian soccer fan by a man from Russia's North Caucasus region. Thousands of young people began an extended riot close to Red Square, chanting "Russia for Russians" and racial slurs.

In 2014, Russia hosted the Winter Olympics in the Black Sea resort of Sochi, almost on the doorstep of insurgent unrest in the Caucasus. Security always had been tight in Sochi, where Mr. Putin has a presidential residence that he uses often and where he frequently hosts visiting foreign leaders. The government further tightened security before the games, which officially began February 7, 2014. The games proceeded without serious incident.

Religion

Tsarist Russia was overwhelmingly Russian Orthodox, with the tsar serving as spiritual head of the church. In reaction, the Soviet Union prohibited religious practices of all kinds, so that most citizens lost their religious affiliations during the 20th century. Boris Yeltsin encouraged the Russian Orthodox Church to reestablish itself, partly as a signal of his break with communism, but also as a reflection of old Russian nationalism. Today most ethnic Russians identify themselves as Russian Orthodox, but they are still largely nonreligious, with only a small percentage regularly attending church services.

The growing acceptance of the church was demonstrated in 2007, when the Russian Church Abroad reunited with the Russian Orthodox Church. The Russian Church Abroad had split off after the Bolshevik Revolution in 1917, vowing never to return as long as the "godless regime" was in power. In a meeting in 2003 in New York, Putin met with leaders of the church to assure them "that this godless regime is no longer there...You are sitting with a believing president." (*New York Times*, May 17, 2007). After the reunion in 2007, Moscow still retained ultimate authority in appointments and other church matters, and many critics say that the church is too much under government control.

Other religions are represented in small percentages – Roman Catholics, Jews, Muslims, and Protestants. Since the current regime is

RELIGION AND ETHNIC GROUPS IN RUSSIA

RELIGION		ETHNIC GROUPS	
Russian Orthodox	15 - 20%	Russian	77.7%
Muslim	10 - 15%	Tatar	3.7%
Other Christian	2%	Ukrainian	1.4%
note: estimates are of practicing worshipers; Russia has large		Bashkir	1.1%
numbers of non-practice believers and non-believers, a legacy of Soviet rule		Chuvash	1%
		Other	10.2%

Reference: CIA World Factbook, 2006, 2010 estimates

relatively new and political parties have few ideological ties, no clear patterns have emerged that indicate political attitudes of religious vs. nonreligious citizens. However, in the past Russia has generally followed a pragmatic combination of authoritarianism and flexibility toward minorities.

One pattern worth noting is the rapid rise in the Muslim share of the population in recent years. Russia has more Muslims than any other European state except Turkey, and some estimates show as many as 20 million Muslims in the country. Muslims are concentrated in three areas:

1. **Moscow** – Muslims form a large share of laborers who have migrated to Moscow in recent years to find work.

2. **The Caucasus** – In this area between the Black Sea and the Caspian Sea, many ethnicities (including Chechens) are Muslim. This area is often seen as a hot spot of trouble (along with Palestine, Kashmir, and Bosnia) for Muslims. The repression of Chechens, as well as intermittent violence in the entire region, was the biggest issue for Putin as he tried to cultivate Russia's role in global Muslim affairs. The region remains highly volatile today.

3. **Bashkortostan** and **Tatarstan** – Muslim relations with Russians are generally calmer in these two regions than in the Caucasus. Tatarstan's Muslim president, Mintimer Shaimiev, accompanied Mr. Putin around the Middle East in 2005, as the president tried to restructure Russia's image as a country supportive of Islam.

In 2013, the government conducted several crackdowns on radical Islamists, largely in preparation for the 2014 Winter Olympics in Sochi. In June 2013, the police arrested 300 Muslims in Moscow, 170 of whom were foreigners. The Muslims were found with extremist literature, Radio Free Europe reported, and were considered to be a threat. Putin said in a meeting of security force officers that the country must continue with the systematic arrests in order to "fight against corruption, crime and the insurgency."

Muslims in the Caucasus Region of the Russian Federation. Karachai-Cherkessia (92%), Kabardino-Balkariya (78%), Ingushetia (63%), Chechnya (91%), and Dagestan (85%) all have heavy concentrations of Muslims, a contributing factor to the persisting unrest in the region.

Social Class

The Soviet attempts to destroy social class differences in Russia were at least partially successful. The old noble/peasant distinction in tsarist Russia was abolished, but was replaced by another cleavage: members of the Communist Party and non-members. Only about 7% of the citizenry were party members, but all political leaders were recruited from this group. Economic favors were granted to party members as well, particularly those of the Central Committee and the Politburo. However, egalitarian views were promoted, and the ***nomenklatura*** process of recruiting leaders from lower levels of the party was generally blind to economic and social background. Today Russian citizens appear to be more egalitarian in their political and social views than people of established democracies.

Many observers of modern Russia note that a new socioeconomic class is developing within the context of the budding market economy: entrepreneurs that have recently amassed fortunes from new business opportunities. Although the fortunes of many of these newly rich Russians were wiped away by the 1997 business bust, many survived and new ones have emerged since then. Boris Yeltsin's government contributed to this class by distributing huge favors to them, and a small but powerful group of entrepreneurs sponsored the presidential campaign of Vladimir Putin in 2000. In the Putin era, oligarchs have come under fire for various alleged and real illegal activities, particularly the underpayment of taxes on the businesses they acquired. Vladimir Gusinsky (MediaMost) and Boris Berezovsky were both effectively exiled, and the most prominent, Mikhail Khodorkovsky (Yukos Oil), was arrested in October 2003, and sentenced to eight years in prison, with his company trying to protect itself from being dismantled. In 2011, his prison term was extended, but Putin pardoned him in late 2013.

Rural/Urban Cleavages

Industrialization since the era of Joseph Stalin has led to an increasingly urban population, with about 73% of all Russians now living in cities, primarily in the western part of the country. The economic divide between rural and urban people is wide, although recent economic woes have beset almost all Russians no matter where they live. City dwellers are more likely to be well educated and in touch with western culture, but the political consequences of these differences are unclear in the unsettled current political climate.

Beliefs and Attitudes

In the old days of the Soviet Union, citizens' beliefs and attitudes toward their government were molded by Communist Party doctrines. At the heart of these doctrines was **Marxism**, which predicted the demise of the capitalist West. This belief fed Russian nationalism and supported the notion that the Russian government and way of life would eventually prevail. The ideals of the revolutionary era of the early 20th century envisioned a world transformed by egalitarianism and the elimination of poverty and oppression. As **Stalinism** set in, the ideals shifted to pragmatic internal development, and many of the old tendencies toward absolutism and repression returned. The collapse of the Soviet Union brought out much hostility toward the government that is reflected in the attitudes of Russian citizens today.

- **Mistrust of the government** – Political opinion polls are very recent innovations in Russian politics, so information about citizens' attitudes and beliefs toward their government is scarce. However, the limited evidence does reflect a great deal of alienation from the political system. Most polls show that people support democratic ideals, including free elections and widespread individual civil liberties and rights. However, most do not trust government officials or institutions to convert these ideals to reality. Alienation is also indicated by a low level of participation in interest groups, including trade unions and other groups that people belonged to in the days of the Soviet Union. An interesting bit of contradictory evidence, though, is the high level of approval that Vladimir Putin enjoyed during his first two terms. Even though his approval ratings have vacillated since 2008, they remain high, and other Russian public officials have not shared his relatively high level of popularity.

- **Statism** – Despite high levels of mistrust in government, Russian citizens still expect the state to take an active role in their lives. For most of Russian history, citizens have functioned more as subjects than as participants, and the central government of the Soviet Union was strong enough to touch and control many aspects of citizens' lives. Today Russians expect a great deal from their government, even if they have been disappointed in the progress of reform in recent years.

- **Economic beliefs** – Boris Yeltsin's market reforms created divisions in public opinion regarding market reform. Nearly all parties and electoral groups support the market transition, but those with more favorable opinions of the old Soviet regime are less enthusiastic. At the other end of the spectrum are those that support rapid market reform, including privatization and limited government regulation. The latter approach was favored by Yeltsin, and his "shock therapy" marketization was blamed by his critics for the steep economic decline that characterized the 1990s.

- **Westernization** – Political opinions follow the old divide of **Slavophile vs. Westernizer**. Some political parties emphasize nationalism and the defense of Russian interests and Slavic culture. These parties also tend to favor a strong military and protection from foreign economic influence. On the other hand, reform parties strongly support the integration of Russia into the world economy and global trade.

Economic beliefs and attitudes toward the West also shape attitudes about whether or not the modern regime should integrate elements of the old Soviet government into its policymaking. Some citizens are nostalgic about the "good old days" when everyone had a guaranteed income, and they are most likely to support the Communist Party that still exists within the party system. Some observers see a generational split between those who remember better times under Soviet power, and those who have come of age during the early days of the Russian Federation.

Political Participation

Russian citizens did actually vote during Soviet rule in the 20th century. In fact, their voting rate was close to 100% because they faced serious consequences if they stayed home. However, until Gorbachev brought about reforms in the late 1980s, the elections were not competitive, and citizens voted for candidates that were hand picked by the Communist leadership. Gorbachev created competitive elections in the Soviet Union, but because no alternate political parties existed yet, voter choice was limited to the designated party candidate vs. anyone from within party ranks who wanted to challenge the official candidate. In some cases, this choice made a real difference, because Boris Yeltsin himself was elected as an "alternate candidate" for president of the then Russian Republic.

Protests

After the economic crisis of late 2008, a series of protests were organized around Russia to criticize the government's economic policies as the economy sank to its lowest point since 1997. The largest was in Vladivostok, in the far eastern part of the country, where about 1000 protesters marched through the streets in late January 2009. The Russian Communist Party organized a rally in Moscow and called for a return of the centralized economic policies of the Soviet Union. The authorities approved the rally, and riot police officers watched the march but did not interfere. Other demonstrations against the government, as well as some in support, were held in several cities throughout the country, with none apparently turning violent.

Putin's decision to run for the presidency in 2012 sparked some of the largest protests in recent years. Protests broke out after the parliamentary elections in December 2011, with accusations that United Russia had rigged the elections. Then on the eve of the election in May, about 20,000 people protested in Moscow, according to a Reuters news report. Many were angry that Putin was extending his 12-year domination of Russia with another presidential term, as the crown chanted "Russia without Putin" and "Putin - thief." Opposition leaders were arrested as violence broke out in several cities, including Vladivostok, the Urals city of Kurgan, and Kemerovo in western Siberia. Putin ignored the protests, and since then no major protests have been allowed.

Russia's involvement in the Ukrainian crisis caused much controversy, with many Russians supporting the government but others openly criticizing it. In early 2014, Boris Nemtsov, a leader of Russia's liberal opposition, was shot dead on a bridge by the walls of the Kremlin. A few days earlier, Mr. Nemtsov had been handing out leaflets for an anti-war rally to protest Russia's support of rebels in eastern Ukraine. The march turned into a memorial procession. Six days before Mr. Nemtsov's death, the Kremlin organized protest marchers bearing slogans denouncing Ukraine, the West, and Russian liberals. Alexei Navlny, another opposition leader, described the emergence of "pro-government extremists and terrorist groups" who openly fight the opposition.

Voter Turnout

Since 1991 voter turnout in the Russian Federation has been fairly high: higher than in the United States, but somewhat lower than turnout rates in Britain and France. Political alienation is reflected in the 50.3% rate in the 1993 Duma elections, but those elections followed a failed attempt by the Duma to take over the country. Voter turnout in the Duma election in December 2003 was just under 56%; for the election in December 2007, the turnout was almost 64%; and for the 2011 election, the turnout was just over 60%. Meanwhile, voter turnout for presidential elections declined between 1991 and 2004, with almost 75% of eligible citizens voting in the first round election in 1991, and less that 65% voting in 2004. The turnout in the presidential election of 2008 was almost 70%, but the turnout for 2012 fell to just over 65%, and the turnout in 2018 was 67.5%.

Civil Society

Despite the relatively high voter turnouts, participation in other forms of political activities is low. Part of this lack of participation is due to a relatively undeveloped **civil society**, private organizations and associations outside of politics. For example, most Russians don't attend church on a regular basis, nor do they belong to sports or recreational clubs, literary or other cultural groups, charitable organizations, or labor unions. Only about 1% report belonging to a political party. On the other hand, Russians are not necessarily disengaged from politics. Many report that they regularly read newspapers, watch news on television, and discuss politics with family and friends.

Civil society appears to be growing in Russia, although since Putin's first reelection in 2012, the government appears to be imposing new restrictions. Before the 1917 Revolution, little civil society existed because of low economic development, authoritarianism, and feudalism. Soviet authorities argued that only the party could and should represent the people's interests, and so state-sponsored organizations appeared in a **state corporatist** arrangement with the government clearly in control of channeling the voice of the people. The Russian Orthodox Church was brought tightly under control of the Communist Party. With the advent of *glasnost* in the 1980s, however, civil society slowly began to emerge, and since that time many organizations have formed to express points of view on different issues, including the environment, ethnicity, gender, human rights, and health care.

Despite the proliferation of these groups, the government has placed severe restrictions on their activities, especially on groups that are openly critical of the government's policies. Rather than directly attacking the groups, the government has used a number of tactics to weaken them, such as investigating sources of income, making registration with the authorities difficult, and police harassment. Since Putin's reelection in 2012, nonprofit groups have come under particular pressure with new laws that severely restrict foreign financing and require them to register as "foreign agents." In addition, the definition of high treason has been expanded to include assisting foreign organizations.

Russian Youth Groups

As president, Vladimir Putin created a handful of youth movements to support the government. The largest is **Nashi,** and others are the Youth Guard and Locals. All are part of an effort to build a following of loyal, patriotic young people and to defuse any youthful resistance that could have emerged during the sensitive presidential election of 2008. Nashi organized mass marches in support of Mr. Putin and staged demonstrations over foreign policy issues that resulted in the physical harassment of the British and Estonian ambassadors. For example, after Estonia relocated a Soviet-era war memorial in April 2007, Nashi laid siege to the Estonian Embassy in Moscow, throwing rocks, disrupting traffic, and tearing down the Estonian flag. Members of the group attacked the Estonian ambassador, and her guards had to use pepper spray to defend her. In May 2011, some 50,000 members of Nashi gathered for a rally against corruption in downtown Moscow, where they concentrated on the corruption of government opponents, not on government officials. When anti-Putin protests broke out in late 2011, Nashi countered with rallies in support of Putin and United Russia.

Nashi's opponents deride the organization as a modern version of Komsomol, the youth wing of the Communist Party of the Soviet Union. Nashi receives grants from the government and large state-run businesses, so critics of the group see it as an arm of an increasingly authoritarian state.

POLITICAL INSTITUTIONS

Russian history includes a variety of regime types, but the tradition is highly authoritarian. The reforms that began in the early 1990s are truly experimental, and only time will tell whether democracy and a free market economy will take root. Even if they do, the nature of the regime must take into account Russian political culture and traditions. Current political parties, elections, and institutions of government are all new, and their functions within the political system are very fluid and likely to change within the next few years. However, the Russian Federation survived its first few rocky years, and many experts believe that at least some aspects of Russian government and politics are settling into a pattern.

Even though the Soviet Union was highly centralized, it still maintained a **federal government structure**. The Russian Federation has retained this model, and the current regime consists of eighty-nine regions, twenty-one of which are ethnically non-Russian by majority. Each region is bound by treaty to the Federation, but not all – including Chechnya – have signed on. Most of these regions are called "republics," and because the central government was not strong under Yeltsin, many ruled themselves almost independently. In the early 1990s, several republics went so far as to make claims of sovereignty that amounted to near or complete independence. Many saw the successful bid of the former Soviet states for independence as role models, and they believed that their own status would change as well. Chechnya's bid for independence and the war that followed are good examples of this sentiment. Some regions are much stronger than others, so power is devolved unequally across the country, a condition called **asymmetric federalism**.

As president, Vladimir Putin has cracked down on regional autonomy, ordering the army to shell even Chechnya into submission. Several measures that Putin imposed were:

- **Creation of super-districts** – In 2000 seven new federal districts were created to encompass all of Russia. Each district is headed by a presidential appointee, who supervises the local authorities as Putin sees fit.

- **Removal of governors** – A law allows the president to remove from office a governor who refuses to subject local law to the national constitution.

- **Appointment of governors** – Putin further centralized power in Moscow in late 2004 with a measure that ended direct election of the eighty-nine regional governors. Instead, the governors now are nominated by the president, and then confirmed by regional legislatures.

- **Changes in the Federation Council** – Originally the Federation Council (the upper legislative house) was comprised of the governors and Duma heads of each region. In 2002 a Putin-backed change prohibited these officials from serving themselves, although they were still allowed to appoint council members.

- **Elimination of single-member-district seats in the Duma** – Many minor political parties were able to capture Duma seats under the old rules that allowed half of the 450 seats to be elected by single-member districts and half by proportional representation. In 2005, Putin initiated a change to a pure proportional representation electoral system that eliminated candidates that were regionally popular. The new rules first applied to the election of 2007.

As a result of all these changes, the "federation" is highly centralized.

Linkage Institutions

Groups that link citizens to government are still not strong in Russia, a situation that undermines recent attempts to establish a democracy. Political parties were highly unstable and fluid during the 1990s, and since Putin's election in 2000, more power has concentrated in his party, so that after the parliamentary elections of late 2003 and presidential elections of early 2004, no strong opposing political parties were in existence. Opposition groups emerged in more recent elections. For example, in the Duma elections of 2016, United Russia won 343 seats, winning 54.2% of the popular vote. The Communist Party won 42 seats, with 13.34% of the popular vote, and the Liberal Democrats won 39 seats, with 13.14% of the popular vote. Other parties that garnered votes were A Just Russia, Rodina, and Civic Platform. Interest groups have no solid footing in civil society since private organizations are weak, and the media has come more under government control.

Parties

Most established democracies had many years to develop party and electoral systems.   However, Russians put theirs together almost overnight after the Revolution of 1991.   Many small, factional political parties ran candidates in the first Duma elections in 1993, and by 1995, 43 parties were on the ballot.   Many of the parties revolved around a particular leader or leaders, such as the "Bloc of General Andrey Nikolaev and Academician Svyaloslav Fyodorov," the "Yuri Boldyrev Movement," or "Yabloko," which is an acronym for its three founders.   Others reflected a particular group, such as the "Party of Pensioners," "Agrarian Party of Russia," or "Women of Russia."   By 1999 the number of parties who ran Duma candidates had shrunk to 26, but many of the parties were new ones, including Vladimir Putin's Unity Party.   Needless to say, with these fluctuations, citizens have had no time to develop party loyalties, leadership in Russia continues to be personalistic, and political parties remain weak and fluid.

New election rules initiated by Vladimir Putin in 2005 solidified this trend toward fewer political parties.   Before 2007, half of the Duma's 450 seats were elected by proportional representation and half by single-member districts.   The rules changed so that all seats – starting in the 2007 election – are elected by proportional representation, with all parties required to win a minimum of 7% of the national vote in order to win any seats.   Smaller parties with regional support lost representation, and only four parties gained seats in the elections of 2007 and 2011: United Russia, the Communist Party, the Liberal Democrats, and A Just Russia.   In 2016 six parties gained seats.

United Russia

The party was founded in April 2001 as a merger of Fatherland All-Russia Party, and the Unity Party of Russia.   The Unity Party was put together by oligarch Boris Berezovsky and other entrepreneurs to support then Prime Minister Vladimir Putin in the presidential election of 2000.   The merger put even more political support behind Putin.   United Russia won 221 of the 450 Duma seats in the election of 2003, although this figure underestimated the party's strength since many minor parties were Putin supporters or clients. Putin, running as United Russia's candidate, won the presidential election of 2004 with 71% of the vote with no serious challengers from any other political parties. In the fall of 2007, Putin announced his willingness to head the party list at the general Duma election in 2007. Since Duma election rules had been changed at his initiative in 2005 to pure proportional representation, this move insured that he would be elected to the Duma, and so eligible to become prime minister. United Russia gained more than 64% of the vote in the election of 2007, which translated to 315 of the 450 seats in the Duma. Putin's hand-picked successor, Dmitri Medvedev, won the presidential election of 2008 with about 70% of the vote, and "chose" Putin as his prime minister.

Putin's decision to run for president in 2012 was controversial enough that United Russia lost seats (315 in 2007 compared to 238 in 2011) and Putin won the presidential election with 64% of the vote, as compared to Medvedev's 70% in 2008. Ideologically, United Russia is hard to define except that it is pro-Putin.

The Communist Party of the Russian Federation (CPRF)

The Communist Party of the old Soviet Union survives today as the second strongest party in the Duma, even though it has not yet won a presidential election. After the election of 1995, it held 157 of the Duma's 450 members, and even though the party lost seats in the 1999 election, it remained an important force in Russian politics. However, the party's support dropped significantly in the parliamentary elections of 2003 and 2007, winning only 51 of the 450 Duma seats in 2003 and 57 in 2007. However, the party won 92 seats in 2011, benefitting from the discontent with Putin and United Russia. The party's leader, **Gennady Zyuganov**, came in second in the 1996 and 2000 presidential elections, but his percentage in the second round fell from 40.3% in 1996 to 29.21% in 2000. Zyuganov dropped out of the presidential election of 2004, and in July 2004, a breakaway faction led by Vladimir Tikhonov weakened the party further. In 2008, the party's candidate was again Zyuganov, who gained less than 18% of the vote, second to Medvedev's more than 70% of the vote. Zyuganov's share in 2012 was more than 17%, compared to Putin's almost 64%. In 2018, the party ran Pavel Grudinin for president, who won 11.77% of the popular vote.

The CPRF is not like the old Communist Party, but it is far less reformist than other parties are. Zyuganov opposed many reforms during the Gorbachev era, and he continues to represent to supporters the stability of the old regime. The party emphasizes centralized planning and nationalism, and implies an intention to regain territories lost when the Soviet Union broke apart.

Liberal Democrats

This misnamed party is by far the most controversial. It is headed by Vladimir Zhirinovsky who has made headlines around the world for his extreme nationalist positions. He regularly attacks reformist leaders, and particularly disliked Yeltsin. He has implied that Russia under his leadership would use nuclear weapons on Japan, and he makes frequent anti-Semitic remarks (despite his Jewish origins). He has also brought the wrath of Russian women by making blatantly sexist comments. His party was reformulated as "Zhirinovsky's bloc" for the 2000 presidential election, when he received only 2.7% of the vote. The party did pick up seats in the 2003 Duma elections, receiving about 11% of the total vote, as well as 37 seats. The rule changes for the 2007 elections did not impact the party's representation significantly, although they won 40 seats, a gain of 3 over the 2003 election. In 2012, the party benefited from Putin's controversial power play, winning 56 seats. In 2016, the party lost 17 seats, winning a total of 39.

A Just Russia

A Just Russia was formed in 2006 by the merger of Motherland People's Patriotic Union with the Party of Pensioners and the Party of Life. The party is led by the Speaker of the Federation Council Sergei Mironov. Motherland formed in 2003 with the merger of 30 organizations, but its leaders quarreled over whether or not to challenge Putin in the 2004 presidential race, and the party split in two, with one faction forming Fair Russia. The party passed the 7% threshold in the

Duma election of 2007 with 7.74% of the vote, enough to gain them 38 seats. A Just Russia did much better in 2011, winning 64 Duma seats, but they only won 23 seats in 2016.

Overall, since 1993 ideological parties have faded in importance and have been replaced by **parties of power**, or parties strongly sponsored by economic and political power-holders. For example, United Russia is Putin's party, created by powerful oligarchs to get him elected. As long as Putin is in power, United Russia will be, too, especially since he was able to orchestrate who his successor would be in 2008. At the time of the election, Putin was tremendously popular, as was reflected in United Russia's landslide in the Duma elections of 2007. The two elections confirmed that the party of power remains the voters' choice. Even though Putin and United Russia lost some support in the elections of 2011 and 2012, they remained firmly in control of the government, with 343 of 450 seats in the Duma after the Duma election of 2016.

Elections

The Russian political system supports three types of national votes:

- **Referendum** – The Constitution of 1993 allowed the president to call for national referenda by popular vote on important issues. Even before the Constitution was written, Boris Yeltsin called for a referendum on his job performance. The people clearly supported his reforms, but his majorities were not overwhelming. The second referendum was held later in the year, and the people voted in favor of the new Constitution. A regional referendum was held in Chechnya in 2003 to approve a constitution for the area. The constitution was approved, including the phrase that declared Chechnya to be an "inseparable part" of Russia.

- **Duma elections** – Russian citizens have gone to the polls seven times to elect Duma representatives (1993, 1995, 1999, 2003, 2007, 2011 and 2016). The Duma has 450 seats, and until 2007, half were elected by proportional representation, and the other half by single-member districts. As of 2007, the 225 single-member districts were abolished, so that all Duma seats now are assigned exclusively by proportional representation. Also eliminated was the "against all" option that allowed voters to reject all candidates. Parties must get at least 7% (raised from 5% before 2007) of the total vote to get any seats according to proportional representation. The election changes were initiated by Putin, who argued that the new rules would reduce the number of parties in the Duma and thus make policymaking more efficient. Since 1993 parties have merged and disappeared, so that only a few have survived to the present.

- **Presidential elections** – Presidential elections follow the two-round model that requires the winning candidate to receive more than 50 percent of the vote. In 2000 Putin received 52.94% of the vote, so no run-off election was required, since he captured a majority on the first round. Communist Gennady Zyuganov received 29.21%, and no other candidates garnered more than 5.8%. Some observers have questioned the honesty of elections, particularly since the media obviously promoted Yeltsin in 1996 and Putin in 2000. A 2001 law seriously restricted the right of small, regional parties to run presidential candidates, so critics questioned how democratic future presidential elections might be. The presidential election of 2004 added credence to the criticism, since Vladimir Putin won with 71% of the vote, again requiring no run off. His closest competitor was Nikolay Kharitonov, who ran for the Communist Party and received less than 14% of the vote. In 2008 Putin was ineligible to run, but his chosen successor, Dmitri Medvedev, won the election with more than 70% of the vote. In 2012, Putin's share of the vote slipped to 64%, but he still managed to avoid a run-off election as he did in 2018, when he ran as an independent, winning 76.69%.

Interest Groups

Of course, interest groups were only allowed in the Soviet Union under **state corporatism** and were controlled by the government. Decision-making took place within the Central Committee and the Politburo, and if any outside contacts influenced policy, they generally were confined to members of the Communist Party. When market capitalism suddenly replaced centralized economic control in 1991, the state-owned industries were up for grabs, and those that bought them for almost nothing were generally insiders (members of the *nomenklatura*) who have since become quite wealthy. This collection of **oligarchs** may be defined loosely as an interest group because they have been a major influence on the policymaking process during the formative years of the Russian Federation.

The Oligarchy

The power of the oligarchy became obvious during the last year of Boris Yeltsin's first term as president of the Russian Federation. The tycoons were tied closely to members of Yeltsin's family, particularly his daughter. Together they took advantage of Yoltsin's inattention to his presidential duties, and soon monopolized Russian industries and built huge fortunes. One of the best known oligarchs was Boris Berezovsky, who admitted in 1997 that he and six other entrepreneurs controlled over half of the Russian GNP. Berezovsky's businesses had giant holdings in the oil industry and in media, incuding a TV network and many newspapers. He used the media to insure Yeltsin's reelection in 1996, and he and the family clearly controlled the presidency.

RUSSIAN DUMA ELECTIONS 2016

PARTY	SEATS WON	POPULAR VOTE	PERCENTAGE
United Russia	343	28,527,828	54.2%
Communist	42	7,019,752	13.34%
Liberal Democrats	39	6,917,063	13.14%
A Just Russia	23	3,275,053	6.22%
Rodina	1	792,226	1.51%
Civic Platform	1	115,433	.22%

Duma Election Results of 2016. United Russia gained 105 seats since the last election; the Communist Party lost 50 seats; the Liberal Democrats lost 17; A Just Russia lost 41; and Rodina and Civic Platform each gained a seat, having no seats before.

RUSSIAN PRESIDENTIAL ELECTION, 2018

Candidate	Party	Votes	%
Vladimir Putin	Independent	56,430,712	76.69
Pavel Grudinin	Communist	8,659,206	11.77
Vladimir Zhirinovsky	Liberal Democratic	4,154,985	5.65
Ksenia Sobchak	Civic Initiative	1,238,031	1.68
Grigory Yavlinsky	Yabloko	769,644	1.05
Boris Titov	Party of Growth	556,801	0.76
Maxim Suraykin	Communists of Russia	499,342	0.68
Sergey Baburin	Russian All-People's Union	479,013	0.65

Voter Turnout - 67.5%

When Yeltsin's ill heath and alcoholism triggered events that led to his resignation in 2000, Berezovsky went to work with other oligarchs to put together and finance the Unity Party. When Unity's presidential candidate Vladimir Putin easily won the election with more than 50% of the vote in the first round, it looked as if the oligarchs had survived Yeltsin's demise.

Putin, however, has shown some resistance to oligarchic control. He has clashed with the entrepreneurs on several occasions, and when television magnate Vladimir Gusinsky harshly criticized Putin's reform plans, Gusinsky was arrested for corruption and his company was given to a state-owned monopoly. Both Berezovsky and Gusinsky are now in exile, but they still have close political and economic connections in Russia. In October 2003, Mikhail Khodorkovsky, the richest man in Russia and chief executive officer of Yukos Oil Company, was arrested as a signal from Putin that the Russian government was consolidating power. The government slapped massive penalties and additional taxes on Yukos, forcing it into bankruptcy. In 2011, Khodorkovsky was sentenced to jail, this time for stealing oil, while during the first trial he was convicted for avoiding taxes on the sale of oil. In late 2013, Putin pardoned him, and he left the country.

The other oligarchs heeded the warning from Khodorkovsy's example and largely withdrew from political activities, leaving Putin in control but probably with a narrower base of support from economic leaders. However, as the Russian economy sank during the recession that began in late 2007, oligarchs have found themselves heavily in debt and have looked to the state for loans. Even though the government has been cash-strapped as well, the economic climate has the potential for weakening the power of the oligarchs and giving the government more control over them. Putin's choice for president, Dmitri Medvedev, was Chairman of Gazprom until he was elected president of the Russian Federation in May 2008, and he was replaced at Gazprom by Viktor Zubkov, the prime minister who was in turn replaced by Vladimir Putin.

State Corporatism

Under Putin's leadership **state corporatism**, where the state determines which groups have input into policymaking, has become well established. The Russian government has established vast, state-owned holding companies in automobile and aircraft manufacturing, shipbuilding, nuclear power, diamonds, titanium, and other industries. If companies appear to be too independent or too rich the government has not forced owners to sell, but has cited legal infractions (such as with Yukos) to force sales. Either government-controlled companies, or companies run by men seen as loyal to Mr. Putin, are the beneficiaries. Another term for such an arrangement is **insider privatization**.

The Russian Mafia

A larger and even more shadowy influence than the oligarchs is known as the "mafia", but this interest group controls much more than underworld crime. Like the oligarchs, they gained power during the chaotic time after the Revolution of 1991, and they control local businesses, natural resources, and banks. They thrive on payoffs from businesses ("protection money"), money laundering, and deals that they make with Russian government officials, including members of the former KGB. They have murdered bankers, journalists, businessmen, and members of the Duma.

STATE CORPORATISM IN RUSSIA

State Owned Company	Chairman	Benefits
Gazprom (natural gas)	Viktor A Zubkov (former prime minister)	Sibneft oil company Sakhalin II oil company (controlling stakes) Yukos Oil assets
Vneshtorgbank (VTB)	Andrei Kostin (close friend of Putin and on the board of Rosneft)	International investment opportunities; funding for power generation
Rosneft (oil)	Igor I. Sechin (presidential deputy chief of staff)	the Yuganskneftegaz oil fields (Yukos assets) Refineries, oil fields from Yukos
Russian Technology (weapons trader)	Sergey Chemezov (former KGB colleague of Putin)	Avtovaz, Russia's largest car maker VSMPO, a titanium aircraft parts maker

State Corporatism in Russia. It is interesting to note that the former Chairman of Gazprom was Dmitri Medvedev, the president of Russia from 2008-2012. The chart also reflects Russia's **patron-client system**, where individuals in power give favors to subordinates, in return for political support.

The huge fortunes made by the oligarchs and mafia offend the sensibilities of most Russian citizens, who tend to value equality of result, not equality of opportunity. In Russia's past, lawlessness has been dealt with by repressive, authoritarian rule, and these groups represent a major threat to the survival of the new democracy.

The Russian Media

For years the official newspaper of the Soviet Union's Communist Party, **Pravda,** only printed what government officials wanted it to, and so it became an important propaganda tool for the Communist Party. After the coup of 1991 and the dissolution of the country, Pravda continued as an independent newspaper with more freedom of the press than the country had ever allowed. Under Putin, the government again tightened its hold on the press, but Pravda has reinvented itself as a tabloid with a huge audience. Today it has little to fear from official censorship because its investigative journalism tends toward exposés of incompetent police work, corrupt low-level officials, and dirty train stations. Its biggest stories focus on celebrities, such as fashion models, radio hosts, and a hockey player hit with a cake. For serious journalists, however, who want to investigate the top layers of political power, it is a different story.

During a joint press conference with Vladimir Putin in early 2005, two Russian reporters challenged comments by U.S. President George Bush about the lack of a free press in Russia. Of course, the reporters were hand picked to accompany Putin on his trip to the United States, but they argued that the Russian media often criticizes the government. It is true that newspapers and television stations are now privately owned in Russia, although the state controls many of them. There are also many instances of reporters commenting on political actions and decisions, but how much real freedom they have is not clear. One example occurred when the Kremlin used a state-controlled company to take over the only independent television network, NTV. When the ousted NTV journalists took over a different channel, TV-6, the state shut it down. Russian media circles also were suspicious of the alleged poisoning of Anna Politkovskaya, one of the most outspoken critics of the government's policies in Chechnya. In March 2007 correspondent Ivan Safronov, who worked for the business daily *Kommersant*, died in a fall from the window of his Moscow apartment.

The status of freedom of the press in Russia is illustrated by media coverage of the school seizure at Beslan in 2004. As the tragedy unfolded on a Friday, two of Russia's main TV channels did not mention what was happening until an hour after explosions were first heard at the school. When state-owned Russia TV and Channel One finally reported it, they returned to their regularly scheduled programs. However, NTV, which is owned by state-controlled Gazprom, did have rolling coverage for three hours, even though it started late.

State corporatism appears to impact the media business, just as it has oil, gas, aircraft building, and auto companies. For example, in May 2007 the Russian Union of Journalists was evicted from its headquarters in Moscow to make space for the Russia Today television channel. According to the general secretary of the RUJ, the eviction was based on an order from President Vladimir Putin to accommodate the expansion plans of the state-owned English-language channel, which aims to promote a positive image of Russia abroad. One newspaper, the Novaya Gazeta, has blatantly criticized the Russian government. Since 2000 five employees of Novaya Gazeta have died under violent or suspicious circumstances. The latest were in January 2009, when the newspaper's lawyer, Stanislav Markelov, and a young reporter, Aanstasia Baburova were fatally shot by a masked gunman. The editor, Dmitri Muratov, put two of his reporters under armed protection and instituted a policy that any article with sensitive information was to be published immediately, reducing the benefit of killing the reporters. No one blames the government directly for the attacks, but the message is clear: don't criticize the government.

The social media played an important role in the protests that surrounded the legislative election of 2011. One of the leaders, Aleksei Navalny, trained as a real estate lawyer, became famous before the election with his online exposes of corruption within state-owned companies. His following on Twitter and LiveJournal grew into the tens of thousands, and he summoned supporters to gather in protest of the Putin-dominated Duma elections. In 2013, Navalny went on trial for embezzling $500,000 from a timber company that led to a five-year prison sentence. Putin critics claimed that Navalny was being punished because of his criticisms and because he announced his candidacy for mayor of Moscow shortly before his arrest.

Institutions of Government

The current structure of the government was put in place by the Constitution of 1993. It borrows from both presidential and parliamentary systems, and the resulting hybrid **semi-presidential** government is meant to allow for a strong presidency, but at the same time place some democratic checks on executive power. Its early history was stormy, but it is hard to say whether the difficulties centered on Yeltsin's ineffective presidency, or if they reflected inherent flaws within the system. The relationships among the branches have stabilized, but in Putin's and Medvedev's administrations the executive has clearly dominated the other branches, and Putin has commanded the executive branch.

The President and the Prime Minister

The executive branch separates the **head of state** (the president) from the **head of government** (the prime minister). Unlike the Queen's role in British politics, the president's position has been far from ceremonial. Although the Constitution provided for a strong presidency, under Putin the president clearly came to dominate the prime minister. However, once Putin stepped aside to allow Dmitri Medvedev to run for and win the presidency and Putin became prime minister, the relationship between the two positions clearly changed, with Putin continuing to assert his influence. Since Putin's reelection in 2012, the president once again dominates the prime minister.

Russian voters directly elect the president for a six-year (starting in 2012) term, with a limit of two terms. Since Russian political parties are in flux, anyone who gets a million signatures can run for president. In 1996, 2000, and 2004, many candidates ran on the first ballot, and in 2000, 2004, and 2012, Putin won without a second-round vote. In 2008, Medvedev also won without a second-round vote. The president has the power to:

- **Appoint the prime minister and cabinet** – The Duma must approve the prime minister's appointment, but if they reject the president's nominee three times, the president may dissolve the Duma. In 1998, Yeltsin replaced Prime Minister Kiriyenko with Viktor Chernomyrdin, and the Duma rejected him twice. On the third round – under threat of being dissolved – they finally agreed on a compromise candidate, Yevgeni Primakov. Putin was prime minister when he ran for president, and when he became president, he appointed Mikhail Kasyanov as prime minister. Kasyanov served for four years, and was eventually replaced by Mikhail Fradkov, and then Viktor Zubkov. Putin became prime minister in 2008, and in 2012, Medvedev switched places with Putin to become prime minister.

- **Issue decrees that have the force of law** – The president runs a cabinet that has a great deal of concentrated, centralized power. For example, Putin created the state-owned United Aircraft Corporation by decree, a decision that the legislature had no control over. According to the **Constitution**, the Duma has no real power to censure the cabinet, except that it may reject the appointment of the prime minister.

- **Dissolve the Duma** – This power was tested even before the Constitution was put in place. In 1993, Yeltsin ordered the old Russian Parliament dissolved, but the conservative members staged a coup, and refused to leave the "White House" (the parliament building). He ordered the army to fire on the building until the members gave up, but the chaos of the new regime was revealed to the world through the images of a president firing on his own parliament. No such chaos has occurred under Putin or Medvedev.

There is no vice-president, so if a president dies or resigns before his term is up, the prime minister becomes acting president. This situation occurred in 1999 when Prime Minister Putin took over presidential duties when Yeltsin resigned. Prime ministers are not appointed because they are leaders of the majority party (as they are in Great Britain); instead most have been career bureaucrats chosen for their technical expertise or loyalty to the president. However, during the four years when Medvedev was president and Putin took the prime minister's position, there is little doubt that Putin was still in charge, and so even though Medvedev was the head of state, policies did not change from those of Putin's presidency.

A Bicameral Legislature

So far, the Russian legislature has proved to be only a very weak check on executive power. The lower house, the **Duma**, has 450 deputies, who since 2007, are all selected by proportional representation.

THE RUSSIAN LEGISLATURE

DUMA	FEDERATION COUNCIL
450 deputies all selected by proportional representation (since 2007); Passes bills, approves the budget, confirms president's political appointments; Has limited power since president's party dominates and president has the power of decree; Function is to provide popular representation	Two members from each of the 89 federal regions; One representative selected by the governor and another by the regional legislature; Function is to represent regions; Has almost no power because the Duma may override the Council if it rejects legislation passed by the Duma

The Duma passes bills, approves the budget, and confirms the president's political appointments. However, these powers are very limited, since the president may rule by decree, and the Duma's attempts to reject prime ministers have failed. In another confrontation with Yeltsin, the Duma tried to use its constitutional power to impeach him, but the process is so cumbersome that it failed. Although the Duma has been controlled by Putin because his party (United Russia) has most of the seats, it still wields some power in the drafting of legislation. Most legislation originates with the president or prime minister, just as it does in Great Britain and most other parliamentary systems, but the Duma debates bills that must pass the deputies' vote before they become laws.

The upper house, called the **Federation Council**, consists of two members from each of the 89 federal administrative units. Since 2002 one representative is selected by the governor of each region and another by the regional legislature. The Federation Council serves the purpose that most upper houses do in bicameral federalist systems: to represent regions, not the population as such. However, like most other upper houses in European governments, it seems to mainly have the power to delay legislation. If the Federation Council rejects legislation, the Duma may override the Council with a two-thirds vote. On paper, it also may change boundaries among the republics, ratify the use of armed forces outside the country, and appoints and removes judges. However, these powers have not been used yet.

The Judiciary and the Rule of Law

No independent judiciary existed under the old Soviet Union, with courts and judges serving as pawns of the Communist Party. The Constitution of 1993 attempted to build a judicial system that is not controlled by the executive by creating a **Constitutional Court**.

The Court's nineteen members are appointed by the president and confirmed by the Federation Council, and it is supposed to make sure that all laws and decrees are constitutional. Under Putin, the court has taken care to avoid crossing the president. However, even the possibility that it might have independent political influence led Putin to propose moving the seat of the court to St. Petersburg, away from the political center in Moscow. The Constitution also created a Supreme Court to serve as a final court of appeals in criminal and civil cases. The court, though, does not have the power to challenge the constitutionality of laws and other official actions of legislative and executive bodies; the Constitutional Court has that power. Both courts have been actively involved in policymaking, although their independence from the executive is questionable. One problem is that many prosecutors and attorneys were trained under the Soviet legal system, so the judiciary currently suffers from a lack of expertise in carrying out the responsibilities outlined in the Constitution.

Vladimir Putin came into office with a mission to revive the great period of law reform under the tsars, including jury trial, planned for all regions except Chechnya by 2007. Russia brought in procedural codes for criminal and civil rights, and spent a great deal of money on law reform. However, the system is still very much in transition, and corruption is a serious problem. The advent of juries is a real change, but the presumption of innocence is far from a reality. The independence of the judiciary is still not apparent, especially since no courts have challenged Putin in his pursuit of the oligarchs and the dismantling of their empires.

The trials of Mikhail Khodorkovsky and Platon Lebedev, the former controlling shareholders of the Yukos Oil Company, indicate that the courts are still under the political control of Putin. Before the 2011 verdict was read that sentenced Khodorkovsky until 2019, Putin declared that the crime had been proven in court and that "a thief must stay in jail". Hillary Clinton, the U.S. secretary of state, protested, "Attempts to exert pressure on the court are unacceptable," causing Russia's foreign ministry to challenge her statement.

The Russian legal system has often been used as an instrument of the state's power, rather than as a tool for protecting citizens. In August 2013, three women from a feminist punk-rock group, Pussy Riot, were sentenced to two years each in prison for an anti-Putin stunt in a Moscow cathedral. In 2013, the Duma passed new laws that raised fines for unsanctioned demonstration and required foreign-funded non-governmental organizations to register as "foreign agents". Another law created a blacklist of offensive websites.

The Rule of Law and Corruption

Movement toward the rule of law continues to be blocked by corruption in state and society and by the political tradition of allowing the security police to continue to operate autonomously. In the Soviet period, domestic security was carried out by the **KGB** (State Security Committee), but since 1991 its functions have been split up among several agencies. The main domestic security agency is called the Federal Security Service, and no member or collaborator of the Soviet-era security services has been prosecuted for violating citizens' rights. Although the security police are generally regarded as one of the least corrupted of the state agencies, society-wide corruption is a major problem in Russia. One large-scale survey by a Moscow research firm found that at least half the population of Russia is involved in corruption in daily life. For example, people often pay bribes for automobile permits, school enrollment, proper health care, and favorable court rulings. This corruption not only impedes the development of rule of law; it also puts a drag on economic development, since so much money is siphoned off for bribes.

Putin initiated some high-profile battles against corruption in 2012, beginning with the dismissal of Anatoly Serdyukov as defense minister. He was fired after investigators linked a company spun off from the ministry to fraud, and state-run television publicly revealed that other high-level bureaucrats had misappropriated funds. However, corruption is so embedded in the Russian political system that these efforts have not gotten to the root of the problem, and corruption remains a stubborn problem that is very difficult to eliminate.

The Military

The army was a very important source of Soviet strength during the Cold War era from 1945 to 1991. The Soviet government prioritized financing the military ahead of almost everything else. The armed forces at one time stood at about 4 million men, considerably larger than the United States combined forces. However, the military usually did not take a lead in politics, and generals did not challenge the power of the Politburo. Even though some of the leaders of the attempted coup of 1991 were military men, the armed forces themselves responded to Yeltsin's plea to remain loyal to the government.

Under the Russian Federation, the army shows no real signs of becoming a political force. It has suffered significant military humiliation, and many sources confirm that soldiers go unpaid for months and have to provide much of their own food. Even as early as 1988, under Gorbachev, Soviet forces had to be withdrawn in disgrace from Afghanistan, and in 1994-1996, Chechen guerillas beat the Soviet forces. More recently, the army partially restored its reputation by crushing Chechen resistance in 1999-2000.

One prominent former general, **Alexander Lebed**, gained a political following before the election of 1996, and Yeltsin had to court his favor in order to win reelection. However, most political leaders have been civilians, so a military coup appears to be unlikely in the near future. Even so, some observers were wary of a military takeover, especially considering the tentative nature of the "democracy" during the 1990s.

Recently, Russia's army has reasserted its old vigor, with Putin's 2007 announcement that, for the first time in 15 years, the Russian Air Force would begin regular, long-range patrols by nuclear-capable bombers again. The move was seen by some observers as one of several signs that Russia is rising in strength and wishes to assert its influence internationally again. Military spending has increased significantly over the past few years, and the invasion of Georgia in 2008 was successful, with soldiers who appeared to be better trained than those who fought in earlier wars in Chechnya. However, the armed forces rely on factories with outdated technology and production methods, and recruitment of personnel remains low.

PUBLIC POLICY AND CURRENT ISSUES

The first few years of the Russian Federation were very difficult ones, characterized by a great deal of uncertainty regarding the regime's future. Any regime change creates legitimacy issues, but Russia's case was extreme, with public policy directed at some very tough issues and seemingly intractable problems. The abrupt change in leadership goals and style between Yeltsin and Putin also has made it difficult to follow continuous patterns in policy over the years, although alternating between reform and authoritarianism is an old theme that goes back to the days of the tsars.

The Economy

The Soviet Union faced many challenges in 1991, but almost certainly at the heart of its demise were insurmountable economic problems. Mikhail Gorbachev enacted his **perestroika** reforms, primarily consisting of market economy programs inserted into the traditional centralized state ownership design of the Soviet Union. These plans were never fully implemented, partly because dissent within the Politburo led to the attempted coup that destroyed the state.

Today leaders of the Russian Federation face the same issue: How much of the centralized planning economy should be eliminated, and how should the market economy be handled? Yeltsin's "shock therapy" created chaotic conditions that resulted in a small group of entrepreneurs running the economy. In 1997 the bottom fell out of the economy when the government defaulted on billions of dollars of debts. The stock market lost half of its value, and threatened to topple other markets around the globe. Meanwhile, the Russian people suffered from the sudden introduction of the free market. Under the Soviet government, their jobs were secure, but now the unemployment rate soared. The ruble – once pegged by the government at $1.60 – lost its value quickly, so that by early 2002, it took more than 30,000 rubles to equal a dollar. The oligarchs and mafia members prospered, but almost everyone else faced a new standard of living much worse than what they had before.

Between 1997 and 2007, the Russian economy steadily improved, particularly in the new areas of privatized industries, but it suffered a tremendous blow when oil prices plummeted in 2008. In 2004 the economy had shown strong indications of recovery, with a growth of about 7%, and the standard of living was rising even faster, although real incomes improved more rapidly in neighboring countries, such as Ukraine. For example, very few people, rich or poor, had running hot water for several weeks in the summer of 2007 in Moscow because the plants and network of pipelines shut down for maintenance every year. Although Russia ended 2008 with GDP growth of 6% – down only slightly from 10 years of growth averaging 7% annually – many economic problems presented themselves after the global economic crisis in September 2008. The Russian stock market dropped roughly 70%, as Russian companies were unable to pay loans called in as the market fell. The government responded with a rescue plan of over $200 billion for the financial sector, and also proposed a $20 billion tax cut plan for Russian citizens. Even so, the ruble fell in value, while unemployment grew and production dropped. Many people are still disillusioned with the new regime, and question the wisdom of current policymakers.

Russia's economy has been fueled by its huge oil and gas reserves, and the corporations (mostly state run) that own them. As long as oil prices remained high, Russia's GNP rose, and the economy was healthy.

However, in 2014, the price of oil fell precipitously, and the Russian ruble lost about half its value, as confidence levels in the country's economic health plummeted. Investors pulled billions of dollars from Russia, and even though oil prices stabilized in 2015, they were still too low for an economic recovery. Inflation has jumped, wages have fallen, and foreign-exchange reserves of the Central Bank of Russia have fallen. Overall, the economy was shrinking, and without a significant increase in oil prices, Russia's economic prospects remained grim.

A continuing economic issue is privatization vs. state control. In 2010, Medvedev announced plans to sell off up to $100 billion of state assets. However, under Putin, the emphasis has shifted back to a state-capitalist model, with the government playing a strong role in the economy. State-owned companies, such as Rosneft (oil), Gazprom (natural gas), an Russian Technologies (weapons, warfare systems), all monopolize their industries, and many supporters of privatization claim that they block entrepreneurial efforts of smaller companies.

Foreign Policy

The Soviet Union held hegemony over huge portions of the world for much of the 20th century, and when it broke apart in 1991, that dominance was broken. The 1990s were a time of chaos and humiliation, as Yeltsin had to rely on loans from Russia's old nemesis, the United States, to help shake its economic doldrums. As the 21st century began, the new president, Vladimir Putin, set out to redefine Russia's place in the world, a two-dimensional task that required a new interpretation of the country's relationship with the west, as well as its role among the former Soviet States.

The CIS

The weak **Commonwealth of Independent States** united the fifteen former republics of the Soviet Union, and Russia has been the clear leader of the group. However, the organization has little formal power over its members, and today only nine former republics remain tied to it. Russia's motives are almost always under strict scrutiny by the other countries. Still, trade agreements bind them together, although nationality differences keep the members from reaching common agreements. These nationality differences also threaten the Federation itself, with the threat of revolution from Chechnya spreading to other regions. In short, the CIS is a long way from being a regional power like the European Union, and many experts believe that the confederation will not survive.

The Troubled Caucasus Region. The map above shows many points of conflict both within the Russian Federation and outside its borders. Chechnya has long been an area of conflict, where many still support Chechen independence from Russia. Georgia, now an independent country, has separatist problems of its own in Abkhazia and South Ossetia, and Russia has supported those regions in their attempts to break away from Georgia. A root of the conflict is the variety of small cultural groups that have long inhabited the area, and over the years hostilities have built up among them.

A controversy erupted between Russia and Estonia in 2007 when the Estonian government removed a Soviet-era statue from a public place in its capital, Tallinn. The Estonian move met with a reaction from ethnic Russians living in Estonia, with hundreds of them attacking the main theater and the Academy of Arts in the capital. Events took a strange turn when computers went down all over Estonia the day after the protests. The Estonians accused Russia of orchestrating the computer attacks, and young protesters in Moscow reacted by attacking Estonia's embassy with eggs and harassing the Estonian ambassador. The old ethnicities of the culturally heterogeneous Soviet Union are still at odds, even though they are no longer united under one central government.

More recently, Russia's relationships with countries in the near abroad (former Soviet states) have been affected by its invasion of Georgia in 2008. Russian troops and armored vehicles rolled into South Ossetia, a "breakaway region" of Georgia that sought its independence. The move marked the growing aggressiveness of the Russian military, but it also reflected years of growing tensions between Georgia and Russia, especially between Georgia's president Mikheil Saakashvili and Putin. Georgia had long been viewed by Moscow as a wayward province, and after Georgia gained its independence when the Soviet Union fell apart, distrust grew, even though traditional bonds continued. However, Saakashvili allied Georgia with the United States, even naming a main road after George W. Bush. Russia responded by announcing its support for separatist regions of Georgia and then invaded South Ossetia and other areas of Georgia. A cease-fire agreement and a peace plan was brokered by Nicolas Sarkozy, the president of France and the European Union, but on August 26, 2008, Medvedev signed a decree recognizing South Ossetia and Abkhazia (another breakaway region) as independent states.

Crisis in the Ukraine

The breakup of the Soviet Union in 1991 into fifteen separate countries resulted in sovereignty issues, especially in regard to Russia's ongoing dominance of the region. The relationship between Russia and Ukraine has been particularly problematic, with conflicts erupting – often along ethnic lines – between Ukrainians who favor stronger ties to the West and those with allegiances to Russia. During the 2004 presidential election campaign in Ukraine, challenger Viktor Yushchenko accused Russian President Putin of providing financing and political advisors for Prime Minister Viktor Yanukovich's campaign for the presidency. Putin himself went to Ukraine twice to campaign for Yanukovich. Popular protests broke out after Yanukovich won, with claims that the election was fraudulent. The elections were held again, and Yushchenko's victory in this round increased ethnic tensions within Ukraine.

Yanukovich eventually was elected president in 2010, but the Ukraine's internal and external tensions eventually led to his ouster in 2014. In late 2013, Yanukovych rejected an agreement with the

European Union that would bolster integration and trade between the EU and the Ukraine. Instead, he agreed to take a $15 billion loan from Russia that would move the country toward a "Eurasian Union" with Belarus, Kazakhstan, and Russia. The decision sparked protests in Kiev by EU supporters, and clashes grew so violent that Yanukovych fled to Russia, and a coalition government formed that supported EU agreements. This turn of events led to opposition in Crimea, a region of Ukraine with a large number of ethnic Russians. Armed men, presumably Russian soldiers, in unmarked uniforms and masks seized airports and regional government buildings, and a new government of pro-Russian leaders decided to hold a referendum on Crimea's future in March 2014. The Russian parliament authorized deploying troops in Ukraine, and 97% of the voters in the extremely controversial referendum supported joining Russia. Putin signed a treaty formally annexing Crimea, and the U.S. and the EU ordered sanctions imposed on Russia. Fighting between government forces and pro-Russian separatists continued despite domestic and international efforts to de-escalate the crisis. However, in 2015, many Russian troops withdrew from Ukraine, fighting diminished, and the area settled into an uneasy peace.

Relations with the West

The biggest adjustment for Russia since 1991 has been the loss of its superpower status from the Cold War era. The United States emerged as the lone superpower in 1991, and the two old enemies – Russia and the United States – had to readjust their attitudes toward one another. U.S. Presidents George H. W. Bush and Bill Clinton both believed that it was important to maintain a good working relationship with Russia. They also knew that the economic collapse of Russia would have disastrous results for the world economy. Both presidents sponsored aid packages for Russia, and they also encouraged foreign investment in the country's fledgling market economy. The United States and the other G-7 political powerhouses of Europe welcomed Russia into the organization, which became known as the G-8, acknowledging the political importance of Russia in global politics. After the crisis in Ukraine, Russian membership in the G-8 was revoked, returning the organization to its previous G-7 status. Russia supported France in blocking the U.N. Security Council's approval of the U.S.-sponsored war on Iraq in early 2003. Whether the move was a wise one is yet to be seen, but it does indicate Russia's willingness to assert its point of view, even if it opposes that of the United States.

For almost two decades, Russia negotiated for membership in the World Trade Organization (WTO), a powerful body responsible for regulating international trade, settling trade disputes, and designing trade policy through meetings with its members. Russia's bid to join the WTO finally succeeded in 2012, an event that almost certainly was a milestone in the country's integration with the international economic community. Putin hopes that the move will win more favorable trade terms for Russian companies and harness the nation's potential by attracting capital and diversifying the economy.

Russia's relations with countries of the West and the near abroad are strongly defined by the clout of its oil and gas industries. In an ongoing dispute about gas lines that cross Ukraine, Belarus, and other nearby countries, Russia's state-run gas company, Gazprom, has instituted gas price hikes that have been met by stiff resistance. In 2006, Gazprom reduced pressure in the Ukrainian pipeline system so that Ukrainian gas customers had no gas to use, even for basics, such as heating their homes. Europeans were affected because the pipelines eventually provide gas to them, and their governments put pressure on Putin's government until the pressure was restored.

Russia's relations with the European Union are sometimes undermined by individual countries pursuing their own interests, opening the way for Russia to play divide-and-rule, especially over energy. Russian leaders have also shown signs that they are more interested in maintaining their relationships with other fast-growing BRIC economies than they are in cooperating with the aging European countries. Still, Russia depends on the EU for half its trade, even though its trade with China has increased substantially in recent years.

Tensions Between Russia and Britain/Espionage

In March 2018, a former Russian spy, Sergei Skripal, who lived in Britain, fell ill and was taken to hospital, suffering from exposure to a nerve-agent, a deadly poison often associated with Russian espionage. Prime Minister Theresa May gave Putin until the end of the following day to produce an explanation before she concluded that Britain had been the victim of "an unlawful use of force". Putin made no attempt to meet the deadline, dismissing the allegations and refusing to respond. May expelled 23 Russian diplomats, and several other western nations also sent Russian diplomats home. The incident heightened tensions not only between Russia and Britain, but other western nations as well.

Relations with the United States

After the September 11th terrorist attacks, Putin's solidarity with the United States seemed to mark the beginning of a new era in Russian-American relations. However, the real breaking-point in Russia's relationship with America came after 2003. Putin saw America's invasion of Iraq as an intolerable encroachment on Russian national interests, and he condemned President Bush for telling other people how to live. Meanwhile, the Bush administration insulted Russian pride by ignoring its relationship with the country, focusing instead on the war in Iraq. Tensions between the two countries escalated after Russia invaded South Ossetia in 2008. Putin had hoped that Bush would rein in Georgia's president as Saakashvili brushed off Russian prerogatives in the near abroad, and the attack affirmed Russia's strength.

Under U.S. President Barak Obama, relationships between the United States and Russia became more tense, especially after the crisis in Ukraine. In reaction to America's threat to sanction Russian officials directly involved in human rights abuses, the Kremlin banned American couples from adopting Russian orphans. The protests against the Duma election in December 2011 sparked anti-Americanism in Russia, with the Kremlin putting at least some of the blame on the United States. Under Obama, the United States downplayed the importance of its relationship with Russia, almost certainly stoking even more anti-American feelings.

Russia has encouraged international efforts to challenge America's global leadership. In the summer of 2015, Putin hosted the BRICS (Brazil, India, China, and South Africa) at a summit in the Russian city of Ufa. According to Russia's state media, the BRICS meeting was a new step in the construction of a counter-weight to the western financial system. Western countries are also concerned about Russia's naval expansion, especially its development of new types of conventional and nuclear-capable submarines. Some westerners fear that this new initiative might threaten NATO's control of western oceans.

Russia and the 2016 U.S. Presidential Election

In the summer of 2016, as the presidential election campaign in the U.S. was in full swing, evidence emerged that Russians had "meddled" in the campaign, with the purpose of swinging the election away from the Democratic candidate, Hillary Clinton, toward the Republican candidate, Donald Trump. Accusations included the hacking of emails exchanged among Clinton campaigners and the Democratic National Committee. A special counsel, Robert Mueller, was appointed to head an investigation into the allegations. At first, Democrats and Republicans agreed that the evidence warranted the investigation. However, President Trump did not agree, and he repeatedly cast doubt on whether Russia had actually meddled. The question remained as to whether or not anyone within the Trump campaign had colluded with the Russians – a possibility that Mr. Trump has fervently disavowed.

Terrorism

Just as has happened in the United States and Britain, Russia has had a number of acts of terror in recent years, with the Beslan school siege in southern Russia in 2004 being the most well known. Just prior to Beslan, a suicide bombing occurred near a subway station in Moscow, and bombs went off in two Russian airplanes almost simultaneously. As the government tried to break the Beslan siege by militants, 360 people died, many who were children. President Putin responded with a reform package to boost security. In an emergency gathering of regional and national leaders in late 2004, Putin argued that only a tighter grip from the central government would foil terrorists whose aim it was to force the country's disintegration. He laid out not just security measures, but also a sweeping political reform – top officials (including regional governors) would no longer be directly elected, but would be selected by the president, and then approved by regional legislatures. The Duma approved the president's plan later in the year. Terrorist attacks in the Caucasus calmed for a few years, but reasserted themselves in the summer of 2009.

Population Issues

In recent years, Russia has suffered a dramatic drop in its overall population. The population peaked in the early 1990s with about 148 million people, and the United Nations predicts that the country will fall to 116 million people by 2050, from the 141 million now, an 18% decline. The U.N. cites two reasons for the decline: a low birth rate and poor health habits. The low birth rate goes back to the Soviet era, when abortion was quite common and was used as a method of birth control. Economic hardship has not encouraged large families, and health issues have also created a very high death rate of 15 deaths per 1000 people per year, far higher than the world's average death rate of just under 9. Alcohol-related deaths in Russia are very high and alcohol-related emergencies represent the bulk of emergency room visits in the country. Life expectancy is particularly low for men at 59, as compared to women's life expectancy of 72. The difference is usually attributed to high rates of alcoholism among males.

A bit of good news came in late 2012, when new data showed that from January through October 2012 the Russian population naturally grew by about 800 people. Compared with the relevant period in 2011, births are up by 6.5% and deaths are down by 1.5%. Although the growth is very slight, it is the first time since 1992 that population hasn't actually declined.

To combat this overall decline the Russian government is encouraging Russians who live abroad to return to their homeland. Moscow has spent $300 million since 2007 to get a repatriation program started, and official estimated that more than 25 million people were eligible. Many are ethnic Russians who live in former Soviet republics, but the government is trying to attract people around the world. It is unclear how the financial crisis and Russia's recent economic woes have affected the program's appeal. However, economic issues have discouraged many Russians from expanding the size of their families.

Re-centralization of Power in the Kremlin

Some critics believe that Putin's reforms for the Duma and the selection of regional governors are more than a response to terrorism, but are part of a re-centralization of power in the Kremlin. Putin's party now has most of the seats in the Duma, and his government has taken important steps toward controlling the power of the oligarchs. The Kremlin now controls major television stations, as well as the Russian gas giant Gazprom. It is not clear whether these moves mark the beginning of the end of democratic experimentation in Russia, or simply a reaction to terrorism similar to those of the U.S. and British governments after major attacks in those countries. Another possibility is that Russia is simply going through yet another of its age-old alternations between reform and conservatism.

The presidential election of 2008 also provided evidence that Russia's political power remains centralized, even though the presidential succession technically went according to the provisions of the Constitution of 1993. Dmitri Medvedev was hand-picked by Putin, and Putin's role as prime minister did not change the fact that he still was in charge of the Russian political system. Putin's reelections in 2012 and 2018 insured that he would maintain control of policymaking until 2024.

Development of a Civil Society

The notion of civil society starts with the acceptance of two areas of life: a public one that is defined by the government, and a private one, in which people are free to make their own individual choices. In a country with a strong civil society, people follow rules, operate with a degree of trust toward others, and generally have respectful dealings with others even if the government is not watching. Even though these ideals may not always be met, citizens are aware of both the rule of law in the public realm and their own privacy that exists outside it. Democracy and capitalism both depend on civil society for their successful operation.

Russians do not necessarily share the assumptions that civil society rests on: the inherent value of life, liberty, and property. Instead, they have been much more influenced by traditions of **statism** – have a strong government or die. Their history began with this truth: survival amidst the invasions across the Russian plains and the rebellions of the many ethnicities depends on a strong, protective government. In the 20th century, Russia became a superpower in the same way – through a strong, centralized government. Is it possible for stability, power, and prosperity to return to Russia through a democratic state and a capitalist economy?

In many ways the answer to that question tests the future of democracy as a worldwide political model. Were John Locke and other Enlightenment philosophers correct in their assumptions that it is in "human nature" to value freedom above equality? That people "naturally" have the right to own property and to live private lives? If so, can these values thrive among a people who have traditionally valued government protection and equality? So far, the spread of democracy has taken many forms. If it takes hold in the Russian Federation, it is indeed a hardy, versatile, and potentially global philosophy.

IMPORTANT TERMS AND CONCEPTS

asymmetric federalism
Berezovsky, Boris
Bolsheviks
boyars
Catherine the Great
Central Committee
civil society in Russia
collective farms, collectivization
Commonwealth of Independent States
conflict in Chechnya
Constitution of 1993
Constitutional Court
Crimean War
CPRF
cultural heterogeneity in Russia
Decembrist Revolt
decrees

democratic centralism
de-Stalinization
Duma
equality of result in Russia
federal government structure
Federation Council
Five Year Plans
general secretary
glasnost
Gorbachev, Mikhail
Gorbachev's three-pronged reform plan
Gosplan
head of government, head of state
Khrushchev, Nikita
kulaks
Lebed, Alexander
Lenin, V.I.
Liberal Democrats
mafia
Marxism-Leninism
Medvedev, Dmitri
Mensheviks
nationality
near abroad
New Economic Policy
nomenklatura
oligarchy
Patriots of Russia
perestroika
Peter the Great
politburo
presidential-parliamentary system
proportional representation
Putin, Vladimir
Red Army/White Army
Russian Orthodox Church

"secret speech"
"shock therapy"
Slavophile vs. Westernizer
Stalinism
state corporatism
statism in Russia
totalitarianism
tsars
United Russia Party
"Window on the West"
Yobloko
Yeltsin, Boris
zemstvas
Zhirinovsky, Vladimir
Zyuganov, Gennady

Russia Questions

1. The tendency of Russian citizens to value the existence of a strong government to protect them is called

A) statism
B) perestroika
C) democratic centralism
D) corporatism
E) militarism

2. Which of the following appears to be a significant difference between the political views of Russian citizens and citizens of most established democracies?

A) Russians are more trusting of government officials.
B) Russians have less faith in competitive, regular elections.
C) Russians are less likely to be swayed by the charisma or popularity of their leaders.
D) Russians are more likely to believe in equality of result rather than equality of opportunity.
E) Russians have a narrower range of political ideologies; they tend to have attitudes to the "left" of center.

3. Which of the following political parties in Russia is most often associated with ultra-nationalism?

A) United Russia
B) Liberal Democratic Party
C) A Just Russia
D) Communist Party
E) Rodina

4. Which of the following communist leaders of the 20th century was the most open to western-style reforms?

A) V.I. Lenin
B) Joseph Stalin
C) Nikita Khrushchev
D) Leonid Brezhnev
E) Mikhail Gorbachev

5. Marx predicted that proletarian revolutions would occur first in

A) weak imperialist countries such as Russia
B) industrial capitalist countries such as Great Britain
C) traditional peasant countries such as China
D) developed agrarian countries such as Argentina
E) racially divided countries such as South Africa

6. Russia's difficulties with the Chechen region are based primarily on

A) disputes over the central government's rights to natural resources
B) borderlines among the regions of the Caucasus
C) trading rights with the Ukraine
D) unpaid taxes
E) nationality

7. *What is to be Done?* is a famous book that promoted Lenin's arguments in support of

A) the development of russian civil society
B) implementation of the first Five Year Plan
C) creation of *zemstvas*
D) the vanguard of the revolution
E) collectivization of agriculture

8. All of the following are geographic features that have drastically affected Russian society and government EXCEPT:

A) a long growing season in most areas
B) a lack of ice-free ports
C) a huge amont of land space
D) a great proportion of land that is unusable or nearly so
E) broad plains that sweep across the country east to west

9. The Constitution of 1993 gave the Russian Duma the power to

A) censure the cabinet
B) issue laws by decree
C) vote for and schedule a national referendum
D) appoint the Prime Minister
E) veto the President's appointment of the Prime Minister

10. One of the most frequently heard current criticisms of Vladimir Putin's presidency is that he is

A) displaying too much unpredictable and unstable behavior to be a good president
B) allowing the Russian mafia to exert too much power in making political decisions
C) centralizing so much power in the presidency that Russia's democratic reforms are in jeopardy
D) allowing the legitimacy of the government to diminish because he has never received a majority of the votes in a presidential election
E) paying too much attention to the actions and political power of the U.S. President

11. In comparison to the European Union, the Commonwealth of Independent States is

A) much weaker
B) much stronger
C) stronger in terms of trade among its member states, but weaker in terms of trade outside the organization
D) much more dependent on directives from the United Nations
E) very similar in power and types of regulations over member states

12. In contrast to non-communist countries, communist countries usually place more value on

A) equality rather than liberty
B) liberty rather than equality
C) acquisition of material wealth
D) decentralization of government responsibilities
E) religion

13. Which of the following is a change that societies influenced by Marxism generally encourage?

A) more emphasis on ethnic identities of sub-groups
B) more equal roles in society for men and women
C) a smaller proportion of the population that depend on state welfare
D) less centralized control by the government
E) privatization of major industries

14. All of the following structures/positions are part of the current Russian government EXCEPT:

A) president
B) prime minister
C) bicameral legislature
D) Politburo
E) Supreme Court

15. Which of the following is an accurate comparison of British and Russian judicial systems?

A) Both systems have mechanisms for judicial review.
B) Both systems have strong judicial branches that overshadow their respective legislatures.
C) Britain's judiciary exercises judicial review, but Russia's does not.
D) In both countries, strong legislatures have kept strong judicial systems from developing.
E) Britain's judiciary does not exercise judicial review, but the Russian Constitution of 1993 created a structure to exercise judicial review.

16. Which of the following accurately compares the electoral systems for the British House of Commons and the Russian Duma since 2007?

A) Britain uses a first-past-the-post system; Russia uses proportional representation.
B) Britain uses a first-past-the post system; Russia combines single-member districts with proportional representation.
C) Both Britain and Russia use single-member district plurality systems.
D) Britain combines first-past-the post and proportional representation; Russia uses first-past-the-post only.
E) Both Britain and Russia use proportional representation.

17. Which of the following is NOT a significant issue for either the British or Russian political systems?

A) the price of oil
B) rapidly increasing populations
C) funding the military
D) terrorism
E) relationship with the United States

18. Which of the following accurately compares the British and Russian executive branches?

A) Britain's executive is separated between a head of state and a head of government; Russia combines the two roles into one position.

B) Russia's executive is separated between a head of state and a head of government; Britain combines the two roles into one position.

C) Both Britain and Russia have an executive branch that is separated between a head of state and a head of government, but Russia's head of state has more real power.

D) Both Britain and Russia have an executive branch that is separated between a head of state and a head of government, but Britain's head of state has more real power.

E) Both Britain and Russia combine the roles of head of state and head of government into one position.

19. Which of the following is an accurate comparison of party systems in Britain and Russia?

A) Britain has a multi-party system; Russia has a two-party system.

B) Britain has no regionally-based parties; Russia does.

C) Russia's political parties are more likely to be organized around a personality or a powerful individual.

D) More of Russia's political parties are based on liberal ideologies.

E) In Russia, political parties are more important in determining voter choices among candidates for public office.

20. Which of the following is an accurate comparison of voting rates during Soviet rule and voting rates in the Russian Federation?

A) Under Soviet rule, citizens did not vote, but citizens of the Russian Federation vote in comparable numbers to those in the west.

B) Voter turnout during both eras was/is very low.

C) Voter turnout during Soviet rule was considerably higher that it has been in the Russian Federaltion.

D) Voter turnout during Soviet Rule was considerably lower than it has been in the Russian Federation.

E) Voter turnout during both eras was/is above 80% of those eligible.

21. Both Britain and Russia have seen significant demographic increases in their percentages of

A) Catholics
B) Sub-Saharan Africans
C) Muslims
D) Scandinavians
E) Southeast Asians

22. Compared to Great Britain, Russia's civil society is

A) growing less rapidly
B) less regulated by the government
C) more dominated by intellectual groups
D) less well developed
E) more likely to support popular elections

23. Which of the following is an accurate comparison of Russia's and Britain's government structures?

A) Russia is a unitary state; Britain is a democratic state.
B) Russia is a confederal state; Britain is a federalist state.
C) Britain and Russia are both unitary states.
D) Britain is a unitary state; Russia is a federalist state.
E) Britain and Russia are both federalist states.

24. The main purpose of the Federation Council, according to the Russian Constitution, is to

A) adjudicate disputes between the Duma and the president
B) represent individual citizens in the national legislature
C) represent regions in the national legislature
D) advise the president on foreign policy
E) check the powers of the regional governments

25. Which of the following do the British and Russian military have in common?

A) Both are major sources of recruitment for political leaders.
B) Neither actively participates in the policymaking process.
C) Both are much stronger and better equipped than they were twenty years ago.
D) Both consider the United States military its biggest foe.
E) Neither has been well-funded by the central government in recent years.

26. All of the following political institutions are present in BOTH Britain and Russia EXCEPT:

A) bicameral legislature
B) Supreme Court
C) prime minister
D) bureaucracy
E) president

27. Which of the following is a common characteristic of upper legislative houses in Britain and Russia?

A) Some of their members hold hereditary seats.
B) Both have significant powers to check the actions of their respective lower houses.
C) Some of their members are appointed by the president.
D) Both have very little policymaking power in the political system.
E) Both have the power to request that new policies and laws be subject to judicial review.

28. The use of judicial review in Russia is limited because

A) judicial review violates the principle of parliamentary sovereignty
B) the judiciary has been dominated by the chief executive
C) legal systems in Russia are based on common law
D) the Constitution does not provide for a constitutional court
E) the Federation Council refuses to pay attention to court rulings

29. The region shown in the map above has long been an area of conflict based primarily on

A) border disputes
B) ethnic differences
C) control of natural resources
D) competition for foreign aid
E) access to sea-based trade

30. The societal cleavage that most influenced the organization of Russia into a "federation" in the early 1990s was

A) social class
B) religion
C) nationality
D) rural/urban differences
E) racial groups

Free-Response Question:

In electing their legislatures, countries may use a plurality electoral system, proportional representation, and some combination of the two.

(a) Describe a plurality electoral system. Describe proportional representation as an electoral system.

(b) Identify the electoral system currently used for the House of Commons in Britain, and explain one impact that the use of this electoral system has on the political party system in Britain.

(c) Identify the electoral system currently used for the Duma in Russia, and explain one impact that the use of this electoral system has on the political party system in Russia.

.

**CHAPTER FIVE:
GOVERNMENT AND
POLITICS IN CHINA**

"Let China sleep. For when China wakes, it will shake the world."
Napoleon Bonaparte

Ancient China was arguably one of the strongest, richest empires in existence – so much so that often rulers saw little value in contacting anyone else in the world. Even though China's power was much diminished by the era of Napoleon, his words describing China as a sleeping giant prophesied the China of the early 21st century – a great civilization on the rise again.

Since western countries first began exploring the world several centuries ago, they have tended to either ignore or exploit China in world politics. And yet the presence of China is deeply felt, sometimes promising riches and cooperation, and other times threatening competition and destruction. Today China stands as one of the few remaining communist nations, with no signs of renouncing communism. China is by some standards a less developed country, but on the other hand the country is now a major world power, partly because of recent dramatic improvements in GNP and standards of living. China no longer sleeps. Its leaders claim membership in the World Trade Organization, travel frequently to other countries, and take active part in the United Nations. The world now comes to China for its vast array of products, and more and more, China is going outside its borders for investments, labor supplies, and raw materials. Its steady move toward capitalism has led some to argue that democratization will follow, yet the government remains highly authoritarian, providing evidence that marketization and privatization do not always go hand in hand with democracy.

SOVEREIGNTY, AUTHORITY, AND POWER

Until the 20th century China's history was characterized by **dynastic cycles** – long periods of rule by a family punctuated by times of "chaos", when the family lost its power and was challenged by a new, and ultimately successful, ruling dynasty. Power was determined by the **mandate of heaven**, or the right to rule as seen by the collective ancestral wisdom that guided the empire from the heavens above. For many centuries public authority rested in the hands of the emperor and an elaborate bureaucracy that exercised this highly centralized power. After a time of chaos in the early 20th century, Communist leader Mao Zedong took over China in 1949, bringing in a new regime with values that often disagreed with traditional concepts of power. How different is the new China from the old? Have the changes brought instability, or have they successfully transformed the country into a modern world power?

China's political structures reflect many modern influences, but the weight of tradition has shaped them in unique ways. For example, China is technically governed by a constitution that grants formal authority to both party and state executive and legislative offices. However, the country is still governed by authoritarian elites who are not bound by rule of law. As long as the rulers are above the law, the constitution will not be a major source of legitimacy for the state.

Legitimacy

Under dynastic rule, Chinese citizens were subjects of the emperor. Legitimacy was established through the mandate of heaven, and power passed from one emperor to the next through hereditary connections within the ruling family. As long as things went well, the emperor's authority was generally accepted, but when problems occurred and the dynasty weakened, rival families challenged the throne, claiming that the emperor had lost the mandate. Legitimacy was not for peasants to determine, although popular rebellions and unrest in the countryside served as signs that the emperor was failing.

The Revolution of 1911 gave birth to the Chinese Republic, with western-educated **Sun Yat-sen** as its first president. The new regime was supposed to be democratic, with legitimacy resting on popular government. However, regional warlords challenged the government, much as they always had done in times of political chaos. Emerging from the mayhem was **Mao Zedong**, with his own version of authority, an ideology known as **Maoism**. The **People's Republic of China** was established in 1949, and Mao led the Communist Party as the new wielder of power until his death in 1976.

Inspired by Marxism, Maoism was idealistic and egalitarian, and even though it endorsed centralized power exercised through the top leaders of the party, it stressed the importance of staying connected to the peasants through a process called **mass line**. Mass line required leaders to listen to and communicate with ordinary folks, and without it, the legitimacy of the rulers was questionable. Despite this important difference between Maoism and Leninism (which based its authority on the urban proletariat), the organizing principle for both ideologies was democratic centralism. Democratic centralism allowed leaders to make decisions that could not be questioned by the people, and gave both Lenin and Mao almost complete control over policymaking.

Since Mao's death, the Politburo of the Communist Party remains the legitimate source of power in China, but the leadership has come under a great deal of criticism in recent years. The Party is said to be corrupt and irrelevant, holding authoritarian power over an increasingly market-based economy. In truth, rebellions against the party have flared up throughout PRC history, but the rumblings have been louder and more frequent since the Tiananmen incident in 1989. How serious a threat these criticisms are to the current regime is a matter of some debate, and current Communist leaders show no signs of loosening the party's hold on the government and the economy.

One important source of power in the People's Republic of China has been the military. The military played an important role in the rise of the Communist Party, and it is represented in the government by the **Central Military Commission**. The head of this commission plays an important role in policymaking. For example, long-time leader Deng Xiaoping was never general secretary of the Communist Party, but he directed the Central Military Commission.

Historical Traditions

Despite the fact that the last dynasty (the Qing) fell in the early 20ᵗʰ century, many traditions from the dynastic era influence the modern political system:

- **Authoritarian power** – China's borders have changed over time, but it has long been a huge, land-based empire ruled from a central place by either an emperor or a small group of people. Chinese citizens have traditionally been subjects of, not participants in, their political system. Despite the many dynasties in China's history, the ruling family was always subject to attack from regional warlords who challenged their right to the mandate of heaven. This tendency toward decentralization is apparent in the modern regime as a centralized Politburo attempts to control its vast population and numerous policies and problems.

- **Confucianism** – This philosophy has shaped the Chinese political system since the 6ᵗʰ century B.C.E. It emphasized the importance of order and harmony, encouraged Chinese citizens to submit to the emperor's power, and reinforced the emperor's responsibility to fulfill his duties conscientiously. This aspect of Confucianism may be tied to **democratic centralism**, or the communist belief in a small group of leaders who make decisions for the people. Confucianism is still a major influence on Chinese society today as it contradicts the egalitarian ideology of communism with its central belief in unequal relationships and mutual respect among people of different statuses, especially within families.

- **Bureaucratic hierarchy based on scholarship** – The emperors surrounded themselves with highly organized bureaucracies that formed an elite based on Confucian scholarship. Government jobs were highly coveted and extremely competitive, with only a small percentage of candidates mastering the examination system. The exams were knowledge-based, and bureaucrats had to be well-versed in Confucianism and many related philosophies. A major social divide in Ancient China was between a large peasant population and the bureaucratic elite.

- **The "Middle Kingdom"** – Since ancient times, the Chinese have referred to their country as ***zhongguo***, meaning "Middle Kingdom", or the place that is the center of civilization. Foreigners were seen as "barbarians" whose civilizations were far inferior to China's, not just in terms of power, but also in terms of ethics and quality of life. All countries are ethnocentric in their approaches to other countries, but China almost always assumed that no one else had much to offer. After the empire's 19th-century weakness was exploited by imperialist powers, these traditional assumptions were challenged, but not destroyed.

CHINA: SOVEREIGNTY, AUTHORITY, AND POWER

CONFUCIANISM	MAOISM
Mandate of heaven (responsibility of ruler to the people)	Democratic centralism (responsibility of ruler to the people)
Vision of an ideal society based on harmony and obedience	Vision of ideal society based on self reliance and struggle
Hierarchical social and political organization; rulers and subjects have uneqal positions	Egalitarian social structure; mass line between rulers and subjects
Emphasis on loyalty to family	Emphasis on loyalty to the state, Mao

- **Communist ideologies** – The 20th century brought the new influence of Maoism that emphasized the "right thinking" and moralism of Confucianism, but contradicted the hierarchical nature of the old regime with its insistence on egalitarianism. The late 20th century brought **Deng Xiaoping Theory**, a practical mix of authoritarian political control and economic privatization.

Political Culture

China's political culture is multi-dimensional and deep, shaped by geographical features and by the many eras of its history: dynastic rule, control by imperialist nations and its aftermath, and communist rule.

Geographic Influences

Today China has the largest population of any country on earth, and its land surface is the third largest, after Russia and Canada. Some of its important geographical features include:

- Access to oceans/ice free ports
- Many large navigable rivers
- Major geographical/climate splits between north and south
- Geographic isolation of the western part of the country
- Mountain ranges, deserts, and oceans that separate China from other countries

These geographic features have shaped Chinese political development for centuries. China's location in the world and protective mountain ranges allowed the Chinese to ignore the rest of the world whenever they wanted to until the 19th century. The rugged terrain of the western part of the country has limited population growth there. The large navigable rivers and good harbors of the east have attracted population, so that the overwhelming majority of people in China have lived in these areas for centuries. Differences in climate and terrain have also created a cultural split between the north and the south.

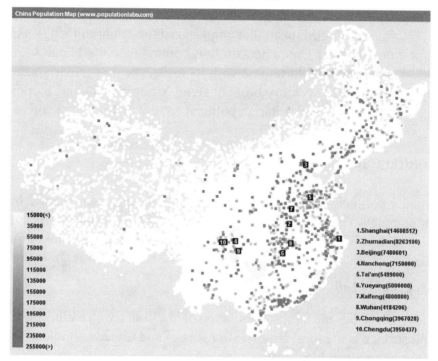

Population concentrations in China. The vast majority of people live in urban areas in the east, with many cities located along rivers and in coastal areas. Large stretches of mountains and deserts make the western and northern parts of the country less habitable.

Historical Eras

1. **Dynastic rule** – The political culture inherited from centuries of dynastic rule centers on **Confucian values**, such as order, harmony, and a strong sense of hierarchy – "superior" and "subservient" positions. China has traditionally valued scholarship as a way to establish superiority, with mandarin scholars filling bureaucratic positions in the government. China's early relative isolation from other countries contributes to a strong sense of cultural identity. Related to Chinese identity is a high degree of ethnocentrism – the sense that China is central to humanity (the "middle kingdom") and superior to other cultures. Centuries of expansion and invasion have brought many other Asian people under Chinese control, resulting in long-standing tensions between "Han" Chinese and others groups. A modern example is Tibet, where a strong sense of Tibetan ethnicity has created resistance to Chinese control.

2. **Resistance to imperialism** – During the 19th century China's strong sense of cultural identity blossomed into nationalism as it resisted persistent attempts by imperialist nations – such as England, France, Germany, and Japan – to exploit China's natural resources and people. This nationalism was secured by the Revolution of 1911, and the hatred of **"foreign devils"** has led China to be cautious and suspicious in its dealings with capitalist countries ever since.

3. **Maoism** – Mao Zedong was strongly influenced by Karl Marx and V.I. Lenin, but his version of communism is distinctly suited to China. Whereas Lenin emphasized the importance of a party vanguard to lead the people to revolution and beyond, Mao resisted the inequality implied by Lenin's beliefs. He believed in the strength of the peasant, and centered his philosophy on these values:

   - **Collectivism** – Valuing the good of the community above that of the individual suited the peasant-based communities that have existed throughout Chinese history. It contrasts to the beliefs of scholars (valued by the old culture) who have often been drawn to individualism.

   - **Struggle and activism** – Mao encouraged the people to actively pursue the values of socialism, something he understood would require struggle and devotion.

   - **Mass line** – Mao conceptualized a line of communication between party leaders, members, and peasants that would allow all to struggle toward realization of the goals of a communist state. The mass line involved teaching and listening on everyone's part. Leaders would communicate their will and direction to the people, but the people in turn would communicate their wisdoms to the leaders through the mass line.

- **Egalitarianism** – Hierarchy was the key organizing principle in Chinese society before 1949, and Mao's emphasis on creating an egalitarian society was in complete opposition to it.

- **Self-reliance** – Instead of relying on the elite to give directions, people under Maoist rule were encouraged to rely on their own talents to contribute to their communities.

4. **Deng Xiaoping Theory** – "It doesn't matter whether a cat is white or black, as long as it catches mice." This famous statement by Deng reflects his practical approach to solving China's problems. In other words, he didn't worry too much about whether a policy was capitalist or socialist as long as it improved the economy. The result of his leadership (1978-1997) was a dramatic turnaround of the Chinese economy through a combination of socialist planning and the capitalist free market. His political and social views, however, remained true to Communist tradition – the party should supervise all, and no allowances should be made for individual freedoms and/or democracy.

The Importance of Informal Relationships

Especially among the political elite, power and respect depend not so much on official positions as on who has what connections to whom. During the days of the early PRC, these ties were largely based on reputations established during the **Long March**, a 1934-1936 cross-country trek led by Mao Zedong as Chiang Kai-shek's nationalist army pursued his communist followers. Today those leaders are dead, but **factions** of their followers still compete for power, and informal relationships define each change in leadership. This informal network – a version of **patron-clientelism** – is not apparent to the casual outside observer. As a result, whenever new leaders come to power, such as the 2003 and 2013 transitions, it isn't easy to predict how policymaking will be affected. However, an important principle is to study their relationships with past leaders. For example, it is significant that Hu

Yaobang, a reformer whose death was mourned by the students that led the Tiananmen Square protest in 1989, mentored Hu Jintao, who later became general secretary of the CCP. Also important is the fact that, before he died, Deng Xiaoping designated Hu Jintao as his "4th generation" successor.

Chinese Nationalism

The identity of Han Chinese – the predominant ethnic group in China – goes back to ancient times. During the late 19th and early 20th centuries, Chinese nationalists fought hard against the western imperialists that dominated China, and they eventually won their country's independence. This pride in Chinese culture and accomplishments is apparent in China today, especially in recent years, by sensitivity to Westerners who have often reacted to it as a third world country. Whereas Mao encouraged his people to ignore the outside world and concentrate on growing the country from within, China has become increasingly involved in world politics and trade since the early days of Deng Xiaoping's rule.

The 2008 Olympics were intended to showcase China's growing place in the world, and many Chinese people reacted strongly to the protests that erupted in some western cities as the Olympic torch passed through on its way to Beijing. Chinese nationalists used the internet to express their anger toward pro-Tibetan western press coverage of the unrest in Tibet. Tibetans and other minority groups are seen as inferior people by some strong nationalists, and their pride in being Han Chinese is often apparent. Another indication that Chinese nationalism is on the rise is the reaction that some have had to the global economic crisis of late 2008. As the West has suffered, many have predicted the demise of the United States, a situation which Chinese nationalists have seen as an opportunity to reassert the new global ascendancy of the Middle Kingdom. At the G-20 meeting of the 20 largest national economies in April 2009, Chinese nationalists saw significance in the fact that President Hu Jintao stood to the right of host Gordon Brown (Britain) in the front center of the official photograph of the leaders gathered for the summit. Others proclaimed that the G-20 meeting was irrelevant, and the only significant summit was the "G-2" meeting between Presidents Barack Obama and Hu Jintao. As China's economic star has risen in recent years, it has been supported by a large dose of traditional pride in the glory of one of the world's oldest civilization as it reclaims what is believed to be its rightful position in the world.

Attitudes Toward the West

The Chinese have long held conflicting attitudes toward westerners. When the British statesman Earl Macartney arrived in China in the late 1700s seeking trade, the Chinese emperor rejected his overtures, believing that China had little to gain from the less wealthy and cultured British. Once China was carved up by foreign powers during the 19th century, many educated Chinese wondered whether western culture might be superior. During the early 20th century, a major source of tension among Chinese leaders was between those who promoted Chinese self-reliance and those seeking modernization through contacts with the West. In the mid-20th century, Mao Zedong rejected western notions of human rights and electoral democracy and banished most foreign residents. Since the late 1970s, China has opened up to both western trade and culture, but the conflicting attitudes still remain.

These tensions are apparent in modern-day China, and they sometimes spill over into the media. In 2012, *Xinhua*, the state-run news agency, ran an editorial that accused other governments of using reporters from their countries to control China's image in the overseas news media. About the same time, *People's Daily*, the ruling Communist Party paper, described western efforts to export democracy and human rights to China as a new form of colonialism. However, western countries – with their rule of law and individual freedoms – still have an enduring appeal to many educated Chinese.

POLITICAL AND ECONOMIC CHANGE

Like Russia, China is an old civilization with a long, relatively stable history that experienced massive upheavals during the 20th century that resulted in regime changes. Unlike Russia, however, China rose to regional **hegemony** (control of surrounding countries) very early in its history and has ranked as one of the most influential political systems in the world for many centuries. Russia's history as a great power is much shorter than China's.

Until the 19th century, dynastic cycles explained the patterns of political and economic change in China. A dynasty would seize power, grow stronger, and then decline. During its decline, other families would challenge the dynasty, and a new one would emerge as a sign that it had the mandate of heaven. This cycle was interrupted by the Mongols in the 13th century, when their leaders conquered China and ruled until the mandate was recaptured by the Ming who restored Han Chinese control. The Manchu were also a conquering people from the north, who established the Qing (or "pure") dynasty in the 17th century. This last dynasty toppled under European pressure in the early 20th century.

Change during the first half of the 20th century was radical, violent, and chaotic, and the result was a very different type of regime: communism. Did European intrusions and revolutions of the 20th century break the Chinese dynastic cycles forever? Or is this just another era of chaos between dynasties? It is hard to imagine that dynastic families might reappear in the 21st century or beyond, but Chinese political traditions are strong, and they almost certainly will determine what happens next in Chinese political development.

Change Before 1949

China's oldest cultural and political traditions have long provided stability and longevity for the empire/country. These traditions come from the dynastic rule that lasted for many centuries. However, in recent years two disruptive influences – control by imperialistic nations (19th century) and revolutionary upheavals (20th century) have threatened that stability and provide challenges to modern China.

Control by Imperialistic Countries

During the 19th century, the weakened Qing Dynasty fell prey to imperialist nations – such as England, Germany, France, and Japan – who carved China into "**spheres of influence**" for their own economic gain. This era left many Chinese resentful of the "**foreign devils**" who they eventually rebelled against.

Revolutionary Upheavals

Major revolutions occurred in China in 1911 and 1949, with many chaotic times in between. Three themes dominated this revolutionary era:

- **Nationalism** – The Chinese wished to recapture strength and power from the imperialist nations that dominated them during the 19th century. The Revolution of 1911 – led by Sun Yat-sen – was a successful attempt to reestablish China as an independent country.

- **Establishing a new political community** – With the dynasties gone and the imperialists run out, what kind of government would modern China adopt? One answer came from **Chiang Kai-shek**, who founded the **Nationalist Party (Guomindang)** and the other from **Mao Zedong**, the founder of the Chinese Communist Party.

- **Socioeconomic development** – A major challenge of the 20th century has been the reestablishment of a strong economic and social fabric after the years of imperialistic control. During the 1920s, the newly formed Soviet Union served as a model for policymaking, but the Nationalists broke with them in 1928. Chiang Kai-shek became the president of China, and Mao Zedong and his communists were left to form an outlaw party.

The Legend of the Long March

Strength for Mao's Communist Party was gained by the Long March – the 1934-36 pursuit of Mao's army across China by Chiang and his supporters. Chiang tried to depose his rival, but his attempt to find and conquer Mao had the opposite effect. Mao eluded him until finally Chiang had to turn his attentions to the invading Japanese. Mao emerged as a hero of the people, and many of his loyal friends on the March lived to be prominent leaders of the People's Republic of China after its founding in 1949.

MARKER EVENT: THE CHINESE COMMUNIST REVOLUTION AND WOMEN'S RIGHTS

The important philsophical influence of Confucianism throughout China's long history encouraged a hierarchical society that assumed inequalities as basic to an orderly society with men and women playing very traditional, family-based roles. As the revolutionary spirit erupted in China during the early 20th century, women's rights became an important issue, resulting in a ban on foot binding and an increase in educational and career opportunities for women. When Mao Zedong instituted the egalitarian values of communism in China, one effect was to create more equal roles for men and women. Mao was committed to women's equality because, in his words, "women hold up half of the heavens."

Even before Mao's Communist Party took over the country, women actively advanced the revolutionary cause by serving as teachers, nurses, spies, laborers, and occasionally as soldiers on the front line. Mao's commitment to women's rights extended to his personal life as well, with his wife, Jiang Qing, playing an increasingly prominent role as an adviser and eventually implementer of his policies. Despite these changes, after Mao's death traditional values remained, with foot binding still practiced among some elites. However, the expectation that women work outside the home continued, and opportunities for educational and professional careers have remained open to women.

The Founding of the People's Republic of China – 1949-1966

The Japanese occupied China during World War II, but after the war ended, the forces of Chiang and Mao met in civil war, and Mao prevailed. In 1949 Chiang fled to Taiwan, and Mao established the People's Republic of China under communist rule.

The People's Republic of China was born from a civil war between the Nationalists under Chiang Kai-shek and the Communists under Mao Zedong. After many years of competitive struggle, Mao's army forced Chiang Kai-shek and his supporters off the mainland to the island of Taiwan (Formosa). Mao named his new China the "People's Republic of China," and Chiang claimed that his headquarters in Taiwan formed the true government. The **"Two Chinas"**, then, were created, and the PRC was not to be recognized as a nation by the United Nations until 1972. The PRC, like the Soviet Union, was based on the organizing principle of democratic centralism.

The early political development of the PRC proceeded in two phases:

1) **The Soviet model** (1949-1957) – The Soviet Union had supported Mao's efforts since the 1920s, and with his victory in 1949, it began pouring money and expertise into the PRC. With this help, Chairman Mao and the Chinese Communist Party (CCP) quickly turned their attention to some of the country's most glaring social problems.

- **Land reform** – This campaign redistributed property from the rich to the poor and increased productivity in the countryside.

- **Civil reform** – They set about to free people from opium addiction, and they greatly enhanced women's legal rights. For example, they allowed women to free themselves from unhappy arranged marriages. These measures helped to legitimize Mao's government in the eyes of the people.

- **Five-Year Plans** – Between 1953 and 1957, the CCP launched the first of its Soviet-style Five-Year Plans to nationalize industry and collectivize agriculture, implementing steps toward socialism.

2) **The Great Leap Forward** (1958-1966) – Mao changed directions in 1958, partly in an effort to free China from Soviet domination. The spirit of nationalism was a force behind Mao's policy, and he was still unhappy with the degree of inequality in Chinese society. The Great Leap Forward was a utopian effort to transform China into a radical egalitarian society. Its emphasis was mainly economic, and it was based on four principles:

- **All-around development** – not just heavy industry (as under Stalin in the U.S.S.R.), but almost equal emphasis on agriculture.

- **Mass mobilization** – an effort to turn sheer numbers of people into an asset – better motivation, harder work, less unemployment.

- **Political unanimity and zeal** – an emphasis on party workers running government, not bureaucrats. **Cadres** – party workers at the lowest levels – were expected to demonstrate their party devotion by spurring the people on to work as hard as they could.

- **Decentralization** – encouraged more government on the local level, less central control. The people can do it!

The Great Leap Forward did not live up to its name. Mao's efforts ran counter to the traditional political culture (bureaucratic centralism), and many people lacked skills to contribute to industrialization. Some bad harvests conjured up fears that the mandate of heaven might be lost.

The Cultural Revolution – 1966-1976

Between 1960 and 1966, Mao allowed two of his faithful – Liu Shaoqi and Deng Xiaoping – to implement market-oriented policies that revived the economy, but Mao was still unhappy with China's progress toward true egalitarianism. And so he instituted the Cultural Revolution – a much more profound reform in that it encompassed political and social change, as well as economic. His main goal was to purify the party and the country through radical transformation. Important principles were:

- the ethic of struggle
- mass line
- collectivism
- egalitarianism
- unstinting service to society

A primary goal of the Cultural Revolution was to remove all vestiges of the old China and its hierarchical bureaucracy and emphasis on inequality. Scholars were sent into the fields to work, and universities and libraries were destroyed. Emphasis was put on elementary education – all people should be able to read and write – but any education that created inequality was targeted for destruction.

Mao died in 1976, leaving his followers divided into factions:

- **Radicals** – This group was led by Mao's wife, Jiang Qing, one of the "Gang of Four," who supported the radical goals of the Cultural Revolution.

- **Military** – Always a powerful group because of the long-lasting 20th century struggles that required an army, the military was led by Lin Biao, who died in a mysterious airplane crash in 1971.

- **Moderates** – Led by Zhou Enlai, moderates emphasized economic modernization and limited contact with other countries, including the United States. Zhou influenced Mao to invite President Richard Nixon to China in 1972. He died only a few months before Mao.

Members of these factions were not only tied to one another through common purposes, but also through personal relationships, illustrating the importance of informal politics throughout Chinese history.

Deng Xiaoping's Modernizations (1977-1997)

The Gang of Four was arrested by the new CCP leader, Hua Guofeng, whose actions helped the moderates take control. Zhou's death opened the path for leadership from the moderate faction. By 1978, the new leader emerged – Deng Xiaoping. His vision drastically altered China's direction through **Four Modernizations** articulated by Zhou Enlai before his death – **industry, agriculture, science, and the military**. These modernizations have been at the heart of the country's official policy ever since. Under Deng's leadership, then, China experienced economic liberalization, and these policies have helped to implement the new direction:

- **"Open door" trade policy** – trade with everyone, including capitalist nations like the U.S., that would boost China's economy

- **Reforms in education** – higher academic standards, expansion of higher education and research (a reversal of the policy during the Cultural Revolution)

- **Institutionalization of the Revolution** – restoring the legal system and bureaucracy of the Old China, decentralizing the government, modifying elections, and infusing capitalism

Despite the major reforms that Deng Xiaoping instituted, he did not support political liberalization, and China has followed this path ever since.

CITIZENS, SOCIETY AND THE STATE

As leadership of the country has passed from Mao to Deng to Jiang Zemin to Hu Jintao and then to Xi Jinping, the relationship of Chinese citizens to the state has changed profoundly. Under Maoism, virtually no civil society was allowed, and the government controlled almost every facet of citizens' lives. Since a transition to a market-based economy began in 1978, important transformations have occurred in citizen-state relationships.

Party leaders realize that most citizens no longer see communist ideology as central to their lives. As a result, the Chinese Communist Party now appeals to patriotism and the traditional pride in being Chinese. The message is that China's economic resurgence in recent years is a reemergence of the great ancient Chinese Empire, but now under communist leadership. For example, the party-state has done all it could to tout its leading role in China's economic achievements, winning the 2008 Summer Olympics for Beijing, and returning Hong Kong to Chinese control.

Ethnic Cleavages

China's ethnic population is primarily **Han Chinese**, the people that historically formed the basis of China's identity, first as an empire, and eventually as a country. China's borders have long included other ethnicities, primarily through conquest and expansion of land claims in Asia. Minority groups now comprise only about 8% of the PRC's population, but their "autonomous areas" (such as Tibet and Xinjiang) make up more than 60% of China's territory and have a long history of resistance to the Chinese government. There are 55 officially recognized minority groups, and no one minority is very large. Even so, the Chinese government has put a great deal of time and effort into its policies regarding ethnic groups.

Most minorities live on or near China's borders with other countries, and most of their areas are sparsely populated. For example, Mongols live in both Mongolia and China, and Kazakhs live in both the Kazakh Republic and China. Because dissidents are a long way from areas of dense population, China is worried that they may encourage independence, or join with neighboring countries.

Even though the percentages are not high, China does have about 100 million citizens who are members of minorities groups, a huge number by anyone's calculations. By and large, the government's policy has been to encourage economic development and suppress expressions of dissent in ethnic minority areas. Most of China's minorities are in the five **autonomous regions** of Guangxi, Inner Mongolia, Ningxia, Tibet, and Xinjiang. The Chinese constitution grants autonomous areas the right of self-government in some matters, such as cultural affairs, but their autonomy is in fact very limited. Ethnic dissent continues to the present, although many groups appear to be content to be part of the Chinese empire.

Tibetans

Tibet – with its long history of separate ethnic identity – has been especially problematic since the Chinese army conquered it in the early days of the PRC. The former government of Tibet never recognized Chinese authority, and many Tibetans today campaign for independence, while others demand enhanced autonomy under Chinese sovereignty. The movement rallies around the Dalai Lama, the spiritual leader who fled to India in 1959 after Tibet's failed uprising against China. There he set up a Tibetan government-in-exile that the Chinese Communist Party has never recognized. A series of riots and demonstrations took place in Tibet in March of 2008 on the 49th anniversary of the failed uprising, a situation that increased tensions between the Chinese government and the Dalai Lama. The Tibetan cause was highlighted in 2008 by protests that greeted the Olympic torch in some Western cities, as the runners made their way to Beijing, where the Olympics were held. In 2011, the government-in-exile elected a prime minister, signaling the withdrawal of the Dalai Lama from political leadership, although his spiritual roles remain intact.

In July 2013, the Chinese government announced its intension to intensify a crackdown again illegal publications, such as pamphlets, text messages and books in Tibetan regions in an attempt to control pro-Dalai Lama literature and publicity. Government figures show that more than 1.3 million illegal publications and promotional items were confiscated from 2011 to mid-2013 in the Tibet Autonomous Region.

Uyghurs

A second group of people that has shown increasing unrest are the Uyghurs, who are Muslims of Turkish descent living in Xinjiang, very close to the borders with Afghanistan and Pakistan and the Central Asian states of the former Soviet Union. Some Uyghur militants want to create a separate Islamic state and have used violence to support their cause. In the post-September 11 world, the Chinese have become very concerned with these Muslim dissidents. Their fears were confirmed in July 2009 when riots broke out in Urumqi, the capital city of Xinjiang. The riots were sparked by Uyghur dissatisfaction with the Chinese central government's handling of the deaths of two Uyghur workers during previous disruptions, but the violence was part of the ongoing ethnic tensions between the Han and the Uyghurs.

Although no large-scale riots have broken out since 2009, Uyghur unrest remains an issue. Discrimination remains a barrier for any Uyghurs who leave Xinjiang, and many find it difficult to get and hold a job because employers do not want Uyghurs as employees. The Chinese government has sponsored education and affirmative action programs, but most Uyghurs remain in Xinjiang, where job opportunities are limited.

Linguistic Diversity

Even among the Han Chinese there is great linguistic diversity, although they have shared a written language for many centuries. Since its inception the Communist regime has tried to make Mandarin the official language of government and education. For example, in early 2006 China stepped up its repression of Shanghainese, a language which, in its various forms, is native to close to 100 million people, especially around Shanghai, China's largest city. Rules required most people in the public sector, including teachers and members of the broadcast media, to use Mandarin when addressing the public. In 2008, the education minister of Hong Kong lifted restrictions that forced many secondary schools to teach in Cantonese, reversing a policy adopted shortly after Hong Kong's return to China in 1997. One motivation was probably the results of a study that showed that students from English-speaking schools did far better in getting into universities than did those from Cantonese-speaking schools. Despite restrictions such as this, dialects remain embedded in Chinese society, and demonstrate the difficulty that the centralized state has in imposing its will on its huge territorial space.

Urban-Rural Cleavages

An increasingly important divide in Chinese society is between rural and urban areas. Most of China's tremendous economic growth over the past few decades has taken place in cities. As a result, the gap between urban and rural incomes has grown to the point that some observers have redefined the meaning of "two Chinas" – this time, a rural and an urban one. The proportion of urban to rural population has also changed dramatically, with about 80 percent of Chinese living in the countryside in the early 1980s compared to about 47% today. The divide is not just economic, but also includes social lifestyle differences that form the basis for growing resentments across the countryside.

One result has been an upsurge in protests in rural areas, where some believe that the government is not looking out for their interests. For example, a few years ago in Hunan Province, thousands of angry farmers marched on the township government headquarters to protest excessive taxes and corruption of local officials. Shortly afterward, nine people suspected of being leaders of the protests were arrested. In reaction to this discontent, Prime Minister Wen Jiabao announced in 2006 a new government emphasis on **"a new socialist countryside,"** a program to lift the lagging rural economy. He recognized the following year that the rural poor had an array of problems not shared by urban residents.

One recent issue has to do with rural-born urban workers who are reaching retirement age. Under the *hukou* system, their pensions are far less than those for city-born workers, requiring many to work past retirement age.

Political Participation

According to Chinese tradition before 1949, citizens are subjects of government, not participants in a political system. The communist state redefined political participation by creating a relationship between the Communist Party and citizenship, and by shaping the economic relationship between citizens and the government. Nevertheless, old traditions that governed personal ties and relationships still mold China's political processes and influence the actions and beliefs of elites and citizens alike. In recent years popular social movements that support democracy, religious beliefs, and community ties over nationalism have influenced Chinese politics and helped to define China's relationships with other countries.

Party and Participation

The **Chinese Communist Party** (CCP) is the largest political party in the world in terms of total formal membership, with about 8,450,000 members in 2018. However, as was true in the U.S.S.R., its members make up only a small minority of the country's population. Only about 6% of the total population are members of the CCP. Only those that are judged to be fully committed to the ideals of communism and who are willing to devote a great deal of time and energy to party affairs may join. Party membership is growing, with new members recruited largely from the CCP's **Youth League.** About 109 million Chinese youths belonged to the Youth League by 2018.

The economic reforms begun by Deng Xiaoping paved the way for a milestone transition in the backgrounds of party members. During the Maoist era (before 1976) revolutionary **cadres** whose careers depended on party loyalty and ideological purity led the CCP at all levels. Most cadres were peasants or factory workers, and few were intellectuals or professionals. Since Deng's reforms, **"technocrats,"** people with technical training who climbed the ladder of the party bureaucracy, led the party increasingly. Over time, backgrounds of leaders have broadened, and many are the sons of earlier leaders. The Standing Committee members selected in 2012 have educations in economics, chemistry, engineering, and history, and all have long careers as party leaders. Today less than 40 percent of party members come from the peasantry, although peasants still make up the largest single group within the CCP. The fastest growing membership category consists of officials, intellectuals, technicians, and other professionals. At the 19th National Congress in 2017, 549 of the 2280 delegates were women, about 24.1%. However, women are far rarer in leadership positions, with only 10 of the 204 members in the latest Central Committee. The number of women in the 25-member Politburo inducted in 2012 doubled, to two, but currently only one member is a woman. No woman has ever been appointed to the highest tier of the Communist Party: the Politburo Standing Committee.

A significant change in party membership came in 2001 with the decision to allow capitalists to become members. In a repudiation of Maoist principles, President Jiang Zemin argued that the CCP ought to represent not just workers and peasants but business interests as well. According to some estimates, between a quarter and a third of all Chinese entrepreneurs are CCP members, a fact that significantly alters the traditional concept of "cadre."

The Growth of Civil Society

In recent years the control mechanisms of the party have loosened as new forms of associations appear, like Western-style discos and coffeehouses. Communications through cell phones, fax machines, TV satellite dishes, and internet have made it more difficult for the party-state to monitor citizens. An important new development is the growth of civil society – the appearance of private organizations that do not directly challenge the authority of the state but focus on social problems, such as the environment, AIDS, and legal reform. For example, recently activist organizations have protested government-sponsored dam projects that would flood the farmland of millions of peasants. The government is trying to harness waterpower for further industrial development, and even though the protesters will probably not block the projects, the very existence of these groups represents a major change. Hu Jintao announced a policy of "harmonious development" that allows the state to solicit public opinion before expanding the country's infrastructure or sponsoring economic development. However, citizens still complain that the government lacks transparency because it reveals its plans too late and in very obscure places. Such attitudes sparked demonstrations in early 2008 in Shanghai when the government extended its train lines without notifying people whose property would be affected by the project. Many observers believe that the rising middle class in China is awakening to the responsibilities and privileges of citizenship. Activists had virtually no say in the Chinese political system until the 1990s when Beijing allowed **non-governmental organizations (NGOs)** to register with the government. Today China has thousands of NGOs, ranging from ping-pong clubs to environmentalist groups. A key test of China's tolerance is religion. Today Christianity and Buddhism are rebounding, after years of communist suppression of religion. Despite these changes, the government still keeps close control of these groups, with their 1999-2001 crackdown on the religious movement Falon Gong a good example of the party's limited tolerance of activities outside the political realm.

Protests

The Tiananmen Square massacre of 1989 showed the limits of protest in China. Massive repression was the government's message to its citizens that democratic movements that defy the party leadership will not be tolerated. In recent years, religious groups, such as Falon Gong, have staged major protests, but none have risen to the level of conflict apparent in 1989. Village protests have made their way into the news, and thousands of labor strikes have been reported. Some observers believe that protests will pose serious threats to the party in the near future.

Riots in Tibet and Protests to the Torch Relay

In recent years the most serious protest movements have occurred in Tibet and Xinjiang, both autonomous regions in western China. In Tibet, a series of riots and demonstrations took place in Lhasa, Tibet's capital city, on March of 2008 on the 49th anniversary of the failed uprisings against China in 1959. The protests became violent after 300 Buddhist monks demanded the release of other monks who had been detained for several months. More political demands followed, as Tibetans and non-Tibetan ethnic groups quarreled, and rioting, looting, burning, and killing began. China's Premier Wen Jiabao accused the Dalai Lama of orchestrating the uprisings, a charge that the Dalai Lama denied, and tensions mounted between the two men. Riots followed in other provinces with Tibetan populations, and became serious enough that they drew international attention.

One series of reactions to the Tibetan riots occurred along the route of the 2008 Summer Olympics torch relay, called by the organizers a "Journey of Harmony" that was supposed to showcase the Olympics as China's symbolic connections to the rest of the world. In many cities along the route, the torch relay was met by protesters inspired most directly by the Tibetan riots, but who also objected to China's human rights record, the political status of Taiwan, and trade policies with Darfur, Myanmar, and Zimbabwe. The protests were particularly strong in Paris, where Chinese security officials were forced to extinguish the flame. Large-scale counter-protests were held by overseas Chinese nationals, and in some places (San Francisco, Australia, Japan, and South Korea) the number of counter-protesters was higher than the number of protesters. Despite the chaos, the Olympics went on as planned without further major disruptions.

Riots in Xinjiang

In July 2009 riots broke out in Urumqi, the capital city of Xinjiang, in northwest China. The riots were sparked by Uyghur dissatisfaction with the Chinese central government's handling of the deaths of two Uyghur workers during previous disruptions. Protesters clashed with police, and after three days of rioting, President Hu Jintao left the G-8 summit to return to China to give his full attention to the violence.

Western Riots in 2008 and 2009. Two serious riots broke out in the far western region of China in recent times. In 2008 rioting took place in Lhasa, the capital city of the Tibetan Autonomous Region, and in 2009 protests turned violent in Urumqi, the capital city of the Xinjiang Autonomous Region. Both areas have heavy concentrations of ethnic minorities, and had a great deal of ethnic unrest that preceded the riots.

The police tried to stop the rioters with tear gas, water hoses, road-blocks, and armored vehicles, and the government strictly enforced curfews in most urban areas. Internet services were shut down and cell phone service was restricted. Although the number of casualties was disputed, **Xinhua,** China's official news media, reported that the death toll from the riots was 197, and hundreds more were hospitalized.

The Chinese government responded to riots in Tibet and Xinjiang with large numbers of arrests, followed by court hearings. The head of the Communist Party in Xinjiang promised that those who have "committed crimes with cruel means" would be executed.

Although the vast majority of protests each year take place in rural areas, urban unrest – such as recent riots by factory workers in the southern province of Guangdong, is now more common. Part of the unrest has to do with *hukou*, China's traditional household registration system that makes it difficult to move from one place to another. In the early days of Deng Xiaoping's reforms, *hukou* restrictions were loosened, allowing migrations from rural to urban areas. However, the largest cities now find themselves overcrowded, and so they are shutting down shelters for workers who have recently migrated from rural areas and erecting other barriers to entry for unskilled workers. For example, in Beijing, the number of automobile license plates issued in 2011 was limited to just 1/3 the number in 2010 and new rules also forbid partitioning flats for rent.

With the government's announcement of its intentions to sponsor a massive program to move people from rural to urban areas, the *hukou* system almost certainly will change. One reaction to growing pressure to loosen restrictions comes from Shanghai, where migrant workers are divided into classes: Class A – the most educated and talented – get the Shanghai hukou, and the slightly less talented – Class B – might get a hukou after seven years of paying into the social security system. Everyone else has to wait longer.

POLITICAL INSTITUTIONS

China's political regime is best categorized as authoritarian, one in which decisions are made by **political elites** – those that hold political power – without much input from citizens. Leaders are recruited through their membership in the Communist Party, but personal relationships and informal ties to others are also important in deciding who controls the regime. However, this authoritarian regime has the same problem that emperors of past dynasties had – how to effectively govern the huge expanse of land and large population from one centralized place. As China has moved away from a command economy toward a market economy, this centralization has become even more problematic in recent years. As a result, a major feature of economic decision-making is now **decentralization**, or devolution of power to subnational governments. Local governments often defy or ignore the central government by setting their own tax rates or building projects without consulting the central government.

The political framework of the People's Republic of China is designed to penetrate as many corners of the country as possible through an elaborately organized Chinese Communist Party (CCP). As in the old Soviet Union, party personnel control government structures. Unlike the Soviet Union, however, the CCP also integrates its military into the political hierarchy. Political elites are frequently recruited from the military, and the head of the Central Military Commission is often the most powerful leader in China.

The Chinese Communist Party (CCP)

Despite the many changes that China has experienced in recent years, the Chinese Communist Party is still at the heart of the political system. The party bases its claim to legitimacy not on the expressed will of the people but on representation of the historical best interests of all the people. Society is best led by an elite vanguard party with a superior understanding of the Chinese people and their needs (democratic centralism).

The Organization of the CCP

The **Chinese Communist Party** (CCP) is organized hierarchically by levels – village/township, county, province, and nation. At the top of the system is the supreme leader (Deng Xiaoping's phrase was "the core"), who until 1976 was Chairman Mao Zedong. The title "chairman" was abandoned after Mao's death, and the head of the party is now called the "general secretary." The party has a separate constitution from the government's Constitution of 1982, and its central bodies are:

- **National Party Congress** – This body consists of more than 2000 delegates chosen primarily from congresses on lower levels. It only meets every five years, so it is obviously not important in policymaking. It usually rubber-stamps decisions made by the party leaders, although in recent years it has acted somewhat more independently. Its main importance remains the power to elect members of the Central Committee.

- **Central Committee** – The Committee has about 340 members (some of whom are alternates) that meet together annually for about a week. They carry on the business of the National Party Congress between sessions, although their size and infrequent meetings limit their policymaking powers. Their meetings are called **plenums**, and they are important in that they are gatherings of the political elites, and from their midst are chosen the Politburo and the Standing Committee.

- **Politburo/Standing Committee** – These most powerful political organizations are at the very top of the CCP structure. They are chosen by the Central Committee, and their decisions dictate government policies. The Politburo has 25 members and the Standing Committee – chosen from the Politburo membership – has only 7. They meet in secret, and their membership reflects the balance of power among factions and the relative influence of different groups in policymaking.

Non-Communist Parties

Even though China effectively has a one-party system, the CCP does allow the existence of eight "democratic" parties. Each party has a special group that it draws from, such as intellectuals or businessmen. Their total membership is about a half million, and they are tightly controlled by the CCP. They do not contest the CCP for control of the government, but they do serve an important advisory role to the party leaders. Some members even attain high government positions, but organizationally these parties serve only as a loyal non-opposition. Attempts to establish independent democratic parties outside CCP control have been squashed, with the party doling out severe prison sentences to independent-minded leaders.

Elections

The PRC holds elections in order to legitimize the government and the CCP. The party controls the commissions that run elections, and it reviews draft lists of proposed candidates to weed out those it finds politically objectionable. The only direct elections are held at the local level, with voters choosing deputies to serve on the county people's congresses. The people's congresses at higher levels are selected from and by the lower levels, not directly by the people. Since the 1980s the party has allowed more than one candidate to run for county positions, and most candidates are nominated by the people. One move toward democracy has occurred at the village level, where local officials are no longer appointed from above, but are chosen in direct, secret ballot elections.

The Political Elite

Mao Zedong's place in Chinese history was sealed by the Long March of 1934-36. He emerged from the ordeal as a charismatic leader who brought about great change. His compatriots that made the journey with him became known as the "Old Guard," a group of friends that networked with one another for many years through *guanxi*, or personal connections. These personal connections are still the glue that holds Chinese politics together today.

China, like the U.S.S.R., recruits its leaders through *nomenklatura,* a system of choosing cadres from lower levels of the party hierarchy for advancement based on their loyalty and contributions to the well-being of the party. However, Chinese leaders communicate with one another through a **patron-client network** called *guanxi.* These linkages are similar to "good old boys networks" in the West, and they underscore the importance of personal career ties among individuals as they rise in bureaucratic or political structures. Besides bureaucratic and personal ties, *guanxi* is based on ideological differences and similarities, and as a result, has been the source of factions within the party. *Guanxi* is also pervasive at the local level, where ordinary people link up with village leaders and lower party officials.

Factionalism

Factionalism in the years before Mao's death in 1976 is demonstrated in the splits among the radicals (led by Jiang Qing and the Gang of Four), the military under Lin Biao, and the reformers under Zhou Enlai. All three men (Mao, Lin, and Zhou) were part of the "Old Guard" that went on the Long March in the 1930s, but by 1976, all were dead. Deng Xiaoping emerged as the new leader of China, partly because he was able to unite the factions in a course toward economic reform.

Even before Deng's death in 1997, however, factional strife was apparent within the leadership, most notably during the 1989 Tiananmen Square incident. In general, the factions split in two ways:

- **Conservatives** – Although all factions supported economic reform, conservatives worried that perhaps the power of the party and the central government has eroded too much. They were particularly concerned about any movement toward democracy and generally support crackdowns on organizations and individuals who act too independently. Their most prominent leader was **Li Peng,** the former premier and chair of the National People's Congress. His retirement in 2003 left this faction with less influence than they had before.

- **Liberals** – This faction went out of power after the 1989 Tiananmen Square incident, but they were generally more accepting of political liberties and democratic movements than are the other factions. They supported economic and political reform. The two most famous leaders of this faction were **Hu Yuobang** – whose death started the protests in 1989 – and **Zhao Ziyang** – the Premier and General Secretary who was ousted for being too sympathetic with the Tiananmen protestors. Hu Yuobang was the mentor of China's current president, Hu Jintao, but during his presidency he showed little support for democratic movements.

The fact that factions in Chinese politics have little connection with ideology became apparent during the presidency of Jiang Zemin, who stepped down in 2003. Although he supported major capitalist infusion into the PRC's economy and generally promoted an open door trade policy, his faction was – and still is – based on a patron-client system with Jiang at the top. His so-called "**Shanghai Gang**" is made up of associates from his time as mayor of Shanghai. These leaders pushed for membership in the World Trade Organization and courted the U.S. to grant "most-favored trading" status to China.

Other factions that have emerged in recent years include:

- **"Princelings"** – Many of China's recent leaders come from the "princeling" class, an aristocracy of families with revolutionary credentials from the days of Mao Zedong. Their policy preferences are not always clear: some have been big beneficiaries of China's economic reforms, using their political connections and Western education to build lucrative business careers. Other princelings are critical of China's stark inequality and call for a return to socialist principles. Former President Hu Jintao's son, Hu Haifeng, who headed a big provider of airport scanners, is a prominent princeling, as is **Xi Jinping,** who took over as party chief in 2012 and as president in 2013. Another princeling is Wen Yunsong, a financier who is the son of Wen Jiabao, the former prime minister.

- **Chinese Communist Youth League ("tuanpai")** – This faction is led by former President Hu Jintao, whose allies come from the CCYL, the party's nation-wide organization for youth aged 14-28. Some analysts characterize the tuanpai faction as promoters of the concerns of the urban and rural poor, but others see few ideological commonalities among its leaders.

The leadership team selected in 2012 has strong representation from the "Shanghai Gang" and the princelings, with five of the seven members of the Standing Committee aligning with Jiang Zemin and the remaining two (including Xi Jinping) aligning with the princelings. However, leaders from both groups are rapidly aging, and so it is difficult to predict how long they will be influential. It is important to note that factional lines are often unclear and constantly shifting and overlapping. They are determined by a complex array of old alliances, family connections, and pragmatic considerations. Despite President Xi Jinping's associations with the princelings, he almost certainly will establish his own network of patronage that will not erase his old ties but will build new ones. As leadership changes, so do factional lines, and the government's lack of transparency makes it difficult to know exactly what those changes are.

The factions follow the process of *fang-shou* – a tightening up, loosening up cycle – a waxing and waning of the power of each. In some ways, the cycle is similar to the old dynastic cycle, when ruling families were challenged as they lost the mandate of heaven. Part of the dominance of economic reformers has to do with the lingering influence of Deng Xiaoping, who designated before his death in 1997 that Jiang Zemin would be the "3rd generation" (after Mao and Deng) leader, and Hu Jintao would be the "4th generation" leader. As the party and government changed hands in 2012 and 2013, factional alliances were clearly continuing to shift.

Corruption

The combination of *guanxi* and the economic boom of the past few decades have brought about rampant corruption within the Chinese economic and political system. Bribes are common, and corruption is widely regarded as a major problem. President Jiang Zemin acknowledged in 1997, "The fight against corruption is a grave political struggle vital to the very existence of the party and the state...If corruption cannot be punished effectively, our Party will lose the support and confidence of the people." In 2004 the Communist Party's Central Committee published a policy paper that warned its members that corruption and incompetence could threaten its hold on power. The anti-corruption statement bore the mark of then President Hu Jintao, who responded to popular perception of widespread corruption among party members. Under his watch, thousands of officials were punished for corruption, although the problem continues to plague the regime.

In 2007 the Chinese government was embarrassed by international publicity about tainted food, health products, and drugs that were making their way through the world market. In reaction, the head of Beijing's most powerful food and drug regulating agency was arrested, imprisoned, and eventually executed. In his confession he acknowledged that he had accepted gifts and bribes valued at more than $850,000 from eight drug companies that sought special favors. Because the Chinese media hardly every report corruption cases without official approval, many speculated that this arrest was meant to be a warning from the government. In 2011, the minister responsible for building the high-speed rail network was dismissed for skimming huge amounts of money in bribes, and another top official in the railways ministry also stepped down amid accusations of corruption. Despite government attempts to curtail corruption, the practice of bribing government officials – by both other government officials and private businessmen – is so widespread that luxury goods producers have come to count on it as an increasingly important revenue source. Still, the government's response is to condemn corruption, and when asked whether such gift-giving takes place, Chinese officials offer strong denials.

In early 2012, shortly before the leadership transition, a major scandal emerged that surrounded Bo Xilai, one of the top party officials in China. Mr. Bo's wife, Gu Kailal, was arrested for the murder of a business partner, Neil Heywood, because of differences over a business deal. Mr. Bo was jailed for his role in covering up events, with charges that included bribery, corruption, and abuse of power. Ms. Gu was convicted of the murder, and Mr. Bo was found guilty of corruption, stripped of his assets, and sentenced to life imprisonment. His downfall is seen as one of the biggest political shake-ups of China's ruling elite in decades.

In 2012, Xi Jinping announced a new anti-corruption program, and he acknowledges the seriousness of the problem. Xi's campaign has continued, and in 2014, officials stepped up efforts to pursue those who have fled the country with illegally-obtained money. In early 2015, the Chinese government released a wanted list of 100 people, many of whom were senior officials in their work place. Chinese officials report that hundreds of fugitives have been returned to China to face charges. However, corruption continues to be pervasive in many areas of Chinese corporate life, including both multinational and domestic companies.

Interest Groups

Organized interest groups and social movements are not permitted to influence the political process unless they are under the party-state authority. The party-state tries to preempt the formation of independent groups by forming mass organizations in which people may express their points of view within strict limits. These mass organizations often form around occupations or social categories. For example, most factory workers belong to the All-China Federation of Trade Unions, and women's interests are represented in the All-China Women's Federation. In urban areas, the party maintains social control through *danwei* – social units usually based on a person's place of work. People have depended on the units for their jobs, income, and promotion, but also for medical care, housing, daycare centers, and recreational facilities. The *danwei* system was crucial to implementing the one child policy, since workers not complying with the policy could have their pay docked or incentives withheld. With the increasing liberalization of China's economy, the role of the work unit has changed, so that by the early 21st century, the power of the work unit has diminished as more private enterprises developed, including multinational corporations. For, example, it now is possible for a worker to marry or divorce without first getting permission from the work unit.

Despite the ever-present control of the state, in the last 25 years China has gone from having virtually no independent groups of any kind to more than 300,000 nongovernmental organizations, by official count. But that understates the true number. Counting unregistered groups, some estimates place the number as high as two million. Still, their impact on the policymaking process is not clearly felt. For example, in 2007 China's legislature passed a new labor law to protect workers, requiring employers to provide written contracts and restricting the use of temporary laborers to help give more employees long-term job security. However, the law also enhanced the power of the All-China Federation of Trade Unions, a monopoly union for the Communist Party. It is an official state organization charged with overseeing workers, and it alone was given the power to collectively bargain for wages and benefits. Workers are not allowed to form independent unions. It is important to note that no legitimate organizational channel exists for farmers. As a result Chinese farmers are more likely than are most other citizens to express their concerns to the government through petitions and protests.

These organizations and the state's relationship with them reflect **state corporatism** (p. 73), as well as the logic of Lenin's democratic centralism Most organizations are created, or at least approved, by the state, and many have government officials as their leaders. In yet another demonstration of corporatism, the state only allows one organization for any given profession or activity. In cases where two groups with similar interests exist in a community, local officials will force them to merge or will disband one in favor of the other. This practice prevents competition between the associations and limits how many associations are allowed to exist, making it easier for the state to monitor and control them.

Media

From 1949 until the 1980s, almost all media – television, newspapers, radio, and magazines – were state-run. Since then some independent media has emerged, but state-run media outlets still hold the largest share of the market. The official press agency of the government, **Xinhua,** is huge, employing more than 10,000 people, who are stationed not only in China but abroad as well. Independent newspapers depend on Xinhua for many of their stories. The **People's Daily,** the official newspaper of the Central Committee of the CCP, also depends on Xinhua for much of its information. Chinese Central Television, or **CCTV,** is the major state television broadcaster, and it broadcasts a variety of programs to more than one billion people. The internet is also used by many people, with internet cafes popular in most urban areas. However, all media outlets are subject to heavy censorship by the government, which has several regulatory agencies that constantly monitor for subjects that are considered taboo by the government. Despite this censorship, Chinese media has become increasingly commercialized as economic liberalization has taken place, resulting in growing competition, a wider diversity of content, and an increase in investigative reporting.

INSTITUTIONS OF GOVERNMENT

The political structure of the People's Republic of China can best be seen as three **parallel hierarchies** that are separate yet interact:

- The **Communist Party**
- The **state** or **government**
- The **People's Liberation Army**

The party dominates the three yet the organizations are separate. The relationship between the party and the government is controlled by the principle of **dual role** – *vertical* supervision of the next higher level of government and *horizontal* supervision of the Communist Party at the same level.

The organization of party and state are similar on paper to those of the former U.S.S.R., largely because the PRC's structure was designed by the Soviets during the period between 1949 and 1958. In reality, China's policymaking is governed more directly by factions and personal relationships. Although the Chinese state remains highly centralized, rapid economic development (including infusion of capitalism) has encouraged some devolution of power to sub-governments.

The Structure of the Government

The government structure of the People's Republic of China has three branches – a legislature, an executive, and a judiciary. But all branches are controlled by the party, so they are not independent, nor does a system of checks and balances exist. All top government positions are held by party members, as are many on the lower levels.

The People's Congresses

Government authority is formally vested in a system of people's congresses, which begins with a **National People's Congress** at the top and continues in hierarchical levels down through the provincial, city, and local congresses. Theoretically they are the people's legislatures, but in reality they are subject to party authority. The National People's Congress chooses the president and vice president of China, but there is only one party-sponsored candidate for each position. Although the Congress itself has little power, its meetings are important because the Politburo's decisions are formally announced then. For example, during the 12th National People's Congress in 2013, China's new president **(Xi Jinping)** was announced, although his appointment was widely known before the meeting began (partly because his position as general secretary had been announced at the 2012 CCP meeting), the National People's Congress meeting was the chosen format for formally introducing the new leader to the world.

Executive/Bureaucracy

According to the original Constitution, the **president** and **vice president** serve five-year terms, are limited to two terms, and must be at least 45 years old. The positions are largely ceremonial, though senior party leaders have always held them. In 2013, President Hu Jintao complied with the Constitution, and stepped down after two terms as president. Currently, Xi Jinping is both the president and the general secretary of the CCP, and a significant change was made to the Constitution in early 2018, when the constitutional provision for the two-term limit was lifted. This move leaves open the probability that Xi Jinping will not step down after his second term is up in 2023. If so, the centralization of power in the hands of one man – Xi Jinping – is accelerating rapidly.

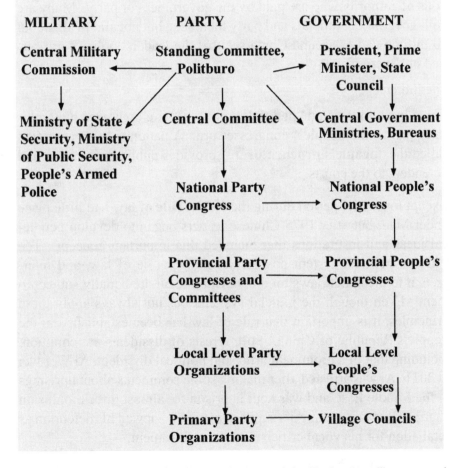

PARALLEL HIERARCHIES IN CHINA

MILITARY   **PARTY**   **GOVERNMENT**

Central Military Commission

Standing Committee, Politburo

President, Prime Minister, State Council

Ministry of State Security, Ministry of Public Security, People's Armed Police

Central Committee

Central Government Ministries, Bureaus

National Party Congress

National People's Congress

Provincial Party Congresses and Committees

Provincial People's Congresses

Local Level Party Organizations

Local Level People's Congresses

Primary Party Organizations

Village Councils

Parallel Hierarchies. The chart illustrates some important relationships between military, party and government structures in China. Parallel hierarchy involves both vertical supervision and horizontal supervision.

The **premier** is the head of government, formally appointed by the president, but again, the position is always held by a member of the Standing Committee. The current premier is **Li Keqiang**, who officially took over in March 2013. He directs the State Council, which is composed of ministers who direct the many ministries and commissions of the bureaucracy. These are controlled by the principle of **dual role** – supervision from higher bodies in the government and by comparable bodies in the CCP.

The bureaucracy exists on all levels – national, provincial, county, and local. The lower level positions are held by **cadres**, people in positions of authority who are paid by the government or party. Many are both government officials and party members, but not all. In all, about 30 million cadres around China see that the leaders' policies are carried out everywhere.

The Judiciary

China has a four-tiered "**people's court**" system, organized hierarchically just as the people's congresses are. A nationwide organization called the "**people's procuratorate**" provides public prosecutors and defenders to the courts.

Except for a brief period during the 1950s, **rule of law** had little place under Mao, but after 1978 Chinese leaders began to develop new legal ideas and institutions that included this important concept. The Chinese political system now acknowledges rule of law, and interprets it to mean that laws bind behavior and all are equally subject to them. Even though the judicial system does not always apply these principles, it is important that rule of law has been established in the People's Republic of China. Still, arrests of dissidents are common, including that of a prominent artist and political dissident, Ai Wei-wei in 2011. Ai was arrested after making some comments about uprisings in the Middle East, and was kept in prison for almost three months on charges of tax evasion. Ai's supporters widely viewed his detention as retaliation for his vocal criticism of the government.

The criminal justice system works swiftly and harshly, with a conviction rate of more than 99% of all cases that come to trial. Prison terms are long and subject to only cursory appeal. Hundreds, perhaps thousands of people have been executed during periods of government-sponsored anti-crimes campaigns. Human rights organizations criticize China for its extensive use of the death penalty.

The People's Liberation Army (PLA)

"Political power grows out of the barrel of a gun."
Mao Zedong

The military grew hand in hand with communism, as Mao's famous statement reflects. The People's Liberation Army encompasses all of the country's ground, air, and naval armed services. The army is huge, with about 2.3 million active personnel and about 12 million reserves. Yet in proportion to its population, the Chinese military presence is smaller than that of the United States. The United States spends about four and a half times as much on defense, but China's military budget has been growing at double-digit rates for years. According to SIPRI, a research institute, annual defense spending rose from over $30 billion in 2000 to almost $120 billion in 2010. Exactly how China might use its growing military power isn't clear, but the long-held aim of once again controlling Taiwan is at least part of the incentive. The PLA is skeptical about military connections to the United States, and China cut off all top-level military exchanges in January 2010 in response to Barack Obama's approval of $6.4 billion of arms sales to Taiwan.

The military has never held formal political power in the People's Republic of China, but it has been an important influence on politics and policy. All of the early political leaders were also military leaders. For example, Mao and the other members of the "Old Guard", led the Long March of the 1930s primarily by military moves.

The second half of Mao's famous quote above is less often quoted:

"Our principle is that the party commands the gun, and the gun must never be allowed to command the party."

Clearly, the military has never threatened to dominate the party. It is represented in the government by the Central Military Commission, which has been led by many prominent party leaders, including Deng Xiaoping.

The Tiananmen crisis in 1989 greatly harmed the image of the PLA, since the military was ordered to recapture the square and do so with brutal force. But the PLA continues to play an important role in Chinese politics. Two of the 24 members of the Politburo are military officers, and PLA representatives make up over 20 percent of the Central Committee membership. In 2003, Jiang Zemin's retention of his position as head of the Central Military Commission despite his stepping down as president, indicated that he still had significant policymaking power. When Hu Jintao replaced Jiang in 2004, the shift signaled that the transition of power was complete, and that Hu then had full control of the parallel hierarchies. Likewise, in 2012, Xi Jinping replaced Hu Jintao as CMC chairman, again reflecting the shift of power.

POLICYMAKING AND POLITICAL ISSUES

Since the beginning of Deng Xiaoping's rule in 1979, policymaking in China has centered on reconciling centralized political authority with marketization and privatization of the economy. Many political scientists who have assumed that democracy and capitalism always accompany one another have waited for China to democratize, an event that has yet to occur. After all, that pattern occurred in the countries that industrialized first, and the fall of the Soviet Union confirmed the notion that authoritarian states cannot be capitalistic. China has defied these theorists, and has found its own path to economic prosperity.

One important trend since 2012 has been the growing concentration of power in the hands of the president, Xi Jinping. He has removed key power figures, including Zhou Yongkang, a member of the Standing Committee who was in charge of the entire law-enforcement apparatus, including the police and the judiciary. As a result, China's leadership has recently evolved from collective decision making by the Standing Committee to more control by one man – Xi Jinping.

Policymaking Process: Fang-shou

Deng Xiaoping's carefully balanced blend of socialist central planning with a capitalist market economy has not been without its critics. The tensions within the system – both economic and political – are evidenced in *fang-shou*, a letting go, tightening-up cycle evidenced even under Mao in his reaction to the Hundred Flowers Move--

FANG-SHOU IN MODERN CHINA

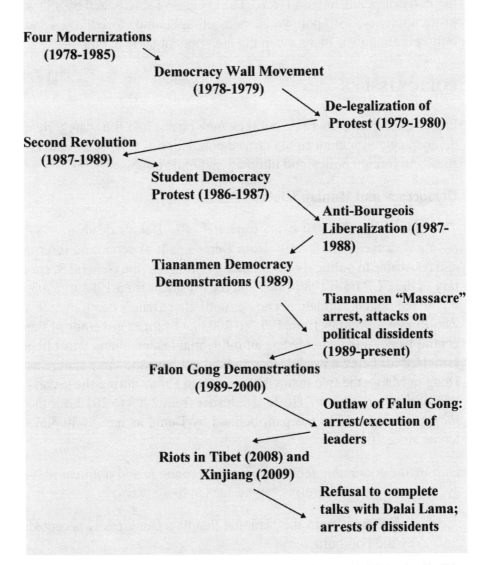

**ECONOMIC   POLITICAL MOVEMENTS   CCP RESPONSE
LIBERALIZATION**

**Four Modernizations
  (1978-1985)**

**Democracy Wall Movement
  (1978-1979)**

**De-legalization of
Protest (1979-1980)**

**Second Revolution
 (1987-1989)**

**Student Democracy
Protest (1986-1987)**

**Anti-Bourgeois
Liberalization (1987-
1988)**

**Tiananmen Democracy
Demonstrations (1989)**

**Tiananmen "Massacre"
arrest, attacks on
political dissidents
(1989-present)**

**Falon Gong Demonstrations
  (1989-2000)**

**Outlaw of Falun Gong:
arrest/execution of
leaders**

**Riots in Tibet (2008) and
Xinjiang (2009)**

**Refusal to complete
talks with Dalai Lama;
arrests of dissidents**

Tensions in China's political economy. The process of *fang-shou* gives some insight into how the Chinese government has managed the tensions between capitalism and democracy. The two rounds of economic reform shown (The Four Modernizations and the Second Revolution) were each followed by political movements that were repressed by the government. Since 1989, the economic reforms have been incremental yet significant, but the government's response to political movements has remained constant.

ment. The cycle consists of three types of actions/policies – economic reform, political movements (letting go), and a tightening-up by the CCP. With each new reform that reflects economic liberalization, liberal factions react with a demand for political liberalization, which the Party responds to with force. The cycle is characterized by a lack of transparency, with policymakers meeting behind closed doors and only revealing their plans when the government takes action.

POLICY ISSUES

Policy issues are numerous, but they may be put into four categories: democracy and human rights issues, population issues, economic issues, and foreign policy and international trade issues.

Democracy and Human Rights

The Chinese leaders that came to power after Deng's death in 1997 have not strayed significantly from Deng's path of economic reform and resistance to political reform. Jiang Zemin was the General Secretary of the CCP from 1989-2003 and the President from 1993 to 2003, but he did not consolidate his power until after Deng's death in 1997. Zhu Rongji – Premier from 1998 to 2003 and former governor of the central bank – also emerged as an influential leader. Jiang was often criticized for being a weak leader and did not have the same stature as Deng or Mao – the two men who dominated China during the second half of the 20th century. Hu Jintao, leader from 2003 to 2012, for the most part also held to the path defined by Deng, as has Xi Jinping, leader since 2012.

Despite the continuing tensions between economic and political policy, some democratic reforms can be seen in these ways:

- Some input from the National People's Congress is accepted by the Politburo.

- More emphasis is placed on laws and legal procedures.

- Village elections are now semi-competitive, with choices of candidates and some freedom from the party's control.

The Tiananmen Crisis began as a grief demonstration for the death of Hu Yaobang – a liberal who had earlier resigned from the Politburo under pressure from the conservatives. Most of the original demonstrators were students and intellectuals, but other groups joined them, and the wake turned into democratic protests. They criticized corruption and demanded democratic reforms, and hundreds of thousands joined in. Protests erupted all over China, and Tiananmen became the center of international attention for almost two months. How would the Politburo react?

The answer came with guns, as Deng sent the People's Liberation Army to shut down the protests, using whatever means necessary. The army shot its way to the square, killing hundreds of protesting citizens. They recaptured control, but the fatalities and arrests began a broad new wave of international protests from human rights advocates. Unofficial estimates of fatalities range from 700 to several thousand.

Since then, China has been under a great deal of pressure from international human rights organizations to democratize their political process and to abide by human rights standards advocated by the groups. Deng Xiaoping showed little impulse to liberalize the political process, as did the government that followed under Jiang Zemin, at least publicly. Factional disagreements are kept from the public eye, yet Hu Jintao followed the same path. China's human rights record came under international spotlight in 2010 when the Nobel Peace Prize Committee bestowed its award on Liu Xiaobo, a jailed Chinese activist who has been a vocal critic of the government, and was imprisoned after calling for an end to Communist one-party rule. News of the award was immediately censored in China, the Chinese government called Liu a criminal who didn't deserve the prize, and Liu's wife was put under house arrest. China asked that other countries boycott the Nobel ceremonies, and as a result, 15 countries declined to attend.

The Rule of Law

The principle of **rule of law**, almost always associated with liberal democracies, is based on the belief that rulers should not have absolute power over their subjects, and that their actions should be constrained by the same principles that control ordinary citizens. From the communist point of view, law is part of politics that the bourgeoisie uses to suppress the proletariat. Early Communist leaders, then, never acknowledged rule of law as a legitimate principle. For example, during the Cultural Revolution, in an effort to bring about his dream of a new egalitarian society, Mao Zedong set about to destroy the old legal codes of dynastic China. However, since 1978 legal codes have begun to revive, partly because the new economic growth and investments have required that consistent regulations be in place that allow China to trade internationally and attract foreign companies.

Criminal law, almost nonexistent in 1978, has also developed because of the new opportunities for bribery, theft, and inside stock market trading created by the economic boom. As a result, **procuratorates**, officials who investigate and prosecute official crimes, were recreated from earlier days, and they have played a role in Hu Jintao's crackdown on corruption within the Communist Party. The 1982 Constitution, theoretically at least, commits the party to the authority of law. Today the Chinese state is more constrained by law and Chinese citizens freer by law from political whim than ever before. However, this trend does not change the fact that Chinese justice is harsh by the standards of most other nations, and the death penalty is often enforced for smuggling, rape, theft, bribery, trafficking in women and children, and official corruption. It is also true that no independent judiciary has ever existed in the People's Republic of China, but remains under the tight control of the CCP.

In very recent years, a new trend has emerged, according the Dua Hua Foundation, an American NGO that tracks trends in China. Over the past decade, the number of people China executes has fallen sharply – from 12,000 executions in 2002 to 3,000 people in 2012. However, the 2012 rate is roughly four times more than the rest of the world put together (excluding Egypt and Syria, where numbers are hard to assess). These figures have not been officially disclosed by the Chinese government, but in 2012 a deputy minister of health cited the decline in executed prisoners as a reason for a shortage in organs available for transplant in China.

As part of a strong anti-corruption campaign, the 2014 Central Committee plenum focused on the rule of law. While the committee mad clear that China would not copy foreign rule-of-law concepts, a resolution emphasized the importance of the Chinese Constitution. It declared December 4 as National Constitution Day and proclaimed that officials have to swear an oath of allegiance to the Constitution. The plenum also ruled that all regulations which violate the Constitution must be revised. Despite this new emphasis, the party continues to punish those who challenge it directly.

Civil Rights and Liberties

Since the protests at Tiananmen Square in 1989, the status of civil rights and liberties in China has been widely debated. Many people believed that because Hu Jintao was mentored by Zhao Ziyang and Hu Yaobang (leaders of the liberal faction), that he would promote more individual freedoms in China. For example, Hu and former Premier Wen Jiabao took the lead in reversing the party's cover-up of the deadly SARS outbreak, pledging greater accountability and transparency in government. However, Hu showed few signs of changing the government's basic political policies toward individual civil liberties and rights. For example, he adopted new measures to regulate discussions on university internet sites. Several dissident writers who criticized the government were arrested, and a professor who posted highly critical comments of the government on the internet was dismissed from Beijing University. Hu also called for "ideological education" in universities, a phrase that is reminiscent of the Maoist era. Xi Jinping has continued the crack-down on promoters of western ideas. In March 2015, two members of a group promoting the rule of law were arrested, and during 2015 several hundred civil rights lawyers were detained.

Population Policy

In 1965 Chinese leader Mao Zedong announced that an ever-expanding population is a "good thing," and in 1974 he denounced population policies as "imperialist tools" designed to weaken developing countries. At the time of Mao's death in 1976, China had about 850 million people with a birth rate of 25. His successors recognized that population growth was consuming more than half of the annual increase in the country's gross domestic product, so China introduced a campaign advocating the "two-child family." The government provided services – including abortions – that supported the program, resulting in a drop in China's birth rate to 19.5 by the late 1970s.

The One Child Policy

In 1979, China's new leader, Deng Xiaoping, went even further by instituting the **"one child policy."** This program included both incentives and penalties to assure that couples produced only one child. Late marriages were encouraged, and free contraceptives, abortions, and sterilizations were provided to families that followed the policy. Penalties, including steep fines, were imposed on couples that had a second child. In 1984 the policy was relaxed in rural areas, where children's labor was still important, but it was reinstated in 2002 in reaction to reports that many rural births were not being reported to the government. In contrast, Chinese people in cities were generally more accepting of the one-child policy since it better suited urban life styles and needs. By 1986 the birth rate had fallen to 18, a figure far below those in other less developed countries.

However, the policy has had other consequences. One was a rise in female infanticide, or the killing of baby girls. Because traditional Chinese society has always valued males above females, many couples have wanted their one child to be a boy. If a girl is born instead, some choose to end the child's life so that they can try again to have a boy. The incidence of female infanticide is almost impossible to tally, but the practice has led to a disproportionate number of male to female children. In more recent years, as technology has allowed parents to know the gender of the child before birth, female infanticide has been replaced – at least in urban areas – with selective abortions. Over the years China's population pyramid has developed a lopsided number of young adult males to young adult females. The problem is so serious that many young men are unable to find women to marry. Some projections suggest that by the mid-21st century China's population numbers will start falling. If that occurs, it almost certainly will change the cultural tradition of sons taking care of their aging parents. There could be too few sons to carry out the responsibility, leaving

China with a problem of what to do about a growing number of elderly people with no one to take care of them.

Census figures from 2010 indicate that demographics in China have changed rapidly in recent years. Not only is the ratio of baby boys to baby girls out of proportion, but China's population is dramatically aging. People above the age of 60 now represent 13.3% of the total, up from 10.3% in 2000, and those under the age of 14 declined from 23% to 17%. An increasingly vocal group of academic demographers has called for a relaxation of the one-child policy, and in 2011, one Chinese official in Guangdong – China's most populous province – joined in the criticism by advocating a "two-child" policy. By 2015, many exceptions existed, such as the allowance of two children for couples in which both partners are single children. Minorities – such as Tibetans and Uyghurs – were permitted a second child, whatever the sex of the first born, and the regulations are most relaxed in rural areas, where population pressures are minimal. Finally, in late 2015, the Party announced the end of the one-child policy, replacing it with a two-child policy starting in 2016.

Population Movement

The broad trend of population movement from rural to urban areas began decades ago. In the early 1980s, about 80 percent of Chinese lived in the countryside versus 47 percent today. The government has long had plans to speed up this process of urbanization much faster than would occur naturally. The primary motivation is to change China's economic structure, with growth based on domestic demand for products instead of relying as much on export.

The government that took power in 2012 has identified urbanization as one of its top priorities by sponsoring a plan that moves people from rural to urban areas. One motivation for the plan is to find a new source of growth for an economy that depends on increasing consumption of productions by city dwellers. The plan involves moving millions of rural residents into newly constructed towns and cities over the next few years and tearing down and paving over vast swaths of farmland. This program at least alters the old *hukou* tradition (pp. 295-296) that requires that most peasants remain tied to their original plots of land.

According to the *New York Times* in an article published in June 2013, the ultimate goal of the government's modernization plan is to integrate about 900 million rural residents into city living by 2025. The transplanting of such a large number of people requires spending on new roads, hospitals, schools, and community centers that will cost the government a great deal of money.

Economic Policy

From 1949 to 1978, China followed a communist political economic model: a command economy directed by a central government based on demo**cratic centralism**. Mao Zedong called this policy the **"iron rice bowl**," or cradle-to-grave health care, work, and retirement security. The state set production quotas and distributed basic goods to consumers. When this model failed, Deng Xiaoping began a series of economic reforms that make up the **socialist market economy** – gradual infusion of capitalism while still retaining state control.

Agricultural policy

- **The people's communes** – During the early days of the PRC – in an effort to realize important socialist goals – virtually all peasants were organized into collective farms of approximately 250 families each. During the Great Leap Forward, farms merged into gigantic **people's communes** with several thousand families. These communes were one of the weakest links in Mao's China, with production and rural living standards showing little improvement between 1957 and 1977. Many communes were poorly managed, and peasants often didn't see the need to work hard, contrary to Mao's hopes of developing devotion through the mass line.

- **Household responsibility system** – In the early 1980s, Deng dismantled the communes and replaced them with a **household responsibility system**, which is still in effect today. In this system individual families take full charge of the production and marketing of crops. After paying government taxes and contract fees to the villages, families may consume or sell what they produce. Food production improved dramatically, and villages developed both private farming and industry.

"Private Business"

In 1988, the National People's Congress officially created a new category of **"private business"** under the control of the party. It included urban co-ops, service organizations, and rural industries that largely operate as capitalist enterprises. Today this system of state-controlled private businesses is sometimes called "bamboo capitalism." The importance of China's state sector has gradually diminished, although private industry remains heavily regulated by the government. Price controls have been lifted, and private businesses have grown by leaps and bounds since the 1980s, and are far more profitable and dynamic than are the state-owned ones.

During the first years of Deng Xiaoping's rule, the fastest growing sector of the Chinese economy was rooted in **township and village enterprises** (TVEs), rural factories and businesses that vary greatly in size, and are run by local government and private entrepreneurs. Although they are called collective enterprises, they make their own decisions and are responsible for their profits and losses. The growth of the TVE system slowed the migration of peasants to the cities, and became the backbone of economic strength in the countryside. However, under Jiang Zemin, a large number of TVEs were dismantled as restrictions of private businesses lessened. Many were privatized or restructured because of increased foreign ownership of enterprises within China. TVEs remain strongly tied to local governments and the loans they can afford, so they appear to be increasingly less important to the overall economy.

Economic Problems

The reforms have brought several important economic problems:

- **Unemployment and inequality** – Under Maoism, everyone was guaranteed a job, but marketization has brought very high rates of unemployment to China today. The Chinese leadership hopes that the booming economy will eventually take care of the unemployed, once the economy has had time to adjust to the reforms. Economic growth has also made some people very rich, and has barely affected others. As a result, economic inequality has increased significantly. The growing inequality has created a **floating population** of rural migrants seeking job opportunities in cities. As cities grow larger, crime rates have increased and infrastructures are strained, leaving urban residents with the tendency to blame the new migrants for their problems. Many critics believe that China will not be able to sustain its growth unless its poor begin to share the prosperity, earning enough money to buy goods and services that will broaden the economy.

- **Inefficiency of the state sector** – Over the years the state-owned sector of the economy has gradually declined so that today almost three-fourths of industrial production is privately owned. The state sector is still large, however, and it is plagued by corruption, inefficiency, and too many workers. Without state subsidies these industries would almost surely fail, bringing about even higher unemployment rates, so the government has continued to support them.

- **Pollution** – As China has industrialized, air and water pollution have become increasingly serious problems. Beijing and Shanghai have some of the most polluted air in the world, and sulfur dioxide and nitrogen oxides emitted by China's coal-fired power plants fall as acid rain on the neighboring countries of South Korea and Japan. Experts once thought China would overtake the United States as the world's leading producer of greenhouse gases by 2010, but now the International Energy Agency believes that happened by 2008. The issue is a real dilemma for the government because China is still a poor country in many ways, and to reduce industrial output could ruin the economic progress of the past few decades. However, evidence that China's air and water are unhealthy for the population is mounting. The government has set targets for energy efficiency and improved air and water quality, but so far they have gone unmet. However, at a summit meeting in late 2014, China and the United States announced an agreement on greenhouse gases. President Obama agreed that the United States will cut emissions by 26-28% by 2025, compared to 2005 levels, and Xi promised China's emissions will peak around 2030. Setting such a date is a first for China.

- **Product Safety** – In 2007 Chinese factories were caught exporting poisonous pharmaceutical ingredients, bogus pet food, faulty tires, and unhealthy shellfish. An international outcry followed, and the government has been pressured to do something about it. A big part of the problem lies with the tension between central government authority and capitalism. In order to allow the market economy to grow, authority has been decentralized, so that local officials have gained a great deal of decision-making power. As a result, the central government has lost direct control over production, and some faulty products have made their way into the international market.

When the global economic crisis occurred in September 2008, many observers believed that China's economy would suffer more than most, especially since its prosperity was solidly based on exports to western nations, especially the United States. Since many Chinese products were sold to Americans, the decline in American consumption struck at the heart of the Chinese economy, with the country's GDP dropping sharply during the last months of 2008. However, China and many other Asian nations rebounded impressively in 2009, and its economy expanded by more than 10% in 2010. By 2017, China's GDP growth had eased to 6.9%, smaller than increases in previous years, but still far better than the figures for most western nations. This economic recovery led many to believe that China's economy was less dependent on American consumers than they had previously thought.

Foreign Policy and International Trade

Since 1998 Chinese foreign policy has undergone profound changes that have brought the country closer into the mainstream of international politics. China still resists pressure from other countries to improve its human rights record, and Chinese leaders continue to threaten to invade Taiwan now and again. However, especially in terms of trade, China has integrated with the world community in almost unprecedented ways. It is quickly replacing Japan as the most powerful economy in Asia, and is now Asia's central economy that affects all others.   Chinese-Japanese relations have been problematic since the late 19ᵗʰ century when Japan began to rise as a world power, generally at China's expense. Both countries are particularly sensitive about Japan's invasion of China during World War II, and formal relations were called off for several months in 2006 because the Japanese prime minister visited a controversial war memorial. Now the two countries are on speaking terms again, but tensions still remain. China also has trading partners all over the world, and that trade is an integral part of the growing economy.

Foreign Policy under Mao

Until Mao's death in 1976, the PRC based its foreign policy on providing support for third world revolutionary movements. It provided substantial development assistance to a handful of the most radical states. Examples are Korea and Vietnam. Under Mao, China's relationship with the U.S.S.R. changed dramatically in the late 1950s from one of dependence to independence.

During the 1920s and 1950s, the U.S.S.R. gave large amounts of money, as well as technical and political advice to China. The countries broke into rivalry during the late 1950s when Mao decided that the Soviets had turned their backs on Marx and revolution. The Great Leap Forward and the Cultural Revolution affirmed China's independent path from Moscow's control.

US/Chinese Relations

The chill in China/Soviet relationships encouraged the U.S. to eye the advantages of opening positive interactions with China. As long as Mao was in control, his anti-capitalist attitudes – as well as U.S. containment policy – meant that the countries had no contacts until the early 1970s. Then, with Mao sick and weak, reformist Zhou Enlai opened the door to western contact. President Nixon and Secretary of State Henry Kissinger engineered negotiations, and Nixon's famous 1972 visit to China signaled a new era. Relations opened with a ping-pong match between the two countries, but after Deng Xiaoping's leadership began in 1978, his open door policy helped lead the way to more substantial contact. Today the U.S. imports many more products from China than it exports, and is concerned about the imbalance between exports and imports. The U.S. has pressured China to devalue their currency and to crack down on illegal exports, but so far, China has not cracked down on illegal exports. However, it did devalue the renminbi in August 2015, making its exports cheaper and imports more expensive.

Another issue between China and western nations has been internet hacking, with western governments and companies long suspecting that Chinese hackers besieging their networks have links to the country's armed forces. In early 2013, an American security company, Mandiant, offered evidence to substantiate the suspicions, with a report that tracked individual members of one Chinese hacker group for six year. This group, with aliases such as Ugly Gorilla and SuperHard, was linked to a district in residential Shanghai that is home to Unit 61398 of the People's Liberation Army. The Chinese government condemned the Mandiant report.

Made in China 2025/"Trade Wars" of 2018

In 2015, the Chinese government announced its "Made in China 2025" program, in which it revealed its goal to dominate cutting-edge technologies like advanced microchips, artificial intelligence and electric cars, among many others, by 2025. Since 2015, China has enlisted some important technology players to help it reach its goals. This push has alarmed the United States, since China could threaten the U.S. advantage in developing and using cutting-edge technologies.

Trade relationships between China and the United States have changed considerably since 2017, with President Donald Trump asserting his belief that the United States has not benefitted as it should from international trade. His plans to increase tariffs have put China (and other countries) on alert, and the Chinese government has threatened to retaliate with an equivalent amount of tariffs. A full-blown trade war between these two countries would have serious consequences for the global economy.

International Trade and Business

Another integral part of the economic reform of the past quarter century has been the opening of the Chinese economy to international forces. Four **Special Economic Zones (SEZs)** were established in 1979. In these regions, foreign investors were given preferential tax rates and other incentives. Five years later fourteen more areas became SEZs, and today foreign investments and free market mechanisms have spread to most of the rest of urban China.

Since 1978 China's trade and industry have expanded widely. With this expansion has come a rapidly growing GDP, entrepreneurship, and trade with many nations. A wealthy class of businessmen has emerged, and Chinese products have made their way around the world. China is now a member of the World Trade Organization, and it also has "most favored nation status" for trading with the U.S. A monumental recognition of China's new economic power came in 1997, when the British officially "gave" the major trading city of Hong Kong back to Chinese control.

Deng Xiaoping emphasized economic reform, but he continued to believe that the Party should be firmly in command of the country. In general, he did not support political reforms that included democracy and/or more civil liberties for citizens. Freedoms and incentives were granted to entrepreneurs, but they have operated largely under the patron-client system (*guanxi*).

Hong Kong

In 1997 the British ceded control of Hong Kong to mainland China under a **"one country, two systems"** agreement signed by Britain and China in 1984. Under this policy, Hong Kong is subject to Chinese rule, but continues to enjoy "a high degree of autonomy," meaning that it maintains its capitalist system, legal system, and ways of life. Since the handover, Beijing authorities have been less heavy-handed than feared, and Hong Kong today enjoys the same civil liberties as under British rule. Even though many Hong Kongers fear that the situation might change, their city is still one where people can openly talk politics, speak against the government, and choose a legislature in multi-party elections. In Hong Kong's case, the central Chinese government has devolved considerable powers to local officials. Despite these change, pro-democarcy groups in Hong Kong still push for more significant reforms.

In September 2014, a campaign known as the "**Umbrella Revolution**" began, with protesters demanding greater citizen input in elections than Beijing would allow. For weeks, protesters occupied important intersections of Hong Kong's roads, and the occupation lasted till December. Beijing responded with a plan for the election of the next chief executive in 2017 that permitted direct election, but left nominations in the hands of a 1200-member pro-establishment committee. Pro-democracy lawmakers defeated the election packet in June 2015, agreeing that it was meaningless. As a result, nothing changed, with the selection of Hong Kong's chief executive still under Beijing's control.

Hong Kong's international trade was seriously impacted by the global economic crisis of late 2008, and its GDP shrank by 7.8% in the first quarter of 2009. To add to the city's economic woes in 2009, the Chinese government approved a plan to turn Shanghai into a global financial and shipping center by 2020, presenting competition to Hong Kong as the international star of the region. However, Hong Kong's elite remains staunchly pro-business, and the Chinese government has supported the city's economic development, and so its future as a leading international trading center is most likely secure.

Taiwan

The island of Taiwan was the destination of Chiang Kai-shek after being driven from mainland China by Mao Zedong in 1949. Since post-World War II, Taiwan has claimed to be the Republic of China, separate from the People's Republic of China ruled by the Communist Party. Taiwan's autonomy was protected by the United States in a Cold War tactic against Communist China, and until the 1970s, Taiwan was recognized by western nations as the sole legitimate representative of China. However, in 1971, Taiwan lost its membership in the United Nations and its seat on the Security Council to the People's Republic of China, and in 1979, the United States recognized mainland China diplomatically. Today only a few countries recognize Taiwan's sovereignty.

In recent years, the Chinese government has made its claim to Taiwan clear. Chinese leaders assert the belief that Taiwan is historically and legitimately a part of China and should be returned to its control. The

Taiwanese government does not agree, but political parties in Taiwan are split in their attitudes about how to respond to China's claims. One point of view is that Taiwan should stand up to, or even defy China, but an opposite sentiment is that Taiwan should try to reconcile its differences with its giant neighbor. The fact that China is Taiwan's biggest trade partner has encouraged the Taiwanese leadership to explore the possibility of bringing the island closer to the mainland.

Starting in 2008, negotiations began to restore the "three links" (transportation, commerce, and communications) between the two sides, cut off since 1949. Party-to-party talks between the CPC and Taiwan's Kuomintang (KMT), have resumed and semi-official negotiations through third party organizations have taken place. An important change came when regular crossings across the Taiwan Strait began for aircraft and mail. Weekend charter flights began in July 2008, and weekday services were added by the end of the year. These changes now allow for more regular communication between the island and the mainland and almost certainly will ease trade and business exchanges as well. Still, relations are prickly, as evidenced by China's cutting off top-level military exchanges with America in 2010 in response to U.S. approval of $6.4 billion of arms sales to Taiwan. In 2013, China offered 31 new measures to better integrate Taiwan economically.

Will China continue to expand its international contacts and its free market economy? If so, will tensions increase between economic and political sectors of the country? During the 20th century many countries have struggled to define the relationship between free market economies and political leadership styles. Most obviously, the Soviet Union collapsed rather than reconcile market liberalization with centralized political power. Will the same thing happen to China, or will its policy of introducing market principles gradually work out in the end? This challenge and many more await answers from Xi Jinping and his leadership team.

IMPORTANT TERMS AND CONCEPTS

"3rd generation leader", "4th generation leader"
autonomous regions
cadres

Central Committee
Central Military Commission
Chiang Kai-shek
collectivism
Chinese Communist Party (CCP)
Confucianism
Cultural Revolution
danwei
decentralization
democratic centralism
Deng Xiaoping Theory
dual role
dynastic cycles
egalitarianism
ethic of struggle
factions, factionalism
fang-shou
floating population
"foreign devils"
Four Modernization
free market socialism
"Gang of Four"
guanxi
Great Leap Forward
Han Chinese
hegemony
household responsibility system
Hu Jintao
hukou
Hu Yaobang
iron rice bowl
Jiang Zemin
Li Peng
The Long March
mandate of heaven
Mao Zedong
Maoism
mass line

mass mobilization
"Middle Kingdom" (*zhongguo)*
Nationalist Party (Goumindang)
National Party Congress
"a new socialist countryside"
nomenklatura
Non-governmental organizations (NGOs)
"one country, two systems"
parallel hierarchies
patron client system in China
People's Courts, procuratorate
People's Liberation Army
People's National Congress
plenums
Politburo/Standing Committee
political elites
"private business"
rule of law and China
self-reliance
socialist market economy
Special Economic Zones (SEZs)
state corporatism
Sun Yat-sen
technocrats
township and village enterprises (TVEs)
"Two Chinas"
"Umbrella Revolution"
unstinting service
Wen Jiabao
Youth League
Zhao Ziyang

China Questions

1. In traditional China before the 20th century, an important source of political legitimacy was

A) the mandate of heaven
B) democratic centralism
C) ethic of struggle
D) parallel hierarchies
E) collectivism

2. The Chinese philosophy that emphasizes the importance of order and harmony and defines the duties of rulers and subjects is

A) Daoism
B) Buddhism
C) Shintoism
D) Confucianism
E) Maoism

3. Which of the following political plans had as its main goal the removal of all vestiges of the old China?

A) the Long March
B) the Great Leap Forward
C) the Cultural Revolution
D) Four Modernizations
E) open door policy

4. Which of the following is the best explanation for the high degree of corruption within the Chinese economic and political system?

A) combination of *guanxi* and the economic boom of the past 30 years
B) appointment of leaders through the *nomenklatura* system
C) absence of any viable religions in China
D) weak enforcement of laws and a weak military
E) new restrictions on entrepreneurs

5. An important difference between Russia and China in the process of political and economic change is that

A) China established itself as a major world power much earlier in its history than Russia did.

B) Russia established itself as a major world power much earlier in its history than China did.

C) during the 20th century, Russia experienced regime change; China did not.

D) Russia moved from hereditary, authoritarian rule to communism in the 20th century; China never had hereditary, authoritarian rule.

E) change in Russian history can best be explained by dynastic cycles; China experienced no similar pattern of change.

6. Which of the following democratic reforms has been enacted in China?

A) Citizens now vote for leaders on both the local and national levels.

B) Other political parties openly compete with the Communist Party for leadership positions.

C) Patron-client relationships are now much weaker than before, and many political leaders come from peasant stock.

D) Village elections are now semi-competitive, with some choices of candidates.

E) The Chinese president, as well as regional leaders, may be removed from office through impeachment proceedings.

7. Mikhail Gorbachev and Deng Xiaoping, leaders of Russia and China respectively in the late 20th century had which of the following in common?

A) Both renounced commnist rule.

B) Both led movements that promoted ideological purification.

C) Both led military revolutions against their governments.

D) Both lost control of their governments amidst opposition to their policies.

E) Both were reformers that supported an infusion of capitalism into their command economies.

8. The regime type that currently exists in the People's Republic of China is

A) corporatism
B) democracy
C) authoritarianism
D) oligarchy
E) monarchy

9. "Political power grows out of the barrel of a gun."

With this statement, Mao endorsed the

A) aggressive takeover of other East Asian countries
B) power of the People's Liberation Army to command the Communist Party
C) power of the People's Liberation Army as commanded by the Communist Party
D) People's Liberation Army's attack on the Tiananmen Square protesters in 1989
E) attempt to take Taiwan from Chiang Kai-shek's control

10. The patron-client system in China may best be described as

A) a strong sense of nationalism based on identity as Han Chinese
B) an informal network of leaders whose factions compete for power
C) a formal network of leadership positions defined by the Chinese Communist Party
D) a set of rules that defines recruitment of elites for leadership positions
E) a set of traditions that defines the relationship between Confucianism and Maoism

11. Which of the following is an accurate comparison of 20th century change in Russia and China?

A) Both countries experienced gradual reform but no major revolutions.
B) Russia experienced gradual reform but China had several important coups d'état.
C) Russia experienced two major revolutions but China did not.
D) Both countries experienced major revolutions during the first half of the century.
E) Russia experienced a major revolution during the early part of the century, and China experienced a major revolution during the last years of the century.

12. Which of the following is an important contributing factor to urban/rural cleavages in China?

A) steady migration of people from urban to rural areas
B) tendency for protests to occur in urban areas only
C) growing gap between urban and rural incomes
D) recent increases in international contacts with people in rural areas
E) policies in many urban areas that encourage people in rural areas to move to cities

13. Which of the following is an accurate comparison of British and Chinese governments?

A) Neither government has a high level of transparency.
B) The British government has a higher level of legitimacy than the Chinese government has.
C) Both British and Chinese governments have become less stable during the early 21st century.
D) The Chinese government has a higher level of stability than the British government does.
E) The British government has a higher level of transparency than the Chinese government has.

14. The Chinese government usually allows only one organization for any given profession or activity. This arrangement is best described as

A) state corporatism
B) communism
C) fragmentation
D) interest group pluralism
E) neo-corporatism

15. Which of the following statements accurately compares Mao Zedong to Deng Xiaoping?

A) Mao was a communist; Deng Xiaoping was not.
B) Mao wished to keep capitalism out of China; Deng supported a gradual infusion of capitalism.
C) Mao led China before it became the People's Republic of China; Deng was a leader of the People's Republic of China.
D) Mao supported a directly elected legislature for China; Deng Xiaoping did not.
E) Neither Mao nor Deng supported contact or trade with western countries.

16. In Chinese politics *fang-shou* is the process of

A) decentralizing policymaking powers to regional levels
B) establishing a line of communication between party leaders and ordinary citizens
C) a tightening up/loosening up cycle that reflects factional power
D) allowing capitalist competition within the Special Economic Zones
E) vertical supervision of each level of government by a higher level

(Questions 17 and 18 are based on the following chart):

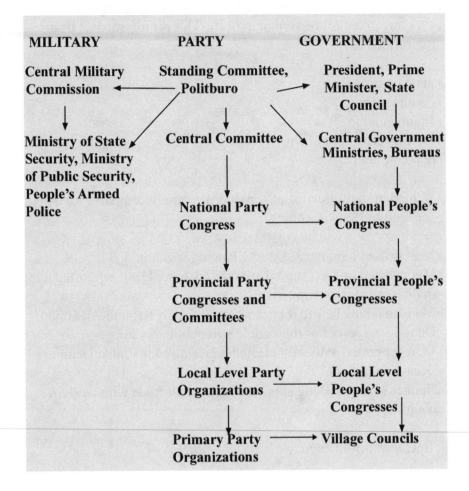

17. The chart illustrates the principle of

A) parallel hierarchy in China
B) corporatism in China
C) *fang-zhou* in China
D) patron clientelism in China
E) the federal government structure in China

18. The most important policymaking body on the chart is the

A) Central Military Commission
B) Standing Committee of the Politburo
C) State Council
D) People's National Congress
E) National Party Congress

19. Which of the following is an accurate comparison of civil society in Russia and China?

A) Chinese citizens are more likely to participate in non-governmental organizations than Russian citizens are.
B) Chinese civil society is less developed than Russian civil society.
C) Chinese civil society is more likely to be organized in urban areas; Russian civil society is more likely to be organized in rural areas.
D) Chinese nongovernmental organizations are more likely to be religious in nature than Russian nongovernmental organizations are.
E) The Russian government more closely controls nongovernmental organizations than the Chinese government does.

20. Which of the following is a basic difference between Maoism and Leninism?

A) Leninism was based on the importance of a party vanguard; Maoism emphasized the strength of the peasant.
B) Leninism is based on Marxism; Maoism is not.
C) Leninism does not support collectivization of agriculture; Maoism does.
D) Leninism does not support capitalism; Maoism does.
E) Leninism emphasizes equality and the ethic of struggle more than Maoism does.

21. Which of the folowing is an acurate statement regarding the judiciary in China?

A) No nationwide system of courts exists in China.
B) Rule of law has never had a place in the Chinese legal system.
C) Although the police make many criminal arrests, the rate of convictions is very low.
D) China has an extensive list of penalties for crimes, but the death penalty is seldom used.
E) The rule of law had little place under Mao, but now the Chinese political system acknowledges it.

22. Which of the following is an accurate description of the judicial system in modern day China?

A) The higher courts have the power of judicial review.
B) The Chinese Communist Party controls Court procedures and decisions.
C) Local courts have a great deal of autonomy, although higher courts are dominated by the CCP.
D) Most judges that sit on courts on all levels make independent decisions.
E) All judges are members of the CCP, but they have the final say in the decisions that they make.

23. The main reason that the government has established Special Economic Zones over the years since 1979 is to

A) establish government regulation of trade
B) stimulate foreign trade
C) encourage domestic trade
D) set up state-owned industries

24. Riots and other types of unrest in Tibet and Xinjiang may be most directly linked to differences based on

A) relations with the West
B) social class
C) ethnicity
D) age
E) political philosophy

25. Which of the following is an accurate comparison of Russian and Chinese politicay hierarchies?

A) The Chinese hierarchy is less authoritarian than the Russian hierarchy.
B) The military is integrated into the Chinese political hierachy; the military in Russia is not.
C) One party dominates the Chinese hierarchy; no single party dominates the Russian hierarchy.
D) The Russian political hierarchy is less centrally controlled than the Chinese hierarchy is.
E) The Russian hierarchy is more likely to include peasants than the Chinese hierarchy is.

26. *Hukou* restrictions in China have most heavily impacted

(A) the government's ability to tax citizens
(B) population growth
(C) media coverage of the government's activities
(D) trade with other countries
(E) rural to urban migrations

27. Since the 1989 Tiananmen Square incident, protest in China has

A) all but disappeared
B) become an acceptable type of political participation
C) re-emerged on a smaller scale, but has been suppressed
D) not been reported to international media sources
E) been confined to major cities, such as Beijing and Shanghai

28. During which time in its history has the Chinese government most strongly endorsed gender equality?

A) during dynastic times
B) during the 19th century, under the influence of western imperialism
C) under Mao Zedong
D) under Deng Xiaoping
E) in modern day

29. Which of the following economic policies is most associated with Mao Zedong?

A) household responsibility system
B) socialist market economy
C) iron rice bowl
D) special economic zones
E) town village enterprises

30. One consequence of the one-child policy has been

(A) a lopsided number of young adult males to young adult females
(B) an even reduction in the number of boy and girl babies who survive infancy
(C) shorter life expectancies
(D) falling overall population numbers since the 1980s
(E) falling birth rates in rural areas but not in cities

Country-Context Free-Response Question:

The modern Chinese political system has been shaped by both Mao-ism and Deng Xiaoping Theory.

(a) Describe two central values of Maoism.

(b) Describe Deng Xiaoping Theory, and identify one government program since 1978 that reflects Deng Xiaoping Theory.

(c) Identify two tensions in the Chinese political system today, and explain how the tensions have been created by conflicts between Maoism and Deng Xiaoping Theory.

**UNIT THREE:
NEWLY INDUSTRIALIZING
AND LESS DEVELOPED
COUNTRIES**

So far, we have investigated countries that represent two types of political systems – advanced democracies and communist and post-communist countries. However, the vast majority of countries in the world have had neither liberal-democratic nor communist regimes. They are often categorized by political scientists and other observers as "less-developed countries", or LDCs. Formerly they were known as "third world countries," but since the Cold War ended in the early 1990s, the term is obsolete. Their very categorization invites students to overlook the vast differences that exist among them. LDCs exist on most continents, and they have a wide array of ethnicities, racial characteristics, political cultures, and political economies.

What do these countries have in common? Most obviously, they all struggle with economic issues, including poverty, low GNP, trade dependency, and weaknesses in infrastructure. And, despite a wide variety of government types, most LDCs are currently developing fragile democracies. Many are still ruled by dictators, military leaders, or hereditary monarchs, but most absolute rulers have been challenged in some way by democratic movements.

TWO CATEGORIES

We will begin by dividing this huge category of countries in two: **newly industrializing countries** and **less-developed countries**. During the last few decades, some countries, mostly in Asia and parts of Latin America, have experienced both economic growth and democratization. As a result, they now exhibit many characteristics of advanced democracies, including relative political and social stability. An example is South Korea, a country that only a few decades ago was a poor agricultural country. During the late 20th and early 21st century, South Korea developed into one of the world's largest economies and also experimented with democratic institutions. The process that it experienced is sometimes called **compressed modernity** – rapid economic and political change that transformed the country into a stable nation with democratizing political institutions, a growing economy, and an expanding web of nongovernmental institutions. In this book, newly-industrializing countries are represented by Mexico, a country that has experienced this compressed modernity over the past 40 years or so, and Iran, that has partially industrialized but has not democratized as Mexico has.

Less-developed countries form a larger category than newly-industrializing countries do, and we will examine Nigeria as an example. Nigeria has experienced political and economic change, but it has not developed distinct characteristics of advanced democracies. It has had economic difficulties, political instability, and authoritarian rule during the past few decades.

ECONOMIC DEVELOPMENT

Economic development by itself cannot explain the differences among the core countries of the AP Comparative Government and Politics Course, but it is an important consideration since economic and political development most often reinforce one another. In recent years in most countries, economic development has been based on free market capitalism, with **economic liberalization** taking place through privatization (expanding private ownership of property) and marketization (allowing free-market principles to govern the economy). Economic development is often measured by the **Gross National Product** (the total market value of all goods and services produced in the country), but GNP gives us a limited amount of information about the economic or human conditions of the people living in an economy. Another way to measure economic development is by using **purchasing power parity (PPP)**, a statistical tool that estimates the buying power of income across different countries by using prices in the United States as a benchmark. It is generally a better indicator than **Per Capita Gross National Product (GNP)**, which merely divides the total market value of all goods and services produced by the population of the country. PPP takes into consideration the fact that some countries are more expensive to live in than others, and it is usually expressed as a per capita figure.

Clearly, our three countries in this section (Mexico, Nigeria, and Iran) vary widely in terms of PPP, with Nigeria falling far behind any other countries on the chart. One notable variation is the size of PPP in the United Kingdom compared to any of the others. It is also worth noting that despite its recent economic development, China's PPP is still relatively low, far behind those of Mexico and Iran, although China's PPP is rising at a faster rate. For comparison's sake, the highest PPP in the world is that of Liechtenstein at $139,000, followed by Qatar at $124,900, and then by Luxembourg at $109,100, (The U.S. is $59,500). Most of the top PPP countries are advanced democracies, although Qatar is ruled by an authoritarian hereditary Amir. The variations among communist, post-communist, newly-industrializing, and less-developed countries are huge.

COMPARATIVE PPP, 2017

Country	PPP (in U.S. dollars)
United Kingdom	$43,600
Russia	$27,900
China	$17,000
Mexico	$19,500
Iran	$20,000
Nigeria	$5,900

Source: *The CIA World Factbook*, 2017 estimates

COMPARATIVE ECONOMIC SECTORS
(as percentage of labor force by occupation)

Country	Primary (Agriculture)	Secondary (Industry)	Tertiary (Services)
China	28.3%	29.3%	42.4%
Iran	16.3%	35.1%	48.6%
Mexico	13.4%	24.%	61.9%
Nigeria	70%	10%	20%
Russia	9.4%	27.6%	63%
United Kingdom	1.3%	15.2%	83.5%
United States	.7%	20.3%	79.1%

Source: *CIA World Factbook* 2011-2016 (except Nigeria 1999)

Source: *The CIA World Factbook, 2008-2016 (except Nigeria, 1999)*

Another way to consider economic development is by examining economic sectors:

- **The primary sector (agriculture)** is the part of the economy that draws raw materials from the natural environment. The primary sector – agriculture, raising animals, fishing, forestry, and mining – is largest in low-income, pre-industrial nations.

- **The secondary sector (industry)** is the part of the economy that transforms raw materials into manufactured goods. This sector grows quickly as societies industrialize, and includes such operations as refining petroleum into gasoline and turning metals into tools and automobiles. As a country's industrial sector grows, its population begins to migrate from rural to urban areas to take advantage of growing urban job opportunities created by industrialization.

- **The tertiary sector (services)** is the part of the economy that involves services rather than goods. The tertiary sector grows with industrialization and comes to dominate **post-industrial societies**, or countries where most people are no longer employed in industry. Examples of tertiary jobs include construction, trade, finance, real estate, private services, government, and transportation.

Because the sectors represent necessary economic activities, most countries have some people employed in all three. However, the percentages vary widely, especially if you compare percentages of people employed in each sector.

By comparing economic sectors, the United Kingdom is the best example of a post-industrial society, with only 1.3% of its population engaged in agriculture, and 83.5% in services. Even though Russia's PPP was fairly low ($18,000), Russia appears to have moved into post-industrialism as well. Likewise, Mexico has moved away from agriculture (13.4%) toward services (61.9%), as has Iran to a lesser extent. Despite its recent economic boom, 28.3% of China's population is still employed in agriculture, and Nigeria, along with its sagging PPP ($5,900) has the largest percentage of its people (70%) employed in the primary sector.

Theories of Economic Development

What factors explain the lack of economic development in LDCs, and what is in store for their future? Their condition is often referred to as **neocolonialism**, or an unequal relationship in a world in which new indirect forms of imperialism are at play. Two conflicting theories have guided political scientists in answering these questions:

- **Westernization (modernization) model** – According to this theory, Britain was the first country to begin to develop its industry. The Industrial Revolution was spurred by a combination of prosperity, trade connections, inventions, and natural resources. Once started, the British model spread to other European nations and the United States, which prospered because they built on British ingenuity and economic practices. By extension, any country that wants its economy to grow should study the paths taken by the industrial nations, and logically they too can reap the benefits of modernization, or "westernization." According to this model, the biggest obstacle for LDCs is tradition because holding on to old values and beliefs often hinders progress.

- **Dependency theory** – In contrast to the westernization model, dependency theory holds that economic development of many countries in the world is blocked by the fact that industrialized nations exploit them. How can a country develop when its resources (natural and human) are controlled by a handful of prosperous industrialized countries? Dependency theory is an outgrowth of Marxism, which emphasizes exploitation of one social class by the other. The same dynamic is at work in assessing relationships among countries. Problems, then, cannot be solved by westernization, but must be addressed by establishing independence. In reaction to this theory, many LDCs have experimented with forms of socialism with the intent of nationalizing industry and narrowing the gap between the rich and the poor.

Most political scientists today do not adhere to one theory or the other, but instead take a pluralist approach: a country's problems have many sources, and no one formula will work for all. Many LDCs today have "mixed" economies – with some elements of capitalism and some of socialism – and they take a variety of approaches in trying to solve their problems. Political leaders are influenced by both theories, with left-leaning governments usually preferring dependency theory, and more conservative governments looking to westernization as a model.

Economic Policies in the Less-developed World

Two distinct types of economic policies have been applied throughout the less-developed world in an effort to jump-start their economies:

- **Import substitution** is based on the belief that governments in poorer countries must create more positive conditions for the development of local industries. If these countries are to compete successfully with the advanced industrialized democracies, the governments must restrict imports by setting quotas or imposing heavy import taxes. The reasoning is that people then will have to buy locally, and that demand will stimulate the growth of domestic businesses. Eventually these businesses will develop the ability to compete in the international market because they will have built the capital and the infrastructure necessary for success. Beginning in the 1930s, import substitution was used widely in Latin America, and later in parts of Africa, and Asia.

- **Export-oriented industrialization** has been used by the so-called "**Asian tigers**" – Hong Kong, South Korea, Taiwan, and Singapore – whose economies boomed starting in the 1960s. This strategy seeks to directly integrate the country's economy into the global economy by concentrating on economic production that can find a place in international markets. The countries have watched the "product life cycle" that follows stages: first an innovator country produces something new; next that country moves on to other innovations. Meanwhile, other countries think of ways to make the first product better and cheaper, and export it back to the innovator country. For example, Asian countries have prospered from this strategy with automobiles and electronics in their trade with the United States.

POLITICAL DEVELOPMENT

As we explored briefly in the introductory review chapter of this book, a major political trend of the 20th and early 21st centuries is **democratization**, or the process of developing a political system in which power is exercised either directly or indirectly by the people. A state that progresses from procedural democracy (regular competitive elections) to substantive democracy (with civil liberties, rule of law, and open civil society) through democratic consolidation is said to experience **political liberalization**, which eventually leads other states to recognize them as liberal democracies.

Characteristics of liberal democracies include regular competitive elections, civil liberties, rule of law, neutrality of the judiciary, open civil society, and civilian control of the military. It is true that most countries that have high PPPs and developed tertiary sectors are also liberal democracies. However, does this correlation mean that economic development cannot occur without democratization? If not, then Russia's recent move toward centralized authority is not a good sign for the future of the Russian economy. China has experienced an almost unprecedented economic boom since 1978, but the political system is still authoritarian. Does this situation spell trouble for China's current political regime? The answers to these questions are uncertain, but they have tremendous implications for the countries that we will study in this section. For example, might it be correct to categorize Iran as a "less developed country" because it has an authoritarian government? Economically its PPP is a relatively healthy $17,100, and 48.6% of its people are employed in the tertiary sector. These statistics imply stronger economic development than China. Our categories are imperfect, partly because no one knows for sure if postindustrial societies are by necessity democracies. Many developing nations may be categorized as "**hybrid regimes**," which have some characteristics of a democracy, but in many ways are still authoritarian regimes.

One important threat to some newly developing and less developed countries is the possible collapse into a **failed state**, a situation in which the very structures of the state may become so weak that it collapses, resulting in anarchy and violence that erupts as order breaks down. Somalia is a clear example of a failed state today, where a civil war has raged for almost two decades. Even though several foreign interventions have attempted to reverse the anarchy, ethnicity-based factions continue to kill Somalians in one of the world's most dramatic humanitarian catastrophes in recent years. Of the three case studies of the AP Comparative Government and Politics Course that fall into this category, the weakest state is Nigeria, which suffers from economic stagnation, regional rebellions, and government corruption.

In the pages that follow, three very different countries illustrate some of the common characteristics and issues facing newly-industrialized and less-developed countries today. In the late 20th century Mexico was declared by some observers to be a poster child for the benefits of westernization, only to have their economy come crashing down with the oil bust of the early 1980s. Since then, the economy has improved, but the country is still riddled with political and economic problems. Nigeria, as Africa's most populous nation, illustrates the perils of new democracies, especially in countries with strong military traditions. Iran represents a part of the world where democracy has very little

TWO CATEGORIES FOR COMPARISON

Newly industrializing countries have experienced both economic growth and democratization, a process known as **compressed modernity.** Representative for this category is **Mexico.**	**Less developed countries (LDCs)** form a larger category than newly industrializing countries. They have experienced political and economic change but have not developed distinct characteristics of advanced democracies. LDCs are represented by **Nigeria.**

Iran is harder to categorize because it has experienced economic growth but its government has not democratized.

foothold. However, countries of Southwest Asia have asserted themselves in many ways in recent years, and they have profoundly affected the balance of power among nations of the world.

IMPORTANT TERMS AND CONCEPTS

"Asian tigers"
compressed modernity
democratization
dependency theory
economic liberalization
economic sectors: primary, secondary, tertiary
export-oriented industrialization
failed state
GNP
GNP per capita
"hybrid regimes"

import substitution
political liberalization
PPP
westernization model

CHAPTER SIX:
GOVERNMENT AND POLITICS
IN MEXICO

Not too many years ago, observers considered Mexico to be a model for LDCs (less-developed countries) around the world. The "**Mexican miracle**" described a country with a rapidly increasing GNP in orderly transition from an authoritarian to a democratic government. Then, the economy soured after oil prices plummeted in the early 1980s, the peso took a nosedive, and debt mounted during the decade. Ethnic conflict erupted in the mid-1990s when the Zapatistas took over the capital of the southern state of Chiapas and refused to be subdued by the Mexican army. On the political front, the leading presidential candidate was assassinated, and top political officials were arrested for bribery, obstructing justice, and drug pedaling. Then under new leadership, Mexico surprised the world by recovering some financial viability through paying back emergency money it borrowed from the United States. In 2000, under close scrutiny by western democracies, Mexico held an apparently honest, competitive presidential election, and confirmed the emergence of a competitive electoral system. Then, just as pundits were declaring Mexico's path to capitalism and liberal democracy a successful one, the contentious presidential election of 2006 threatened to rock the government's legitimacy to its core. Once again, Mexico survived the uproar, only to be hit hard by the global economic crisis in late 2008.

Today it is the BRICS countries – Brazil, Russia, India, China, and South Africa – that attract world consideration, while Mexico draws attention for the drug-fueled violence that has plagued it in recent years. Still, recent elections have confirmed the existence of a competitive party system, with the presidency recaptured in 2012 by the party that dominated Mexico during the 20th century, and then won by a popular left-leaning political leader in 2018.

Despite its uncertain path, Mexico may be seen as a representative for the category of "newly-industrializing countries." Its purchasing power parity ($19,500) is fairly high, and about 62% of its workers are employed in the service sector. This "developing" nation is full of apparent contradictions that make its politics sometimes puzzling, but always interesting and dynamic. Mexico is generally described economically as a developing country and politically as a "transitional democracy." In both cases it is at an "in-between" stage when compared with other countries globally, but the transition has had its surprises, and its successes and challenges may well serve as beacons for other nations to follow.

SOVEREIGNTY, AUTHORITY, AND POWER

Like many other Latin American countries, Mexico's sources of public authority have fluctuated greatly over the centuries. From the time that the Spanish arrived in the early 16th century until independence was won in 1821, Mexico was ruled by a viceroy, or governor put in place by the Spanish king. The rule was centralized and authoritarian, and it allowed virtually no participation by indigenous people. After Mexican independence, this ruling style continued, and all of Mexico's presidents until the mid-20th century were military generals. The country was highly unstable during the early 20th century, and even though a constitution was put in place, Mexico's presidents dictated policy until very recently. Significant economic growth characterized the late 20th century, followed by democratization that is currently reshaping the political system.

Legitimacy

In general, Mexican citizens consider their government and its power legitimate. An important source of legitimacy is the **Revolution of 1910-1911**, and Mexicans deeply admire revolutionary leaders throughout their history, such as Miguel Hidalgo, Benito Juarez, Emilio Zapata, Pancho Villa, and Lazaro Cardenas. Revolutions have been accepted as a path to change, and charisma is highly valued as a leadership characteristic.

The revolution was legitimized by the formation of the **Institutional Revolutionary Party (PRI)** in 1929. The constitution that was written during that era created a democratic, three-branch government, but PRI was intended to stabilize political power in the hands of its leaders. PRI, then, served as an important source of government legitimacy until other political parties successfully challenged its monopoly during the late 20th century. After the election of 2000, PRI lost the presidency and one house of Congress, so that by 2006, the party held only a minority of seats in both houses of the legislature. Then, in the 2009 mid-term election, PRI showed that it was still a viable party by capturing a plurality of seats in the Chamber of Deputies. In 2012, the party won the presidency for the first time since 1994, although it still did not dominate the legislature. In 2018, the presidency was won by Andres Manuel Lopez Obrador, a populist who established Morena, a new political party. PRI remains a viable political party; however, Mexican voters are clearly disillusioned with the governmet's handling of major problems. Today, sources of public authority and political power appear to be changing rapidly. However, some characteristics carry through from one era to the next.

Historical Traditions

Mexico's historical tradition may be divided into three stages of its political development – colonialism, the chaos of the 19th and early 20th century, and the emphasis on economic development during its recent history.

- **Authoritarianism** – Both from the colonial structure set up by Spain and from strong-arm tactics by military-political leaders such as Porfirio Diaz, Mexico has a tradition of authoritarian rule. Currently, the president still holds a great deal of political power, although presidential authority has been questioned during the past few years.

- **Populism** – The democratic revolutions of 1810 and 1910 both had significant peasant bases led by charismatic figures that cried out for more rights for ordinary Mexicans, particularly Amerindians. The modern Zapatista movement is a reflection of this historical tradition, which is particularly strong in the southern part of the country.

- **Power plays/divisions within the elite** – The elites who led dissenters during the Revolutions of 1810 and 1910, the warlords/caudillos of the early 20th century, and the *politicos vs. tecnicos* of the late 20th century are all examples of competitive splits among the elite. Current party leaders are often at odds, as displayed during the election crisis of 2006. Presidential candidate Andres Manuel Lopez Obrador's challenge of the election results threatened to destroy fragile democratic structures, although the crisis passed without destabilizing the country. Obrador won the presidential election of 2018, and in doing so, he created new political dynamics, especially by creating a new political party on the left – **Morena.**

- **Instability and legitimacy issues** – Mexico's political history is full of chaos, conflict, bloodshed, and violent resolution to political disagreements. As recently as 1994, a major presidential candidate was assassinated. Even though most Mexicans believe that the government is legitimate, the current regime still leans toward instability, and the current outbreak of gang-related violence – especially in the north – seriously challenges the government's authority.

Political Culture

Mexicans share a strong sense of national identification based on a common history, as well as a dominant religion and language.

- **The importance of religion** – Until the 1920s, the Catholic Church actively participated in politics, and priests were often leaders of populist movements. During the revolutionary era of the early 20th century, the government developed an anti-cleric position, and today the political influence of the church has declined significantly. However, a large percentage of Mexicans are devout Catholics, and their beliefs strongly influence political values and actions.

- **Patron-clientelism** – The system of cliques based on personal connections and charismatic leadership has served as the glue that has held an agrarian Mexico together through practicing "you scratch my back, I'll scratch yours." The network of **ca-**

marillas (patron-client networks) extends from the political elites to vote-mobilizing organizations throughout the country. **Corruption** is one by-product of patron-clientelism. Democratization and industrialization have put pressure on this system, and it is questionable as to whether or not modern Mexico can continue to rely on patron-clientelism to organize its government and politics. The defeats of PRI for the presidency in 2000, 2006, and 2018 are indications that clientelism may be on the decline, but corporatism still plays a big role in policy-making.

- **Economic dependency** – Whether as a Spanish colony or a southern neighbor of the United States, Mexico has almost always been under the shadow of a more powerful country. In recent years Mexico has struggled to gain more economic independence.

Geographic Influence

Mexico is one of the most geographically diverse countries in the world, including high mountains, coastal plains, high plateaus, fertile valleys, rain forests, and deserts within an area about three times the size of France.

Some geographical features that have influenced the political development of Mexico are:

- **Mountains and deserts** – Because large mountain ranges and vast deserts separate regions, communication and transportation across the country is often difficult. Rugged terrain also limits areas where productive agriculture is possible. Regionalism, then, is a major characteristic of the political system.

- **Varied climates** – Partly because of the terrain, but also because of its great distance north to south, Mexico has a wide variety of climates – from cold, dry mountains to tropical rain forests.

- **Natural resources** – Mexico has an abundance of oil, silver, and other natural resources, but has always struggled to manage them wisely. These resources undoubtedly have enriched the country (and the United States), but they have not brought general prosperity to the Mexican people.

Geographic Influences. The geography of Mexico varies widely – mountains, deserts, coastal plains, and valleys. The country also has a long border with the United States to its north, although most large cities are far away from the border. The largest city in the north in Monterrey.

- **A long** (2000-mile-long) **border with the United States** – Contacts – including conflicts and migration and dependency issues – between the two countries are inevitable, and Mexico has often been overshadowed by its powerful neighbor to the north.

- **131 million people** – Mexico is the most populous Spanish-speaking country in the world, and among the ten most populous of all. Population growth has slowed significantly to about 1.1%, but population is still increasing.

- **Urban population** – Mexico has urbanized rapidly, as people have moved to cities from rural areas. Today about 3/4 of all Mexicans lives in cities of the interior or along the coasts. Mexico City is one of the largest cities in the world, with about 21 million inhabitants living in or close to it. The shift from rural to urban population areas during the late 20th century disrupted traditional Mexican politics, including the patron-client system.

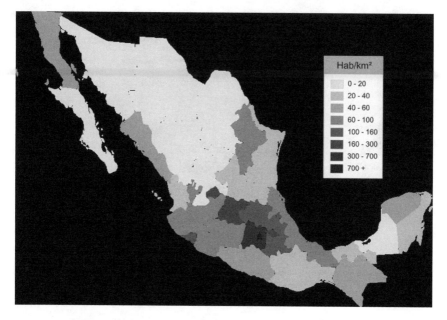

Population Density in Mexico. The population of Mexico is unevenly distributed across the country, with a vast majority of the people living in the mid-section, centered on Mexico City but spreading to several other major cities, such as Guadalajara and Puebla.

POLITICAL AND ECONOMIC CHANGE

Mexican history dates back to its independence in 1821, but many influences on its political system developed much earlier. Over time, Mexico has experienced authoritarian governments first under the colonial control of Spain, and then under military dictatorships during the 19th century. The 19th century also saw populist movements influenced by democratic impulses, accompanied by violence, bloodshed, and demagoguery. The first decades of the 20th century saw an intensification of violence as the country sank into chaos, and the political system was characterized by serious instability and rapid turnover of political authority. Stability was regained by resorting to authoritarian tactics that remained in place until the latter part of the century. In recent years, Mexico has shown clear signs of moving away from authoritarianism toward democracy.

Economic changes in Mexico have been no less dramatic. For most of its history, Mexico's economy was based on agriculture, along with other primary sector activities such as mining. However, Mexico was strongly influenced by the industrialization of its northern neighbor, the United States, starting in the late 1800s. Under the dictatorship of Porfirio Diaz, U.S. business interests were encouraged to develop in Mexico, and a strong dependency on the U.S. economy was put in place. Mexican nationalists have reacted against U.S. participation in the Mexican economy at various times since those days, so that anti-U.S. sentiments have become one dynamic of political and economic interactions. During the late 20th century, Mexico industrialized rapidly, with its rich natural resource of oil serving as the wind that drove the economic expansion. Mexico has struggled since then to break its dependency on one product, especially after the sudden drop in oil prices during the early 1980s sent the Mexican economy into a tailspin. Today Mexico has moved rapidly from an agricultural society to an industrial one, and even in some ways toward post-industrialism.

We will divide our study of historical influences into three parts:

- Colonialism

- Independence until the Revolution of 1910

- 1910 to the Present

Colonialism

From 1519 to 1821 Spain controlled the area that is now Mexico. The Spanish placed their subjects in an elaborate social status hierarchy, with people born in Spain on top and the native Amerindians on the bottom. Colonialism left several enduring influences:

- **Cultural heterogeneity** – When the Spanish arrived in 1519 the area was well populated with natives, many of whom were controlled by the Aztecs. When the conquistador Hernan Cortés captured the Aztec capital of Tenochtitlan, the Spanish effectively took control of the entire area. Even though status differences between natives and Spanish were clearly drawn, the populations soon mixed, particularly since Spanish soldiers were not allowed to bring their families from Spain to the New World. Today about 60% of all Mexicans are **mestizo** (a blend of the two peoples), but areas far away from Mexico City – particularly to the south – remain primarily Amerindian.

- **Catholicism** – Most Spaniards remained in or near Mexico City after their arrival, but Spanish Catholic priests settled far and wide as they converted the population to Christianity. Priests set up missions that became population centers, and despite the differences in status, they often developed great attachments to the people that they led.

- **Economic dependency** – The area was controlled by Spain, and served the mother country as a colony, although the territory was so vast that the Spanish never realized the extent of Mexico's natural resources.

Independence/New Country (1810-1911)

As part of a wave of revolutions that swept across Latin America during the early 1800s, a Mexican parish priest named **Miguel Hidalgo** led a popular rebellion against Spanish rule in 1810. After eleven years of turmoil (and Father Hidalgo's execution), Spain finally recognized Mexico's independence in 1821. Father Hidalgo, though of Spanish origins, was seen as a champion of the indigenous people of Mexico. He still symbolizes the political rights of the peasantry, and statues in his memory stand in public squares all over the country. However, stability and order did not follow independence, with a total of thirty-six presidents serving between 1833 and 1855.

Important influences during this period were:

- **Instability and legitimacy issues** – When the Spanish left, they took their hierarchy with them, and reorganizing the government was a difficult task.

- **Rise of the military** – The instability invited military control, most famously exercised by Santa Anna, a military general and president of Mexico.

- **Domination by the United States** – The U.S. quickly picked up on the fact that its neighbor to the south was in disarray, and chose to challenge Mexican land claims. By 1855, Mexico had lost half of its territory to the U.S. What is now Texas, New Mexico, Arizona, California, Utah, and part of Colorado fell under U.S. control after the Treaty of Guadalupe Hidalgo was signed in 1848.

- **Liberal vs. conservative struggle** – The impulses of the 1810 revolution toward democracy came to clash with the military's attempt to establish authoritarianism (as in colonial days). The Constitution of 1857 was set up on democratic principles, and a liberal president, **Benito Juarez**, is one of Mexico's greatest heroes. Like Father Hidalgo, Juarez was very popular with ordinary Mexican citizens, but unlike Hidalgo, he was a military general with a base of support among elites as well. Conservatism was reflected in the joint French, Spanish, and English takeover of Mexico under Maximilian (1864-1867). His execution brought Juarez back to power, but brought no peace to Mexico.

The "Porfiriato" (1876-1911)

Porfirio Diaz – one of Juarez's generals – staged a military coup in 1876 and instituted himself as the president of Mexico with a promise that he would not serve more than one term of office. He ignored that pledge and ruled Mexico with an iron hand for 34 years. He brought with him the *cientificos*, a group of young advisors who believed in bringing scientific and economic progress to Mexico. Influences of the "Porfiriato" are:

- **Stability** – With Diaz the years of chaos came to an end, and his dictatorship brought a stable government to Mexico.

- **Authoritarianism** – This dictatorship allowed no sharing of political power beyond the small, closed elite.

- **Foreign investment and economic growth** – The *cientificos* encouraged entrepreneurship and foreign investment – primarily from the United States – resulting in a growth of business and industry.

- **Growing gap between the rich and the poor** – As often happens in developing countries, the introduction of wealth did not insure that all would benefit. Many of the elite became quite wealthy and led lavish lifestyles, but most people in Mexico remained poor.

Eventually even other elites became increasingly sensitive to the greed of the Porfirians and their own lack of opportunities, and so Diaz's regime ended with a coup from within the elite, sparking the Revolution of 1910.

1910 - Present

The Revolution of 1910 marked the end of the "Porfiriato" and the beginning of another round of instability and disorder, followed by many years of attempts to regain stability.

The Chaos of the Early 20th Century

In 1910, conflict broke out as reformers sought to end the Diaz dictatorship. When Diaz tried to block a presidential election, support for another general, Francisco Madero – a landowner from the northern state of Coahuila – swelled to the point that Diaz was forced to abdicate in 1911. So the Revolution of 1910 began with a movement by other elites to remove Diaz from office. In their success, they set off a period of warlordism and popular uprisings that lasted until 1934.

The influence of this era include:

- **Patron-client system** – In their efforts to unseat Diaz, **caudillos** – political/military strongmen from different areas of the country – rose to challenge one another for power. Two popular leaders – **Emiliano Zapata** and **Pancho Villa** – emerged to lead peasant armies and establish another dimension to the rebellion. Around each leader a **patron-client** system emerged that encompassed large numbers of citizens. Many caudillos (including Zapata and Villa) were assassinated, and many followers were violently killed in the competition among the leaders.

- **Constitution of 1917** – Although it represents the end of the revolution, the Constitution did not bring an end to the violence. It set up a structure for democratic government – complete with three branches and competitive elections – but political assassinations continued into the 1920s. The constitution also sought to limit foreigners' rights to exploit natural resources by declaring that all subsoil rights are the property of the nation.

- **Conflict with the Catholic Church** – The Cristero Rebellion broke out in the 1920s as one of the bloodiest conflicts in Mexican history, with hundreds of thousands of people killed, including many priests. Liberals saw the church as a bastion of conservatism and put laws in place that forbid priests to vote, restricted church-affiliated schools, and suspended religious services. Priests around the country led a rebellion against the new rules that contributed greatly to the chaos of the era.

- **The establishment of PRI** – Finally, after years of conflict and numerous presidential assassinations, President Calles brought caudillos together for an agreement in 1929. His plan – to bring all caudillos under one big political party – was intended to bring stability through agreement to "pass around" the power from one leader to the next as the presidency changed hands. Each president could only have one six-year term (**sexenio**), and then must let another leader have his term. Meanwhile, other leaders would be given major positions in the government to establish their influence. This giant umbrella party – **PRI** (Institutional Revolutionary Party) – "institutionalized" the revolution by stabilizing conflict between leaders. Other parties were allowed to run candidates for office, but the umbrella agreement precluded them from winning.

The Cardenas Upheaval – 1934-1940

When Calles's term as president was up, **Lazaro Cardenas** began a remarkable sexenio that both stabilized and radicalized Mexican politics. Cardenas (sometimes called "the Roosevelt of Mexico" by U.S. scholars) gave voice to the peasant demands from the Revolution of 1910, and through his tremendous charisma, brought about many changes:

COMPARATIVE REVOLUTIONS
EARLY 20TH CENTURY

Country	Motivations	Characteristics	Outcomes
Russia (1917)	Defeat authoritarian government; carry forward Marxist ideology	Led by V.I. Lenin, Bolsheviks; violent, sudden change; carried out in middle of World War I	Four years of civil war; triumph of Marxism-Leninism; one-party state
China (1911)	Drive out "foreign devils"; defeat authoritarian, weak government; assert nationalism	Regional warlordism, violent, sudden change; chaotic, competing forces	Years of chaos; two competing forces; triumph of Maoism; one-party state
Mexico (1910)	Defeat authoritarian government; break dependency on foreign governments; elite power struggle	Began as a conflict among elites; joined by populist forces; sudden, violent change; chaotic competing forces	Years of violence, instability; elites "umbrellaed" under PRI for stability; one-party state

Origins of one-party states. Although the early 20th century revolutions of Russia, China, and Mexico had some very different motivations, characteristics, and outcomes, they had a few things in common, including the outcome of a one-party state.

- **Redistribution of land** – Land was taken away from big land-lords and foreigners and redistributed as *ejidos* – collective land grants – to be worked by the peasants.

- **Nationalization of industry** – Foreign business owners who had been welcomed since the time of Diaz were kicked out of the country, and much industry was put under the control of the state. For example, **PEMEX** – a giant government-controlled oil company – was created.

- **Investments in public works** – The government built roads, provided electricity, and created public services that modernized Mexico.

- **Encouragement of peasant and union organizations** – Cardenas welcomed the input of these groups into his government, and they formed their own camarillas with leaders that represented peasants and workers on the president's cabinet.

- **Concentration of power in the presidency** – Cardenas stabilized the presidency, and when his sexenio was up, he peacefully let go of power, allowing another caudillo to have the reins of government.

The strategy of state-led development that Cardenas followed is called **import substitution industrialization.** ISI employs high tariffs to protect locally produced goods from foreign competition, government ownership of key industries, and government subsidies to domestic industries. Since there was relatively little money in private hands to finance industrialization, the government took the lead in promoting industrialization. Although including peasant and union organizations in the policymaking process is a populist touch, the Cardenas government is still an example of **state corporatism**, with the president determining who represents different groups to the government.

The Emergence of the *Tecnicos* and the Pendulum Theory

Six years after Cardenas left office, Miguel Aleman became president, setting in place the **Pendulum Theory**. Aleman rejected many of Cardenas' socialist reforms and set Mexico on a path of economic development through economic liberalization, again encouraging entrepreneurship and foreign investment. He in turn was followed by a president who shifted the emphasis back to Cardenas-style reform, setting off a back-and-forth effect – socialist reform to free-market economic development and back again. As Mexico reached the 1970s the pendulum appeared to stop, and a new generation of *tecnicos* – educated, business-oriented leaders – took control of the government and PRI with a moderate, free-market approach to politics. In many ways, the pendulum swung between modernization and dependency theories (see p. 324-325), with the government eventually settling on modernization theory. By the 1980s, Mexico practiced **neoliberalism**, a strategy that calls for free markets, balanced budgets, privatization, free trade, and limited government intervention in the economy.

By the 1950s, Mexico was welcoming foreign investment, and the country's GNP began a spectacular growth that continued until the early 1980s. This **"Mexican Miracle"** – based largely on huge supplies of natural gas and oil – became a model for less developed countries everywhere. With the "oil bust" of the early 1980s, the plummeting price of oil sank the Mexican economy and greatly inflated the value of the peso. Within PRI, the division between the *"politicos"* – the old style caciques who headed camarillas – and the *tecnicos* began to grow wider, as demands for political liberalization grew in intensity.

CITIZENS, SOCIETY, AND THE STATE

For many years Mexican citizens have interacted with their government through an informal web of relationships defined by patron-clientelism. Because the camarillas are so interwoven into the fabric of Mexican politics, most people have had at least some contact with the government during their lifetimes. However, interactions between citizens and government through clientelism generally have meant that the government has had the upper hand through its ability to determine which interests to respond to and which to ignore. The role of citizens in the Mexican political system is changing as political parties have become competitive and democracy seems to be taking root, yet the old habits of favor-swapping are ingrained in the political culture.

Cleavages

Cleavages that have the most direct impact on the political system are social class, urban v. rural, mestizo v. Amerindian, and north v. south. These cleavages are often **crosscutting**, with different divisions emerging as the issues change, but in recent years they have often **coincided** (see p. 46) as urban, middle-class mestizos from the north have found themselves at odds with rural, poor Amerindians from the south.

- **Urban v. rural** – Mexico's political structure was put into place in the early 20th century – a time when most of the population lived in rural areas. PRI and the patron-client system were intended to control largely illiterate peasants who provided political support in exchange for small favors from the *politicos.* Today Mexico is more than 75% urban, and the literacy rate is about 95%. Urban voters are less inclined to support PRI, and they have often been receptive to political and economic reform.

- **Social class** – Mexico's Gini coefficient is .48 (2017 estimate), which means that economic inequality is high. In 2010, the richest 10% earned 37.5% of all income, reflecting the unequal distribution of income. This economic divide translates into higher infant mortality rates, lower levels of education, and shorter life expectancies among the poor. In very recent years Mexico's middle class has been growing, even in poorer sections of the country. Some are from the **informal economy** (businesses not registered with the government), and others from new industries or service businesses. Until 2018, middle and upper class people have been more likely to support PAN, and are more likely to vote than the poor, especially as PRI-style patron-client ties unwind.

- **Mestizo v. Amerindian** – The main ethnic cleavage in Mexico is between mestizo (a blend of European and Amerindian) and Amerindian. Only about 10% of Mexicans actually speak an indigenous language, but as many as 30% think of themselves as Amerindian. Amerindians are more likely to live in marginalized rural areas and to live in poverty. This cleavage tends to define social class, with most of Mexico's wealth in the hands of mestizos.

- **North v. south** – In many ways, northern Mexico is almost a different country than the area south of Mexico City. The north is very dry and mountainous, but its population is much more prosperous, partly because many are involved in trade with the United States. The north has a substantial middle class with relatively high levels of education. Not surprisingly, they are generally more supportive of a market-based economy. The south is largely subtropical, and its people are generally less influenced by urban areas and the United States. Larger numbers are Amerindian, with less European ethnicity, and their average incomes are lower than those in the north. A typical adult in the south has only six years of schooling, as compared to 8.1 years on average in the north. Although their rural base may influence them to support PRI, some southerners think of the central government as repressive. The southernmost state of Chiapas is the source of the Zapatista Movement, which values the Amerindian heritage and seeks more rights for natives.

One recent change worth noting is that the incomes of the poorest half of the population are growing faster than the average. Poverty levels as defined by the government have fallen, and income distribution is becoming less unequal. For example, Mexico's Gini coefficient has dropped from more than .54 in 2002 to .48 in 2017. If significant numbers of the poor begin making enough money to move them into the middle class, cleavages that define political behavior will certainly be affected. Likewise, if job opportunities in the formal sector (businesses recognized by the government) spread into new regions of the country as the economy grows, regional and ethnic divisions may also change.

Political Participation

Political participation in Mexico has been characterized by revolution and protest, but until recently, Mexican citizens were generally subjects under authoritarian rule by the political elite. Citizens sometimes benefited from the elaborate patronage system, but legitimate channels to policymakers were few. Today, citizens participate through increasingly legitimate, regular elections.

The Patron-Client System

Traditionally, Mexican citizens have participated in their government through the informal and personal mechanisms of the **patron-client system**. Since the formation of PRI in 1929, the political system has emphasized compromise among contending elites, behind-the-scenes conflict resolution, and distribution of political rewards to those willing to play by the informal and formal rules of the game.

The patron-client system keeps control in the hands of the government elite, since they have the upper hand in deciding who gets favors and who doesn't. Only in recent years have citizens and elites begun to participate through competitive elections, campaigns, and interest group lobbying.

Patron-clientelism has its roots in warlordism and loyalty to the early 19th century **caudillos.** Each leader had his supporters that he – in return for their loyalty – granted favors to. Each group formed a **camarilla,** a hierarchical network through which offices and other benefits were exchanged. Until the election of 2000, within PRI most positions on the president's cabinet were filled either by supporters or by heads of other camarillas that the president wanted to appease. Peasants in a camarilla received jobs, financial assistance, family advice, and sometimes even food and shelter in exchange for votes for the PRI.

Despite trends toward a modern society, the patron-client system is still very important in determining the nature of political participation. Modernization tends to break up the patron-client system, as networks blur in large population centers, and more formal forms of participation are instituted. However, vestiges of the old patron-client system were at work in the controversy surrounding the 2006 presidential election, with the losing candidate Andres Manuel Lopez Obrador accusing the winning candidate's PAN party of election fraud. Polls indicate that between a quarter and a third of voters believed Obrador, since decades of one-party rule had sustained fraudulence under the patron-client system. As a result, many Mexicans still deeply distrust government officials and institutions. Obrador's election as president in 2018 reflected voters' disillusionment with established political leaders and parties.

Protests

When citizen demands have gotten out of hand, the government has generally responded by not only accommodating their demands, but by including them in the political process through **co-optation.** For example, after the 1968 student protests in Mexico City ended in government troops killing an estimated two hundred people in **Tlatelolco Plaza,** the next president recruited large numbers of student activists into his administration. He also dramatically increased spending on social services, putting many of the young people to work in expanded antipoverty programs in the countryside and in urban slums.

Social conditions in Mexico lie at the heart of the Chiapas rebellion that began in 1994. This poor southern Mexican state sponsored the **Zapatista (EZLN) uprising**, representing Amerindians that felt disaffected from the more prosperous mestizo populations of cities in the center of the country. The Chiapas rebellion reminded Mexicans that some people live in appalling conditions with little hope for the future. President Vicente Fox (2000-2006) made some efforts to incorporate the Zapatistas into the political system, but the group only recently called off its rebellion. The federal government currently supplies electricity and water to the villages the Zapatistas still control, a measure that may have helped to quiet the movement.

Some protests have been staged by drug gangs. For example, on May Day 2015, the Jalisco New Generation, a relatively new organization, defied the federal government by burning buildings, creating road blocks, and shooting down an army helicopter. Fifteen people died in the violence. The incident calls into question the success of the government's strategy of going after gang leaders with the assumption that the groups will be dismantled. New Generation formed from the remnants of defeated groups, suggesting that the gangs will not go away just because leaders are captured.

Voter Behavior

Before the political changes of the 1990s, PRI controlled elections on the local, state, and national levels. Voting rates were very high because the patron-client system required political support in exchange for political and economic favors. Election day was generally very festive, with the party rounding up voters and bringing them to the polls. Voting was accompanied by celebrations, with free food and entertainment for those who supported the party. Corruption abounded, and challengers to the system were easily defeated with "tacos," or stuffed ballot boxes.

Despite PRI's control of electoral politics, competing parties have existed since the 1930s, and once they began pulling support away from PRI, some distinct voting patterns emerged. Voter turnout was probably at its height in 1994, when about 78% of all eligible citizens actually voted. This is up from 49% in 1988, although any comparisons before 1988 have to be considered in light of corruption, either through fraudulent voting or simply the announcement from PRI of inflated voter participation rates. Voter rates have declined since 1994, but a respectable 64% of those eligible actually voted in the election of 2000, 60% in 2006, and 63% in 2012 and 2018.

Some factors that appeared to influence voter behavior in recent elections are:

- **Region** – Regional differences are quite dramatic, with PRI usually dominant in the north/northeast and in the Yucatan. It usually competes with PRD in southern Mexico, and with PAN in the north. PRD has built its strongest support bases in and around Mexico City, which it has governed since mayors were first elected in the city in 1997. In the 2012 presidential election, PRI candidate Enrique Peña Nieto performed well all over the country, winning in 21 of 32 states, whereas PRD candidate López Obrador did well in and around Mexico City and also in the southern states. Pan candidate Josefina Vásques Mota only won three states in northern and central Mexico. The election of 2018 upended these patterns as voters all over the country supported Obrador and his newly-formed Morena Party.

- **Poverty/marginalization** – Traditionally, PRI benefitted from strong electoral support in the rural, marginalized parts of the country, with votes secured through clientelism and assistance that obligated peasants to vote for PRI. During 12 years of PAN presidents, government poverty alleviation programs expanded and clientelism weakened, so that the results of the election of 2012 show that PAN, and to a lesser extent PRD, have expanded their popularity in rural parts of the country. Again, the election of 2018 defied these patterns, with Morena gaining support from voters in almost all areas of the country.

Civil Society

Despite the fact that PRI formed an umbrella party over elites in the years that it ruled, Mexico has always had a surprising number of groups who have refused to cooperate. These groups have formed the basis for a lively civil society in Mexico, which also has provided an atmosphere where public protests have been acceptable. PRI practiced **state corporatism,** with the state mediating among different groups to ensure that no one group successfully challenged the government. PRI formally divided interest groups into three sectors: labor, peasants, and the middle class ("popular"), with each dominated by PRI-controlled groups. However, The Confederation of Employers of the Mexican Republic (a labor group) was an autonomous group that vocally and publicly criticized the government.

PRI's downfall started in civil society with discontented businessmen who were not incorporated into the government's system. This group was behind the formation of PAN in 1939, and though the party did not successfully challenge PRI for many years, PAN's 2000 presidential candidate – Vicente Fox – emerged to successfully challenge PRI partly because he had the backing of powerful business interests. With the narrow PAN victory in 2006, business interests again benefitted, so PRI's old state corporatism clearly has been broken up, and even though PRI candidate Enrique Peña Nieto won the presidency in 2012, PRI did not capture either legislative house. In the election of 2018, voters rejected all traditional parties and overwhelmingly supported Obrador's Morena Pary.

In recent years, the number of non-governmental organizations (NGOs) has increased significantly. Many have pressured the government to crack down on gang-related violence, and some are supported by powerful business interests and are well funded. Others focus on campaigns for clean government. After the murder of 43 students in late 2014 by a drug gang, NGOs pushed the president to back a constitutional reform to tackle corruption. However, corruption only grew worse under Peña Nieto, leading voters to back Obrador, the populist candidate.

What will emerge in the place of PRI's domination is now the question – state corporatism, neo-corporatism (where interests, not the government controls), or pluralism (independent interests have input, but don't control).

POLITICAL INSTITUTIONS

Mexico is a country in economic and political transition. As a result, it is difficult to categorize its regime type. For many years its government was highly authoritarian, with the president serving virtually as a dictator for a six-year term. Mexico's economy has also been underdeveloped and quite dependent on the economies of stronger nations, particularly that of the United States. However, in recent years Mexico has shown strong signs of economic development, accompanied by public policy supportive of a free market economy. Also, the country's political parties are becoming more competitive, and the dictatorial control of PRI has been soundly broken by elections since 1997. Although the political structures themselves remain the same as they were before, significant political and economic reforms have greatly altered the ways that government officials operate.

Regime Type

Traditionally, Mexico has had a **state corporatist structure** – central, authoritarian rule that allows input from interest groups outside of government. Through the camarilla system, leaders of important groups, including business elites, workers, and peasants, actually served in high government offices. Today political and economic liberalization appears to be leading toward a more open structure, but corporatism is still characteristic of policymaking. Is the modern Mexican government authoritarian or democratic? Is the economy centrally controlled, or does it operate under free market principles? The answers are far from clear, but the direction of the transition is toward both economic and political liberalization.

"Developed," "Developing," or "LDC"?

Categorizing the economic development of countries can be a tricky business, with at least four different ways to measure it:

- **GNP per capita** – This figure is an estimate of a country's total economic output divided by its total population, converted to a single currency, usually the U.S. dollar. This measure is often criticized because it does not take into account what goods and services people can actually buy with their local currencies.

- **PPP** (Purchasing Power Parity) – This measure takes into account the actual cost of living in a particular country by figuring what it costs to buy the same bundle of goods in different countries. Mexico's figure is $19,500 per year.

- **HDI (**Human Development Index) – The United Nations has put together this measure based on a formula that takes into account the three factors of longevity (life expectancy at birth), knowledge (literacy and average years of schooling), and income (according to PPP). Mexico's literacy rate is 95.5% for men and 93.5% for women, and life expectancy is 73.3 for men and 79 for women.

- **Economic dependency** – A less developed country is often dependent on developed countries for economic support and trade. Generally speaking, economic trade that is balanced between nations is considered to be good. A country is said to be "developing" when it begins relying less on a stronger country to keep it afloat financially. Despite recent attempts to change the balance, Mexico is still quite dependent on the U.S. for trade, jobs, and business.

- **Economic inequality** – The economies of developing countries usually benefit the rich first, so characteristically the gap between the rich and poor widens. This trend is evident in Mexico with its high Gini coefficient of .48.

No matter which way you figure it, Mexico comes out somewhere in the middle, with some countries more developed and some less. Since these indices in general are moving together upward over time for Mexico, it is said to be "developing."

A Transitional Democracy

Politically, Mexico is said to be in transition between an authoritarian style government and a democratic one. From this view (modernization theory), democracy is assumed to be a "modern" government type, and authoritarianism more old-fashioned. Governments, then, may be categorized according to the degree of democracy they have. How is democracy measured? Usually by these characteristics:

- **Political accountability** – In a democracy, political leaders are held accountable to the people of a country. The key criterion is usually the existence of regular, free, and fair elections.

- **Political competition** – Political parties must be free to organize, present candidates, and express their ideas. The losing party must allow the winning party to take office peacefully.

- **Political freedom** – The air to democracy's fire is political freedom – assembly, organization, and political expression, including the right to criticize the government.

- **Political equality** – Signs of democracy include equal access to political participation, equal rights as citizens, and equal weighting of citizens' votes.

Mexico – especially in recent years – has developed some democratic characteristics, but still has many vestiges of its authoritarian past, as we have seen. *The Economist,* in its 2017 democracy index (p. 27), categorizes Mexico as a "flawed democracy," ranking it 66th of 167 countries in terms of its functioning as a democracy, its electoral process, political participation, political culture, and civil liberties. Another often used standard for considering a country a democracy is the longevity of democratic practices. If a nation shows *consistent* democratic practices for a period of 40 years or so (a somewhat arbitrary number), then it may be declared a stable democracy. Mexico does not fit this description.

Linkage Institutions

Before the trend toward democratization took hold during the late 20th century, Mexico's political parties, interest groups, and mass media all worked to link Mexican citizens to their government in significant ways. This linkage took place under the umbrella of PRI elite rulers so that a true, independent civil society did not exist. However as democratization began and civil society developed, the structures were already in place, so that activating democracy was easier than it would have been otherwise.

Political Parties

For most of the 20th century, Mexico was virtually a one-party state. Until 2000 all presidents belonged to PRI, as did most governors, representatives, senators, and other government officials. Over the past twenty years or so other parties have gained power, so that today competitive elections are a reality, at least in many parts of Mexico.

Until 2018, the three largest parties in Mexico today are PRI, PAN, and PRD. Morena's victories in 2018 promised to alter the traditional political party system considerably.

PRI

The *Partido Revolucionario Institucional* was in power continuously from 1920 until 2000, when an opposition candidate finally won the presidency. PRI was founded as a coalition of elites who agreed to work out their conflicts through compromise rather than violence. By forming a political party that encompassed all political elites, they could agree to trade favors and pass power around from one cacique to another. The party traditionally was characterized by:

- **A corporatist structure** – Interest groups are woven into the structure of the party. The party has the ultimate authority, but other voices are heard by bringing interest groups under the broad umbrella of the party. This structure is not democratic, but it allowed input into the government from party-selected groups whose leaders often held cabinet positions when Mexico was a one-party state. Particularly since the Cardinas sexenio (1934-1940), peasant and labor organizations have been represented in the party and hold positions of responsibility, but these groups are carefully selected and controlled by the party.

- **Patron-client system** – The party traditionally gets its support from rural areas where the patron-client system is still in control. As long as Mexico remained rural-based, PRI had a solid, thorough organization that managed to garner overwhelming support. Until the election of 1988, there was no question that the PRI candidate would be elected president, with 85-90% victories being normal.

PRI lost the presidency in 2000 to The National Action Party's Vicente Fox, and it trailed the other two major parties in the election of 2006. However, in the mid-term election of 2009, it picked up major support in the legislature and – by forming a coalition with a minor party – held a majority of seats in the lower house of the legislature. In 2012, PRI candidate Enrique Peña Nieto won the presidency, but PRI lost a significant number of seats in the Chamber of Deputies.

PAN

The National Action Party, or PAN, was founded in 1939, making it one of the oldest opposition parties. Although PAN provided little competition for PRI for many years, it began winning some guberna-torial elections in the north in the 1990s. It was created to represent business interests opposed to centralization and anti-clericism (PRI's practice of keeping the church out of politics.) PAN is strongest in the north, where the tradition of resisting direction from Mexico City is the strongest. Under Felipe Calderón's presidency, the party also gain support in the south, partly because Calderón, and Vicente Fox before him, expanded poverty assistance programs that helped indigenous people in the southern states.

PAN's platform includes:

- Regional autonomy

- Less government intervention in the economy

- Clean and fair elections

- Good rapport with the Catholic Church

- Support for private and religious education

PAN is usually considered to be PRI's opposition to the right. PAN's candidates won the presidency in 2000 and 2006, and between the 2006 and 2009 (mid-term) elections it had more deputies and sena-tors in the legislature than any other party. Although Felipe Calderón remained popular as president, the party experienced a major setback when it lost more than 60 seats in the lower house of the legislature in 2009, and 28 more seats in 2012. PAN's hold in the Senate increased slightly in 2012, with a gain of three seats (33 senators). The PAN candidate for president in 2012, Josefina Vásques Mota, came in third, gaining majorities in only four states.

PRD

The Democratic Revolutionary Party, or PRD, is generally thought of as PRI's opposition on the left. Its presidential candidate in 1988 and 1994 was **Cuauhtemoc Cárdenas**, the son of Mexico's famous and revered president Lazaro Cárdenas. He was ejected from PRI for demanding reform that emphasized social justice and populism, and he responded by switching parties. In 1988 Cárdenas won 31.1% of the official vote, and PRD captured 139 seats in the Chamber of Deputies (out of 500). Many observers believe that if the election of 1988 had been honest, Cárdenas actually would have won.

PRD has been plagued by a number of problems that have weakened it since 1988. It has had trouble defining a left of center alternative to the market-oriented policies established by PRI. Their leaders have also been divided on issues, and have sometimes publicly quarreled. The party has been criticized for poor organization, and Cárdenas is not generally believed to have the same degree of charisma as did his famous father. PRD's standard-bearer has been **Andres Manuel López Obrador**, the popular mayor of Mexico City that barely lost the presidential elections in 2006 and 2012. However, Obrador's refusal to accept the results of the election of 2006 split PRD once again into factions – those that support Obrador and those that oppose him. The party made significant gains in the legislative elections of 2006, but the disarray after the election caused it to lose more than half its seats in the lower house in 2009. In 2012, the party regained some of those seats: 100 deputies, up from 69 in 2009. However, in 2015, it lost those gains, only winning 56 seats. Obrador lost the presidency of the party in 2008, and announced his resignation from the party in 2012. He has supported smaller parties on the left, including National Regeneration Movement (Morena) and Citizens' Movement.

Elections

Citizens of Mexico directly elect their president, Chamber of Deputy representatives, and senators, as well as a host of state and local officials. Although the parties have overlapping constituencies, typical voter profiles are:

- PRI – small town or rural, less educated, older, poorer
- PAN – from the north, middle-class professional or business, urban, better educated (at least high school, some college), religious (or those less strict about separation of church and state); lost support in the 2012 presidential election to PRI
- PRD – younger, politically active, from the central states, some education, small town or urban; drew some middle-class and older voters in 2006; gained support in 2012 in southern states; strongest in Mexico City area

LINKAGE INSTITUTIONS IN MEXICO: POLITICAL PARTIES

Party to PRI's left; First won support during the late 1980s; Has had trouble defining a left of center alternative to the market-centered policies set by PRI; Appeals to the young, populists, some intellectuals: threatened by Morena's 2018 victories	Ruled as a one-party system from 1929 to the late 20th century; Corporatist structure that brought competing elites into the cabinet; Patron-client system that included most people in the country; Appeal to rural people, residents of southern Mexico	Party to PRI's right; PRI's oldest opposition party, created to represent business interests; Advocates regional autonomy, less government intervention in the economy; good rapport with the Catholic Church; Appeals to middle class, northerners, and those with higher levels of education

Elections in Mexico today tend to be most competitive in urban areas, but more competition in rural areas could be seen in the presidential and legislative elections of 2006 and 2012. Under PRI control, elections were typically fraudulent, with the patron-client system encouraging bribery and favor swapping. Since 1988, Mexico has been under pressure to have fairer elections. Part of the demands have come from a more urban, educated population, and some have come from international sources as Mexico has become more and more a part of world business, communication, and trade.

The elections of 2000 brought the PAN candidate, **Vicente Fox**, into the presidency. PAN captured 208 of the 500 deputies in the lower house (Chamber of Deputies), but PRI edged them out with 209 members. 46 of the 128 senators elected were from PAN, as opposed to 60 for PRI. The newly created competitive electoral system has encouraged coalitions to form to the left and right of PRI, and the split in votes may be encouraging gridlock, a phenomenon unknown to Mexico under the old PRI-controlled governments.

COMPARATIVE PARTY SYSTEMS

	BRITAIN	RUSSIA	MEXICO
Type of system	multi-party system	multi-party system	multi-party system
relationship to the legislature	2 parties dominate the legislature	1 party dominates the legislature	several parties represented in the legislature.
relationship to the executive	1 party dominates the executive	1 party dominates the executive	unclear pattern, appears competitive
Types of parties	parties on the left, center, and right; regional parties relatively strong	parties of power common; party in the previous one-party system is still competitive.	parties on left and right; party in the previous one-party system is still competitive.

The Elections of 2006

When the votes were counted in the presidential election on July 2, 2006, PAN candidate Felipe Calderón and PRD candidate Andres Manuel Lopez Obrador were virtually tied for the lead, with PRI candidate Roberto Madrazo trailing far behind. The official vote tally put Calderón ahead by about 230,000 votes, out of 41.5 million votes cast, about a half percentage point difference. Obrador challenged the results as fraudulent and demanded a recount. The election tribunal investigated his allegations, and for more than two months the election was held in the balance until the tribunal gave its report. In early August the tribunal ordered recounts on only about 9% of the precincts, not the full recount demanded by Obrador. In early September, the tribunal announced that the recount did not change the outcome, despite some errors in math and some cases of fraud. During the entire process Obrador held rallies for supporters, and he refused to accept the tribunal's decision, claiming that the election was "stolen" by a broad conspiracy between business leaders and the government. He encouraged his supporters to protest, and he claimed to be the legitimate president. Obrador's challenge drew strength from well established traditions from the political culture – populism and dissent among the elites – but by 2007 the crisis had passed.

The legislative elections of 2006 changed the power balance as PRI lost heavily in both houses, PAN received modest gains in the Chamber of Deputies, and PRD gained many seats in both houses.

The Election of 2012

PRI's prospects for the 2012 presidential election were enhanced by the popularity of Enrique Peña Nieto, who stepped down from the governorship of Mexico State in 2011. PRI capitalized on a growing sense among voters that neither PAN nor PRD is any less corrupt than PRI, and many think that PRI is more able to deliver on political promises. About 30% of Mexican voters were younger than 18 when PRI lost power in 2000, so they do not remember some of the party's worst excesses when it dominated government and politics in Mexico.

In 2012, the presidency was recaptured by PRI, with Peña Nieto winning with more than 38% of the vote. Andres Manuel López Obrador, the PRD candidate, came in second with less than 32% of the vote, and Josefina Vásquez Mota, the PAN candidate, was third with just over 25% of the vote. The election of 2012 affirmed the fact that Mexico has developed a competitive multi-party electoral system, with PRI still playing an important, but not dominant, role in Mexican politics.

Elections of 2018

In 2018, Obrador's newly established Morena Party swept the presidential, legislative, and regional elections, potentially upending the party system. The fate of PRD, especially, is uncertain. Obrador won more than 53% of the vote, the first time a candidate won an outright majority since 1988. His closest competitor, Ricardo Anaya of PAN (in alliance with PRD) won just over 22%, and the PRI candidate, Jose Antonio Meade won only 16.4%. This sweeping victory for Obrador reflected voter concern over drug and gang-related violence and corruption in the government. Morena won large number of seats in both the Senate and the Chamber of Deputies, but did not win a majority in either house.

Electoral System

The president is elected through the **"first past the post"** (plurality) system with no run-off elections required. As a result, the current Mexican president, Enrique Peña Nieto, was elected with only a little more than a third of the total popular votes. Members of congress are elected through a dual system of "first-past-the-post" and **proportional representation**. Proportional representation was increased in a major reform law in 1986, a change that gave power to political parties that have challenged PRI's control. Each of Mexico's 31 states elects three senators. Two of them are determined by plurality vote, and the third is determined by whichever party receives the second highest number of votes. Also, thirty-two Senate seats are determined nationally through a system of proportional representation that divides the seats according to the number of votes cast for each party. In the lower house (the Chamber of Deputies), 300 seats are determined by plurality within single-member districts, and 200 seats are chosen by proportional representation.

Interest Groups and Popular Movements

The Mexican government's corporatist structure generally responds pragmatically to the demands of interest groups through accommodation and co-optation. As a result, political tensions among major interests have rarely escalated into the kinds of serious conflict that can threaten stability. Where open conflict has occurred, it has generally been met with efforts to find a solution. Because private organizations have been linked for so long to the government, Mexico's development of a separate civil society has been slow.

In the past 30 years or so, business interests have networked with political leaders to protect the growth of commerce, finance, industry and agriculture. Under **state corporatism,** these business elites have become quite wealthy, but they were never incorporated into PRI. However, political leaders have listened to and responded to their demands. Labor has been similarly accommodated within the system. Wage levels for unionized workers grew fairly consistently between 1940 and 1982, when the economic crisis prompted by lower oil prices caused wages to drop. The power of union bosses is declining, partly because unions are weaker than in the past, and partly because union members are more independent. Today with PAN recently controlling the presidency, business interests may exhibit more characteristics of **neo-corporatism,** but there is no clear evidence that businesses are controlling the government.

One powerful interest group is the Educational Workers' Union, Latin America's largest trade union. It has long had the power to negotiate salaries for teachers each year, and many see it as a neo-corporatist group that has a great deal of power over government decisions in education. In early 2013, Peña Nieto's government sent a message to the union when it arrested a powerful leader, Elba Esther Gordillo. Federal prosecutors charged her with the embezzlement of 2 billion pesos of union funds that she allegedly spent on designer clothes, art, property, and cosmetic surgery. The arrest came the day after Peña Nieto had signed into law an education reform designed to pry control of schools from the union. The government promised that teachers' jobs would no longer be for sale or inherited, and teachers who failed assessments would be fired.

In rural areas, peasant organizations have been encouraged by PRI, particularly through the *ejido* system that grants land from the Mexican government to the organizations themselves. Since the 1980s these groups have often demanded greater independence from the government, and have supported movements for better prices for crops and access to markets and credit. They have joined with other groups to promote better education, health services, and environmental protections.

Urban popular movements also abound in Mexico, with organizations concerned about social welfare spending, city services, neighborhood improvements, economic development, feminism, and professional identity. As these groups have strengthened and become more independent, the political system has had to negotiate and bargain with them, transforming the political culture and increasing the depth of civil society.

The Media

As long as PRI monopolized government and politics in Mexico, the media had little power to criticize the government or to influence public opinion. The government rewarded newspapers, magazines, radio, and television stations that supported them with special favors, such as access to newsprint or airwaves. The government also subsidized the salaries of reporters, writers, and media personalities who strongly supported PRI initiatives. A considerable amount of revenue came from government-placed advertisements, so few media outlets could afford to openly criticize the government.

The media began to become more independent starting in the 1980s at the same time that PRI began losing its hold in other areas. Today there are several major television networks in the country, and many people have access to international newspapers and networks, such as CNN and BBC. Several news magazines now offer opinions of government initiatives, just as similar magazines do in the United States. One indication of freedom of the press came early in the Fox administration when the media publicized "Toallagate," a scandal involving the purchase of some significantly overpriced towels for the president's mansion. The Mexican press also criticized President Fox for his *"Comes y te vas"* (eat and leave) instructions to Fidel Castro after a United Nations gathering, so as not to offend U.S. President George W. Bush with Castro's presence. So, for better or for worse, Mexican citizens now have access to a much broader range of political opinions than they ever have had before.

During the presidential campaign in 2012, protests took place in Mexico City against alleged bias toward PRI and Peña Nieto in the print and television media, particularly Televisa, the largest multimedia company in North America. The movement, *Yo Soy 132* ("I am 132") formed, accusing Peña Nieto as the candidate of "corruption, tyranny and authoritarianism." Mass protests organized by university students then took place across the country, and the movement successfully demanded that, unlike the first presidential debate, the second debate be broadcast on national television.

Mexico is one of Latin America's biggest internet markets. There were 85 million internet users by 2017, 65% of the population. Facebook is the most popular social network. During the presidential campaign in 2018, social media helped to spread voter outrage over corruption and drug/gang-related violence.

GOVERNMENT INSTITUTIONS

Mexico is a federal republic, though the state and local governments have little independent power and few resources. Historically the executive branch with its strong presidency has had all the power, while the legislature and judiciary followed the executive's lead, rubber-stamping executive decisions. Though Mexico is democratic in name, traditionally the country has been authoritarian and corporatist. Since the 1980s, the government and its citizens have made significant changes, so that – more and more – Mexico is practicing democracy and federalism. An important consequence of growing party competition has been that state governors have become more willing to exercise their formal powers.

According to the Constitution of 1917, Mexican political institutions resemble those of the U.S. The three branches of government theoretically check and balance one another, and many public officials –

including the president, both houses of the legislature, and governors – are directly elected by the people. In practice, however, the Mexican system is very different from that of the United States. The Mexican constitution is very long and easily amended, and the government can best be described as a strong presidential system.

The Executive

A remarkable thing happened in the presidential election of 2000. The PRI candidate did not win. Instead, Vicente Fox, candidate for the combined PAN/PRD parties won with almost 43% of the vote. He edged out Francisco Labastida, the PRI candidate, who garnered not quite 36%. This election has far-reaching implications, since the structure of the government is built around the certainty that the PRI candidate will win. This election may have marked the decline of patron-clientelism and the beginning of a true democratic state. The election of Felipe Calderón in 2006 secured PAN's control of the presidency, but since he only received about 36% of the vote – only .5% more than PRD's Obrador – he had to build a coalition cabinet. In 2012, Enrique Peña Nieto recaptured the presidency for PRI, but only with 38% of the vote. Peña Nieto's cabinet was a mix of business-oriented technocrats and veteran PRI party insiders, but a few members were from outside the party. PRI failed to win a majority in either house of the legislature.

Since the formation of PRI, policymaking in Mexico had centered on the presidency. The president – through the patron-client system – was virtually a dictator for his **sexenio**, a non-renewable six-year term. The incumbent always selected his successor, appointed officials to all positions of power in the government and PRI, and named PRI candidates for governors, senators, deputies, and local officials. Until the mid 1970s, Mexican presidents were considered above criticism, and people revered them as symbols of national progress and well-being. As head of PRI, the president managed a huge patronage system and controlled a rubber-stamp Congress. The president almost always was a member of the preceding president's cabinet. Despite recent changes, the Mexican president remains very powerful.

During his sexenio, Vicente Fox had to manage Mexico without the supporting patron-client system of PRI behind him. His predecessor, Ernesto Zedillo, had responded to pressure to democratize by relinquishing a number of the traditional powers of the presidency. For example, Zedillo announced that he would not name his PRI successor (the candidate in 2000), but that the party would make the decision. Even so, President Fox inherited a job that most people still saw as all-powerful, and they often blamed him for failing to enact many of his promised programs, despite the fact that he did not have a strong party in Congress or many experienced people in government. Although PRI won the presidency in 2012, no single party had a majority in the legislature, and Mexico's evolution of a multi-party system continues, a trend that impacts the president's ability to control policymaking.

The Bureaucracy

Almost 1 1/2 million people work in the federal bureaucracy, most of them in Mexico City. More government employees staff the schools, state-owned industries, and semi-autonomous agencies of government, and hundreds of thousands of bureaucrats fill positions in state and local governments.

Officials are generally paid very little, but those at high and middle levels have a great deal of power. Under PRI control, all were tied to the patron-client system and often accepted bribes and used insider information to promote private business deals.

Under PRI, the **para-statal** sector – composed of semiautonomous or autonomous government agencies – was huge. These companies often produce goods and services that in other countries are carried out by private individuals, and the Mexican government owned many of them. The best-known para-statal is PEMEX, the giant state-owned petroleum company. After the oil bust of the early 1980s, reforms eliminated many para-statals, and the number has continued to dwindle, so that many of them are now privately owned. President Fox pushed for privatization of PEMEX, but did not succeed, and President Enrique Peña Nieto has proposed significant reforms that would effect the operation of the energy giant and its relationship to the government.

The Legislature

The Mexican legislature is bicameral, with a 500-member **Chamber of Deputies** and a 128-member **Senate**. All legislators are directly elected: deputies have three-year terms and senators have six-year terms. Like the Russian Duma until 2007, the Chamber of Deputies includes some deputies (300) who are elected from **single-member districts**, and others (200) who are elected by **proportional representation**. Unlike the Russian upper house – the Federation Council, which is filled with appointed representatives – the Mexican Senate is also directly elected by a combination of the electoral methods: three senators are elected from each of 31 states and the federal district (Mexico City), with the remaining senators selected by proportional representation. Although legislative procedures look very similar to those of the United States, until the 1980s the legislature remained under the president's strict control.

PRI's grip on the legislature slipped earlier than it did on the presidency. The growing strength of opposition parties, combined with legislation that provided for greater representation of minority parties (proportional representation) in Congress, led to the election of 240 opposition deputies in 1988. After that, presidential programs were no longer rubber-stamped, but were open to real debate for the first time. President Salinas's reform programs, then, were slowed down, and for the first time, the Mexican government experienced some gridlock. In 1997, PRI lost a majority in the Chamber of Deputies when 261 deputies were elected from opposition parties. The election of 2000 gave PRI a bare plurality – but far from a majority – in both houses. In the election of 2006, PRI's support slipped in both houses, PAN gained some seats in the Chamber of Deputies, and PRD made big gains in both houses. In 2012, PRI' representation in the Chamber of Deputies slipped by 32 seats, and in the Senate, the party gained two, resulting in 52 seats out of 128. In 2018, Obrador's Morena Party captured the most seats in both houses, but did not earn a clear majority in either.

The developing multi-party system also encouraged the implementation in 2002 of an election law that required political parties to sponsor women candidates. Parties must run at least 30% women for both lists for the proportional representation election, as well as candidates for the single-member districts/states. In an effort to regain some of its lost clout, PRI has exceeded the requirements by instituting a 50% quota for its candidates. A minor party – Social-Democrats and Farmers – ran Patricia Mercado in 2006 for the presidency, and in 2012, PAN's candidate was Josefina Vásquez Mota, who came in third, with just over 25% of the vote.

As a competitive multiparty system begins to emerge, the Mexican Congress has become a more important forum for various points of view. Competitive elections are the rule in many locales, and the number of "safe seats" is declining. The legislature has challenged recent presidents on a number of occasions, but whether or not a true system of checks and balances is developing is still unclear.

SENATE SEATS – ELECTION OF 2018*

MORENA	42.97%
PAN	18.75%
PRI	10.16%
PRD	6.25%

* Several other parties – Citizens' Movement, Ecologist Green Party, Labor Party Social Encounter Party, and New Alliance Party –won between 1 and 5 seats each.

CHAMBER OF DEPUTIES SEATS ELECTION OF 2018*

MORENA	38.2%
PAN	16.4%
LABOR (PT)	12.2%
SOCIAL ENCOUNTER (PES)	11%
PRI	9%
PRD	4.2%

* Other parties – Citizens Movement, Ecologist Green Party, and New Alliance – won small percentages of seats.

Judiciary

A strong judicial branch is essential if a country is to be ruled by law, not by the whim of a dictator. Mexico does not yet have an independent judiciary, nor does it have a system of judicial review. Like most other non-English speaking countries, it follows code law, not common law (see p. 29). Even though the Constitution of 1917 is still in effect, it is easily amended and does not have the same level of legitimacy as the U.S. Constitution does.

Mexico has both federal and state courts, but because most laws are federal, state courts have played a subordinate role. If states continue to become more independent from the central government, the state courts almost certainly will come to play a larger role.

The **Supreme Court** is the highest federal court, and on paper it has judicial review, but in reality, it almost never overrules an important government action or policy. Historically, then, the courts have been controlled by the executive branch, most specifically the president. As in the United States, judges are officially appointed for life. In practice, judges resign at the beginning of each sexenio, allowing the incoming president to place his loyalists on the bench as well as in the state houses, bureaucratic offices, and party headquarters.

The administration of **Ernesto Zedillo** (1994-2000) tried to strengthen the courts by emphasizing the rule of law. Increasing interest in human rights issues by citizens' groups and the media has put pressure on the courts to play a stronger role in protecting basic freedoms. Citizens and the government are increasingly resorting to the courts as a primary weapon against corruption, drugs, and police abuse. President Zedillo often refused to interfere with the courts' judgments, and Vicente Fox promised to work for an independent judiciary, although the results were disappointing to many people.

The strength of the judiciary is limited by the general perception that judges are corrupt, especially at the local level, where many decisions are made. In areas of Mexico where drug wars currently rage, many judges are afraid to rule against gang leaders for fear of reprisal, and others almost certainly are bribed into compliance. As part of a Calderón reform package, federal and state courts conducted oral trials, in which lawyers have to argue before the bench rather than simply push papers across a clerk's desk. It is hoped that the change will improve methods of gathering and presenting evidence in court. Calderón also pushed through a change in the criminal appeals system that makes it harder for the accused to frivolously block or delay prosecutions. In 2011, the president stated that his long-term goal is for "judicial institutions that Mexico has too long lacked and without which the advance of criminals is understandable – and a future for Mexico is incomprehensible."

The fate of the court system under Obrador is uncertain, since he openly scorns it. As mayor of Mexico City, he refused to enforce rulings from the supreme court, including one to clear a bottling factory taken over by striking workers. He explained his behavior by asserting that the court lacked "social sensitivity". Obrador's commitment to checks and balances, including an independent court system, is far from clear.

Military

Military generals dominated Mexican politics throughout the 19th century and into the early 20th century. The military presided over the chaos, violence, and bloodshed of the era following the Revolution of 1910, and it was the competitiveness of its generals that caused PRI to dramatically cut back the military's political power. Although all presidents of Mexico were generals until the 1940s, they still acted to separate the military from politics. Even critics of PRI admit that gaining government control of the military is one of the party's most important accomplishments. Over the past fifty years, the military has developed into a relatively disciplined force with a professional officer corps.

Much credit for de-politicizing the military belongs to Plutarco Calles and Lazaro Cardenas, who introduced the idea of rotating the generals' regional commands. By moving generals from one part of the country to another, the government kept them from building regional bases of power. And true to the old patron-client system, presidents traded favors with military officers – such as business opportunities – so that generals could enjoy economic, if not political power.

GOVERNMENT INSTITUTIONS IN MEXICO

EXECUTIVE BRANCH	LEGISLATIVE BRANCH	JUDICIAL BRANCH
First non-PRI president elected in 2000, also in 2006 President still has a great deal of power through informal political ties Large, poorly paid bureaucracy, susceptible to bribes	Chamber of Deputies (500 members) Senate (128 members) Deputies and senators come from all three major political parties Number of women legislators has increased since 2002 implementation of law that requires parties to sponsor women candidates.	The Supreme Court is the highest court, and on paper has judicial review. Traditionally judges have been controlled by the president, resigning at the end of each sexenio. In recent years, attempts have been made to strengthen, but judges still are seen as corrupt.

The tendency to dole out favors to the military almost certainly has led to the existence of strong ties between military officers and the drug trade. In recent years, the military has been heavily involved in efforts to combat drug trafficking, and rumors abound about deals struck between military officials and drug barons. In 2009, Calderón created an entirely new police force that formed part of Mexico's first national crime information system, which stores the fingerprints of everyone arrested in the country. This force has assumed the role of the army in several parts of the country. The federal police enjoy greater public confidence than do state and local police, and President Peña Nieto promised to draft 40,000 soldiers to serve on the federal police force.

POLICIES AND ISSUES

Mexican government and politics has changed dramatically since the 1980s. Today Mexico has taken serious steps toward becoming a democracy, but the economy that had shown signs of improvement since the collapse of 1982 took a nosedive after the global economic crisis in 2008. The country is trying to move from regional vulnerability to global reliability, but those connections to other parts of the world made the Mexican economy responsive to the contraction of the U.S. economy.   Stubborn problems remain, both economic and political. PRI has been entangled with the government so long that creating branches that operate independently is a huge task. The gap between the rich and poor is still wide in Mexico, despite the growth of the middle class in the north. President Peña Nieto faces a big challenge in shaping Mexico's relationship with the United States and in controlling violence associated with the drug trade. How does Mexico retain the benefits of trade and cooperation with its neighbor to the north, and yet steer its own independent course?

The Economy

Mexico's economic development has had a significant impact on social conditions in the country. Overall, despite the economic downtown of 2008, the standard of living has improved greatly since the 1940s. Rates of infant mortality, literacy, and life expectancy have steadily improved. Health and education services have expanded, despite severe cutbacks after the economic crisis of 1982 and again in 2008.

"The Mexican Miracle"

Between 1940 and 1960 Mexico's economy grew as a whole by more than 6% a year. Industrial production rose even faster, averaging nearly 9% for most of the 1960s. Agriculture's share of total production dropped from 25% to 11%, while that of manufacturing rose from 25% to 34%. All this growth occurred without much of the inflation that has plagued many other Latin American economies, but it meant that large numbers of people have moved from rural to urban areas, creating new urban issues.

Problems

- **A growing gap between the rich and the poor** was a major consequence of rapid economic growth. Relatively little attention was paid to the issues of equality and social justice that historically had led to revolutions in the first place. Social services programs were limited at best. From 1940 to 1980, Mexico's income distribution was among the most unequal of all the LDCs, with the bottom 40% of the population never earning more than 11% of total wages. Today inequality has lessened slightly, but it is still an important issue.

- **Rapid and unplanned urbanization** accompanied the growth. In recent years, millions have migrated to cities, and as a result, the Federal District, Guadalajara, and other major cities became urban nightmares, with many people living in huge shantytowns with no electricity, running water, or sewers. Poor highway planning and no mass transit means that traffic congestion is among the worst in the world. Pollution from cars and factories make Mexico City's air so dirty that it is unsafe to breathe.

The Crisis

In its effort to industrialize, the Mexican government borrowed heavily against expectations that oil prices would remain high forever. Much of the rapid growth was based on oil, especially since Mexico's production began increasing just as that of OPEC countries was decreasing during the early 1970s. When the price of oil plummeted in 1982, so did Mexico's economy. By 1987, Mexico's debt was over $107 billion, making it one of the most heavily indebted countries in the world. The debt represented 70% of Mexico's entire GNP.

Reform

President Miguel de la Madrid began his sexenio in 1982 with all of these economic problems before him. He began a dramatic reform program that reflected the values of the new *tecnico* leaders. This program continued through the presidencies of Salinas and Zedillo, and it brought about one of the most dramatic economic turnarounds in modern history.

- **Sharp cuts in government spending** – According to agreements with the International Monetary Fund, the World Bank, the U.S. government, and private banks, Mexico began an austerity plan that greatly reduced government spending. Hundreds of thousands of jobs were cut, subsidies to government agencies were slashed, and hundreds of public enterprises were eliminated.

- **Debt reduction** – Debt still continues to plague Mexico, although the U.S. spearheaded a multinational plan to reduce interest rates on loans and allow more generous terms for their repayment. Mexico still pays an average of about $10 billion a year in interest payments.

- **Privatization** – In order to allow market forces to drive the Mexican economy, Madrid's government decided to give up much of its economic power. Most importantly, the government privatized many public enterprises, especially those that were costing public money. President Salinas returned the banks to the private sector in 1990. By the late 1980s a "mini Silicon Valley" was emerging in Guadalajara where IBM, Hewlett-Packard, Wang, and other tech firms set up factories and headquarters. Special laws – like duty-free importing of components – and cheap labor encouraged U.S. companies to invest in Mexican plants.

Today, Mexico's economy has diversified significantly, and is not as dependent on oil production. Still, the problems persist today, particularly those of income inequality, urban planning, and pollution. As a businessman, Vicente Fox made a campaign promise to oversee a 7% annual growth in the Mexican economy during his sexenio, but his hopes fell short. Between 2001 and 2003, Mexico's economic slowdown can be partially explained by the U.S. recession after the September 11 attacks. In 2004, the economy grew by 4.1%, but an estimated 40% of the Mexican population was still below the poverty line, despite some new initiatives by the government to provide benefits and pensions for those not covered by jobs in the formal economy.

Energy Reform and the Economic Crisis of 2008

When Felipe Calderón became president in 2006, oil production in Mexico was falling off, largely because little exploration for new oil fields had taken place for decades. PEMEX was a large, inefficient para-statal that provided almost 40% of the budget, but its technical capabilities had atrophied. President Fox had tried to privatize PE-MEX, but had met with too much resistance, so Calderón tried another approach. In early 2008, he announced a reform to give PEMEX greater budgetary autonomy and strengthen government regulations on the oil industry. However, his plan also enabled private contracting of refining, and would allow PEMEX to hire private contractors for the distribution and storage of refined products. The reform included a large bond issue to raise money for two new refineries. His plan met opposition in the legislature, especially from PRD, whose leaders accused Calderón of privatizing PEMEX. However, the president's plans were foiled by an even deeper problem: the effects of the global economic crisis of 2008.

By early 2009, the Mexican economy was shrinking quickly, with experts estimating the rate at 5.9% reduction during the first quarter of 2009, four times the predicted fall in Latin America as a whole. The main cause was the nation's close integration with the United States, since exports across the Rio Grande River are equivalent to a fifth of Mexico's GDP. These exports fell by 36% in 2008 as demand from the U.S. dried up. U.S. investors also froze their operations in Mexico as they tried to resuscitate their businesses at home, which in turn caused a depreciation of the Mexican peso. The recent explosive growth of Brazil has led the Inter-American Development Bank, the biggest lender in the region, to describe a "two speed" Latin America, in which economies, such as Mexico, which do most of their trade with developed countries, lag behind those, such as Brazil, that have forged links with emerging markets. Whereas Brazil sent 16% of its exports in 2009 to fellow BRICs (Russia, India, and China), only 3% of Mexico's exports went to the BRICs. Once again, Mexico has found that events to the north dictate the country's economic development, keeping it from charting the independent course so necessary for its prosperity.

During the 2012 election campaign, Enrique Peña Nieto promised to reform PEMEX, not to privatize it, but to allow joint ventures with private firms. PRD has vowed to keep PEMEX's monopoly intact, and Obrador prepared to take his populist battle against energy reform to the streets. In recent years, PEMEX has been plagued by deficits and two explosions in 2013, one of which claimed 37 lives. In late 2014, the government began the process of inviting private oil companies to bid for new oil exploration blocks. The fate of PEMEX is unclear, with the election of Obrador in 2018.

Telecommunications Reform

In June 2013, Peña Nieto signed into law a far-reaching reform of the telecommunications and broadcast industries that aimed to curb the market power of big companies in order to increase competition and investment in the industries. The law created a new regulatory body, Ifetel, which has the power to regulate and even force dominant players to sell assets. According to the Wall Street Journal, the company expected to be the most affected by new regulations is America Movil, which is controlled by billionaire Carlos Slim, and has 70% of the country's wireless customers and more than 70% of the fixed phone lines. Televisa SAB, which controls close to 70% of the broadcast television market, and TV Azteca SAB, which has around 30%, faced competition from two new planned digital networks.

Foreign Policy

The crisis that began in 1982 clearly indicated that a policy of encouraging more Mexican exports and opening markets to foreign goods was essential. In the years after 1982 the government relaxed restrictions on foreign ownership of property and reduced and eliminated tariffs. The government courted foreign investment and encouraged Mexican private industry to produce goods for export. Mexico's foreign policy is still more concerned with the United States than with any other country, but in recent years Mexican leaders have asserted themselves in international forums, such as the United Nations and the World Trade Organization.

Maquiladora

A manufacturing zone was created in the 1960s in northern Mexico just south of the border with the United States. Workers in this *maquiladora* district have produced goods primarily for consumers in the U.S., and a number of U.S. companies have established plants in the zone to transform imported, duty-free components or raw materials into finished industrial products. Industrialization of the zone was promoted by the North American Free Trade Agreement (NAFTA), a treaty signed in 1995 by Mexico, the United States, and Canada, that eliminated barriers to free trade among the three countries. Today hundreds of thousands of workers are employed in the *maquiladora* district, accounting for over 20% of Mexico's entire industrial labor force. U.S. companies have been criticized for avoiding employment and environmental regulations imposed within the borders of the U.S., hiring young women for low pay and no benefits who work in buildings that are environmentally questionable.

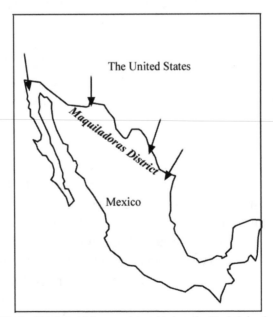

The Maquiladoras District. This industrial zone exists right along the Mexican border with the United States.

Trade Agreements

Since the mid-1980s, Mexico has entered into many trade agreements
and organizations in order to globalize its economy and pay its way
out of debt:

- **GATT/WTO** – In 1986, Mexico joined the General Agreement on Tariffs and Trade (GATT), a multilateral agreement
  that attempts to promote freer trade among countries. The
  World Trade Organization was created from this agreement,
  and Mexico has been an active member of the WTO. Under
  WTO agreements, Mexico has expanded the diversity of its
  exports beyond oil, and has developed new trade relationships
  with countries other than the United States.

- **NAFTA** – The North American Free Trade Agreement was
  signed by Mexico, Canada, and the United States. Its goal
  is to more closely integrate the economies by eliminating tariffs and reducing restrictions so that companies can expand
  into all countries freely. Mexico hopes to stimulate its overall
  growth, enrich its big business community, and supply jobs for
  Mexicans in new industries. U.S. firms gain from access to
  inexpensive labor, raw materials, and tourism, as well as new
  markets to sell and invest in. Mexico runs the risk of again
  being overshadowed by the United States, but hopes that benefits will outweigh problems. The fate of NAFTA is uncertain,
  with American President Donald Trump threatening to either
  do away with or significantly revise the agreement. Obrador's
  position on NAFTA is also far from clear.

Immigration Policy

Unlike the agreement among member nations of the European Union,
the NAFTA agreement currently does not allow free flow of labor
across borders. Early in his term, Vicente Fox pushed hard to solve
tensions between the United States and Mexico regarding immigration policy. Fox proposed a bold immigration initiative that included
a guest worker program, amnesty for illegal immigrants, an increase
in visas issued, and movement to an eventual open border. The plan

would have allowed Mexicans to work legally in the U.S., while amnesty for illegal immigrants would have eventually offered a green card as well as legal citizenship to over three million undocumented Mexicans living in the U.S. In exchange, Fox pledged to tighten the Mexican border to prevent additional illegal immigration. President George W. Bush responded positively to Fox's initiatives, but the plan fell through after the September 11, 2001 attacks in the United States. President Bush reevaluated the security risks involved with Fox's plan, and the whole thing unraveled within weeks, and only recently came to life again.

In 2014, after Congress took no action on immigration policy, U.S. President Barack Obama announced by executive order that his administration would provide up to four million undocumented immigrants the ability to live and work in the U.S. without fear of deportation. However, a conservative legal campaign blocked the president's actions while judges considered their legality. The delay has held up the implementation of the plan, and it appears as if Obama will leave office before the courts rule.

Another immigration issue has to do with the route that Central American migrants take through Mexico on their way to the United States. In 2014, Mexican authorities began cracking down on those following "La Bestia" (the Beast), a train route that goes through Mexico south to north. The plan included replacing large stretches of track so that trains go faster, making them harder for migrants to board.

Drug Trafficking

Drug trafficking between Mexico and the United States has been a major problem for both countries for many years. The drug trade has spawned corruption within the Mexican government, so that officials have often been bribed to look the other way or even actively participate in the trade. The depth of drug-related problems was evident in early 2005, when the government staged a raid on its own maximum-security prison, *La Palma*, in an effort to regain control of the prison from drug lords who had engineered the murder of a prominent fellow inmate. Fox vowed to stamp out the corruption and some major arrests were made, but the problem remained far from resolved at the end of his sexenio.

When Felipe Calderón took office he stepped up the war on drugs, sending troops and federal agents into areas where gangs control local officials. He also promised to remake the nation's police departments, root out corrupt officers, and support legislation that makes it possible for the local police to investigate drug rings. The immediate reaction has been one of the worst waves of drug-related violence ever. The number of brutal murders, often of policemen, has increased significantly. One cause of the violence is a fierce competition between competing drug rings that want exclusive control of very lucrative smuggling routes between Mexico and the United States.

Calderón reacted to these problems by turning to the army, sending thousands of troops to patrol the streets in the most troubled cities. It was supposed to be an emergency measure, but the troops have remained, and some have criticized them for brutality against ordinary citizens. In May 2008 the violence reached a fevered pitch after Mexico's police chief was gunned down as he arrived home late at night. Other top officials have also been assassinated, including the police second-in-command in the border town of Juárez and a top policeman from Mexico City. This targeting of senior law-enforcement officials is unprecedented in Mexican history. U.S. President Bush pushed for government assistance to Mexico to fight the drug wars, but the funding became bogged down in the U.S. Congress. On a visit to Mexico in early 2009, U.S. Secretary of State Hillary Clinton frankly admitted that America's "insatiable demand for illegal drugs fuels the drug trade" and that "our inability to prevent weapons from being illegally smuggled across the border to arm these criminals causes the deaths of police officers, soldiers, and civilians" in Mexico. She promised Black Hawk helicopters for the Mexican police, but funding for them was cut by the U.S. Congress.

By 2011, the U.S. widened its role by sending new C.I.A. operatives and retired military personnel to a military base in Mexico, where security officials from both countries work side by side in collecting information about drug cartels and helping plan operations. In another operation, the U.S. Drug Enforcement Administration and a Mexican counter-narcotics police unit collaborated on an operation that led to the arrest of a prominent drug trafficker. However, in 2010 the murder rate in Mexico was 17 per 100,000 people, up more than two-thirds from 2007. The fighting was concentrated in a few areas, most notably in Ciudad Juárez, a center of *maquila* factories just across the border from El Paso, Texas. There the murder rate had climbed to one of the highest in the world as two cartels battle for control of the border crossing. Since 2010, many drug lords have been killed or arrested, and in 2012, the national murder rate fell for the first time since 2008. President Peña Nieto vowed to reduce it by half during his six-year tenure.

After taking office in December 2012, President Peña Nieto moved to end the widespread access that U.S. security agencies had in Mexico to tackle the violence that affects both sides of the border. Since then U.S. law enforcement has had to go through Mexico's federal Interior Ministry, the agency that controls security and domestic policy.

Despite these efforts, a tragedy occurred in 2014 with the disappearance of 43 students in the southwestern state of Guerrero. The Mexican attorney-general's office held that the students had been handed over by local police to a drug gang, which killed them, apparently because they believed the students were members of a rival gang. The government's report was disputed, and as of 2018, the murders were still under investigation. By the end of Peña Nieto's term in 2018, the murder rate had gone even higher, and the frustration levels with the government's inability to solve the problems led voters to turn to Obrador for leadership.

Ethnic Rebellions

In his first year in office, Fox made several efforts to negotiate with the **Zapatistas** to settle their dispute with the government. The **EZLN** (Zapatista National Liberation Front) began in 1994 in the southern state of Chiapas in protest to the signing of the NAFTA treaty. Zapatistas saw the agreement as a continuation of the exploitation of voracious landowners and corrupt PRI bosses. Their army captured four towns, including a popular tourist destination, and they demanded jobs, land, housing, food, health, education, independence, freedom, democracy, justice and peace. Their rebellion spread, and Zapatista supporters wear black ski masks to hide their identity from the government. Today the rebellion is technically still on, but has quieted down considerably.

The Zapatista rebellion was based on ethnicity – the Amerindian disaffection for the mestizo, urban-based government. It has since spread to other areas and ethnicities, and it represents a major threat to Mexico's political stability. The 2006 uprising in Oaxaca is another indication that hostilities toward the rich and the government are still quite strong in the south, particularly toward PRI leaders.

Democracy and Electoral Reform

Part of the answer to Mexico's economic and foreign policy woes lies in the development of democratic traditions within the political system. Mexico's tradition of authoritarianism works against democratization, but modernization of the economy, the political value of populism, and democratic revolutionary impulses work for it. One of the most important indications of democracy is the development of competitive, clean elections in many parts of the country. The Mexican political system went through a series of reforms during the 1990s that solidly directed the country toward democracy.

The **IFE (Instituto Federal Electoral)** was created as an independent regulatory body to safeguard honest and accurate election results. Although it was dominated by PRI in its early years, in recent elections it appears to be operating as it should. Some election reforms include:

- Campaign finance restrictions – laws that limit contributions to campaigns

- Critical media coverage, as media is less under PRI control

- International watch teams, as Mexico has tried to convince other countries that elections are fair and competitive

- Election monitoring by opposition party members

The 1994 campaign for the presidency got off to a very bad start when PRI candidate Luis Donaldo Colosio was assassinated in Tijuana. PRI quickly replaced him with Ernesto Zedillo, but the old specters of violence and chaos threatened the political order. The incumbent president's brother was implicated in the assassination, and high officials were linked to drug trafficking. Despite this trouble, Zedillo stepped up to the challenge, and PRI won the election handily. Many observers believe that the elections of 1994 and 2000 have been the most competitive, fair elections in Mexico's history. The election of 2000 broke all precedents when a PAN candidate – Vicente Fox – won the presidency, finally displacing the 71-year dominance of PRI.

The controversial election of 2006 was clearly competitive, but it also threatened to tear the fragile base of democracy apart. Obrador questioned the very legitimacy of the process, and the strong support he received from his followers is evidence that instability is still a part of the Mexican political system. However, the fact that the election tribunal followed the process set by law is a step toward becoming a liberal democracy. Members of Obrador's own party – the PRD – eventually came to criticize him for his behavior. Even more significant is the eventual acceptance by most Mexican citizens of its decisions, evidence that the country successfully passed through the crisis.

During the 2013 state and local election campaigns, violence broke out that resulted in the death of six candidates, with another wounded and numerous assaults of family members and party and campaign officials. The violence was an embarrassment for Peña Nieto's new government, and opposition leaders called on the president to put the army in the streets in some states to protect voting procedures and voters. Most of the killings took place in small towns, which are less protected and more vulnerable to actions by drug and organized-crime groups. Whereas the motives for the killings are murky, they continue Mexico's tradition of violence associated with political campaigns.

The election of 2018 brought Andres Manuel Lopez Obrador to the presidency, reflecting voter disillusionment with the government, violence, and deeply embedded corruption. The traditional party system was upended, as citizens hoped that the new leader would solve these problems.

What will the future bring? Will Mexico be able to sustain a strong, stable economy? Has the political system fully emerge from its peasant-based patron-client system and authoritarianism as a modern democracy? Will more social equality be granted to peasants and city workers? Many observers await the answers to these questions, including people in less developed countries that look to Mexico as an example for development. More powerful countries – particularly the United States – realize that international global politics and economies are tied to the successes of countries like Mexico. Despite the instabilities of its past, Mexico does have strong traditions, a well-developed sense of national pride, many natural resources, and a record of progress, no matter how uneven.

IMPORTANT TERMS AND CONCEPTS

Amerindians
Calderón, Felipe
camarillas
Chamber of Deputies, Senate
co-optation
Cardenas, Cuauhtemoc
Cardenas, Lazaro
caudillos
Chiapas rebellion
corporatism (state and neo)
Cristeros Rebellion
dependency
Diaz, Porfirio
ejidos
election reform (in Mexico)
EZLN
Father Hidalgo
Federal Election Commission
Fox, Vicente
GATT
GNP per capita
HDI
IFE
import substitution
Juarez, Benito
mestizos
"Mexican Miracle"
NAFTA
neoliberalism

Obrador, Andres Manuel Lopez
para-statals
patron-client system
PEMEX
pendulum theory
plurality (first past the post)/proportional representation electoral
systems
Pact for Mexico
PAN
politicos
Porfiriato
PPP
PRD
PRI
proportional representation in Mexico
Santa Anna
sexenio
technicos
Villa, Pancho
WTO
Zapata, Emiliano
Zapatistas
Zedilla, Ernesto

Mexico Questions

1. According to dependency theory, less developed countries

A) should follow the western model of economic development
B) are blocked by the fact that industrialized countries exploit them
C) must devalue old traditions
D) control the corruption of their leaders
E) should mix their economies with some elements of capitalism and some of socialism

2. A state that progresses from procedural democracy to substantive democracy through democratic consolidation is said to experience

A) compressed modernity
B) westernization
C) political liberalization
D) democratic corporatism
E) economic liberalization

3. The netwok of camarillas that characterized the Mexican political system throughout most of the 20th century was a version of

A) patron-clientelism
B) neoliberalism
C) populism
D) regional autonomy
E) para-statism

4. Which of the following is an accurate description of Mexico's population distribution?

A) Mexico is one of the most sparsely populated states in Latin America.
B) Mexico is urbanizing rapidly, since many people have moved to cities from rural areas.
C) Most Mexicans live in the northern part of the country, close to the U.S. border.
D) Most Mexicans live in the southern part of the country, especially the Yucatan Peninsula.
E) A vast majority of Mexicans live in coastal areas.

5. Since the 1980s, both Mexico and China have experienced significant

A) privatization of the economy
B) political revolutions
C) liberalization of the political system
D) progress in containing pollution and other environmental problems
E) regime changes

6. In comparison to government bureaucrats in Mexico, government bureaucrats in Britain

A) have much more discretionary power
B) are generally more corrupt
C) must bow to the will of cabinet members
D) are less likely to stay in their jobs when a new cabinet is formed
E) are more likely to run for elected office after several years of servic

Questions 7 and 8 are based on the following chart:

COMPARATIVE ECONOMIC SECTORS
(as percentage of labor force by occupation)

Country	Primary (Agriculture)	Secondary (Industry)	Tertiary (Services)
China	28.3%	29.3%	42.4%
Iran	16.3%	35.1%	48.6%
Mexico	13.4%	24.%	61.9%
Nigeria	70%	10%	20%
Russia	9.4%	27.6%	63%
United Kingdom	1.3%	15.2%	83.5%
United States	.7%	20.3%	79.1%

Source: *CIA World Factbook* 2011-2016 (except Nigeria 1999)

7. According to the chart above, the best example of a post-industrial country is

A) China
B) Mexico
C) Nigeria
D) Russia
E) the United Kingdom

8. According to the chart, the least industrialized country is

A) China
B) Iran
C) Mexico
D) Nigeria
E) Russia

9. In China and Mexico, clientelism is almost always accompanied by

A) corruption
B) privatization of the economy
C) growth of the GNP
D) neo-corporatism
E) higher HDI scores

10. An important similarity between the Revolution of 1910 in Mexico and the Revolution of 1911 in China was that both revolutions

A) were led by Communists
B) were led by populists
C) resulted in years of chaos
D) quickly resulted in a one-party state
E) involved conflict with the Catholic Church

11. One reason that it is difficult to categorize Mexico as a liberal democracy is that

A) little political liberalization has taken place
B) little economic liberalization has taken place
C) no competitive party system exists
D) elections are as corrupt as they were when PRI dominated the country
E) consistent democratic practices are relatively new, only dating back to about 1988

12. Both Mexico and Russia have political systems characterized by

A) a federalist structure
B) post-industrialism
C) high levels of transparency
D) democratic consolidation
E) parliamentary structure

13. Like the Federation Council in Russia, the Senate in Mexico is primarily intended to represent

A) different ethnicities
B) urban areas
C) different regions
D) rural areas
E) lower social classes

14. Which of the following is an accurate comparison of Chinese and Mexican judicial systems?

A) The Mexican Constitution provides for judicial review; the Chinese Constitution does not.
B) Both systems have judicial review, but both are characterized by corruption.
C) In China, the president dominates the judiciary; in Mexico, the president does not.
D) Neither judicial system has a Supreme Court.
E) In China, the judiciary has the power to overturn legislation; in Mexico, it does not.

15. Which of the following is the most reliable indication that a country is a "failed state"?

A) a low GNP
B) government corruption
C) a civil war
D) persistent anarchy
E) an authoritarian government

16. Britain's upper house of the legislature differs from Mexico's upper house in that representatives to Britain's upper house

A) have more political experience
B) are elected officials
C) represent regions of the country
D) have to be approved by the head of state
E) are non-elected officials

17. The most important single explanation for Mexico's percentage of women in the lower house of the legislature is that the country has

A) a political culture that de-emphasizes traditional values
B) more women who are interested in politics
C) a patron-client system that encourages participation by all
D) well established democratic values and beliefs
E) a law that requires political parties to sponsor women candidates

18. For most of the 20th century, both Russia and Mexico were ruled by

A) democratically elected presidents
B) one political party
C) military dictators
D) parliamentary government
E) state corporatists

19. The main reason for the signing of the North American Free Trade Agreement was to provide support in Mexico, the United States, and Canada for

A) the development of a common currency
B) a more uniform pricing of products and wages for labor
C) a more intense trade with Europe
D) a reduction in tariffs and trade restrictions
E) the economic unification of the Western Hemisphere

20. Which of the following is the most important reason that the gap between the rich and the poor has grown in Mexico since the mid-20th century?

A) economic dependency on the U.S.
B) escalating drug traffic
C) a decline in the quality of public education
D) rapid economic growth
E) lack of populist traditions

21. Britain, Russia, and Mexico all do NOT have a well-developed

A) electoral system
B) system for judicial review
C) multi-party systems
D) civil society
E) system of linkage institutions

22. The political systems of Britain and Mexico both have

A) More than two parties competing in popular elections
B) two political parties dominating the legislature
C) one party dominating the executive branch
D) parties of power that dominate both the executive and legislative branches
E) coalition parties forming a government

23. Mexico's inclusion of proportional representation in their electoral system directly resulted in

A) a more powerful legislative branch
B) a clear majority in both legislative houses for PAN
C) three well-represented parties in both legislative houses
D) a rubber-stamp legislature
E) growing representation for minority parties in the lower house only

24. The political systems of China, Mexico, and Russia all have

A) legitimacy primarily based on a written constitution
B) code law systems
C) prime ministers
D) active military participation in the policymaking process
E) separation of power among government branches

25. Which of the following is the BEST explanation for why PRI succeeded in monopolizing political power in Mexico after its establishment in 1929?

A) PRI leaders outmaneuvered leaders from other parties, such as PAN and PRD.
B) PRI leaders took advantage of Mexico's independence from Spain to establish a power base.
C) Mexican elites were willing to join together as PRI leaders in order to alleviate the chaos and violence of the early 20th century.
D) By 1929, the Catholic Church in Mexico had lost influence, and could no longer control the government.
E) PRI had the support of the United States government, and so was able to defeat the competing parties of the day.

26. Citizens of Mexico directly elect their

A) president only
B) president and Chamber of Deputies representatives only
C) Chamber of Deputies representatives and senators only
D) local and state officials only
E) president, Chamber of Deputies representatives, senators, and local and state officials

27. Which of the following is the BEST description of the societal cleavages in Mexico between north and south?

A) Northerners are generally more prosperous than southerners, but they are ethnically similar.
B) Southerners are more likely to be Amerindian with less European ethnicity than northerners.
C) Northerners are more likely to be engaged in agriculture as a main occupation than southerners are.
D) Northerners are less likely to support a market-based economy than southerners are.
E) Northerners are generally less educated than southerners are.

28. Which of the following is an accurate contrast of the democratization process in Mexico with the democratization process in Russia?

A) Mexico's democratization process started much later than Russia's.
B) Mexico's democratization process was highly decentralized; Russia's was centralized in Moscow.
C) Russia's democratization process was violent and bloody; Mexico's was not.
D) Since 2000 Mexico's legislative and presidential elections have been more competitive than Russia's elections.
E) Since the early 1990s, Mexico's legislative and presidential elections have been markedly more corrupt than Russia's elections.

29. Which of the following is an accurate description of the electoral system for selecting representatives to the Mexican Chamber of Deputies?

A) All deputies are chosen to represent single member districts.
B) All deputies are chosen by proportional representation.
C) All deputies are chosen by a plurality system, but they do not represent single member districts.
D) Some deputies are chosen to represent single member districts, and some are chosen by proportional representation.
E) All deputies are chosen in a 2-round election with many candidates in the 1st round, and the top two vote getters in the 2nd round.

30. Which of the following is an accurate comparison of the British and Mexican political systems?

A) The British system is characterized by separation of powers among branches; the Mexican system is not.
B) The British system has no checks and balances among branches; the Mexican system theoretically has checks and balances.
C) The British system is a presidential democracy; the Mexican system is a parliamentary democracy.
D) The British system uses proportional representation for elections; the Mexican system uses first-past-the-post for all elections.
E) The British system has a unicameral legislature; the Mexican system has a bicameral legislature.

Free-Response Question:

(a) Describe one similarity and one difference between a procedural democracy and a substantive democracy.

(b) Describe one feature of the Mexican political system that provides support that it is a procedural democracy.

(c) Describe two features of the Mexican political system that provide support that it is a substantive democracy.

CHAPTER SEVEN:
GOVERNMENT AND POLITICS
IN IRAN

"This is the voice of Iran, the voice of the true Iran, the voice of the Islamic Revolution."

Iran National Radio
February 11, 1979

This dramatic announcement came on Iran's national radio the first evening after the coup d'état that deposed Muhammad Reza Shah, who had followed his father in ruling Iran with an iron fist for more than half a century. The announcement struck fear into the hearts of many westerners who today see the 1979 Revolution in Iran as the beginning of a great modern conflict between western and Islamic civilizations. According to this line of reasoning, the events of 1979 started a fundamentalist movement that spread throughout the Islamic world and eventually culminated in the September 11, 2001 attacks on the World Trade Towers and the Pentagon in the United States. For some political scientists, Samuel Huntington foresaw this situation in his 1993 article in *Foreign Affairs* magazine called, "The Clash of Civilizations."

This view of Iran's role in modern world politics, however, ignores the complexities of Iran's political culture, which was so apparent in the reactions within the country to recent presidential elections. Iran's identity is steeped in thousands of years of history that not only includes a deep attachment to Islam, but also a popular revolution in the early 20th century that resulted in a western-style constitution that was intact until 1979. These influences are still at odds today, and they shape the major challenges that face the political system. Is democracy incompatible with Islam, or is true Islam actually based on popular support? The first impulse leads Iran toward a **theocracy**, or a government ruled strictly by religion, and the second leads the country toward **secularization**, or the belief that religion and government should be separated. These political questions are complicated by Iran's developing economy that squarely places it in the global market, but is heavily reliant on one product. Iran is the second largest oil producer in the Middle East and the fourth largest in the world. Should these resources be controlled by clerics, or do economic matters require an expertise outside the realm of religious leaders?

In many ways, Iran is a unique addition to the AP Comparative Government and Politics course because it is the only one of the six countries that currently is governed as a theocracy. However, Iran shares a characteristic with Russia, China, Mexico, and Nigeria in its possession of that all-important modern resource – oil. Like Mexico, its economy may be labeled "developing" rather than "less-developed," as is the case for Nigeria. China also may be seen as having a rapidly "developing" economy. Similar to all the other five countries, Iran's political system is multi-faceted, and cannot be boiled down simply to a monolithic representation of the Islamic world.

SOVEREIGNTY, AUTHORITY, AND POWER

An early Iranian concept of sovereignty may be traced to the days of the ancient Achemenian Empire (called Persia by the Greeks) that existed as the world's largest empire from its founding by Cyrus in the 6th century B.C.E. till its defeat some 200 years later. Iran's greatest rival was ancient Greece, and the two civilizations couldn't have been more different. Greece was divided into quarreling city-states, and its economy and transportation were heavily reliant on the sea. In contrast, Persia emerged from the dry lands north of the Persian Gulf and spread its power through highly centralized military leadership by land as far as the Aegean Sea, where its interests conflicted with those of the Greeks. The clash between two great civilizations may be seen as the first act of a drama that has played out over the centuries: West vs. East. Ironically, both civilizations were conquered by a Macedonian, Alexander the Great, but Alexander's affinity for Greece led him to spread its culture to lands that he conquered. Less well known is the fact that Alexander much admired the Persian political structure, and left it largely in place as he conquered those lands.

The Persian sovereigns were always hereditary military leaders who very much enjoyed the trappings of royalty. One king, Darius, built a magnificent capital at Persepolis, and joined his new city to many parts of the ancient world by an intricate system of roads that carried his armies all over and allowed people from many lands to pay tribute to him. His title was "The Great King, King of Kings, King in Persia, King of countries," and he referred to everyone, even the Persian nobility, as "my slaves." The king's authority was supported by a strong military as well as a state-sponsored religion, **Zoroastrianism**.

Although none of the rulers of empires that followed were able to centralize power so successfully as the Achemenians did, the stage was set for the authoritarian state. Zoroastrianism did not survive as a major religion, but it continued to be sponsored by rulers for centuries, including those of the Sassanid Dynasty (226-651 C.E.)

The Importance of Shiism

From the 7th to 16th centuries C.E., the geographical region of Iran had little political unity, and experienced numerous invasions, including that of Arabs, who brought Islam to the area. What emerged was a new glue that held the Persians together – not political, but religious in nature. As a result, even when their caliphate (an Islamic empire put in place by Arabs) was defeated by the mighty Mongols in the 13th century, the religion survived the chaos as the invaders converted to the religion of the conquered. Despite the changes in political leadership over the years, the religion of Islam has continued to be a vital source of identity for Iranians.

The brand of Islam that distinguishes Iran from its neighbors today – **Shiism** – was established as the state religion in the 16th century by Ismail, the founder of the Safavid Empire. Ismail and his *qizil-*

bash ("redheads," because of their colorful turbans) were supporters of this sect of Islam that had quarreled bitterly with **Sunni** Muslims for centuries. The division originated after the religion's founder, Muhammad, died without a designated heir, a significant problem since his armies had conquered many lands. The Sunnis favored choosing the caliph (leader) from the accepted leadership (the Sunni), but the Shiites argued that the mantle should be hereditary, and should pass to Muhammad's son-in-law, Ali. When Ali was killed in the dispute, the Shiite opinion became a minority one, but they kept their separate identity, and carried the belief that the true heirs of Islam were the descendants of Ali. These heirs, called **imams**, continued until the 9th century, when the 12th descendant disappeared as a child, only to become known as the "**Hidden Imam.**"

When Ismail established Iran as a Shiite state in the 16th century, he distinguished it as different from all Sunni states around him, a characteristic that still exists today. He gave political legitimacy to the belief that the "Hidden Imam" would eventually return, but until he did, the rulers of Iran stood in his place as the true heirs of Islam.

Legitimacy in the Modern State

To a remarkable extent, these historical influences still shape the modern state. Authoritarian leaders played an important role in the 20th century as the **Pahlavi** shahs ("King of Kings," or "shah in shah") ruled from 1925 to 1979. Their attempts to secularize the state, though, were undone by a charismatic leader – the **Ayatollah Khomeini** – who personified the union of political and religious interests from ancient days. His appeal may be likened to that of Ismail – the protector of the "true faith" that unites the Shiite religion with the power of the state. The Ayatollah was hailed as the "Leader of the Revolution, Founder of the Islamic Republic, Guide of the Oppressed Masses, Commander of the Armed Forces, and Imam of the Muslim World" – titles that blend the historical influences into the persona of one very powerful religious/political leader.

The Ayatollah Khomeini led the **Revolution of 1979**, an event that transformed the legitimacy of the state, anchoring it once again in principles of Shiism. The most important document that legitimizes the state today is the **Constitution of 1979**, along with the amendments of 1989, written during the last months of the Ayatollah Khomeini's life. The document and the 40 amendments are a highly complex mixture of theocracy and democracy. The preamble of the constitution reflects the importance of religion for the legitimacy of the state, affirming faith in God, Divine Justice, the Qur'an, the Prophet Muhammad, the Twelve Imams, and the eventual return of the Hidden Imam. Khomeini's doctrine of **jurist's guardianship** (which we'll define later) is included along with the other "divine principles."

In recent years two conflicting ideas – sovereignty of the people and divinely inspired clerical rule – have created a crisis of legitimacy in Iran. During the presidency of Muhammad Khatami (1997-2005), reformers who supported a democratic government came to the forefront, but with the election of Mahmoud Ahmadinejad in 2005, the conservatives who endorsed a theocracy took control. As a result, the rift between these two forces – conservatives and reformers – has illustrated the issue of just how a theocracy can also function as a democracy. The conflict is reflected in differences among clerics in the seminaries of **Qom** (a city south of Tehran) through their interpretations of the true meaning of jurist's guardianship.

Political Culture

Although the Safavid Empire was followed by centuries of weak political organization in Iran, Shiism continued as an important unifying thread to the political culture. However, the dynasty that followed – the Qajars – did not claim the imam's mantle, so Shiite clerical leaders came to be the main interpreters of Islam, and a separation between religion and politics developed. Although the Qajars were never very strong, they did not succumb to European imperialism, and they ruled until the 20th century. These complex historical influences – with roots in ancient times – have formed a multi-faceted political culture characterized by:

- **Authoritarianism, but not totalitarianism** – Beginning with the Safavid Empire, the central political leaders did not control all areas of individuals' lives. While the leaders claimed to be all-powerful, in reality they were not, and people became accustomed to paying attention to local officials and/or to leading their own lives within civil society.

- **Union of political and religious authority** – From the days of the ancient Persians, political and religious leaders were often one and the same. However, starting with the rule of the Qajars (1794-1925), the two types of authority were separated, only to be brought back together by the Revolution of 1979.

- **Shiism and *sharia* as central components** – Today almost 90% of all Iranians identify themselves as Shiite, a fact that links citizens to the government, which is officially a theocracy. Islamic law, the *sharia*, is an important source of legitimacy that the modern government particularly emphasizes.

- **Escape from European colonization** – Unlike most countries of Asia, Africa, and South America, Iran was never officially colonized by Europeans during the imperialist era of the 18th and 19th centuries. Although the area was heavily impacted by European power moves, imperialism did not have the same direct control of Iran that it had of Mexico and Nigeria.

- **Geographic limitations** – A great deal of Iran's land space is unusable for agriculture, with a vast central desert plain, and mountains to the north and northeast. Such geographic restrictions caused the early Persians to seek better lands to the west by expansion and conquest. In modern day, the population of Iran is unevenly distributed, with most living in cities and in the northwest, where the most arable land is located.

- **The influence of ancient Persia** – Differences between Iran and neighboring countries is not only based on Shiite vs. Sunni Islam. Even after the Arabs invaded Iran, people continued to speak Persian rather than Arabic, and many of their other cultural habits remained as well, including distinctive architecture, literary works, poetry, and decorative arts (such as "Persian rugs"). This identity shapes Iranian nationalism today.

The Geography of Iran.

- **Strong sense of Iranian nationalism** – Public opinion surveys show that Iranians in general have a stronger sense of national identity than do citizens of most Arab countries. As a result, they are more likely to identify themselves as Iranians first and Muslims second. Their Persian roots encourage the perception that Iran is a distinct culture, and pride in being Iranian is quite pronounced.

POLITICAL AND ECONOMIC CHANGE

Not surprisingly, with Iran's long, complex history, political and economic change has taken many forms, including both evolution and revolution. Politically, Persia established itself as the first large empire in world history – a military powerhouse with strong leaders and centralized governing structures. Despite the continuity of religious and political union, a gradual separation of religion from politics resulted in declining centralization of political power over time before the 20th century. The 20th century saw two revolutions: one in 1905-1909 that set democratic impulses in place, and one in 1979 that reunified religion with politics in the modern theocracy.

Economically, Iran has both suffered and benefited from natural resources. A lack of arable land has meant that the agricultural basis of the empires was never secure, and geographical location also caused Iran to emphasize trade by land. When world commerce turned to sea-based powers beginning in the 16th century, Iran was marginalized. Although Iran maintained its independence during the age of European imperialism, it did not prosper until its greatest modern natural resource was discovered. However, oil has brought its own set of economic problems to Iran – that of managing this necessary commodity for industrialization in such a way that it benefits not only the state but its people as well.

We will follow political and economic change through four eras: The Safavids (1501-1722); The Qajars (1794-1925); the Pahlavis (1925-1979); and the Islamic Revolution and Republic (1979-the Present).

The Safavids (1501-1722)

As discussed in the previous section, modern Iran traces its Shiite identity to the **Safavid Empire** that began in the 16th century. By the mid-17th century, the Safavids had succeeded in converting nearly 90% of their subjects to Shiism. Sunnism has survived to modern day among ethnic groups along the borders: Kurds in the northwest, Turkmen in the northeast, Baluchis in the southeast, and Arabs in the southwest. Despite their religious fervor, the Safavids tolerated the Sunnis, as well as smaller numbers of Jews, Zoroastrians, and Christians. They shared with other Muslim rulers a special regard for **People of the Book** – monotheistic people who subjected their lives to holy books similar to the Qur'an. They respected all these religions because they had their own books: Jews, the Torah; Christians, the Bible; and Zoroastrians, the Avesta.

The Safavids ruled from Isfahan, a Persian-speaking city, and most of their bureaucrats were Persian scribes. However, the Safavids had serious economic constraints. Trade routes from Iran to the ancient Silk

Route had broken up, and world trade had shifted to the Indian and Atlantic Oceans. Isfahan was far inland with little access to sea-based trade, and agricultural production was hampered by lack of arable land. These economic problems affected the Safavids' ability to rule, since they did not have money for a large bureaucracy or a standing army. As a result, they had to rely largely on local rulers to keep order and collect taxes. In theory, the Safavids claimed absolute power, but in reality they lacked a central state and had to seek the cooperation of semi-independent local leaders. Geographic features fragmented the empire, particularly the mountains, and many clerics lived safely outside the reach of the government. As a result of both political and economic factors, the monarchy became separated from society and lost a great deal of its power by 1722.

The Qajars (1794-1925)

The Safavid Empire ended when Afghan tribesmen invaded Isfahan in 1722. Iran was in disarray for more than a half century, until the land was finally conquered by another Turkish group, the **Qajars.** The Qajars moved the capital to Tehran, and they retained Shiism as the official state religion. However, the Qajar rule marked an important political change. Whereas the Safavids claimed to be descendants of the Twelve Imams, the Qajars obviously could not tie their legitimacy to such a link. As a result, the Shia clerical leaders could claim to be the main interpreters of Islam, and the separation between government and religion widened significantly.

Economically and politically Iran's power eclipsed during the 19th century. The Qajars ruled during the era of European imperialism, and they suffered land losses to the north and northwest to the growing power of Russia. They sold oil-drilling rights in the southwest to Britain, and they borrowed heavily from European banks to meet their considerable court expenses. By the end of the 19th century, the shah had led the country into serious debt, and many Iranians were upset by his lavish lifestyle.

These problems encouraged the **Constitutional Revolution of 1905-1909.** The revolution began with business owners and bankers demonstrating against the Qajars' move to hand over their customs collections to Europeans. Although the Qajars were attempting to settle their debts, middle-class people were fed up, particularly because they suspected that the shah would sacrifice paying domestic debts in order to repay European loans. In 1906 the merchants and local industrialists, affected by British liberalism, demanded a written constitution from the shah. The British, who had many business interests in Iran, encouraged the shah to concede, particularly since Iran did not have an army to effectively put down an insurrection.

The Constitution of 1906 was modeled after western ones, and included such democratic features as:

- Direct elections
- Separation of powers
- Laws made by an elected legislature
- Popular sovereignty
- A Bill of Rights guaranteeing citizens equality before the law, protections for those accused of crimes, and freedom of expression

The revolution sparked a debate about separation of religion from the government – the trend that the Qajars themselves had initiated. The constitution retained the monarchy, but it created a strong legislature to balance executive power. The new assembly was called the *Majles*, and seats were guaranteed to the "People of the Book": Jews, Christians, and Zoroastrians. The *Majles* not only had the authority to make and pass laws, but it also controlled cabinet ministers, who reported to the legislature, not the shah.

The Constitution of 1906 did not turn away from Shiism completely. Shiism was declared the official state religion, and only Shiites could hold cabinet positions. The constitution also created a **Guardian Council** of clerics that had the power to veto any legislation passed by the *Majles*.

These political reforms could do nothing, however, for Iran's economic woes. World events of the early 20th century led to Iran's division into three parts, with one piece for themselves, but another piece occupied by Russia, and another by Britain during World War I. By 1921 Iran was in political and economic disarray, with quarreling factions polarizing the *Majles* into an ineffective ruling body. The country was ready for a strong leader to deliver them from complete chaos.

The Pahlavis (1925-1979)

The Cossack Brigade had been one of the few areas of strength in the latter days of the Qajars, since it was the only force that resembled a real army. The brigade's commander, Colonel **Reza Khan**, carried out a successful coup d'état against the weakened political state in 1921, and declared himself shah-in-shah in 1925, establishing his own Pahlavi dynasty, using a name of an ancient language from Iran's glorious past.

Under Reza Shah, the *Majles* lost its power, and authoritarian rule was reestablished in Iran. He ruled with absolute authority until he turned over power to his son, **Muhammad Reza Shah** in 1941. Despite the fact that the Pahlavis reestablished order in Iran, democratic experimentation resulting from the Constitution of 1906 was not forgotten, and the second shah had to confront some democratic opposition. One group that challenged the shah was the communist **Tudeh** (Masses) **Party** that gained most of its support from working class trade unions. A second group was the **National Front**, led by **Muhammad Mosaddeq**, whose life influenced many later political leaders in Iran. The National Front drew its support from middle-class people who emphasized Iranian nationalism. Mosaddeq advocated nationalizing the British-owned company that monopolized Iran's oil business, and he also wanted to take the armed forces out from under the shah's control. Mosaddeq was elected prime minister in 1951, and his power grew so that the shah was forced to flee the country in 1953. Mosaddeq's career was cut short when the British struck back by co-sponsoring with the U.S. an overthrow of Mosaddeq, and restoring the shah to full power again. The U.S., ever mindful of keeping Soviet power contained in these Cold War days, was motivated to reinstall the shah as a pro-Western force in the Middle East. As a result, many Iranians came to see Britain and the U.S. as supporters of autocracy, and the shah as a weak pawn of foreign powers.

Economically, Iran was transformed into a **rentier state** under the Pahlavis because of the increasing amount of income coming in from oil. A rentier economy is heavily supported by state expenditure, while the state receives rent from other countries. Iran received an increasing amount of income by exporting its oil and leasing oil fields to foreign countries. The income became so great by the 1970s that the government no longer had to rely on internal taxes for its support, but paid most of its expenses through oil income. In short, the government didn't need the people anymore. Iran was quickly transformed into a one-product economy, and was heavily dependent on oil to keep the government afloat. Even though the shah adopted **import substitution industrialization** by encouraging domestic industries to provide products that the population needed, by 1979 oil and its associated industries made up a large percentage of Iran's GNP, and provided 97% of the country's foreign exchange.

The White Revolution

During their rule, the two Pahlavi shahs built a highly centralized state, the first since the ancient days of the Persian Empire. The state controlled banks, the national radio-television network, and most importantly, the National Iranian Oil Company. The armed forces grew into the fifth largest army in the world by 1979, and came to include a large navy and air force as well. The central bureaucracy gained control of local governments, and the *Majles* became a rubber-stamp legislature that let the shah rule as he pleased. Whereas Iran remained a religious state, its courts became fully secularized, with a European-style judicial system and law codes in place. Most controversial of all was the shah's **White Revolution** (so named because it was meant to counter communist, or "red" influences) that focused on land reform, with the government buying land from large absentee owners and selling it to small farmers at affordable prices. The purpose was to encourage farmers to become modern entrepreneurs with irrigation canals, dams, and tractors. The White Revolution secularized Iran further by extending voting rights to women, restricting polygamy, and allowing women to work outside the home.

Patronage and the Resurgence Party

Both Pahlavi shahs bolstered their own personal wealth first by seizing other people's property, and eventually through establishing the tax-exempt **Pahlavi Foundation**, a patronage system that controlled large companies that fed the pocketbooks of the shah and his supporters. In 1975, Muhammad Reza Shah announced the formation of the **Resurgence Party**, and declared Iran to be a one-party state which he headed. He replaced the Islamic calendar with a new one, and adopted two new titles: "Guide to the New Great Civilization," and "Light of the Aryans." The shah also dared to create a Religious Corps, whose duty it was to teach Iranian peasants "true Islam."

The Islamic Revolution and the Republic (1979-Present)

Great revolutions have shaken the world in many places since the late 18th century, and the causes and consequences of Iran's 1979 revolution are in some ways very similar to those in Russia, China, and Mexico in the 20th century. However, Iran's revolution is unique in that it was almost completely religious in nature. The dominant ideology was religion, whereas revolutions in Russia and China revolved around communism. Although the Catholic Church was very much involved in the revolutionary era (early 20th century) in Mexico, the Church did not direct the military, and PRI quickly sidelined the Church once the party gained control of the country. In Iran, the dominant ideology was Shiism, and the most important revolutionary leader was a cleric, who in turned ruled Iran for ten years following the revolution. Perhaps most significantly, Iran's revolution resulted in the establishment of a theocracy, while other revolutions often tried to break religious control of the government.

The shah's behavior disturbed Iranians largely because from many people's points of view, he overstepped the bounds of the political culture in three ways:

- He was perceived as being totalitarian, not just authoritarian, as shahs before the Pahlavis had been. Not unlike Porfirio Diaz in Mexico, the shah set about to create a patrimonial state, with patron-clientelism in place, but without any real input from interest groups. As a result, true corporatism did not develop.

- He broke the balance between the secular and the religious state by secularizing Iran too much too fast, at least from the point of view of the clergy.

COMPARATIVE RULING FAMILIES: IRAN

SAFAVIDS (1501-1722)	QAJARS (1794-1925)	PAHLAVIS (1925-1979)
Characteristics		
Converted Iranians to Shiism	Turkish invaders	Overthrew a representative
Tolerated "People of the Book"	Ruled from Tehran	government;
Ruled from Isfahan	Retained Shiism, but lost	Centralized power in shah
Relied on local rulers	hereditary claims to 12 Imams	Increasing oil income:
Rulers claimed to be	Dominated by other countries;	creation of the rentier state
descendants of the 12 Imams	Loved luxury; fell into debt	Contact with the West
		Secularization of Iran
		Corruption; shah's personal
		enrichment
Influences on modern political system		
Almost 90% of Iranians today	Loosened Shiite influence	Reinforced authoritarian
are Shiite	Tradition of trade/contact	rule; led to resistance to
Tradition of isolation	with others	totalitarianism
Authoritarianism, not	Authoritarianism, not	Modern corruption issues
totalitarianism	totalitarianism	in government, economy
Foundations for a theocracy	Foundations for secularism,	Increased secularization led
	separation between religious	to reestablishment of a
	and political leaders	theocracy
	Failures of regime led to	
	the creation of a representative	
	government	

The Creation of a Conflictual Political Culture. Between 1501 and 1979 Iran was ruled by three families that shaped the modern day clash between the conflicting political goals of authoritarianism, democracy, and theocracy.

- His ties to the West (particularly the United States) offended Iranian nationalists as well as the clergy.

In many ways, the shah created a divide in the political culture, with one side supporting modernization in the sense of establishing closer ties to the West, and the other side staunchly defending traditional ways, in particular Shiism. A clerical elite rose to oppose the shah, lead a revolution, and eventually take over the government.

One more ingredient for the success of the revolution was the charisma of its leader, the **Ayatollah Ruhollah Khomeini**. He not only defended Islamic **fundamentalism**, which emphasized literal interpretation of Islamic texts, social conservatism, and political traditionalism, but he also articulated resentments toward the elite and the United States. His depiction of the United States as the "Great Satan" puzzled many Americans, but resonated with many frustrated people in Iran. The Ayatollah gave new meaning to an old Shia term *velayat-e-faqih* (**jurist's guardianship**). The principle originally gave the senior clergy (including himself) broad authority over the unfortunate people (widows, orphans, mentally unstable) in the society, but Khomeini claimed that the true meaning of jurist's guardianship gives the clergy authority over the entire Shia community.

The Revolution Begins

Revolutions generally need a spark to begin the crisis. Although discontent had been building for a long time, two factors brought the situation to explode in revolution:

- Oil prices decreased by about 10% in the late 1970s at the same time that consumer prices increased about 20% in Iran. According to the theory of the **revolution of rising expectations,** revolutions are most likely to occur when people are doing better than they once were, but some type of setback happens. Iran fits this classic model in the early days of 1979.

- The United States put pressure on the shah to loosen his restraints on the opposition. President Jimmy Carter was a big promoter of human rights around the globe, and the shah's tight control on Iranian civil society was worrisome to his administration. However, in this situation, when the shah let his opponents speak, it encouraged others to voice their frustrations.

Once the reins loosened, many groups supported the revolution – political parties, labor organizations, professional associations, bazaar (merchant) guilds, college students, and oil workers. In late 1978, hundreds of unarmed demonstrators were killed in a central square in Tehran, and oil workers had gone on strike, paralyzing the oil industry. Anti-regime rallies were attracting as many as 2 million protestors. It is important to note that the rallies were organized and led by clerics, but were broadly supported by people from many sectors of society.

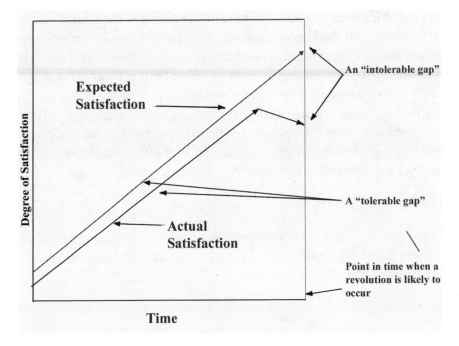

Revolution of Rising Expectations. In this chart the line that dips represents a drop in a standard of living that had been going up for some time. However, expectations rise along with living standards, and when the drop occurs, people are more likely to support a revolution.

(Source: James Davies, "Toward a Theory of Revolution," *The American Sociological Review,* February 1962)

Although Khomeini was in exile in Paris, audiotapes of his speeches were passed out freely at the rallies, where people called for the abolition of the monarchy. The shah fled the country at the beginning of February 1979, and his government officially ended on February 11 with the famous announcement from the national television-radio station quoted at the beginning of this chapter.

The Founding of the Islamic Republic

In late April 1979, a national referendum was held, and the Iranian people officially voted out the monarchy and established the Islamic Republic in its place. A constitution was drawn up late in the year by the **Assembly of Religious Experts**, a 73-man assembly of clerics elected directly by the people. The constitution gave broad authority to Khomeini and the clergy, although Prime Minister Mehdi Bazargan strongly objected. Bazargan advocated a presidential republic based on Islam, but democratic in structure. However, Khomeini's constitution was presented to the people in the midst of the U.S. hostage crisis, a time of high hostility toward Americans. The result was not surprising: 99% of the electorate endorsed it, even though only 75% of the eligible voters actually voted.

Once the constitution was endorsed, the Shia leaders launched the **Cultural Revolution** with goals that were very similar to Mao Zedong's goals as he led China's Cultural Revolution in 1966. The Cultural Revolution in Iran aimed to purify the country from not only the shah's regime, but also from secular values and behaviors, particularly those with western origins. The universities were cleared of liberals and staffed with faculty who supported the new regime. The new government suppressed all opposition, including almost all groups from civil society, and many were executed in the name of "revolutionary justice."

Post-Khomeini – 1989-Present

Until the Ayatollah Khomeini's death in 1989, the clerics consolidated and built their power. Their success was cemented by several important factors that brought them popular support:

- World petroleum prices rebounded, so Iran's economy improved accordingly. The government was able to afford social programs for the people, such as modern improvements for housing and medical clinics.

- Iraq (under Saddam Hussein) invaded Iran in 1980, beginning a war between the two countries that continued throughout the decade. The people rallied around the government in response to this threat.

- The charisma of Khomeini remained strong, and the power of his presence inspired faith in the government.

Khomeini's death in 1989 marked the beginning of a new era for the Republic. His successor, **Ali Khamenei,** does not have the same magnetism of personality, nor does he have the academic credentials that Khomeini had, facts that have encouraged some scholars in Qom to question the legitimacy of the theocracy. The Iran-Iraq War ended in 1988, and world oil prices fell again during the 1990s. Most importantly, many in the population began to criticize the authoritarian rule of the clerics, and to advocate a more democratic government.

In many ways the conflict between theocratic and democratic values played itself out during the presidencies of Mohammad Khatami (1997-2005) and Mahmoud Ahmadinejad (2005-2013). Khatami was a reformist who aimed to end the freeze in relations between Iran and the West, particularly the United States. He believed in a "dialogue among civilizations" that fostered positive relationships with other countries, not just a cessation of hostilities. Although he never advocated changing theocratic political structures, reformers became a strong presence in both the *Majles* and the executive branch. In contrast, Ahmadinejad was a conservative who antagonized western countries, although he did not isolated himself from them. He asserted theocratic values and appealed to Iranian nationalism to solidify his **white** (bloodless) **coup** of the reformists.

CITIZENS, SOCIETY, AND THE STATE

Iranian citizens have had little direct experience with democracy, but they generally understand the importance of civil society. Until the Pahlavi shahs of the 20th century, the authoritarian rulers had very little power to reach into citizens' everyday lives. Local officials were a presence, to be sure, and religious law, *sharia,* set strict rules for behavior. The democratic experiment after the Constitution of 1906 created an elected legislature, the *Majles*, but the new government was so unable to solve the country's problems that chaos followed, inviting authoritarian rule to return with the Pahlavis.

Cleavages

Major divisions in Iranian society are based on:

- **Religion** – Almost 90% of all Iranians are Shia Muslims, but almost 10% are Sunni, and 1% are a combination of Jews, Christians, Zoroastrian, and Baha'i. Although the Constitution recognizes religious minorities and guarantees their basic rights, many religious minorities have left the country since the founding of the Republic in 1979. The Baha'i faith, which many Shiites believe to be an unholy offshoot of Islam, has been a particular object of religious persecution. Its leaders have been executed, imprisoned, and tortured, schools closed, and community property taken by the state. Many Baha'i have immigrated to Canada, as have a large number of Jews and Armenian Christians. The Constitution does not mention Sunnis, and so their rights are often unclear.

- **Ethnicity** – Ethnicity is closely tied to religion, but other cultural differences distinguish minorities in Iran. 51% may be considered Persian, speaking Persian (Farsi) as their first language; 24% are Azeri; 8% are Gilaki and Mazandarani; 7% are Kurds; 3% are Arabi; and the remaining percentages are a mixture of other groups. Many Azeris live in the northwest close to the former Soviet republic of Azerbaijan, creating a worry for the Iranian government that the Azeris will want to form a larger state by taking territory away from Iran. The Azeris do not speak Persian, but they are strongly Shiite, and the supreme leader that followed Khomeini in 1989 – Ali Khameini – is Azeri. Kurds and Arabs tend to be Sunni Muslim, so the religious cleavage is reinforced by ethnicity.

- **Social class** – The peasantry and lower middle class are sources of support for the regime, partly because they have benefited from the government's social programs that have provided them with electricity and paved roads. However, middle and upper-middle class people are largely secularized, and so they tend to be highly critical of the clerics and their control of the society. Many middle-class people have not fared well economically during the years since the Republic was founded. As a result, their cultural and political views of secularism are reinforced by their economic problems, creating discontent and opposition to the regime.

- **Reformers v. conservatives** – A fundamental cleavage in the political culture since the founding of the Republic has to do with a debate about the merits of a theocracy v. a democracy.

The conservatives want to keep the regime as it is, under the control of clerics and *sharia* law, and the reformers would like to see more secularization and democracy. Most reformers do not want to do away with the basic principles of an Islamic state, but they display a wide array of opinions about how much and where secularization and democracy should be infused into the system.

- **Pragmatic conservatives v. radical clerics** – The complicated set of cleavages in Iran is made more complex by distinct divisions among the clergy that have led to many important disagreements at the top levels of policymaking. Pragmatic conservatives are clergy that favor liberal economic policies that encourage foreign trade, free markets, and direct foreign investment. They base their points of view on strong personal ties to middle-class merchants (bazaaris) and rural landowners who have long supported mosques and religious activities. Conservatives argue that private property and economic inequality are protected under Islamic law. They are generally willing to turn over economic management to liberally-inclined technocrats. Radicals are more numerous among younger and more militant clerics, and they call for measures to enhance social justice, especially in terms of providing welfare benefits to Iran's poor. Radicals generally endorse state-sponsored wealth redistribution and price controls.

Civil Society

A major source of unhappiness with the rule of the Pahlavi shahs was the government's incursion into private lives of citizens – the civil society. However, civil society has not been restored under the current regime, and this fact tends to create discontent, especially among middle-class people. The Shiite revolutionary elites launched a campaign that may be compared to Mao's Cultural Revolution in that they sought to impose values of the Islamic state on the general population. University professors with reputations for western preferences were fired and replaced with people that clearly supported the regime. Other professionals quietly left the country to seek refuge in western

IRAN: CITIZEN, SOCIETY, AND THE STATE

Religion – 90% are Shia Muslim;
10% are Sunni Muslim

Ethnicity – 51% Persian, 24% Azeri,
8% Gilaki and Mazandarani; 7% Kurds;
3% Arabi

Social class – the peasantry and lower
middle class are sources of support for
the regime, which sponsors social programs
for them; secularized middle and upper
middle classes most likely to rebel

Reformers v. conservatives – Conservatives
want to keep the regime as it is, under the
control of clerics and sharia law, and the
reformers would like to see more secularization and democracy.

Pragmatic conservatives v. radical clerics –
Pragmatic conservatives are clergy that favor
liberal economic policies that encourage free markets.
Conservatives call for measures to enhance social
justice, especially in terms of providing welfare
benefits to Iran's poor.

Some Major Cleavages in the Iranian Political System

nations. However, the desire to preserve civil society did not disappear – it was too large an influence on the political culture before the takeover by Reza Shah in the early 1920s.

Under the presidency of **Muhammad Khatami** (1997-2005), Iranians experienced the so-called "Tehran spring" – a period of cautious political liberalization, with a loosening of freedom of speech and press, a more open economy, and a friendlier stance towards the outside world. However, the Iranian president has only limited powers, and the reforms were hampered by more conservative elements in the government. When **Mahmoud Ahmadinejad** became president in 2005, the government closed down newspapers, banned and censored books and websites, and did not tolerate the peaceful demonstrations and protests of the Khatami era. Prominent scholars were arrested, including Haleh Esfandiari, the director of the Woodrow Wilson Center in Washington, D.C. Dr. Esfandiari had dual citizenship (the U.S. and Iran), but was arrested in 2007 while visiting her mother in Tehran. She was imprisoned for more than three months before being released to return to the United States. After the election of 2009, the government out of fear of a backlash did not arrest the liberal candidates who officially lost the election, but their political activities were limited to putting out statements on their websites. Less visible opposition figures have were arrested, including three reform-minded journalists, four opposition politicians, and an economist who criticized some of Ahmadinejad's programs. In January 2011, Nasrin Sutoodeh, a human-rights lawyer, was jailed for 11 years, and film-makers around the world protested the six-year sentence imposed in 2011 on Jafar Panahi, a dissident Iranian director.

One indication that civil society is alive and well in Iran may be found among Iran's growing number of young people. Demographically, the young have grown in proportion to old at very dramatic rates, partly because of the Republic's encouragement of large families during the first years after it was founded. Many are the sons and daughters of disillusioned middle-class professionals, and they appear to be very attracted to western popular culture – music, dress, cars, and computers. The regime under Khatami showed some signs of tolerating this behavior, but under Ahmadinejad there was a crackdown against western dress, with arrests of women who show too much hair under their headscarves or wear makeup.

Political Participation

Despite the fact that guarantees for civil liberties and rights were written into the 1979 Constitution, the Islamic Republic from the beginning closed down newspapers, labor unions, private organizations, and political parties. Due process principles were ignored as many were imprisoned without trials. Political reformers were executed, and others fled the country. The regime also banned demonstrations and public meetings.

Protests and Demonstrations

The Republic's actions against public demonstrations did not curtail them, particularly on college campuses. In 1999, protests erupted in universities all across the country when the government shut down a reformist newspaper. In late 2002, similar demonstrations broke out among students when the courts ruled a death sentence for a reformist academic. In Iran in the summer of 2003, student demonstrations escalated into mass protests over the privatization of the university system. The protesters called for the overthrow and even death of Iran's religious and political leaders. Thousands were arrested during 4 days of protest in June. Because more than half of all Iranians alive today have been born since the Revolution of 1979, these youthful protesters may be a force for change in the future. Factory workers also tend to participate in rallies against the government. Their concerns are high unemployment rates, low wages, and unsatisfactory labor laws. AfterAhmadinejad became president in 2005, the government renewed its crackdown on protests and demonstrations. For example, in January 2007 security forces attacked striking bus drivers in Tehran and arrested hundreds of them. Two months later police beat hundreds of men and women who had assembled to commemorate International Women's Day.

Most remarkably, the days of protests that followed the presidential election of 2009 demonstrated the Iranian capacity to react strongly to repressive government. When the election results were announced, supporters of opposition candidates to President Ahmadinejad cried foul, and the biggest popular upheaval since the 1979 revolution began. The announcement that Ahmadinejad had won with 63% of the vote, against 34% for **Mir Hossein Mousavi**, caused the opposition candidates to call for the election to be annulled, and people on both sides of the issue poured out into the streets. Demonstrations and rallies continued for several days, and the government arrested many protesters, including some top leaders of the opposition. The government sent tens of thousands of Revolutionary Guards and voluntary militiamen, known as the Basij, to disperse the crowds, and violence followed The death toll is disputed, with state-controlled media reporting 20 people killed, but others put the figure much higher. The protesters, calling themselves the "Green Movement," after Mousavi's campaign colors, rallied around the image of a young woman, Neda Agha Soltan, who was photographed in a demonstration in Tehran as she lay dying after being shot by an unknown assailant.

The government contained the protesters, and a few months later, the Ayatollah Ali Khamenei declared that the society had been "vaccinated" against these "germs." In December 2009 a huge rally of the regime's supporters seemed to cast the Green Movement into the shadows. However, in early 2011, Mousavi and Mehdi Karroubi (another liberal candidate for president in 2009) revived when they encouraged their supporters to march in honor of freedom-seeking protesters in demonstrations in Egypt and Tunisia, and Green Movement advocates gathered in Tehran in large numbers and began marching, mostly in silence, before the security forces responded. Police and members of the *baseej* militia, using tear-gas and clubs, subdued the crowd, but not before two people were killed and dozens arrested. U.S. President Barack Obama – who had approached the 2009 election aftermath cautiously – called on Iran to let people express their opinions.

Women and the Political System

One of the most frequently heard criticisms of Iran by westerners is the regime's treatment of women. The veil has become a symbol of oppression, but probably more for westerners than for Iranian women themselves. The wearing of veils predates the birth of Islam as a religion in the 7th century, and women of many other religions in Southwest Asia have also worn veils. However, traditionally women in Islamic cultures have stayed home, with little education or opportunity to work outside the home. 20th century Iran is something of an exception because women have had better access to education. Educated women harbor particular resentments toward the regime. Their educations have led them to expect better job opportunities and more political rights than they have been granted. Judges often interpret the *sharia* narrowly, so that women are considered to be wards of their male relatives. However, today more than half of all college students are women, and they are also well represented as doctors and government employees.

The Islamic Republic calls its policy toward women **"equality-with-difference,"** meaning that divorce and custody laws now follow Islamic standards that favor males. Women must wear scarves and long coats in public, and they cannot leave the country without the consent of male relatives. Occasional stoning of women for adultery has also taken place, though the government issued a ban on them. However, women are allowed educations and entrance to at least some occupations. Women now constitute about 33% of the total labor force.

Iranian women are not well represented in the *Majles*, as the chart below shows. Mexico's large representation is partly due to the recent parity laws that require political parties to run women candidates for office. Nigeria's low representation is probably reflective of traditional society there, and China's relatively large representation may be influenced by a lingering communist ideology that emphasizes equality. Russia does not appear to be influenced by its former status as a communist nation.

WOMEN IN NATIONAL PARLIAMENTS

Country	Lower House % Women	Upper House % Women
China	23.6%	___*
Iran	3.1%	___*
Mexico	42.4%	33.6%
Nigeria	5.6 %	6.5%
Russia	13.6 %	17.1%
United Kingdom	29.4%	24.6%

* No directly comparable upper house

Source: *Women in National Parliaments*, www.ipu.org (figures based on last election as of 2015)

POLITICAL INSTITUTIONS

The political system of Iran is unlike any other in the world today in that it blends a theocracy with a democracy. The theocracy is represented in the national government by the supreme leader, and two governmental bodies: the Guardian Council and the Expediency Council. The president, the Assembly of Religious Experts, and the national assembly (the *Majles*) are democratically elected. Linkage institutions are in various stages of development, and tend to be fluid in nature.

Linkage Institutions

The constitution guarantees citizens the right to organize and to express themselves, so some institutions that link people to the government have developed. Some organizations, such as interest groups and the press, developed long before 1979 and continue today. Others, like political parties, had to begin all over again.

Political Parties

The constitution provides for political parties, but the government did not allow them until Muhammad Khatami's election as president in 1997. Since then, multiple parties have formed, with most of them organized around personalities, not issues.

A number of new parties appeared for the *Majles* elections of 2007 and the presidential elections of 2009 and 2013, and only a few have carried over from previous elections, so current parties are highly unstable and very likely to change in the near future. However, the parties usually operate in loose alignments within two main coalitions: the conservative and the reformist. The alliances/parties that sponsored presidential candidates in 201 are:

- **Executives of Construction Party** – This reformist party was founded in the 1990s, and it ran Mostafa Hashemitaba in 2017. He received less than 1% of the vote.

- **Moderation and Development Party** – This political party brands its approach as "moderate." The party's 2017 candidate was Hassan Rouhani, who was running for reelection.

- **Combatant Clergy Association** – This party was supported in 2013 by the Iranian Reform Movement and represented the reformist coalition, and sponsored Hassan Rouhani in 2013. In 2017, however, it supported the conservative candidate, Ebrahim Raisi, the choice of the Ayatollah Khamenei.

- **Islamic Coalition Party** – This party was founded in 1962, so it is one of the oldest, and it generally is seen as part of the conservative coalition. The party's candidate in 2017 was Mostafa Mir-Salim, who gained only about 1% of the vote.

Many political parties of former dissidents are now in exile but still active. The Liberation Movement, a moderate Islamic party, was established by Mehdi Bazargan (Khomeini's first prime minister) in 1961, but was banned in 2002 as a subversive organization. The National Front, headed by the shah's dissident Prime Minister Mossadeq in the 1950s was banned in the late 1980s. Other parties in exile are the Mojahedin, a guerilla organization that fought the shah's regime; the Fedayin, a Marxist guerilla group that modeled itself after Latin American hero Che Guevara; and Tudeh, a communist party.

The party system reflects **factionalism,** or the splintering of the political elites based not just on points of view, but also on personalities. Since parties are fluid and weak, they are not vehicles for discussing policymaking alternatives. Instead, factions tend to coalesce before elections and then break apart if their candidates are chosen. Defeated factions tend to stay together between elections in hopes of reversing their fortunes in the next election.

Elections

On the national level, citizens over the age of eighteen (minimum age changed in early 2007 from fifteen to eighteen) may vote for members of the Assembly of Religious Experts, representatives to the *Majles*, and the president of the Republic. The Republic is a highly centralized regime, although citizens may also vote for officials on the local level. Elections to the *Majles* and the presidency are conducted according to plurality, or winner-take-all, and no proportional representation is used. However, elections consist of two rounds, so that one of the two contenders left in the second round will get a majority of the votes.

The Majles Elections of 2004 and 2008

The first round elections to the *Majles* were held on February 20, 2004, but they took place after the Guardian Council banned thousands of candidates from running, mainly from the reformist parties. Particularly hard hit was the Islamic Iran Participation Front. Out of a possible 285 seats (5 seats are reserved for religious minorities), reformist parties could only introduce 191 candidates. Some reformists refused to vote, and the official turnout was only about 51%. Not surprisingly, conservative candidates won about 70% of the seats. In 2008, conservatives held on to about 70% of the seats, but reformists managed to win 46, an increase over their numbers in 2004.

The Presidential Election of 2005

The Constitution provides that presidents may not run for more than two terms of office, so President Khatami had to step down in 2005. The Guardian Council disqualified about 1000 candidates, leaving only seven to run, some with the support of a party, and some not. The results of the first round were very close, with two candidates going on to the second round: **Akbar Hasemi Rafsanjani,** a former president known for his moderate and pragmatic views (21% of the vote); and **Mahmoud Ahmadinejad**, the conservative mayor of Tehran (19.5% of the vote). Ahmadinejad won in the second round with almost 62% of the vote, since Rafsanjani was not able to organize the reformist vote behind him. Ahmadinejad is known for his populist views, and he announced after his victory that he meant for prosperity to be shared among all classes, not just the elite.

The Presidential Election of 2009

Charges of election fraud were made after the presidential election of 2005, but they were dismissed, even though many were surprised that Ahmadinejad won. One reason for his victory was that many reformists did not vote, since they rejected both major candidates. As the election of 2009 approached, the Iranian reform movement attempted to rally behind one candidate. Many reformists hoped that former President Mohammad Khatami would win the election, but Khatami dropped out of the race and endorsed his former prime minister, Mir-Hossein Mousavi. One other reformist ran, Mehdi Karroubi, and one conservative – Mohsen Rezee – challenged Ahmadinejad for conservative support. The debates leading up to the election focused mainly on the economy, a main concern of Iranian citizens after the global economic crisis of late 2008.

Opinion polls – not always very reliable in Iran – showed a close race between Ahmadinejad and Mousavi as the election approached on June 12, so the official results – nearly 63% for Ahmadinejad and less that 34% for Mousavi – surprised many people. Record numbers (85% of the electorate) turned out for the election, and many reformists that had not voted in 2005 went to the polls in 2009. Mousavi urged his supporters to fight the decision, without resorting to violence, and protests in favor of Mousavi broke out in Tehran. Mousavi appealed the result to the Guardian Council two days after the election, and Supreme Leader Khamenei agreed to an investigation into the fraud. The votes were recounted, but Iran's electoral board concluded that Ahmadinejad won the election. When Khamenei publicly endorsed the decision, many criticized him for shutting down the popular outcry prematurely. The inauguration of Ahmadinejad was held in early August, with protests held outside the Parliament.

In the election's aftermath, many were arrested, and some high-ranked clerics accused foreigners – including some British embassy employees – of stirring up the protests. Moussavi was portrayed as a tool of secular foreigners who plotted for the downfall of the country. The government also claimed to have confessions from top reformers who were arrested, who allegedly pleaded guilty to accusations of organizing a "velvet revolution" to overthrow the country's leaders. Moussavi and Karroubi were not arrested, but accusations soon surfaced that some of those who had been detained were tortured and/or killed by government officials. Mr. Moussavi responded by announcing on his website the formation of a "grass roots and social network" to promote democracy and adherence to the law. The formation of a new party would have required a government permit, which would have been denied.

The election brought many disparate elements of Iran's political culture together for the biggest confrontation since 1979. Although the protests finally cooled, charges of voter fraud continued to circulate, and the legitimacy of the government was shaken to its very core, most profoundly by those who questioned the authority of the supreme leader.

The Elections of 2012 and 2013

As tensions mounted over a number of issues between Supreme Leader Khamenei and President Ahmadinejad, the legislative election in 2012 was described by many journalists and analysts as a contest between the two men, with Khamenei supporters winning a large majority of seats. More than 5,000 candidates registered, but more than a third were disqualified by the Guardian Council. 290 seats were up for election, with alliances shifting into two camps: the United Front of Principalists (UFC – supporters of Supreme Leader Khamenei) and the Resistance Front (FSP – supporters of Ahmadinejad). The UFC won 101 seats (34.8%) and the FSP won 50 seats (17.2%). Even though most reformist candidates had been disqualified by the Guardian Council, the reformist alliance, Democratic Coalition of Reformists, won 43 seats (14.1%).

The presidential election in June of 2013, the first since the disputed election of 2009, took place at a time when international concern for Iran's nuclear programs was high. Western sanctions had weakened the Iranian economy, and Israel had threatened a military strike, so international interest was high. In May, the Guardian Council disqualified two prominent candidates: former president Ali Akbar Hashemi Rafsanjani, and Ahmedinejad's hand-picked choice, Esfandiar Rahim Mashaei. Of the eight candidates selected, one – **Hassan Rouhani**, a former nuclear negotiator – had even slightly different stances from the traditionalists. Three of the qualified candidates had direct links to Supreme Leader Khamenei: Gholam Ali Haddad Adel, a close adviser and relative; Ali Akbar Velayati, his foreign policy adviser; and Iran's top nuclear negotiator, Saeed Jalil. Another candidate, Mohammad Bagher Ghalibaf, mayor of Tehran, had previously served as a commander of the Revolutionary guard, and had played a leading role in the maintenance of Iran's internal security.

Although most analysts projected that someone close to the Ayatollah would win, Mr. Rouhani pulled votes that would have gone to the two disqualified candidates, and in a late surge, he won the election with a majority vote in the first round. Turnout was high, with 72% of the electorate voting, and Rouhani won with 50.7% of the votes, with Bagher Ghalibaf coming in a distant second, with 16.6% of the vote, and Saeed Jalili netting third place with 11.4%. With the backing of former reformist presidents Mohammad Khatami and Ali Akbar Hashami Rafsanjani, Rouhani had a powerful mandate to improve Iran's international relations and attempt to negotiate a settlement of Iran's nuclear activities.

The Presidential Election of 2017

In 2017, Hassan Rouhani was easily reelected, winning over 57% of the vote and avoiding a runoff with conservative candidate Ebrahim Raisi, who received just over 38%. The fluid nature of political parties in Iran was evident in this election, since the party that sponsored Rouhani in 2013 sponsored Raisi in this election. The election was widely seen as an affirmation of Rouhani's course of moderate reform, especially in terms of his approach to international affairs.

Interest Groups

Since political parties are ill-defined in Iran, it is often difficult to draw the line between parties and interest groups. A large number of groups have registered with the government, including an Islamic Association of Women and a Green Coalition. The parties in exile, such as the National Front, the Liberation Movement, and the Mojahedin also have members still in Iran that work for their benefit.

An important interest group for factory workers is called **Workers' House**, that operates with the help of its affiliated newspaper, *Kar va Kargar (Work and Worker)*. Their political party, Islamic Labor Party, backed Khatami in the 2000 election, but its coalition with other reform parties was broken up by the Guardian Council's banning of reformist candidates in 2004 (*Majles* election*)*, and 2005 (presidential election). Workers' House holds a May Day rally most years, and in 1999 the rally turned into a protest when workers marched to parliament to denounce conservatives for watering down labor laws. When bus drivers joined the protest, most of central Tehran was shut down. A bus drivers' protest was crushed by the government in 2007.

Few interest groups have formed for business because private businesses have been crowded out since the Revolution of 1979, when many were taken over by the government. Agriculture, internal trade, and distribution are mostly in private hands, but the government controls between 65% and 80% of the economy.

Mass Media

Over 20 newspapers were shut down shortly after the Revolution in 1979, and by 1981 an additional seven were closed. In 1981 the *Majles* passed a law making it a criminal offense to use "pen and speech" against the government. In more recent years, some of the restrictions have been lifted. The Rafsanjani government permitted some debate in the press on controversial issues during the 1990s, and the Khatami administration issued permits to dozens of new publications, apparently hoping to establish an independent press. However, freedom of the press is still a major issue between conservatives and reformists, and the large-scale student demonstrations in 1999 were sparked by newly imposed restrictions on the media. Shortly after the 2000 *Majles* elections, when many reformists were elected, the outgoing *Majles* approved a press control law, which the Council of Guardians ruled could not be overturned by the new legislature. Some 60 pro-reform newspapers were shut down by 2002.

Radio and television are government-run by the Islamic Republic of Iran Broadcasting (IRIB), but many newspapers and magazines are privately owned. Compared with other regimes in the region, the Iranian press has more freedom to criticize the government. Iran's elite is well educated, and many of these publications cater to their needs as professional journals, sports magazines, and publications for the fine arts, cinema, and health care. Most are nonpolitical, however. A semipublic institution whose directors are appointed by the Supreme Leader runs the country's two leading newspapers, *Ettela'at* and *Kayhan*.

GOVERNMENT INSTITUTIONS

Iran is a highly centralized unitary state, but it is divided administratively into provinces, districts, sub-districts, and local areas. The Islamic Constitution of 1979 promises elected councils on each level of administration, and it also requires governors and other regional officials (who are all appointed) to consult local councils. No steps were taken to hold council elections until 1999 when President Khatami insisted on holding nationwide local elections. The election resulted in a landslide for reformists, presenting a challenge for the conservative clergy. Local elections in December 2006 supported candidates critical of Mahmoud Ahmadinejad, reflecting a weakness in the president's popularity.

The government structure of Iran is complex, but the most important thing to remember is that it attempts to blend theocratic ideals with democratic ones. Every structure has a purpose in terms of one or both of these principles.

Jurist's Guardianship

The supreme leader, the Guardian Council, the Assembly of Religious Experts, and the Expediency Council do not fit into a three-branch arrangement of government institutions. All three have broad executive, legislative, and judicial powers that allow them to supersede all other positions and bodies. They abide by the Ayatollah Khomeini's overarching principle of *velayat-e-faqih* (**jurist's guardianship**) in that they have all-encompassing authority over the whole community based on their ability to understand the *sharia* and their commitment to champion the rights of the people. The Constitution of 1979 specifies the duties of government institutions, including prerogatives and responsibilities of the dual executive: the supreme leader and the president.

The Supreme Leader

This position at the top of Iran's government structure was clearly meant to be filled by the Ayatollah Ruhollah Khomeini, the leader of the 1979 Revolution. The supreme leader is seen as the imam of the whole community, and he represents the pinnacle of theocratic principles of the state. The Constitution specifically put Khomeini in the position for life, and stated that after his death, his authority would pass to a leadership council of two or three senior clerics. This did not occur when Khomeini died in 1989 because his followers did not trust the clerics, so instead they changed the Constitution and selected as Supreme Leader Ali Khamenei, a cleric of the middle rank who had none of Khomeini's formal credentials. Khamenei also was appointed for life, and continues as supreme leader to the present.

The Constitution gives the supreme leader many powers. First and foremost, he is the *faqih*, or the leading Islamic jurist to interpret the meaning of religious documents and *sharia,* Islamic law. He links the three branches of government together, may mediate among them, and is charged with "determining the interests of Islam." His many powers include:

- Elimination of presidential candidates

- Dismissal of the president

- Command of the armed forces

- Declaration of war and peace

- Appointment and removal of major administrators and judges

- Nomination of six members of the Guardian Council

- Appointment of many non-governmental directors, such as the national radio-television network and semi-public foundations

Although the dual executive positions of the Iranian government may be categorized as **head of state** (the supreme leader) and **head of gov-**

ernment (the president), the supreme leader holds ultimate power, and is far from a figurehead.

The Guardian Council

A body that also represents theocratic principles is the Guardian Council, which consists of twelve male clerics. Six are appointed by the supreme leader, and the other six are nominated by the chief judge and approved by the *Majles*. Bills passed by the *Majles* are reviewed by the Guardian Council to ensure that they conform to *sharia*, and the council also has the power to decide who can compete in elections. In 2012, 2013, 2016, and 2017, they disqualified thousands of candidates for both the *Majles* and the presidential elections.

Together the supreme leader and the Guardian Council exercise the principle of **jurist's guardianship**, making sure that the democratic bodies always adhere to Islamic beliefs and laws.

The Assembly of Religious Experts

In 1989 a smaller Assembly of Religious Experts was expanded to be an 86-man house directly elected by the people every four years. The Assembly is given the responsibility, along with the supreme leader and the Guardian Council, of broad constitutional interpretation. One of the new Assembly's first actions was to elect Ali Khamenei as Khomeini's replacement as supreme leader. The Assembly also reserved the right to dismiss him if he was unable to fill Khomeini's shoes. So far, that has not happened. The Assembly's members were required to have a seminary degree equivalent to a master's degree, but in 1998 revisions were made that allowed nonclerics to stand for the Assembly, but the candidates are still subject to approval by the Guardian Council.

In 2007 former President Hashemi Rafsanjani was picked as chairman of the Assembly, a move that many thought would pose a challenge to Mahmoud Ahmadinejad, and possibly even Supreme Leader Khamenei. Rafsanjani, a moderate, was Ahmadinejad's main opponent in the presidential election of 2005, and he also tended to side with pro-democracy reformers who believe the government's authority is derived from popular elections. However, in 2011, Rafsanjani was pressured to step down from his position, leaving many to speculate about how his loss of power would impact opposition movements to the government. Rafsanjani ran for president in 2013 but was disqualified by the Guardian Council.

The Expediency Council

Because the Guardian Council can overturn decisions and proposals for law made by the *Majles*, the two bodies often argued fiercely during the days of the early republic, so Khomeini created a body to referee their disputes. It began as a council with thirteen clerics, including the president, the chief judge, the speaker of the *Majles*, and six jurists from the Guardian Council. The Expediency Council eventually passed some compromise bills, and was institutionalized by the 1989 constitutional amendments. Today it consists of 32 members, and it has many more powers than it had originally. For example, it now may originate its own legislation. Not all of its members today are clerics, but they are still appointed by the supreme leader (Ali Khamenei). Collectively they are the most powerful men in Iran.

The Executive

Iran does not have a presidential system, so the head of the executive branch does not have the same authority as presidents in countries that have a presidential system, such as the U.S., Mexico, and Nigeria. However, the president is the highest official representing democratic principles in Iran, and he functions as the head of government, while the supreme leader serves as head of state.

The president is the chief executive and the highest state official after the Supreme Leader. He is directly elected every four years by Iranian citizens, and he is limited to two consecutive terms in office.

Although he is democratically elected, the Constitution still requires him to be a pious Shiite who upholds Islamic principles.

THEOCRATIC GOVERNMENT INSTITUTIONS IN IRAN

GUARDIAN COUNCIL	ASSEMBLY OF RELIGIOUS EXPERTS	THE EXPEDIENCY COUNCIL
Consists of twelve male clerics: six appointed by the supreme leader and six nominated by the chief judge and approved by the *Majles* Review bills passed by the *Majles* to be sure they adhere to sharia Decides who can compete in elections Along with the *Majles*, the most important policymaking body in Iran	86-man house directly elected by the people every eight years Selects the supreme leader and has the right to dismiss him Until recently, was been headed by Hashemi Rafsanjani, a cleric and former president who has been critical of the regime	32 members appointed by supreme leaders Designed to referee disputes between the Majles and the Guardian Council May originate its own legislation Not all are clerics Until recently, headed by Hashemi Rafsanjani

The President and the Cabinet

Some of the president's powers include:

- Devising the budget

- Supervising economic matters

- Proposing legislation to the *Majles*

- Executing policies

- Signing of treaties, laws, and agreements

- Chairing the National Security Council

- Selecting vice presidents and cabinet ministers

- Appointing provincial governors, town mayors, and ambassadors

All of the six presidents of the Islamic Republic have been clerics, except for two: Abol-Hasan Bani-Sadr, who was ousted in 1981 for criticizing the regime as a dictatorship, and Mahmoud Ahmadinejad, president from 2005 to 2013. The cabinet conducts the real day-to-day work of governance. Practically all new laws and the budget are initiated and devised by cabinet members, and then submitted to parliament for approval, modification, or rejection.

Former president Ahmadinejad and the supreme leader, Ayatollah Ali Khamenei, generally supported one another, but in the last years of Ahmadinejad's presidency, the two were often openly competitive. In 2011, Ahmadinejad fired his minister of intelligence, Heidar Moslehi, for bugging the offices of Ahmadinejad's chief of staff, but Khamenei exercised his authority and quickly reinstated him. The president responded by refusing to attend cabinet meetings, but he resumed his duties after 300 MPs urged him to respect Mr. Khamenei's decision. The two men are both conservative but disagreed on economic policy issues, and a two-headed executive leaves room for internal disputes. The supreme leader, as head of state, is supposed to stay aloof from everyday politics, and Khamenei said as much when he praised the government in a 2011 speech and stressed that he intervened only when he felt that "expediency is ignored." However, each time that the supreme leader gets involved in politics, he risks his ability to rise above the fray and exercise undisputed authority based on jurist's guardianship.

The Bureaucracy

The president heads a huge bureaucracy that has expanded over the years to provide jobs for college and high school graduates. It has doubled in numbers since 1979. Some of the newer ministries include: Culture and Islamic Guidance that censures the media; Intelligence that serves as the chief security organization; Heavy Industry that manages nationalized factories; and Reconstruction that expands social services and sees that Islam extends into the countryside. The clergy dominates the bureaucracy, just as it controls the presidency. The most senior ministries – Intelligence, Interior, Justice, and Cultural and Islamic Guidance – are headed by clerics, and other posts are often given to their relatives.

Semipublic Institutions

These groups are theoretically autonomous, but they are directed by clerics appointed personally by the Supreme Leader. They are generally called "foundations," with such names as the "Foundation for the Oppressed and Disabled," the "Martyrs Foundation," and the "Foundation for the Publication of Imam Khomeini's Works." They are tax exempt and are reputed to have a great deal of income. Most of the property they supervise was confiscated from the pre-1979 elite. Because they are run by people with strong connections to the government, these organizations are called **para-statals,** or **bonyads,** which trace their roots to royal foundations established by Shah Mohammad Reza Pahlavi. These bonyads invested in property development, which catered to the middle and upper classes. After the 1979 Revolution, the bonyads were nationalized and renamed with the intention of redistributing income to the poor and families of martyrs, those killed in the service of the country. They received land confiscated from those who did not support the government, and so many gained considerable wealth as a consequence.

Today, there are over 100 bonyads, and they are criticized for many of the same reasons as the earlier organizations. As charity organizations they are supposed to provide social services to the poor and the needy, but without direct government supervision, no one knows how much or to whom this help is given. They have been accused of funneling their money to support the regime, and of turning to commercial activities since the death of the Ayatollah Khomeini. Others criticize bonyads for unfairly competing with private companies, since bonyad firms have political connections that prevent private firms from succeeding.

The Legislature (The *Majles*)

For most of its recent history Iran has had a unicameral legislature, the *Majles,* although in some ways the Assembly of Religious Experts has functioned as an upper house since 1989, when its membership was expanded to 86 elected representatives. Both the *Majles* and the Assembly are directly elected by the people.

The *Majles* was first created by the Constitution of 1906, when it was part of Iran's early 20th century experiment with democracy. The *Majles* survived the turmoil of its early days as well as the dictatorship of the Pahlavi shahs, and was retained as the central legislative body by the Constitution of 1979. Although the 1989 constitutional amendments weakened the *Majles* in relationship to the presidency, it is still an important political institution with significant powers. Some of these powers are:

- Enacting or changing laws (with the approval of the Guardian Council)
- Interpreting legislation, as long as they do not contradict the judicial authorities
- Appointing six of the twelve members of the Guardian Council, chosen from a list drawn up by the chief judge
- Investigating the cabinet ministers and public complaints against the executive and judiciary
- Removing cabinet ministers, but not the president
- Approving the budget, cabinet appointments, treaties, and loans

The *Majles* has 290 seats, all directly elected through single member districts by citizens eighteen and over. The election of 2000 saw many reformists fill the seats through a coalition of reformist parties called the **Khordad Front**. They won 80% of the vote in a campaign that drew over 70% of the electorate. Many supporters of secular parties, all banned from the campaign, voted for the reformers since they saw them as better alternatives to religious conservatives. Before the 2004 elections, the Guardian Council banned many reformist candidates from entering the race, and the result was an overwhelming victory for conservatives. Significantly, control of the *Majles* flip-flopped dramatically from the hands of reformers to religious conservatives. For the 2012 election, about 1200 of the 5000 candidates for legislative seats were disqualified, mostly reformists.

The Judiciary

The judiciary is headed by a chief justice, who must have an understanding of *sharia*, so by necessity he is a cleric. The chief justice is appointed by the supreme leader for a five-year term, and he is charged with managing the judiciary and overseeing the appointment and removal of judges. Beneath the chief justice is the Supreme Court, which is the highest court of appeals in the land. Judges on the Supreme Court, like the chief justices, are all high-ranking clerics who are familiar with *sharia*.

Two very important things to remember about Iran's judiciary are: 1) the distinction between two types of law: *sharia* and *qanun*; and 2) the principle of jurist's guardianship means that the supreme leader and the Guardian Council have the final say regarding interpretation of law.

Two types of law are:

- **Sharia**, or Islamic law, was built up over several centuries after the death of the religion's founder, Muhammad, in the 7th century. *Sharia* is considered to be the foundation of all Islamic civilization, so its authority goes far beyond Iran's borders. It has incorporated the ideas of many legal scholars, and captures what many Muslims believe to be the essence of Muhammad himself. Overall, *sharia* is meant to embody a vision of a community in which all Muslims are brothers and sisters and subscribe to the same moral values. The very foundations of Iran's political system rest in the belief that *sharia* supersedes all other types of law, and its interpretation is the most important of all responsibilities for political and religious leaders. The principle of jurist's guardianship reflects reverence for *sharia*, and much of the legitimacy of the supreme leader is based on his ultimate authority as the interpreter of this sacred law.

- **Qanun** – Unlike *sharia*, *qanun* has no sacred basis, but instead is a body of statutes made by legislative bodies. In Iran, *qanun* are passed by the *Majles*, and they have no sacred meaning. *Sharia*, then, is divine law derived from God, and *qanun* is law made by the people's elected representatives. Of course, *qanun* must in no way contradict *sharia,* so the *Majles* must pass responsible *qanun,* especially since the Guardian Council (and ultimately the Supreme Leader) review the work of the legislature and apply the interpretation of *sharia* to all laws passed.

In a very different way than we have seen it applied in other countries, judicial review does exist in Iran. However, ultimate legal authority does not rest in the Constitution, but in *sharia* law itself. Because *sharia* is so complex, its interpretation is not an easy task, and it has been applied in many different ways. In Iran, the Ayatollah Khomeini's importance in shaping the political system is that his interpretation of *sharia* came to be the standard that influenced all leaders that followed him – Supreme Leader Khamenei, the seven presidents, and all other high officials. In other words, a core principle of the present-day regime is to accommodate Islam to a constitutional framework, as provided by the Constitution of 1979.

The Islamic Republic Islamized the judiciary code by interpreting the *sharia* very strictly. The new regime passed the Retribution Law, which permitted families to demand "blood money" (compensation to the victim's family from those responsible for someone's death), and mandated the death penalty for a whole range of activities, including adultery, homosexuality, drug dealing, and alcoholism. The law also set up unequal legal treatment of men and women, and Muslim and non-Muslim. The government also banned interest rates on loans, condemning them as "usury," which implies that people in need of loans are taken advantage of by the lenders.

Although Khomeini argued that the spirit of *sharia* calls for local judges to pronounce final decisions, the regime realized that a centralized judicial system was needed to tend to matters of justice in an orderly fashion. The regime retained the court structure from the shah's government, keeping the appeals system, the hierarchy of state courts, and the central government's right to appoint and dismiss judges. Furthermore, the interpretation of *sharia* has broadened gradually, so that the harsh corporal punishments outlined in the Retribution Law are rarely carried out today. Modern methods of punishment are much more common than harsh public retributions, so that most law breakers are fined or imprisoned rather than flogged in the town square.

The Military

Immediately after the 1979 Revolution the Ayatollah Khomeini established the **Revolutionary Guards,** an elite military force whose commanders are appointed by the supreme leader. The shah had built the regular army, navy, and air forces, and so the Revolutionary Guards was created as a parallel force with its own budgets, weapons, and uniforms, to safeguard the Republic from any subterfuge within the military. The supreme leader is the commander in chief, and also appoints the chiefs of staff and the top commanders of the regular military. According to the Constitution, the regular army defends the borders, while the Revolutionary Guards protect the republic. Both regular armed forces and the Revolutionary Guards were greatly taxed during the war with Iraq that finally ended in 1988.

The **Basij** is a loosely-organized military that is formally part of the Revolutionary Guards, and it gained international attention in the aftermath of the disputed presidential election of 2009, when the opposition candidate, Mir-Hussein Moussavi, accused the Basij of brutality as it contained the demonstrations and addressed dissidents. The word Basij means "mass mobilization" in Persian, and it dates back to the Iran-Iraq War, when the Ayatollah Khomeini asked for civilian volunteers to go to the war front. The militia was reinvented in the late 1990s, when the government quelled the street celebrations when Iran advanced to the playoffs in the World Cup soccer championship in

1998. The Basij also helped the government contain students protests in 1999.

THEOCRATIC AND DEMOCRATIC ELEMENTS IN IRAN'S GOVERNMENT STRUCTURE

Structure/Position	Theocratic Characteristics	Democratic Characteristics
Supreme Leader	Jurist guardianship; ultimate interpreter of *sharia;* appointed for life	
Guardian Council	Jurist guardianship; interpreter of *sharia*; six members selected by the supreme leader	Six members selected by the *Majles,* which is popularly elected; indirect democratic tie
Assembly of Religious Experts	Jurist guardianship; interpreter of *sharia*	Directly elected by the people; nonclerics may be members
Expediency Council	Appointed by the supreme leader; most members are clerics	Not all members are clerics
Majles	Responsibility to uphold *sharia*	Directly elected by the people; pass *qanun* (statutes)
Judiciary	Courts held to *sharia* law; subject to the judicial judgments of the supreme leader, Guardian Council	Court structure similar to those in democracies; "modern" penalties, such as fines and imprisonment

Iran currently has about 540,000 active troops, making it the eighth largest military in the world. Much about the military is kept secret, but its advanced abilities and technologies have been shown through the building of long-range missiles. The Revolutionary Guard remains an important political force, with its own ministry, army, navy, and air-force units, and appears to have a great deal of say in Iran's nuclear program. The Guard is becoming increasingly independent, and takes an active role in policymaking. A large number of former Guards sit in the *Majles,* and men with close links to the Guards control principal media outlets, such as the state broadcaster and the powerful Ministry for Islamic Guidance and Culture. In 2004 the Guards showed their strength by deciding on their own authority to close down the airport in Tehran on the grounds that a national security threat was present. The Guards' engineering arm, known as Ghorb, has been granted big state projects, such as a new section of the Tehran metro.

PUBLIC POLICY

The policymaking process in Iran is highly complex because laws can originate in many places (not just the legislature), and can also be blocked by other state institutions. Also, policies are subject to change depending on factional control. The two most powerful policymaking institutions in Iran are the *Majles* and the Guardian Council, with the Expediency Council refereeing disputes between the two.

Policymaking Factions

The leaders of the Revolution of 1979 and their supporters agreed on one thing: they wanted the shah to abdicate. Most people also wanted the Ayatollah Khomeini to lead the country after the shah left. After that, the disagreements began and continue until this day. Two types of factions are:

- **Conservative vs. reformist** – By and large, these factions are created by the often contradictory influences of theocracy and democracy. **Conservatives** uphold the principles of the regime as set up in 1979, with its basis in strict *sharia* law with a minimum of modern modifications. They are wary of influence from western countries and warn that modernization may threaten the tenets of Shiism that provide the moral basis for society, politics, and the economy. They support the right and responsibility of clerics to run the political system, and they believe that political and religious decisions should be one and the same. **Reformists**, on the other hand, believe that the political system needs significant reform, although they disagree on exactly what the reforms should be. They are less wary of western influence, and tend to advocate some degree of international involvement with countries of the West. Most reformers support Shiism and believe it to be an important basis of Iranian society, but they often support the idea that political leaders do not necessarily have to be clerics.

- **Statists vs. free-marketers** – This rift cuts across conservatives and reformers, and has taken different meanings over the years. Basically, though, the **statists** believe that the government should take an active role in controlling the economy – redistributing land and wealth, eliminating unemployment, financing social welfare programs, and placing price ceilings on consumer goods. We have seen this point of view at work in Mexico under Lazaro Cardenas during the 1930s, and in Russia and China under communism. Statists are not necessarily communists (and few in Iran are), but the same philosophy directed the economy of the Soviet Union with its Five-Year Plans, and continues to direct China's "socialist market economy." On the other hand, the **free-marketers** want to remove price controls, lower business taxes, encourage private enterprise, and balance the budget. In many ways they believe in the same market principles that guide the United States, but they envision it working within the context of the theocratic/democratic state.

These factional disputes have often brought about gridlock and instability, such as the flip-flop that occurred in the *Majles* between the election of 2000 and 2004 from reformist to conservative control. The disputes among the factions have led many of Iran's best and brightest to leave the country, and have deprived the reformists in particular of some potentially good leadership. Factions have also led to confusion on the international scene as well. For example, after the September 11, 2001 attacks in the United States, President Khatami almost immediately extended his condolences to the American people. However, Supreme Leader Ali Khamenei forbid any public debate about improving relations with the United States, and also implied that Americans had brought the situation on themselves.

President Hassad Rouhani included a broad number of factions in his cabinet selections in 2013, appointing moderate reformists from President Khatami's administration, technocrats from President Rafsanjani's administration, and moderate conservatives, who are the closest political alignment to a centrist party. Still, factional splits threaten the stability of any president's cabinet, and Rouhani's success also depends on the relationship he forms with Supreme Leader Khamenei, which appear to be mixed.

The Importance of Qom

The legitimacy of the modern Iranian theocracy has its roots in Qom, a desert city about 60 miles south of Tehran. It was from Qom that Ayatollah Khomeini began to denounce the shah, and it was there that he set up his government after returning from exile in France. It is a city of seminaries, and the scholars that inhabit them help to define the very foundation of Iranian society. Ironically, despite the fact that Khomeini's doctrine of *velayat-e-faqih* was devised in Qom, many scholars there are not entirely comfortable with the theocratic state. Their debate frames the factionalism of Iranian politics.

From some perspectives, the only rightful union of religion and politics will occur when the Twelfth Imam (see p. 395) returns from hiding. Until then, these scholars say, men of religion should be careful not to get involved in politics, and no one has special authority to guide society during this period called "occultation" between the disappearance and the return of the twelfth imam. Therefore, *velayat-e-faqih* is invalid, because it endows the supreme leader – and other government structures – with divine authority. President Khatami's reform movement drew heavily on the views of clerics that see politics as an experimental, man-made activity that Islam should respect. These pragmatists, of course, clashed with conservative religious scholars, who agree with the doctrine of *velayat-e-faqih* and the divine authority that it implies, and their points of view are very influential in the reversal of the Khatami reforms under President Ahmadinejad.

The presidential candidates who challenged the 2009 election results appealed directly to the scholars of Qom without challenging *velayat-*

e-faqih as a doctrine. The response from Qom was mixed, with one group of mid-ranking scholars and a few senior clergy denouncing the election as a fraud, but most kept quiet. However, the election and its aftermath no doubt fueled the disagreements among clerics, further factionalizing the country.

Economic Issues

The factional disagreements within the political elite are apparent in Iran's struggles with economic policymaking. On the international scene in 2002, a bill was drafted in the *Majles* that would have permitted foreigners to own as much as 100% (up from 48%) of any firm in the country. Not surprisingly, the bill came from the reformists. Predictably, the bill was not approved by the Guardian Council, a reflection of the tug of war between reformists and conservatives. Domestically, most Iranian leaders want improved standards of living for the people, but conservatives are cautious about the influence of secular prosperity on devout Shiism.

Oil has created a vertical divide in the society, particularly among the elites. On one side are elites with close ties to the oil state. On the other side is the traditional sector of the clergy. It was this divide that was clearly evident during the Revolution of 1979, and despite the fact that the clerics won, the secularists have not gone away. Almost no one denies the benefits that oil has brought to Iran. Money from the rentier state that grew under Muhammad Reza Shah helped to build the economic infrastructure and fuel the growth of a middle class. By the 1970s Iran was clearly an industrializing country with increasing prosperity, and its economy was integrated into the world economy.

The Ayatollah Khomeini famously stated that "**economics is for donkeys**," disdaining the importance of economics for policymakers and affirming the superiority of religious, rather than secular leaders. Even conservatives today don't deny the importance of economic policy decisions, but the factions don't agree on whether or not secularists should be allowed to make policy. The main economic problem plaguing the Islamic Republic has been the instability in the price of oil. The country suffered greatly when oil prices plunged in the early 1980s, rebounded somewhat, and then dropped again in the 1990s. Prices stayed relatively low until the end of the century. After that, oil prices have rebounded, and the Iranian economy benefited but again suffered when prices fell in 2014.

The management of the economy has been criticized, especially under President Ahmadinejad. He was elected based on his promises to provide government subsidies for consumers, and government expenditures on subsidies increased to about 25% of Iran's GDP in 2005-2006. The programs include food, housing, and bank credit, and perhaps most controversially, gasoline. Until 2011, gasoline was priced so low that domestic refiners refused to raise production to meet demand, so Iran had to import about 40% of its oil. This situation encouraged oil smuggling to neighboring countries, and corruption among the quasi-state companies that deal in oil products. The global economic recession that began in late 2007 impacted Iran deeply, especially the dramatic decline in the price of oil in 2008.

In 2010, the government made a bold announcement that major reforms would end many economic subsidies, especially those that encouraged people to waste precious resources. By dropping subsidies, the government allowed prices of oil, gas, electricity, and other basic commodities to reach market levels, and within a month of the president's announcement of the reforms, the price of gasoline had gone up by 75% and that of diesel by more than 2000%. Electricity and water bills also increased, as did the price of some types of bread. Supported by state television, President Ahmadinejad pointed out that the old system favored the rich, whose lifestyles – including heating big houses and fueling multiple cars – were subsidized by the cheap commodities. Indeed, the reforms were structured so that the more water, gas, and electricity an Iranian consumes, the more expensive these utilities become. In order to compensate ordinary Iranians for raising prices closer to world levels, the government has given monthly cash transfers to families. These reforms have reduced waste and encouraged conservation, and yet the cash transfers have kept people from openly protesting or resisting the changes.

Even so, today almost all Iranians receive cash transfers intended for the poor, with the government spending $100 billion in subsidies in 2013. With the arms agreement in mid-2015, many hoped that with the lifting of sanctions, the economy would turnaround, but inefficiencies abound, making Iran's economic future uncertain.

In order for President Rouhani to address the country's economic problems, he turned his attention to foreign policy to find a way to ease international sanctions imposed on Iran because of its nuclear activities. In 2015, Iran's oil exports had dwindled to half their former levels. GDP had fallen, currency rates had plunged, and unemployment had risen sharply. Rouhani's success as president depends heavily on his ability to resuscitate the economy.

Population Policy

One major initiative of the government in recent years has been to bring down the overall birth rate in Iran. The population surged after the Revolution of 1979, when Iranians were encouraged to have large families. As a result, the percentage of young people in the country grew tremendously, placing pressure on schools and eventually the workforce. Unemployment rates increased as too many young people sought the same jobs, so the clergy approved policies to lower the birth rate and reduce long-term burdens from overpopulation. Beginning in the late 1980s, the government reversed its policy and began discouraging large families. This new emphasis occurred at the same time that greater educational and professional opportunities opened to women, so the fertility rate declined, especially in urban areas. Although the population will continue to grow for some time because there are still so many young people of childbearing age, the government appears to have reversed the population crisis.

Today, the effects of these policy shifts is evident, with Iran fast becoming a middle-aged country. Those born in the early years of the republic are now in their late 20s, 30s, and early 40s, and they create an ever-aging bubble in the populations pyramid. Birth rates are down, with experts estimating 1.6-1.9 children per woman of childbearing age, broadly in line with European rates.

Foreign Affairs

Iran's international profile was raised considerably by President Mahmoud Ahmadinejad, whose statements and actions were quite controversial. He became the most polarizing head of government in the Muslim world when he declared the Holocaust a "myth," and argued that Israel should be "wiped away." After that, he threatened to retaliate against American interests "in every part of the world" if the U.S. were to attack Iran. His 2006 letter to George W. Bush inviting him to a televised discussion about their differences was openly published in newspapers, and although Bush declined, Ahmadinejad received a great deal of international publicity for his gesture. He held regular press conferences with western journalists, and he traveled widely. Yet the stance that he generally took was to defend Iran against the rest of the world, particularly the West, reinforcing the historical perception of an isolated country.

President Rouhani has a long record of experience in international relations. He, like many other Iranian leaders, sees the United States and other western countries as permanently in conflict with Iran. However, he has expressed concern over Iran's "brain drain" (exit of scholars to the West), and he has supported membership in the World Trade Organization. During his years as the secretary of the National Security Council, Mr. Rouhani prevented hard-liners from forming an alliance with Saddam Hussein after Iraq invaded Kuwait in 1990. He also directed Iran's negotiations with western countries in 2003, which resulted in an agreement in 2003, the only nuclear deal between Iran and the West before 2015.

The attitudes toward international organizations such as the United Nations, the World Bank, and the World Trade Organization are mixed. Iran's application to join the WTO in 1996 failed in part because of the difficulties in making foreign investments within the country's borders. The application also failed because the United States opposed it, so these hostilities between the two countries have reverberated into many areas of international economic policy. Iran's most important international membership is probably in OPEC (Organization for

Petroleum Exporting Countries) that controls the price of oil exported from its member states.

Iran has long sought to spread its influence throughout the Middle East, an effort that benefited after the United States removed hostile regimes in Iraq and Afghanistan. The Quds Force has exploited the region's instability, carrying out assassinations and bombings, and supplying arms and training to militia's deemed helpful to its interests. Syrian President Assad relies on Iran for cash, advice, and training for its paramilitary fighters.

Nuclear Energy

"States like these [Iran, Iraq, and North Korea], and their terrorist allies, constitute an axis of evil, arming to threaten the peace of the world. By seeking weapons of mass destruction, these regimes pose a grave and growing danger. They could provide these arms to terrorists, giving them the means to match their hatred. They could attack our allies or attempt to blackmail the United States."

U.S. President George W. Bush
State of the Union Address
January 29, 2002

President Bush's "**axis of evil**" statement quoted above created a stir of controversy regarding Iran's international relations with western countries. Iran's nuclear program goes back many decades, but this program has been under serious scrutiny by western nations since the attacks on the United States on September 11, 2001. Iran has maintained that the purpose of its nuclear program was for the generation of power, not for use as weapons. However, in August 2002, a leading critic of the regime revealed two secret nuclear sites, a uranium enrichment facility in Natanz and a heavy water facility in Arak. Late in 2003, the U.S. insisted that Iran be "held accountable" for allegedly seeking to build nuclear arms in violation of international treaties, including the Nuclear Non-Proliferation Treaty that Iran had signed. Then in November 2004, Iran's chief nuclear negotiator announced that Iran had temporarily suspended the uranium enrichment program after pressure from the European Union. This dispute boiled over in August 2005, when the International Atomic Energy Agency announced that Iran had broken seals on one of its nuclear sites – seals that had been placed there by the United Nations in 2004. In 2006 Britain, France, and Germany offered Iran trade, civil-nuclear assistance, and a promise of talks with America if it stopped enriching the uranium that could produce the fuel for a bomb. When Iran refused, diplomacy led in December 2006 to the imposition of formal economic sanctions by the United Nations' Security Council.

Years of diplomacy efforts followed, and finally in mid-2015, Iran, the United States, and five other world powers reached an agreement about the future of Iran's nuclear programs. Important parts of the agreement include:

- Limits on Iran's nuclear programs – Iran agreed to turn its Fordow facility (a site where many experts believe Iran was enriching uranium in centrifuges) into a research center where Iranian and world scientists would work together. Iran also agreed to rebuild its Arak facility so that the production of weapons-grade plutonium would be impossible. Iran also agree to give up most of its centrifuges, which are used to enrich uranium.
- Continuation of enrichment – Iran has long contended that its nuclear program is focused on peaceful purposes, so the agreement allowed Iran to use its Natanz facility for those purposes. However, levels of enrichment were limited, so that the building of weapons would be impossible.
- Extension of the "breakout time" – President Obama argued that the deal extends the time it would take Iran to make enough highly enriched material for a nuclear bomb. However, the agreement has time limits, so it is unclear what might happen when it expires.
- Sanctions may return – If Iran does not comply with the agreement, the U.N. Security Council may vote to reinstate economic sanctions on Iran.
- Comprehensive inspections – Inspectors from the International Atomic Energy Agency would have continual access to Iranian facilities, especially if any suspicious activity occurs.

This agreement will no doubt impact Iran's economic future as well as its relations with other countries, especially the United States. Since the terms of the agreement begin to expire 10 and 15 years from the time of the agreement, critics say that it only delays the Iranians' ability to obtain a nuclear weapon and so is not a long-term solution.

U.S. Withdrawal from the Iran Nuclear Deal

In May 2018, U.S. President Donald Trump announced the withdrawal of the United States from the Iran Nuclear Deal, formally known as the Joint Comprehensive Plan of Action. In a joint statement responding to the withdrawal, the leaders of France, Germany, and the United Kingdom affirmed their support of the United Nations Security Council resolution endorsing the nuclear deal. However, without the backing of the United States, the future of the agreement remains uncertain. The withdrawal was controversial, with conservatives in the United States endorsing it because they considered the deal to be weak. Others – particularly former president Barack Obama and former vice president Joe Biden – criticized the decision to withdraw.

Iran's complex political culture and internal factional debates make it very difficult to predict its future. Oil continues to fill the government's coffers with income, but the economy's dependence on one product is worrisome to economists and politicians alike, especially after the price of oil plummeted in 2008 and again in 2014. Iran's unique political system is a bold experiment, and tests the question as to whether or not it is possible for a theocracy to be democratic. Another major theme in government and politics that Iran's case raises is the relationship between religion and politics. Is a democracy possible without separating the two into different spheres? Does the state benefit from being based in religious principles that are meant to guide human life in general? On the other hand, does religion increase tensions in the relationship between citizens and state so that the government loses its objectivity and essential fairness to its citizens? For these reasons and more, the evolution of Iran's political system is interesting to watch and vital to understand.

IMPORTANT TERMS AND CONCEPTS

Ahmadinejad, Mahmoud
Assembly of Religious Experts
"axis of evil"
Basij
Baha'i
Constitution of 1979
Constitutional Revolution of 1905-09
Cultural Revolution
"economics is for donkeys"
equality-with-difference
The Executives of Construction Party
faqih
fundamentalism
Guardian Council
head of state, head of government
Hidden Imam
imams
import substitution industrialization
Iranian Militant Clerics Society
Islamic Iran Participation Front
Islamic Society of Engineers
jurist's guardianship (*velayat-e-faqih*)
Khamenei, Ayatollah Ali
Khatami, Muhammad
Khomeini, Ayatollah Ruhollah
Khordad Front
Majles
Majles Election of 2004, 2008
Mosaddeq, Muhammad
Mousavi, Mir-Hossein
Muhammad Reza Shah
National Front
qanun
Qajar Empire
Qom
Pahlavi Foundation

Iran Questions

1. Which of the following is the LEAST important influence on the modern state from Iran's political culture?

A) totalitarianism
B) union of political and religious authority
C) *sharia*
D) strong sense of nationalism
E) uneven distribution of population

2. A similarity between China's Revolution of 1949 and Iran's Revolution of 1979 was that both revolutions

A) resisted religious control of the government
B) were directed by military leaders
C) promoted religious freedoms
D) were led by charismatic figures
E) rejected communism as a central ideology

3. Which of the following pairs of countries are unitary states?

A) Russia and China
B) Iran and China
C) Britain and Russia
D) Mexico and Iran
E) Russia and Mexico

4. Which of the following accurately compares the Chinese military to the Iranian military?

A) In China, the military actively participates in policymaking; in Iran, the military does not.
B) In Iran, the military actively participates in policymaking; in China, the military does not.
C) The military in neither country actively participates in policymaking.
D) The military in both countries actively participates in policymaking.
E) The military in both countries controls the government.

5. Presidents in both Iran and Mexico are

A) limited to serve for only one term
B) directly elected by the people
C) heads of state
D) heads of ideological parties
E) commanders of the armed forces

6. The main goal of the Cultural Revolution that followed the adoption of the Constitution of 1979 was to

A) promote liberal values in schools and universities
B) promote the rights of all groups in civil society
C) advocate and define the responsibilities of the dual executive
D) reject Sunni influences from nearby Arabic nations
E) purify the country from secular values and beliefs

7. Which of the following would be most likely to support state-provided welfare benefits for Iran's poor?

A) a pragmatic conservative cleric
B) a middle-class reformer
C) a middle-class merchant
D) an upper-class supporter of democracy
E) a radical cleric

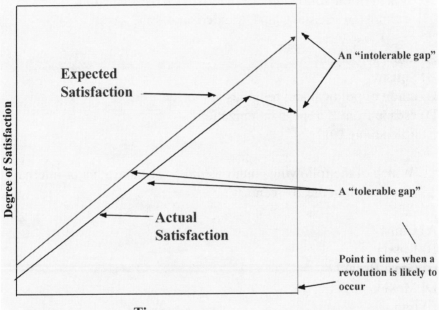

8. According to the "revolution of rising expectations: illustrated above, factor(s) that created he "intolerable gap" that sparked the Iranian revolution of 1979 was

A) the deterioration of the shah's health
B) the shah's crackdown on cvil liberties
C) the return of the Ayatollah Khomeini to Iran
D) the steep drop in oil prices accompanied by a rise in consumer prices
E) the threat that secularism osed to religious fundamentalism

9. A major geographical limitation of Iran is that

A) there is no access to warm water ports
B) it has a climate that is generally too cold for agriculture
C) the densely populated south is separated by mountain ranges from the sparsely populated north
D) much of the land is either desert or mountains
E) it straddles two continents so that citizens are physically separated

10. Which of the following characteristics have shaped the political cultures of Russia, China, Mexico, and Iran?

A) authoritarianism
B) Shiism
C) union of political and religious authority
D) escape from European colonization
E) little arable land

11. Which of the following countries did NOT have a major internal revolution in the 20th century?

A) China
B) Russia
C) Great Britain
D) Mexico
E) Iran

12. Iran's Constitution of 1979 differed from the Constitution of 1909 because it (the Constitution of 1979) put more emphasis on

A) the legislative process
B) democratic electoral processes
C) divinely inspired clerical rule
D) The rule of law
E) civil rights and liberties

13. Which of the following is the best description of the "Tehran spring" that occurred under the presidency of Muhammad Khatami (1997-2005)?

A) a period of state-sponsored wealth redistribution and price controls
B) a period of cautious political liberalization
C) a period of rededication to the Islamic state
D) a period of drastic political and econoic liberalization accompanied by frequent violent protests
E) a period of gradual tightening of government controls over civil society

14. Which of the following is an accurate description of the status of women in Iranian society?

A) Women are well represented in the *Majles*.
B) Women no longer must wear scarves and long coats in public.
C) Women may leave the country without the consent of male relatives.
D) Women are well represented as doctors and government employees.
E) Women now constitute about 10% of the total labor force.

15. Which of the following is the best description of the Iranian party system?

A) Iran has a stable one-party system.
B) Iran has a relatively new two-party system.
C) Iran's party system is factionalized and parties are fluid and weak.
D) One party has dominated Iranian politics in recent years, but other parties are becoming more competitive.
E) Iran has a multi-party system, and most parties are stable and well-established.

16. An important result of the government's population policy that it has held since the late 1980s is that the

A) population has increased significantly
B) fertility rate has declined significantly
C) population has decreased significantly
D) average family size in Iran has grown
E) Iran's population is disproportionately old

17. In Iran ultimate legal authority rests in

A) the Supreme Court
B) the Supreme Leader
C) the Constitution of 1979
D) *sharia* law
E) the *Majles*

18. An important cultural characteristic that separates Iran from most of its near neighbors is its

A) history of authoritarian hereditary rule
B) identity as Shiite rather than Sunni
C) identity as Arab rather than Persian
D) reliance on *sharia* law
E) weak sense of nationalism

19. Under the Pahlavis, Iran was transformed into a rentier state because of its

A) reliance on income from oil
B) high level of agricultural productivity
C) renting of land to its people to use as they saw fit
D) adaptation of western-style democracy
E) one-party system

20. The Ayatollah Khomeini changed the meaning of jurist's guardianship by

A) expanding it to give the clergy authority over the entire Shia community
B) limiting it to the clergy's authority over the unfortunate people in society
C) interpreting it to grant the power to rule to the people
D) creating a Supreme Court to carry out its basic principles
E) interpreting it to reinforce separation of religious and political authority

21. Since 1989, one of the few checks on the supreme leader's power is the right of the

A) president to call for a vote of confidence in the supreme leader
B) Assembly of Religious Experts to remove him from office
C) Guardian Council to overturn the supreme leader's political decisions
D) Supreme Court to declare his actions unconstitutional
E) Expediency Council to side with the *Majles* in disputes between the executive and legislative branches

22. Civil society in Iran expanded most noticeably during the time

A) when the Pahlavi shahs ruled
B) just after the Revolution of 1979
C) just after the death of the Ayatollah Khomeini
D) when Muhammad Khatami was president
E) after Mahmoud Ahmadinejad became president

23. Which of the following are elected to office by direct popular vote in Iran?

A) Guardian Council and the Assembly of Religious Experts
B) Assembly of Religious Experts and the *Majles*
C) Expediency Council and the Guardian Council
D) supreme leader and the *Majles*
E) president and the supreme leader

24. Political parties in both Iran and Russia tend to be organized

A) by positive v. negative attitudes toward the government
B) by religious beliefs
C) by conservative v. liberal political beliefs
D) according to specific interest groups
E) around prominent political leaders/personalities

25. The highest official representing democratic principles in Iran is the

A) president
B) supreme leader
C) chairman of the Assembly of Religious Experts
D) chairman of the Guardian Council
E) leader of the *Majles*

26. Which of the following is a political power held by both the Iranian president and the British prime minister?

A) leading the ruling political party
B) commanding the armed forces
C) declaring war
D) appointing judges
E) devising the budget

27. In contrast to political systems in Britain, Russia, and Mexico, the political system in Iran has a

A) directly elected president
B) Supreme Court
C) unicameral legislature
D) plurality electoral system
E) military with little policy-making power

28. Members of which of the following governing bodies in Iran *must* be clerics?

A) Guardian Council
B) Assembly of Religious Experts
C) Expediency Council
D) *Majles*
E) president's cabinet

29. Which of the following accurately compares elections in Mexico and Iran?

A) Both have direct elections for president.
B) Neither have direct elections for an upper house of the legislature.
C) Mexico has direct elections for the lower house of the legislature, but Iran has no direct elections for legislators.
D) Iran uses proportional representation to elect its legislature; Mexico uses a plurality system to elect its legislature.
E) Elections in Iran are generally less fraudulent than elections in Mexico are.

30. Which of the following is a similarity between the policy-making process in China and Iran?

A) Neither country has a legislature with any real policy-making power.
B) Both countries have fluid weak party systems.
C) In both countries, the military takes an active role in policy-making.
D) The interpretation of law is not an important principle in either country.
E) In both countries, the president has ultimate authority over all other officials.

Free-Response Question: 20 minutes

The political cultures of the Russian Federation and Iran may both be described as conflictual.

(a)   Describe one basic conflict at work within the Russian political culture.

(b)   Explain two political consequences of the conflict you identified in (a) for the modern Russian political system.

(c)   Describe one basic conflict at work within the Iranian political culture.

(d)   Explain two political consequences of the conflict you identified in (c) for the modern Iranian political system.

CHAPTER EIGHT: GOVERNMENT AND POLITICS IN NIGERIA

As Nigeria goes, so goes the rest of sub-Saharan Africa."

a common saying

The quote above reflects both the importance of Nigerian political and economic issues as well as the vulnerability of its political system. With its history of tradition-based kingdoms, colonialism, military dictatorships, and disappointing steps toward democracy, Nigeria faces daunting problems, and it is anyone's guess as to what the future holds. Its importance lies partly in the fact that it is Africa's most populous state, with about 190 million citizens, making it one of the largest countries in the world. Nigeria, like many of its neighbors, is a study in contrasts. The political traditions include strong democracy movements, coupled with a susceptibility to totalitarian military rule. It has vast resources, including one of the largest oil deposits in the world, but 70% of the people live in poverty, with a PPP per capita of about $5900 a year. Nigeria is also a microcosm of worldwide religious tensions, with its population split almost evenly between Islam and Christianity. Yet this division masks an even greater challenge to the nation state: the lack of a coherent national identity that binds together the many ethnicities encompassed within the country's borders. The government's legitimacy was rocked to the core by the flagrantly fraudulent national elections of 2007, which observers declared to be even more flawed than previous elections. However, the elections of 2011 and 2015 appear to have been far cleaner, and hopes for democracy lifted as the crucial element of fair elections were tenuously met.

Is it possible for Nigeria to somehow reconcile a tradition-based and colonial past with the present needs of a modern nation? Will Nigeria's fledgling democracy survive? Will its leaders successfully harness the political muscle once held by the military and learn to better manage the country's resources? Finally, is it possible for the country to stay together, even though its people identify more with individual ethnic groups than with the nation of Nigeria? An examination of these questions, with answers that are far from certain, will help us to understand the dynamics of these issues not only in Nigeria, but in lands far beyond.

SOVEREIGNTY, AUTHORITY, AND POWER

Citizens of all countries have different opinions about how political power should be distributed and how the government should be structured. However, in Nigeria the differences run far deeper than in most other countries. Even though it has been an independent nation since 1960, neither its leaders nor its citizens agree on the basics of who should rule and how. This dilemma is known as the "**national question**" of how the country should be governed, or even if Nigeria should remain as one nation. The issue is magnified by regional disagreements and hostilities and by the tendency to solve problems by military force and authoritarian leaders, not by mutual agreement.

Constitutionalism

Nigeria's first constitution was written in 1914, but since then, eight more constitutions have been written, with the last one introduced in 1999 and heavily amended since. Nigerian constitutions represent attempts to establish a basic blueprint for the operation of the government, but none have lasted for any length of time. As a result, **constitutionalism**, or the acceptance of a constitution as a guiding set of principles, has eluded Nigeria. Military and civilian leaders alike have felt free to disobey and suspend constitutional principles, or to toss out older constitutions for those more to their liking. Without constitutionalism, the "national question" has been much harder to answer.

Legitimacy

The fact that Nigeria is a relatively young country, gaining its independence in 1960, means that establishing the government's legitimacy is a challenging priority. The "national question" is at the heart of the country's legitimacy problems. Nigeria has strong impulses toward fragmentation, or the tendency to fall apart along ethnic, regional, and religious lines. The country's history is full of examples of ethnic and religious conflicts, economic exploitation by the elite, and use of military force. Ironically, the military is one of the few truly national organizations in Nigeria, so despite the problems that it has posed for democracy, it has also been an important source of stability in an unstable country. That stability lends legitimacy to the military's right to rule, and explains why, despite the fact that the last four presidents of Nigeria have been civilians, two (**Olusegun Obasanjo** and **Muhammadu Buhari**) were formerly military generals. Most major candidates for the presidency in recent years have also been drawn from the military, except for two presidents – Umaru Yar'Adua, elected in 2007, and **Goodluck Jonathan**, who became president in 2010.

The legitimacy of the Nigerian government is currently at very low ebb, with many citizens having little or no trust in their leaders' abilities to run an efficient or trustworthy state. Part of the problem lies in the different political impulses originating in contradictory influences from Nigeria's past. As a British colony, Nigerians learned to rely on western rule of law, in which even those that govern are expected to obey and support laws. On the other hand, almost since independence was granted in 1960, Nigerian leaders have used military might to enforce their tentative, personalized authority. These military strong men generally adhered to no discernible rule of law. The corruption associated with General **Ibrahim Babangida**, who ruled from 1985 to 1993, and General **Sani Abacha** (1993-1998) alienated citizens even further. Many people questioned why they should pay taxes when their hard-earned money went straight to the generals' bank accounts. This corruption has tainted civilian rule as well, so that most Nigerians are very skeptical about their government. Yet democratic movements have continued throughout the years, so there is a certain hope beneath the cynicism on the surface.

An important source of legitimacy in the north has been *sharia,* especially since the fall of military rule in 1999. Before that, Islamic law influenced the private sphere for centuries, but in many areas of the north it became public law after 1999. In some areas, Hisbah, a police force charged with enforcing Islamic morality, has searched the streets for violators, and has taken them to Islamic courts to face sentences like death by public stoning. However, in 2008 the federal government cracked down on the Hisbah, enforcing a national ban on religious and ethnic militias, and the secular, federally controlled police force has little interest in enforcing the harshest strictures of *sharia*. It now appears that the application of Islamic law is returning to the role that it has long had – a compromise between the dictates of faith and the realities of modern life in Nigeria. The shift reflects the fact that religious law did not transform society. However, *sharia* is evident in new programs that encourage parents to send their daughters to hybrid public elementary schools that offer traditional Islamic education along with math and reading, an initiative that could significantly improve female literacy rates. State officials are using *sharia* rules on cleanliness to encourage recycling of plastic materials that choke landfills and gutters. If this trend toward moderating Islamic law continues, it is possible that tensions between Muslims and Christians will ease in the future, lessening the pressure on the state to fall apart.

A generation ago novelist Chinua Achebe wrote, "The trouble with Nigeria is simply and squarely a failure of leadership," a statement that strikes at the heart of the country's legitimacy crisis. The deeply flawed election of 2007 reinforced Achebe's statement, as it became apparent that the state and national leaders were selected amidst widespread vote rigging, intimidation, fraud, and violence. As president from 2010 to 2015, Goodluck Jonathan was unable to harness the military to deal with Boko Haram, an Islamic terrorist group in the north. In the election of 2015, the people chose Muhammadu Buhari, a former military general, with the hope of defeating the group and regaining stability.

Political Traditions

Nigerian political traditions run deep and long. Kingdoms appeared as early as 800 C.E., and historical influences may be divided into three eras: the pre-colonial era, the colonial era, and the era since independence.

The Pre-Colonial Era (800-1860)

Centralized states developed early in the geographic area that is now Nigeria, especially in the northern savanna lands. Transportation and communication were easier than in the southern forested area, and the north also needed government to coordinate its need to irrigate crops. Influences from this era include:

- **Trade connections** – The Niger River and access to the ocean allowed contact and trade with other civilizations. Also, trade connections were established across the Sahara Desert to North Africa.

- **Early influence of Islam** – Trade with the north put the early Hausa and other groups in contact with Arabic education and Islam, which gradually replaced traditional customs and religions, especially among the elite. Islamic principles, including the rule of religious law (*sharia*), governed politics, emphasizing authority and policymaking by the elite. All citizens, especially women, were seen as subordinate to the leaders' governance.

- **Kinship-based politics** – Especially among the southern people, such as the Tiv, political organization did not go far beyond the village level. Villages were often composed of extended families, and their leaders conducted business through kinship ties. This political organization contrasts greatly with the tendency toward larger states in the north.

- **Complex political identities** – Unfortunately for those trying to understand Nigeria's political traditions, the contrast between centralized state and local governance is far from clearcut. Even in the south, some centralized kingdoms merged (such as Oyo and Ife), and many small trading-states emerged in the north.

- **Democratic impulses** – One reason why the people of Nigeria today still value democracy despite their recent experiences is that the tradition goes back a long way. Among the Yoruba and Igbo especially, the principle of accountability was well accepted during the pre-colonial period. Rulers were expected to seek advice and to govern in the interest of the people. If they did not, they were often removed from their positions. Leaders were also seen as representatives of the people, and they were responsible for the good of the community, not just their own welfare.

The Colonial Era (1860-1960)

Colonialism came much later to Africa than to many other parts of the world, but its impact was no less important. In contrast to Mexico that gained independence in 1821, Nigeria only broke with its colonial past in 1960. As a result, Nigeria has had much less time to develop a national identity and political stability. Ironically, even though they brought the rule of law with them, the British also planted influences that worked against the democratic patterns set in place in Nigeria during the pre-colonial period.

- **Authoritarian rule** – The British ruled indirectly by leaving chiefs and other natives in charge of governments designed to support British economic interests. In order to achieve their goals of economic domination, the British strengthened the authority of the traditional chiefs, making them accountable only to the British. This new pattern resulted in the loosening of the rulers' responsibility to the people.

- **The interventionist state** – The colonialists trained chiefs to operate their governments in order to reach economic goals. Whereas in Britain individual rights and free market capitalism check the government's power, no such checks existed in Nigeria. This practice set in place the expectation that citizens should passively accept the actions of their rulers.

- **Individualism** – Capitalism and western political thought emphasizes the importance of the individual, a value that generally works well in Britain and the United States. However, in Nigeria it released a tendency for chiefs to think about the personal benefits of governance, rather than the good of the whole community.

- **Christianity** – The British brought their religion with them, and it spread throughout the south and west, the areas where their influence was the strongest. Since Islam already was well entrenched in the north, the introduction of Christianity created a split between Christian and Muslim dominated areas.

- **Intensification of ethnic politics** – During the colonial era, ethnic identities both broadened and intensified into three groups: the **Hausa-Fulani, Igbo,** and **Yoruba**. This process occurred partly because the British pitted the groups against one another in order to manage the colony by giving rewards (such as education and lower-level bureaucratic jobs) to some and not to others. Another factor was the anti-colonial movement that emerged during the 20th century. Independence leaders appealed to ethnic identities in order to gain followers and convince the British to decolonize.

The Era since Independence (1960 to the present)

In the first years after independence, Nigeria struggled to make the parliamentary style of government work, and then settled into military dictatorship by 1966, interspersed with attempts to establish a civilian-led democracy. Traditions established during this era include:

- **Parliamentary-style government replaced by a presidential system** – From 1960 to 1979 Nigeria followed the British parliamentary style government. However, the ethnic divisions soon made it difficult to identify a majority party or allow a prime minister to have the necessary authority. In 1979 the country switched to a presidential system with a popularly-elected president, a separate legislature, and an independent judiciary. However, the latter two branches have not consistently checked the power of the president.

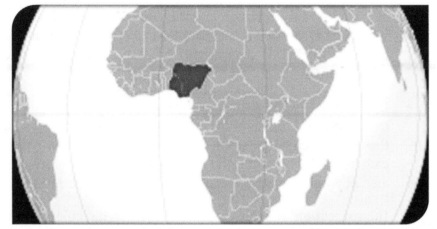

Nigeria's Location in Africa. Nigeria is the most populous country in Africa, with about 140 million people. It is located in the "bight of Africa" along a coastline that Europeans dominated from the late 19th century until the mid-20th century.

- **Intensification of ethnic conflict** – After independence the Hausa-Fulani of the north dominated the parliamentary government by nature of their larger population. To ensure a majority, they formed a coalition with the Igbo of the southeast, which in turn caused resistance to grow among the Yoruba of the west. Rivalries among the groups caused them to turn to military tactics to gain power, and in 1966 a group of Igbo military officers seized power and established military rule.

- **Military rule** – The first military ruler, Agiyi Ironsi, justified his authority by announcing his intention to end violence and stop political corruption. He was killed in a coup by a second general, but the coup sparked the Igbo to fight for independence for their land – called **Biafra** – from the new country of Nigeria. The Biafran Civil War raged on from 1967 until 1970, creating more violence and ethnic-based conflict. Although the country remained together, it did so only under military rule.

- **Personalized rule/corruption** – During colonial rule, native leaders lost touch with the old communal traditions that encouraged them to govern in the interest of the people. Individualism translated into rule for personal gain, and the military regimes of the modern era generally have been characterized by greed and corruption.

- **Federalism** – In an attempt to mollify ethnic tensions yet still remain one country, Nigerian leaders set up a federalist system, with some powers delegated to state and local governments. Although this system may eventually prove to be beneficial, under military regimes it did not work. Theoretically, power was shared. However, military presidents did not allow the sub-governments to function with any separate sovereignty. Instead, the state remained unitary, with all power centered in the capital city of Abuja.

- **Economic dependence on oil** – In many ways, Nigeria's good fortune has been a liability in its quest for political and economic stability. Its rich oil reserves have proved to be too tempting for most of the military rulers to resist, and corruption has meant that oil money only enriched the elite. Abundant oil also has caused other sectors of the economy to be ignored, so that Nigeria's economic survival is based almost exclusively on oil. When the international oil markets fall, so does Nigeria's economy.

Political Culture

All-important historic traditions have shaped a complex modern political culture characterized by ethnic diversity and conflict, corruption, and a politically active military. However, it also includes a democratic tradition and the desire to reinstate leadership that is responsible to the people. Characteristics of the political culture include:

- **Patron-clientelism (prebendalism)** – Nigeria is the third example that we have seen of a political culture characterized by **patron-clientelism.** Just as in China and Mexico, clientelism, the practice of exchanging political and economic favors among patrons and clients, is almost always accompanied by corruption. The patron (or political leader) builds loyalty among his clients (or lesser elites) by granting them favors that are denied to others. For example, in Nigeria, in exchange for their support, a president may grant to his clients a portion of the oil revenues. This practice invites corruption, and it usually means that the larger society is hurt because only a few people benefit from the favors. In Nigeria, patrons are generally linked to clients by ethnicity and religion.

- **State control/rich civil society** – Civil society refers to the sectors of a country that lie outside government control. In Nigerian history, the state has tried to control almost all aspects of life, first under British rule and then under military dictatorship. However, the government has never succeeded in totally dominating civil society. Formal and informal ethnic and religious associations, professional and labor groups, and other NGOs (nongovernmental organizations) have long shaped the society. These groups have related to the government mainly through corporatism and clientelism, but potentially they could form the base of a viable democracy.

- **Tension between modernity and tradition** – Nigeria's colonial past has encouraged it to become a strong, modern nation, but it also has restricted its ability to reach that goal. For many years, Nigeria's status as a colony kept the country in a subservient economic position. Once independence was gained, modernity was difficult to attain because of ethnic-based military conflicts and personalized, corrupt leadership practices. The independence movement itself encouraged Nigerians to reestablish contact with their pre-colonial roots that emphasize communal accountability. Values established in the pre-colonial era conflict with those established in the colonial era, creating the basis for the serious problems that Nigeria faces today.

- **Religious conflict** – Islam began to influence northern Nigeria as early as the 11th century, at first coexisting with native religions, and finally supplanting them. Christianity arrived much later, but spread rapidly through the efforts of missionaries. These two religions have intensified ethnic conflict, and they also have fed political issues. For example, Muslims generally support *sharia,* or religious law, as a valid part of political authority. Christians, of course, disagree. As a result, an ongoing debate about the role of *sharia* in the Nigerian state has sparked religious conflict.

- **Geographic influences** – Nigeria is located in West Africa, bordered on the south by the Gulf of Guinea in the Atlantic Ocean. Its population of 190 million is greater than all the other fourteen countries of West Africa combined, partly because of its size and the lure of employment in its cities and in the oil industry. Nigeria's ethnic groups may be divided into six geographic zones:

    1. Northwest – Dominated by two groups that combined as the Hausa-Fulani people, the area is predominately Muslim.

    2. Northeast – This area is home to many smaller groups, such as the Kanuri, which are also primarily Muslim.

    3. Middle Belt – This area contains many smaller ethnic groups, and it is characterized by a mix of both Muslims and Christians.

    4. Southwest – The large ethnic group called Yoruba dominate this area. The Yoruba are about 40% Muslim, 40% Christian, and about 20% devoted to native religions.

    5. Southeast – This area is inhabited by the Igbo, who are primarily Roman Catholic, but with a growing number of Protestant Christians.

    6. The Southern Zone – This area includes the delta of the huge Niger River, and its people belong to various small minority groups.

POLITICAL AND ECONOMIC CHANGE

Political and economic change in Nigeria may be analyzed by dividing its history into three parts: pre-colonial, colonial, and modern eras. Nigeria's political influences in pre-colonial days varied widely according to ethnicity and region, as did its economic practices. British control during the colonial era brought contradictory political influences – democracy vs. subjugation to colonial rule. Economically Nigeria became highly dependent on British demands, and the colony established a mercantilist role of providing raw materials (like oil) to industrialized nations. Independence in 1960 meant that one of Nigeria's biggest challenges was just that – How does the new country truly become independent, when it has been dependent for so long? The sources of change have varied with each era, but they have all had important consequences for the modern Nigerian state.

The Pre-Colonial Era (800-1860 C.E.)

From the beginning, Nigerian geography has dictated political, social, and economic development. The savanna areas of the north invited easy trade through Saharan Berber traders up to northern Africa, whereas the people of the forested areas of the south were not in contact with the Berbers. Change occurred through cultural diffusion, or contact with and spread of customs and beliefs of other people. Most important was the diffusion of Islam, a change that was gradual, with conversion to the religion occurring slowly but steadily over time.

Despite the overall nature of gradual change, an important group – the Fulani – came to the north through jihad, or Islamic holy war, so this change occurred abruptly. In 1808 the Fulani established the **Sokoto Caliphate**, a Muslim state that encompassed the entire northwest, north mid section, and part of the northeast. The caliphate traded with Europeans, and eventually succumbed to British colonial rule by 1900. However, it put in place the tradition of an organized, central government based on religious faith.

In contrast, people in the south generally lived communally and in closer contact with the Atlantic Ocean trade. As a result, even before the colonial era, they came into contact with Europeans who converted many of them to Christianity. An important consequence of this contact plagued Nigeria from the 16th through the 19th century in the form of the Atlantic slave trade. The first contacts were with the Portuguese, but the real displacement of people began in the 17th century, when the Dutch, British, French, and Spanish traders began transporting Africans in large numbers to the New World from the Nigerian coast. The impact on the people is difficult to quantify, but the very nature of the slave trade meant that countless young males were forced to leave their native lands.

The Colonial Era (1860-1960)

European influence began in the earlier era, but in 1860 the British imposed indirect rule, in which they trained natives, primarily from the south, to fill the European-style bureaucracy. The British established the area that would become Nigeria in 1860 as a trading outlet, where they made use of natural resources and cheap human labor. The British influence was strongest in the south, emanating from the ports along the coast.

Because the north was already organized into political hierarchies according to Islamic tradition, the British left that area's government structures primarily intact. These political changes gave more power to elites, and reinforced their tendencies to seek personal benefit from their positions. It further emphasized differences between north and south, leaving the colony vulnerable to divisions that later caused serious conflict and violence.

Another important influence from the colonial era was the introduction to Nigeria of western-style education. Christian missionaries set up schools subsidized by the British government, primarily for elementary education. In 1934, the first higher education institution was opened, and the first university was founded in 1948. This change had many important consequences, the most obvious being the creation of a relatively literate population. However, it also reinforced some growing cleavages. Elites became more and more separated from the people because they received most of the benefits of education. As a result, they tended to see themselves as privileged leaders who deserved economic rewards. Another consequence was a deepening of the rift between north and south, since most of the British schools were located in the south, and very few northerners had access to western-style education. In turn, northerners came to be seen as backward by southerners, and northerners came to resent this stereotype.

Modern Nigeria (1960-Present)

Nigeria's transition to independence began to take place in the years preceding 1960, with the British trying to "prepare" Nigerians to rule their own country. Indeed, the preparation began early because the British trained natives to join the bureaucracy. Education invariably included the teaching of western political values, including freedom, justice, and equality of opportunity. These lessons were not lost on the native leaders for Nigerian independence, so British education sowed the seeds for decolonization.

An important change in the early post-colonial days came in 1966 when the parliamentary government was replaced by a military dictatorship. This action set in motion the tendency for government to change hands quickly and violently, as the nation began to experience a series of military coup d'états. In 1979 the military dictator, **Olusegun Obasanjo**, willingly stood down for a democratically-elected president, Shehu Shagari, but Shagari was forced out of office in 1983 by a military coup led by General Muhammadu Buhari. Two more coups kept Nigeria under military dictatorship until 1999, when a democratic election brought Obasanjo back to power, but this time as a civilian. The elections of 1999, 2003, and 2007 were rife with fraud and violence, with the election of 2007 probably the worst of all. At the same time, the development of nationalism eluded Nigeria, and created the "**national question**," or the possibility that Nigeria would not survive as a country.

The modern era has also seen ethnic identities become the major basis for conflict in Nigeria. Before the colonial era, these ethnicities certainly existed, but the different identities did not lead to constant conflict. Independence brought on a competition among groups, based on heightened awareness of ethnic differences encouraged by the British. Once the British were gone, competition among military generals for control of the country became based on ethnicity, and the heightened tensions have left reconciliation of differences all the more difficult.

Another change brought about during the modern era has been the institutionalization of corruption among the political elite. This tendency was made much worse by two military presidents: General Ibrahim B. Babangida, president from 1985 to 1993, and General Sani Abacha, from 1993 to 1998. Both generals maintained large foreign bank accounts, with regular deposits being diverted from the Nigerian state. Other funds went to the Nigerian elite through the patron client system. For example, it is estimated that about 2/3 of the windfall Nigeria received in oil sales during the first Persian Gulf War in 1991 ended up in the hands of Nigerian elites.

Each military leader between 1966 and 1999 promised to transfer power to civilians as soon as the country was "stable." In 1993 it seemed as if the time had arrived when civilian Moshood Abiola won the presidential election. However, General Babangida annulled the election, only to lose power to General Sani Abacha in a military coup later that year. When Abacha died suddenly in 1998, a Middle-Belt Muslim General, Abdulsalami Abubakar succeeded him, with the now-familiar promise to eventually hand over the government to a duly elected civilian. He set up a transition team, elections were held in 1999, and the winner, Olusegun Obasanjo, became president. Obasanjo was re-elected in 2003, and some hope that these events indicate the long anticipated arrival of a democratic government. However, two facts made it difficult to claim the triumph of democracy: Obasanjo was a former military general, and both elections were characterized by voting fraud. The election of 2007 was even more questionable than the previous two, and so the potential for instability is still a threat to the country. Even though the elections of 2011 and 2015 were an improvement, no clear trend toward democratization is yet in place.

CITIZENS, SOCIETY, AND THE STATE

The people of Nigeria have some huge challenges in establishing democratic ties with their government. Democratization is always a difficult process because it assumes that citizens have both the time and means to pay attention to political and societal issues. Even in advanced democracies, people often do not link their everyday concerns with those of the government. Many societal characteristics of Nigeria make democratization a challenge:

LEADERSHIP TRANSITIONS IN NIGERIA SINCE 1960

RULER	GOVERNMENT TYPE	REASON FOR TRANSITION
1960-1966 Tafawa Balewa (Prime Minister)	Republic	Military coup; Balewa assassinated
1966 Johnson Aguyi-Ironsi	Military dictatorship	Military coup; Ironsi assassinated
1966-1975 Yakubu Gowon	Military dictatorship	Military coup; Gowon replaced
1975-1976 Murtala Muhammed	Military dictatorship	Military coup; Muhammed assassinated
1976-1979 Olusegun Obasanjo	Military dicatorship	Replaced by democratically elected president
1979-1983 Shehu Shagari	Presidential democracy	Military coup; Shagari replaced
1983-1985 Muhammed Buhari	Military dictatorship	Military coup; Buhari replaced
1985-1993 Ibrahim Babangida	Military dictatorship	Military coup; Babangida resigned under pressure
1993-1998 Sani Abacha	Military dictatorship	Death of Abacha; Abdulsami Abubakar rules temporarily
1999-2007 Olusegun Obasanjo	Presidential democracy	Reached end of two-term presidency
2007-2010 Umaru Yar'Adua	Presidential democracy	Death of Yar'Adua
2010-2015 Goodluck Jonathan	Presidential democracy	Lost election of 2015
2015-Present	Muhammed Buhari	

Leadership transitions. Nigeria's unstable leadership is reflected in the table above as the country first tried parliamentary government that was taken over by military coup, and then changed to a presidential system in 1979, only to have the government seized again by the military in 1983. Since 1999 the country has elected the president in a series of questionable elections (1999, 2003, 2007), although the elections of 2011 and 2015 appeared to be cleaner.

- **A large gap between the rich and the poor** – Like Mexico, the distribution of income in Nigeria is very unequal (Gini index of .43), with a few people being very wealthy and most being very poor. However, Nigeria's economy shows fewer signs of growth, and so the outlook for closing the income gap is much bleaker.

- **Health issues** – Like many other African nations, Nigeria has high rates of HIV/AIDS, with some estimating that one of every 11 HIV/AIDS sufferers in the world lives in Nigeria. The toll that the disease has taken on the African continent is incalculable, and the cost to the Nigerian economy, as well as to society in general, is immeasurable. The government has generally made AIDS a secondary priority, leaving much of the challenge to a small group of underfunded nongovernmental organizations (NGOs). The government has provided medications through a small number of clinics, but they reach only a few thousand people in a country where several million people are estimated to be HIV positive.

- **Literacy** – Nigeria's overall literacy rate is 59.6%, but there is a gap between the male literacy rate at 69.2%; and the female rate of 49.7%. This is higher than for many other nations in Africa, but is below the world average of 89.9% for men, and 82.2%% for women.

Cleavages

Nigeria has one of the most fragmented societies in the world, with important cleavages based on ethnicity, religion, region, urban/rural differences, and social class. Nigeria is similar to Russia in that both have had to contend with ethnic-based civil wars – Russia in the ongoing conflict with Chechnya, and Nigeria with the Biafran Civil War between 1967 and 1970. In both countries, the ethnic conflicts have undermined the basic legitimacy of the government. The consequences of these cleavages for the Nigerian political system have been grave because they have made any basic agreements about governance almost impossible.

- **Ethnicity** – Nigeria has between 250 and 400 separate ethnic groups with their own array of customs, languages, and religions. The three largest groups – the Hausa-Fulani, Igbo, and Yoruba – have very little in common, and generally cannot speak one another's languages. They live separately in their own enclaves, and virtually no contacts take place among the groups.

COMPARATIVE LITERACY RATES

China
Males	98.2%
Females	94.5%

Iran
Males	91.2%
Females	82.5%

Mexico
Males	95.5%
Females	93.5%

Nigeria
Males	69.2%
Females	49.7%

Russia
Males	99.7%
Females	99.6%

United Kingdom
Males	99%
Females	99%

Source: *CIA Factbook,* 2012-2016 estimates

The table above shows that Nigeria's literacy rates for both men and women are significantly lower than those for the other five countries. China and Russia's high rates reflect the emphasis that communist leaders put on literacy, as well as equality between the sexes. Nigeria's rates are not only low, but they also show a large gap between male and female literacy rates, as do the rates for Iran. A related statistic for Nigeria is that each woman bears an average of 4.91 children in her lifetime, which means that women's educational opportunities are often cut short by having children at a young age and remaining at home with offspring.

- **Religion** – In China and the former Soviet Union, ethnic tensions are (were) managed by imposing communism on the society so that some unifying ideology held the people together. Nigeria has had no such ideology, but instead its political culture is made more complex by competing religions. About half of all Nigerians are Muslim, 40% are Christian, and the remaining 10% affiliate with native religions. Ethnic tensions are exacerbated by religious differences among Muslims, Christians, and those that practice native religions. International tensions between Muslims and Christians are reflected in Nigeria, but their arguments are rooted in the preferential treatment that the British gave to Christians. Disputes regarding the religious law of Islam, the *sharia,* and its role in the nation's policymaking practices reflect the significance of religious cleavages.

- **Region/north vs. south** – Although Nigeria's ethnic divisions are multiple, the country was divided into Three Federated Regions in 1955, five years before independence was official. These regions follow ethnic and religious divisions, and they are the basis for setting election and legislative procedures, as well as political party affiliations. Another way to divide Nigeria by region is north vs. south, with the north being primarily Muslim, and the South mainly Christian.

- **Urban/rural differences** – As in many other countries, significant urban/rural differences divide Nigeria. Political organizations and interest groups exist primarily in cities, as well as newspapers and electronic media sources. Although their activities were suppressed by the annulment of the election of 1993 and the execution of rights activist and environmentalist Ken Saro-Wiwa in 1995, most organized protests have taken place in cities.

- **Social class** – The division between elites and ordinary people runs deep in Nigeria. The wealth of the elites stems from control of the state and the resources of the country. They have maintained power through appealing to ethnic and religious identities of the people. The elites generally have found it difficult to abandon their access to the government's treasury for personal gain, and yet many educated elite would like to see Nigeria transformed into a modern nation based on democratic principles.

Public Opinion and Political Participation

Nigeria is not yet a democracy, and despite a historically rich civil society, its citizens have been encouraged to relate to government as subjects, not as active participants. Some activities are now taking

Nigeria's Diversity. The ethno-linguistic map above shows the diversity of Nigeria and its neighboring countries, Benin and Cameroon. The shade variations in the map indicate different languages, and the names show some of the many ethnic groups that inhabit the area. Notice how the political boundaries between countries do not follow ethno-linguistic lines. In recent years, the capital of Nigeria was moved from Lagos (on the coast) to Abuja (in the center of the country) in an effort to create a neutral zone in the center of the country.

place in civil society, or the realm outside the government influence, with some professional associations, trade unions, religious groups, and various other interest groups emerging. Even with the presence of military rule, presidents have generally allowed a free press to exist and interest group membership to be maintained.

Patron-Clientelism (Prebendalism)

Much participation, particularly in rural areas, still takes place through the patron-client system. The special brand of clientelism in Nigerian politics is known as "**prebendalism**," a term borrowed from Max Weber's concept of an extremely personalized system of rule in which all public offices are treated as personal fiefdoms. By creating large patronage networks based on personal loyalty, civilian officials have skewed economic and political management to such an extent that they have often discredited themselves. Local government officials gain support from villagers through dispensing favors, and they in turn receive favors for supporting patron bosses. Of course, most favors are exchanged among the political elite, but the pattern persists on all levels. With patron-clientelism comes corruption and informal influence, but it does represent an established form of political participation in Nigeria.

Civil Society

In Nigeria's postcolonial history, many formal interest groups and informal voluntary associations have actively sought to influence political decisions. Since 1999 many have strengthened, some serving as centripetal forces, encouraging Nigerian unity, and others creating centrifugal influences, causing Nigeria to fragment along ethnic and religious lines. One group that has managed to do both is the Movement for the Survival of the Ogoni People, or MOSOP, founded by dissident **Ken Saro-Wiwa** in the 1990s. MOSOP has worked to apply national laws to secure financial benefits for the Ogoni in the Niger Delta and to hold foreign-operated oil companies to environmental standards.

Trade unions and professional organizations have been particularly active in trying to protect the rights of their members. For example, the National Union of Petroleum and Gas Workers (NUPENG) has been an influential voice for workers in the all-important petroleum industry. Formal associations for legal, medical, and journalism professions articulate the political interests of Nigeria's growing professional class.

Voting Behavior

Nigerian citizens have voted in national elections since 1959, but since many elections have been canceled or postponed by the military and others have been fraudulent, voter behavior patterns are difficult to track. Political parties are numerous and fluid, with most formed around the charisma of their candidates for office, so party loyalty is an imperfect reflection of voter attitudes. Babangida's annulment of the 1993 election also put a damper on political participation during most of the 1990s. However, elections on local, state, and national levels were held in 1999 and 2003, although their results appear to be fraudulent. Nevertheless, Nigerian citizens voted in large numbers in both the 1999 and 2003 elections. One estimate is that close to 2/3 of eligible voters actually voted in 2003, but the widespread corruption around the election make those figures highly unreliable. The participation rates in the 2007 election are almost impossible to calculate because of voter fraud and inability of legitimate voters to cast their ballots. In the more reliable election of 2011 more than 3% of the votes were declared invalid, but the turnout of valid voters was almost 54%. In 2015, 2.8% were declared invalid, but the turnout was less than 44%, partly because of difficulty voting in areas in the northeast where the terrorist organization, Boko Haram, held control at the time of the election.

Attitudes toward Government

Not surprisingly, most Nigerians have a low level of trust in their government. General Abacha was so widely disliked that there was rejoicing and celebration in the street when he died unexpectedly in 1998, with some citizens dubbing the event a "coup from heaven." Nigerians in general are skeptical about the prospects for democracy, and they do not believe that elections are conducted in a fair and honest way. Whether or not Nigerians will remain cynical, however, is yet to be seen. In the early days of independence, attitudes toward the government were generally much more favorable, and many citizens expressed an identity as Nigerians, not just as members of ethnic groups. Perhaps the cynicism results from the notorious rule of Babangida and Abacha in the 1980s and 90s and will soon change. However, without the commitment to democracy from political elites, ordinary citizens are unlikely to see their government in a positive light in the near future.

According to an Afrobarometer survey published in 2013, the majority of citizens (67 percent) describe the present economic condition of the country as "very bad or fairly bad." Additionally, the survey revealed that 81 percent of Nigerians assessed the government's performance in managing the economy as "very badly or fairly bad." 50 percent say they would go to the police for assistance if they were victims of crime (the top reason for not going to the police is the need to pay a bribe). Despite these bleak statistics, many Nigerians thought the quality of the election of 2011 was "better" than the election of 2007. Still, only 38% rated the election "completely free and fair." Nigerian attitudes toward democracy are shared by citizens in many other African countries. According to an Afrobarometer survey published in 2006, 6 in 10 Africans sampled in 18 countries said that democracy was preferable to any other form of government. However, satisfaction with democracy dipped to 45% from 58% in 2001.

Nigerian citizens' negative perceptions of their government are based in some very solid evidence that government officials are quite corrupt. **Transparency International**, a private organization that compiles statistics about corruption in countries around the world, usually ranks Nigeria very low in the "Transparency International Corruption Perceptions Index" that they publish every year. In 2006 Nigeria ranked 142nd out of 146 countries in terms of how "clean" its government is. In 2017, the country's score was 27, ranking it toward the bottom of the list. Mexico's score (29), Russian's score (29), Iran's score (30), and China's score (41) were somewhat higher, but five of the six core countries are low, considering that the scale is 1-100. Only the United Kingdom, with a score of 82, can claim to have a relatively "clean" government, with a rank of 8 out of 178 countries.

CORRUPTION PERCEPTION INDEX 2017

COUNTRY	CPI SCORE*	RANK (178 COUNTRIES TOTAL)
China	41	77
Iran	30	130
Mexico	29	135**
Nigeria	27	148
Russia	29	135**
United Kingdom	82	8

*The Corruption Perception Index Score is compiled every year by Transparency International. Countries are ranked from 1 to 100, with a 100 reflecting a corruption-free government.
**a tie

Source: *Transparency International*, www.transparency.org

China, Mexico, and Nigeria all are characterized by patron-clientelism, so it is not surprising that all have relatively low CPI scores. Since Transparency International considers a score of 1 to be "highly corrupt," the chart supports the fact that corruption is a big problem in all of the six countries except for the United Kingdom. In all five cases (China, Mexico, Nigeria, Iran, and Russia) corruption is part of the political culture, and bribes and favoritism are a part of the ways that governments operate. Nigeria's prebendalism permeates the political system to such a degree that political participation cannot take place outside its influence.

One controversial action taken by Yar'Adua's administration in 2008 was the removal from office of Nuhu Ribadu, the head of the Economic and Financial Crimes Commission (EFCC), a government organization set up to fight corruption. Since 2003, Ribadu had gained a reputation for bravely charging and prosecuting the politicians, particularly the state governors, who are responsible for most of the fraud and looting of public funds. In 2007 the EFCC arrested seven former governors, including James Ibori of the oil-rich Delta States, who was a leader of the ruling People's Democratic Party and a major funder of Yar'Adua's election campaign. Two weeks after Ibori's arrest, the government announced that Ribadu was resigning in order to be "re-educated" in a special training program. Many believe that EFCC had made real progress in addressing Nigeria's corruption, but the agency was not allowed to continue its investigations and arrests.

During the election campaign of 2015, Muhammadu Buhari promised to curb corruption, including theft of public funds by elites and poor government practices and supervision. The high level of corruption is a decades-old pattern, so it is imbedded in the political system and the society in general, so curbing corruption is no easy task.

Protests and Political Participation

Since the return of democracy in 1999, a number of ethnic-based and religious movements have mobilized to pressure the federal government to address their grievances. International oil companies have been major targets, especially in the Niger Delta where the companies and oil fields are centered. A widely publicized protest occurred in July 2002 when a group of unarmed Ijaw women occupied Chevron-Texaco's Nigerian operations for 10 days. The siege ended when ChevronTexaco's officials agreed to provide jobs for the women's sons, and set up a credit plan to help village women start businesses. Although this protest ended peacefully, others were violently suppressed by the Obasanjo government. A major upswing in protests and unrest began in early 2006, with groups organizing to attack the foreign-based oil companies. Armed rebel gangs have blown up pipelines, disabled pumping states, and kidnapped foreign oil workers. These events in Nigeria, the world's eighth largest oil exporter, have affected international energy markets, contributing to higher prices and tighter supplies. As a result, production sites have been shut down, and some companies have left Nigeria, often blaming the government for its inability to stop the problems. An amnesty was signed in 2009, and so in recent years, the conflicts have lessened but the uneasiness remains.

After the election of 2011, when Goodluck Jonathan, a Christian from the south, retained the presidency that he had assumed when Yar'Adua died in 2010, protests erupted in the north among people who believed that the informal rule of alternating presidents from the north and south had been violated. One group, Boko Haram, carried out almost daily shootings and occasional bombings, trying to undermine Jonathan's authority. The group, whose name means "Western education is sinful," says it is fighting for the wider application of *sharia* law in Nigeria, and has claimed responsibility for hundreds of attacks in the north, often aimed at police, churches, and bars. Although Boko Haram's ideology is not widely supported in Nigeria, where most Muslims are moderate, it has built a following by playing on people's frustrations. Amnesty International has criticized the Nigerian military's retaliation to attacks, claiming that unlawful arrests, extra-judicial killings and unexplained disappearances have occurred.

By 2013, Boko Haram had killed more than a thousand people, and so the Nigerian government launched a campaign to crush the insurgency, using thousands of troops, vehicles, and even fighter jets and helicopter gunships. President Jonathan placed a large part of Nigeria's north under a state of emergency, ordering troops to "take all necessary action" to end the terrorism. In May 2013, more than 200 people were killed in what local officials, residents, and human rights groups said was a sweeping massacre by Nigerian forces in Baga, in northern Nigeria. Since much of the area was put under a communications blackout, it was difficult to know what was going on, but the crackdown resulted in thousands of people fleeing across the border to Niger.

In 2014-2015, Boko Haram stepped up the attacks, and gained international attention with the kidnapping and disappearance of 276 schoolgirls from Chibok in April 2014. In mid-2014, the group gained control of territory in their home state of Borno. In 2015, a military coalition, including Chad, Niger and Nigeria displaced the group from most of its territory. However, violence continued as Boko Haram claimed responsibility for further attacks that continued to the present.

POLITICAL INSTITUTIONS

In its long history, Nigeria has experienced many different regime types. In its pre-colonial days, the regime type varied from one area to another. In the north and west, well-developed large states with hereditary monarchs developed, and in the south, small communal kinship-based rule predominated. The Hausa people in the west were organized into powerful trading city-states. Regime-type changed dramatically with colonization, with the British imposition of indirect rule. Where chiefs did not exist, the British created them, and authoritarian rule under British direction was well developed by the mid-20th century. Authoritarian rule has continued into the independence era, when a military-style regime emerged by 1966.

Today the government structure is formally federalist and democratic, but it has not generally operated as such. The British controlled economic life during the colonial era, and the economy remains under state control today. However, international factors have forced Nigeria to turn to international organizations – such as the World Bank and the International Monetary Fund – for help in restructuring the economy.

Linkage Institutions

Because Nigeria's efforts to democratize are so far incomplete, linkage institutions in general are both newly developed and highly fluid. However, Nigerian citizens have organized in a number of ways with varying degrees of impact on Nigerian politics.

Political Parties

Predictably, political parties in Nigeria have almost always been regionally and ethnically based. Unlike Mexico, Nigeria did not develop a one-party system in the 20th century that contributed to political stability. Instead, Nigeria's extreme factionalism led to the development of so many parties that it was almost impossible to create a coherent party system. The resulting multi-party system has reinforced and deepened ethnic and religious cleavages. Parties also form around powerful individuals, and so tend to fade with leadership changes.

Parties have appeared, disappeared, and reorganized frequently. However, in the election of 2015, these two parties supported major presidential candidates:

- **The People's Democratic Party (PDP)** – This is one of the better-established parties, having run candidates for office as early as 1998. The PDP is the party of Olusegun Obasanjo, and in 2003 he received about 62% of the vote for president. In 2007, amidst widespread fraud, Umaru Yar'Adua received almost 70% of the vote. The party also gained the overwhelming majority in the National Assembly, and most of the governors elected were candidates of the PDP. However, because the elections were fraudulent, it is very difficult to know how much real support the PDP actually has. Obasanjo is a Christian and Yoruba from the south, but the party won elections throughout the country. Yar'Adua was a Muslim from the north, and when he died in 2010, his vice president, Goodluck Jonathan, a Southern Christian took over as acting president, and in 2011, Jonathan was elected president in his own right, but he lost the 2015 election to All Progressive Congress candidate Muhammadu Buhari.

- **All Progressive Congress** – Prior to the election the All Progressive Congress was formed as an alliance of four opposition parties – the Action Congress of Nigeria, the Congress for Progressive Change, the All Nigeria People's Party, and the All Progressives Grand Alliance. In primaries held in December 2014, Muhammadu Buhari won the new party's candidacy for president, and eventually won the election.

One trend since 1999 is for parties to lose their regional base and to draw support from many parts of the country. The PDP originated in the Muslim north, but deliberately ran Obasanjo, a Christian Yoruba from the south, as its candidate in 1999 and 2003. As a result, it became the dominant party; however, all three elections before 2011 were fraudulent, and the violence levels were high enough (more than 200 people were killed in protests surrounding the 2007 elections) that it was difficult for PDP to claim legitimacy. Since the 2011 elections were much cleaner, the PDP's legitimacy increased, although the party was criticized for not running a Muslim from the North, since Jonathan – a southern Christian – had been president since 2010. In 2015, the All Progressive Congress made big inroads into the South, insuring the election of Buhari as president.

A flurry of party registrations with the **Independent National Election Commission (INEC)** followed the death of President Abacha in 1998. In order to run candidates for the legislative and presidential elections of 1999, a party had to qualify by earning at least 5% of the votes in two-thirds of the states in the December 1998 local elections. This practice effectively cut the number of parties running to three, and also limited the eligible parties to five in the presidential election of 2003. The INEC was widely accused of corruption in the election of 2007, and of complying with President Obasanjo's desire to keep Vice President Abubakar from running for the presidency. The INEC left his name off the list of official candidates, but his disqualification was overturned by the Supreme Court. Before the election of 2011, President Jonathan asked Attahiru Jega, a respected academic, to head the INEC, and Jega drew up a new voter register, removing names that were obviously fraudulent. For example, a village in Kanduna state that reported 50,000 votes for the PDP in 2007, was shown to contain only 4,000 voters. He also had ballot papers printed abroad to limit their supply, though a later delivery forced a one-week delay in legislative, gubernatorial, and presidential elections. Jega also supervised a switch to the "open secret ballot" system: voters were asked to register at polling stations on election day, and they were encouraged to stay there until results were posted locally in order to verify them and to prevent multiple voting. These reforms contributed to relatively fair and open elections in 2011 and 2015, the first in Nigeria's recent history.

Elections and Electoral Procedures

Citizens vote for candidates on three levels: local, state, and national. On the national level, they vote for the president, representatives to the House of Representatives, and for senators from their states.

National Elections

- **Presidential elections** – The first presidential election after the annulled election of 1993 took place in 1999, followed by a second election in 2003. If a presidential candidate does not receive an outright majority, a second ballot election may take place. A candidate won in the first round for the first time in 2011, when Goodluck Jonathan won almost 59% of the vote. An unusual requirement, however, reflects Nigeria's attempt to unite its people. A president also must receive at least 25% of all the votes cast in 2/3 of the states. In other words, a purely regional candidate cannot win the presidency. The requirement also indicates how difficult unification has been for Nigeria since independence in 1960.

- **Legislative elections** – The **Senate** has 109 senators, three from each of 36 states, and one from the federal capital territory, Abuja. They are elected by direct popular vote. The 360 members of the **House of Representatives** are elected from single member districts by plurality vote. No run-offs take place for these seats. The result in both houses is regional representation, with a wide array of ethnicities that try to form coalitions, even though legislative policymaking power is very weak anyway. Currently, the PDP holds a majority in both houses, although several other parties are represented.

Election Fraud

Many observers believe that Nigeria has made significant progress simply to be able to sustain four regularly scheduled popular elections in a row. During the April 12, 2003 legislative election, about a dozen people died, but many commented that it was not as bad as it could have been. Additionally, several politicians were assassinated, including Marshall Harry, one of the leaders of Mr. Buhari's All Nigeria People's Party. However, the Independent National Electoral Commission (INEC), with outside pressure, made an attempt to cleanse the electoral process when it declared almost six million names to be fraudulent. The names were struck from the voter rolls. On the other hand, international teams that observed the election generally concluded that the election was corrupt, with ballot boxes being vandalized, stolen, and stuffed with fraudulent votes. Some concluded that voting patterns in the south were particularly suspicious.

The elections of 2007 were even worse, with national legislative and presidential races deeply flawed, as were the state and local contests. The year before the election President Obasanjo sponsored a plan to modify the 1999 constitution that would allow him to run for a third term of office, but the National Assembly failed to ratify it. Next, the Independent National Election Committee disqualified Vice President Abubakar from running for president, but the Supreme Court declared that the INEC had no such power. Last-minute ballots were printed and distributed to include him, but the ballots showed only party symbols, not the names of candidates, and lacked serial numbers that help reduce fraud. On election day, international observers, including some from the European Union and some from the United States, witnessed instances of ballot-box theft, long delays in the delivery of ballots and other materials, and a shortage of ballots for the presidential race. Often there was no privacy for voters to mark their ballots in secret. Observers also witnessed unused ballots being marked and stuffed into ballot boxes. Frustrated voters erupted in protest, and the ensuing violence ended in the deaths of about 200 people.

The Elections of 2011

The elections of 2011, however, were considered by most observers to be a big improvement over 2007, at least partly because of reforms initiated by the INEC. Goodluck Jonathan (from the south) won almost 59% of the vote, and Muhammadu Buhari (from the north) won 32%. PDP candidates won majorities in both houses of the legislature, although the ACN, CPC, and several other parties won Senate and House seats. Flaws – such as under-age voting and chaotic local counting centers – were noted, but the reforms apparently controlled the amount of fraud. Despite these changes, the election starkly exposed the ethnic and religious divide between north and south. Mr. Jonathan did not win a single one of the 12 northernmost states, out of Nigeria's total of 36. Mr. Buhari got less than a quarter of the vote in the 20 southernmost ones. Even before the results were tallied, youths began burning buildings in northern cities, and bombs exploded in the days that followed. Human rights groups claimed that hundreds of people were killed, and a heavy military presence and curfews in the worst-hit states of the north restored the calm. Still, the violence reflected the country's cleavages, and almost certainly resulted from discontent fed by high poverty rates in the north, leaving Nigeria's "national question" as open as ever.

The Elections of 2015

The elections were first scheduled to be held on February 14, 2015, but they were postponed to March 28, mainly due to the poor distribution of Permanent Voters' Cards, especially in areas where people had been displaced from their homes by Boko Haram. The government also claimed that the postponement was necessary to allow time to contain the group's insurgency in several northeastern states. Critics claimed that the postponement was a ploy by the incumbent president, Goodluck Jonathan, to buy time to sway support from the main opposition candidate, Muhammadu Buhari. However, Buhari won the election by more than 2.5 million votes, marking the first time an incumbent president has lost re-election in Nigeria. Buhari's party, All Progressives Congress, also picked up seats in the House of Representatives and the Senate, and Jonathan's People's Democratic Party lost seats in both houses.

Boko Haram attempted to disrupt the elections by attacking voting centers, killing 41 people, and an opposition politician, Umaru Ali, was gunned down in one attack. However, the elections were generally peaceful and orderly, according to observers from the African Union, Commonwealth of Nations, Economic Community of West

African States, and the European Union. United Nations Secretary-General Ban Ki-moon congratulated Nigerian citizens and the government for conducting a successful and peaceful election.

Interest Groups

Perhaps surprisingly, interest groups have played an important role in Nigerian government and politics. Although the development of an active civil society has been hampered by prebendalism and corruption, there is an array of civil society organizations that often cooperate with political parties. Some of them are based on religion, such as the Christian Association of Nigeria that protested loudly when Babangida decided to change Nigeria's status in the Organization of the Islamic Conference from observer to member. A large number of Muslim civil society organizations in the north work to support the *sharia* court system. They have had to work around military control, but citizens have sought an impact on political life through labor unions, student groups, and populist groups.

Labor Unions

Labor unions before the military oppression of the 1980s were independent and politically powerful. Organized labor challenged governments during both the colonial and post-colonial eras, but the Babangida regime devised methods to limit their influence. This was established through corporatism, or government-approved interest groups that provide feedback to the government. A central labor organization supplanted the older unions, and only candidates approved by Babangida could be elected as labor leaders. However, the labor movement still is alive, and retains an active membership. If democracy indeed is established, labor unions could play a vital role in the policymaking process. For example, in July 2003, labor unions widely and openly protested the government's attempt to raise oil prices for Nigerian consumers.

By 2007 it was clear that labor unions had regained much of their previous power when the **Nigeria Labor Congress** called and successfully orchestrated a general strike of workers in cities across Nigeria. The strike was organized to protest the government's hike in fuel prices and taxes. The government agreed to rescind their hikes, but strike organizers wanted further reductions. The Nigerian government has subsidized fuel heavily, just as the Iranian government has, and in both cases, the subsidies are quite expensive. Nigeria especially is under international pressure to cut the subsidies so that the immense national debt can be paid.

Business Interests

Business interests have tended to work in collaboration with the military regimes during the last decades, and have shared the spoils of the corruption within the elite classes. However, some business associations have operated outside the realm of government influence in the private sector. Associations for manufacturers, butchers, and car rental firms are only a few groups that have organized. In the 1990s, some of these groups became a leading force in promoting economic reform in Nigeria.

Human Rights Groups

Other interest groups have organized to promote human rights. University students, teachers, civil liberties organizations, and professional groups (doctors, lawyers) protested the abuses of the Babangida and Abacha regimes, and remain active promoters of democratic reform. They staged street demonstrations and protests in 1997-98 as Abacha prepared to orchestrate a campaign to succeed himself. Although the groups are now only loosely connected, their willingness to collaborate and remain active might play an important role in creating a true democracy in Nigeria.

Mass Media

In contrast to most less developed countries, Nigeria has long had a well-developed, independent press. General Abacha moved to muffle its criticisms of his rule when he closed several of the most influential and respected Nigerian newspapers and magazines in 1994. However, the tradition remains intact, although the press reflects, like so many other institutions, the ethnic divisions within the country. Most of the outspoken newspapers are in the south, although a few have been published in the north. Generals from the north have often interpreted criticisms of the press as ethnic slurs reflective of region-based stereotypes. The media actively spread news as the events of the 2007 elections unfolded, and many journalists were highly critical of the government's actions.

Radio is the main source of information for most Nigerians, with newspapers and TV more common in the cities. All 36 states run their own radio stations.

THE INSTITUTIONS OF NATIONAL GOVERNMENT

Nigeria is in theory a federal political system with government organizations on local, state, and national levels. Its various constitutions have provided for three branches of government, but in reality its executive branch has dominated policymaking. In the Second, Third, and Fourth Republics (all since 1979), Nigeria has had a presidential system, with a strong president theoretically checked by a bicameral legislature and an independent judiciary. Each of the 36 state governments and 774 local governments has an executive and a legislative branch, and a network of local, district, and state courts exists. Currently, neither federalism nor checks and balances operate, and state and local governments are totally dependent on the central government.

The Executive

In 1979, with the establishment of the Second Republic, the parliamentary system modeled after Britain was replaced by a presidential system. Nigeria's many ethnicities fragmented its multi-party system and legislature so seriously that a prime minister could not gain the necessary authority to rule. The belief was that a popularly-elected president could symbolize unity and rise above the weak party system. the U.S. presidential model was chosen, including a two-term limit for the chief executive. Nigeria followed the model until 1983, when

Major-General Muhammadu Buhari (also a candidate for president in the 2003, 2007, and 2011 elections) staged a palace coup. He in turn was ousted by General Babangida in 1985, who was replaced by General Abacha in 1993. Civilian rule returned in 1999, and President Obasanjo was reelected in 2003, and in 2007 Nigeria had its first experience of one civilian president handing power to another, no matter how flawed the election. Another civilian, Goodluck Jonathan, was elected in 2011, the 2015 election brought back a former military general – Muhammadu Buhari – as president.

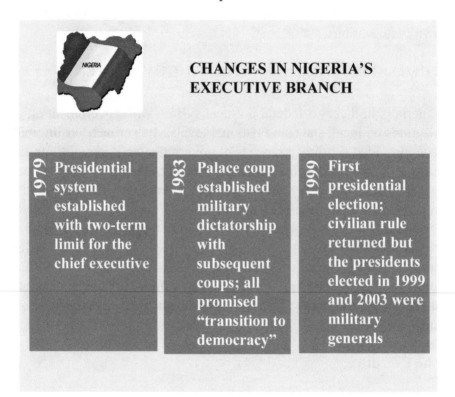

CHANGES IN NIGERIA'S EXECUTIVE BRANCH

1979	1983	1999
Presidential system established with two-term limit for the chief executive	Palace coup established military dictatorship with subsequent coups; all promised "transition to democracy"	First presidential election; civilian rule returned but the presidents elected in 1999 and 2003 were military generals

The Executive under Military Rule

Nigeria's seven military leaders did not all rule in the same fashion. All promised a "transition to democracy," but only two gave power over to elected leaders: General Obasanjo in 1979, and General Abubakar in 1999. Generals Buhari (1983-1985), Babangida (1985-1993), and Abacha (1993-1998) were known for their use of repressive tactics during their rule, but virtually all military and civilian administrations have concentrated power in the hands of the executive. The presidents appointed senior officials without legislative approval, and neither the legislature nor the judiciary has consistently checked executive power.

Patrimonialism

The generals ruled under a system of patrimonialism, in which the president was the head of an intricate patron-client system and dispensed government jobs and resources as rewards to supporters. As a result, cabinet positions, bureaucracy chiefs, and virtually all other government jobs were part of the president's patronage system. The fact that generals repeatedly were overthrown indicates that the system is unstable, or possibly that the impulse toward democracy is keeping patrimonialism from working.

The Bureaucracy

The British put an elaborate civil service in place in Nigeria during colonial days, allowing Nigerians to fill lower-level jobs in the bureaucracy. After independence, the civil service remained in place, and has grown tremendously over the past decades. Many observers believe that the bureaucracy is bloated, and it is a generally accepted fact that it is corrupt and inefficient. Bribery is common, and jobs are awarded through the patron-client system, or prebendalism. Not surprisingly, this system has led to a rapid increase in the number of bureaucratic jobs.

Para-statals

Like Mexican organizations before the 1980s, many Nigerian government agencies are actually **para-statals**, or corporations owned by the state and designated to provide commercial and social welfare services. Theoretically the para-statals are privately owned, but their boards are appointed by government ministers, and their executives are interwoven into the president's patronage system. Para-statals commonly provide public utilities, such as water, electricity, public transportation, and agricultural subsidies. Others control major industries such as steel, defense products, and petroleum.

State Corporatism

As we saw in Mexico in its pre-democracy days, corporatism may function in an authoritarian political system where the government allows political input from selected interest groups outside the government structure. Although corporatism in PRI-dominated Mexico was far from democratic, political leaders generally did take into consideration the opinions of these selected groups. In Nigeria, as in Iran, para-statals provide this input, but because they are controlled by the government, they create state corporatism. Para-statals fulfill important economic and social functions, and they insure that the state controls private interests as well. They serve as contact points between the government and business interests, but the state ultimately controls the interactions. Para-statals generally are inefficiently run and corrupt, and many believe that they must be disbanded if democracy is to survive in Nigeria.

One para-statal, founded by President Obasanjo to provide better electrical service, was known as N.E.P.A., but Nigerians joked that the initials stood for "Never Expect Power Again." When the para-statal was renamed the Power Holding Company, the new joke was that it stood for "Please Hold Candle." Recently, however, Nigeria privatized many state-owned power distribution companies, and many hope that the power infrastructure will improve as a result.

After his election in 2011, President Jonathan promised to make electricity reform a priority, hoping to transform the lives of millions of Nigerians who have no electric power. However, his power minister, Bartholomew Nnaji, resigned in August 2012, when a conflict of interest was exposed. In an effort to privatize the industry, Mr. Nnaji was found to hold shares in one firm that bid for business, although it is not unusual for Nigerian politicians to engage in business overseen by their office. Nevertheless, this scandal was a setback for the president's initiative, especially since it discouraged foreign investments necessary for the project's success.

The Legislature

The Nigerian legislature has taken several different forms since independence, and it has been disbanded a number of times by military rulers. A parliamentary system was in place until 1979, when it was replaced by a presidential system with a bicameral legislature, known collectively as the **National Assembly**. Both representatives and senators serve four-year renewable terms, and elections are held the week preceding the presidential election.

- **The Senate** – Currently the upper house is composed of 109 senators, three from each of 36 states and one from the federal capital territory of Abuja. Senators are elected directly by popular vote. Its equal representation model for states is based on that of the United States Senate, so some senators represent much smaller populations than others do. However, the ethnic and religious diversity of the 36 states means that senators are also a diverse lot.

- **The House of Representatives** – The House of Representatives has 360 members from single-member districts. They are elected by plurality, and like the senators, represent many different ethnicities. After the elections of 2015, only 20 representatives were women, as were only 7 of the 109 senators, giving Nigeria one of the lowest rates of female representation in the legislature in the world.

Nigerian legislatures under military governments have had almost no power, and even under civilian control, the legislature has only recently become an effective check on the president's power. A notable example is the National Assembly's failure to ratify President Obasanjo's plan to alter the Constitution to allow him to run for a third term in 2007. Even though the president's party (PNP) held a majority in the Assembly, the legislative leaders were highly critical of the fraud and violence associated with the election of 2007. Even though the elections of 2011 and 2015 were an improvement, like so many other government officials, representatives and senators have often been implicated in corruption scandals. For example, in 1999 the president of the Senate and the speaker of the House of Representatives were removed from their positions for perjury and forgery. In August 2000, the Senate president was removed on suspicion of accepting kickbacks for government contracts, and in 2011, the speaker of the House of Representatives was investigated for "misappropriating" $140,000,000.

The Judiciary

During the early years of independence the Nigerian judiciary actually had a great deal of autonomy. Courts combined British common law with an assortment of traditional or customary law, including *sharia* in the Northern Region. They were known for rendering objective decisions and for operating independently from the executive. However, the years of military rule ravaged the court system. The judiciary was undermined by military decrees that nullified court decisions, and the generals even set up quasi-judicial tribunals outside the regular system. Judicial review was suspended, and the presidents' cronies were appointed as judges. As a result, many judges today are not well versed in law and render decisions that are manipulated by the government.

Today the judiciary is charged with interpreting the laws in accordance with the Constitution, so judicial review exists in theory. Court structures exist at both federal and state levels, with the highest court in the land being the Supreme Court. The court structure is complicated by the *sharia* courts that exist side by side with courts based on the British model. The 1999 constitution established a Supreme Court, a Federal Court of Appeals, and a single unified court system at the national and state levels. Individual states may also authorize traditional subsidiary courts, with the most controversial being the Islamic *sharia* courts, which now function in twelve of the predominantly Muslim northern states.

Two notorious cases from the 1990s indicate to many people how deeply the Nigerian judiciary fell under the sway of military rulers. **Mshood Abiolao**, the winner of the 1993 election annulled by Babangida, was detained and eventually died while in custody. The presiding judges for his detention changed often, and critics of the government believe that justice was not served. In 1995, activist **Ken Saro-Wiwa** and eight other Ogonis were detained and hanged under orders from a court arranged by the military, consisting primarily of military officers.

The establishment of tribunals to hear accusations of voting fraud during the election of 2007 is an indication that Nigeria's institutions are taking the rule of law seriously. The fact that they actually had the power to remove officials from their positions reflects the fact that the judiciary is stronger and more independent now than in the past. The courts set the bar high for proving election irregularities, and Yar'Adua was not removed from office, but the procedures were followed, and the cases were referred to the Supreme Court.

The Military

It goes without saying that the military has been a strong force behind policymaking in Nigeria. Yet by becoming so active in political affairs, the military lost its credibility as a temporary, objective organization that keeps order and brings stability. Starting in 1966 when the first coup took place, the military made distinctions between the **"military in government"** and the **"military in barracks."** The latter fulfills traditional duties of the military, and its leaders often have been critical of military control of political power. As a result, the military has been subject to internal discord, and the military presidents often had to keep a close eye on other military leaders. Babangida protected his authority by constantly moving military personnel around and by appointing senior officers through his patronage system.

Although the military is a strongly intimidating force in the Nigerian political system that has often blocked democratic reforms, it is important to understand that it is one of the few institutions in the country that is truly national in character. When the deep ethnic cleavages within Nigerian society have threatened instability, the military has been there to restore order. Nigeria's best, brightest, and most ambitious have often made their way by rising through the military, a fact particularly important for the ethnic Muslims of northern Nigeria who have not had the same opportunities that many in the south have had. Because of these factors, generals had the ability to keep control of the government for many years, and it helps to explain why the democracy has been so fragile so far.

The military suffered major setbacks in 2014 and 2015 as Boko Haram gained territory in the north-east and spread their attacks to neighboring countries. The Nigerian military could not contain the group's territorial gains, with some Nigerian soldiers refusing orders and others fleeing the country. In early 2015, a coalition of military forces from Nigeria, Chad, and Niger began a campaign against Boko Haram, and in September the military claimed victory. However, bombings continued as Boko Haram proclaimed its goal of creating a new Islamic caliphate in the region. President Buhari promised to quell corruption in the army, since embezzlement by generals contributed to the army's lack of resources to defeat Boko Haram.

Despite government efforts, Boko Haram's attacks have continued, with another 110 schoolgirls kidnapped in Dapchi, Yobe, in February 2018, although Boko Haram reportedly released all but one of the girls within a month. In April of 2018, a Boko Haram attack on the outskirts of Maiduguri resulted in the death of 18 people and another 84 wounded. In May the Nigerian Army killed 15 Boko Haram insurgents and rescued 49 people in several encounters.

PUBLIC POLICY

Nigeria's years of military rule resulted in a top-down policymaking process. Power is concentrated in the presidency, and much outside input comes to the president and his cabinet ministers through channels established by patron clientelism. Senior government officials are supported by a broader base of loyal junior officials, creating a sort of "**loyalty pyramid**." State control of resources means that those in the pyramid get the spoils, and they alone have access to wealth and influence. These loyal clients have had many nicknames, including the "Kaduna Mafia," "Babangida's Boys," and "Abacha's Boys." Since the military was in control until 1999, the pyramids are backed by guns, so that protesting the corruption could be dangerous.

The system operated under the assumption that the military and political elite rule with only their self-interest in mind. Historically, this pattern of top-down, self-interested rule was put in place during colonial times when the British relied on native chiefs to ensure that Nigerian trade and resources benefited Great Britain. To break this pattern, political elites must get in touch with their older roots – the communalism from pre-colonial days. Democratic rule requires that political leaders are responsible for the welfare of their people, not only to those that they owe favors to.

Economic Issues

One result of the loyalty pyramids has been the squandering of Nigeria's wealth. Currently the country finds itself deeply in debt, and most of its people live in poverty. Tremendous oil revenues have disappeared into the pockets of government officials, and most Nigerians have not profited from them at all. The situation is complicated by ethnic and regional hostilities and by widespread popular distrust of the government. In February 2001, the federal government asked the Supreme Court to allow the federal government to collect oil revenues and pool them into a "federal account." On the surface, this appears to be revenue sharing, or allowing the entire country to benefit from offshore oil profits. However, the areas in the south along the Niger Delta protested the practice strongly, partly because they saw the policy as coming from northerners who wanted to take southern profits away. And without trust in the government, almost no one believed that the profits would benefit anyone except corrupt government officials.

Oil: a Source of Strength or Weakness?

Like Iran, Nigeria is a **rentier state**. A rentier economy is heavily supported by state expenditure, while the state receives rent from other countries. Iran and Nigeria receive income by exporting their oil and leasing out oil fields to foreign companies. The state's main role in the economy is in controlling the nation's revenues, and in spending those earnings, known as **rents**, which come mainly from oil. Individuals, groups, and communities have learned to respond through **rent-seek-**

ing behavior, primarily by competing for the government's largesse. Those that win the competition do so through political connections provided through the patron-client system, with the president having control over who gets what. Most Nigerians struggle along without much access, and participate in the **informal economy** of unreported incomes from small-scale trade and subsistence agriculture.

During the 1970s Nigeria's oil wealth gave it a great deal of international leverage. As an active member of OPEC, Nigeria could make political and economic demands because developed countries needed its oil. Through the years Nigeria has gained clout whenever Middle Eastern tensions have cut off oil supplies from that region, forcing developed countries to rely more heavily on Nigerian oil. However, Nigeria's over reliance on oil has meant that the country's economy suffers disproportionately whenever oil prices go down. During eras of low oil prices, Nigeria has amassed great debt, partly because the profits do not remain in the state's coffers long enough to cover the lean years.

An important issue is the fact that oil is being stolen at record rates, so that no one knows for sure what Nigeria's actual production is. The state-run Nigerian National Petroleum Corporation has often been judged one of the world's most corrupt oil companies. A joint report by Transparency International and the Revenue Watch Institute in New York recently claimed that the NNPC had the worst record of 44 national and foreign companies examined. An external audit said it was "accountable to no one," and it has been called a "slush fund for the government." A Petroleum Industry Bill has been in the works for more than 15 years, intended to overhaul the industry, make it more transparent, and improve regulatory institutions and fiscal policies. However, the bill has yet to be passed.

Another major issue since early 2006 has been the unstable situation in the Niger Delta regarding protests and subterfuge on foreign-based oil companies there. Some groups are idealistic, such as the Movement for the Emancipation of the Niger Delta (MEND), which wants more oil money going to the people of the Delta states. However, the group has chosen violent methods, such as kidnapping foreign workers, and others have joined in the mayhem, including gangs with no such communal goals. MEND has also siphoned oil illegally to sell to refineries overseas, and gun-running is believed to be a big source of the group's revenue. The violence has driven some companies away, such as Willbros, one of the world's largest independent contractors that left Nigeria in the summer of 2006. Other companies have cut production, so that by mid-2007 about a quarter of Nigeria's oil output had been shut down since January 2006.

Dealing with this issue was one of the biggest challenges facing President Jonathan, and he made it one of his priorities. However, despite the army's attempt to contain the rebels, the violence continued. Yar'Adua created a dedicated ministry for the Niger Delta to oversee development in 2008 and convened a committee to look for long-term solutions. The environmental impact of oil production in the delta was the focus of a 2011 report from the United Nations, which declared that it could take 30 years and at least 41 billion to rid the mangroves of a thick carpet of crude oil. About the time that the report was released, Shell Oil admitted liability for the first time for two big leaks in the delta, and the company paid out $1,700,000 in compensation to groups in the delta affected by spills.

In the north, an Islamist group called Ansaru kidnapped several foreign construction workers in the state of Bauchi. The kidnapping rattled foreigners working in the north, so that some companies have transferred family members of workers to the south. An increase in polio has been reported in Nigeria since the rebellion started by Boko Harm about four years ago, according to the World Health Organization. Polio vaccinators have been a particular target of the militant groups, with several health workers killed early in 2013.

Despite these economic problems, Nigeria's economy is growing quickly, with an increase of 6.3% in 2014. The GDP is fast approaching that of South Africa, where growth is about 3% annually, so it is possible that Nigeria will become Africa's biggest economy within a decade. However, the economy slowed by 2017, when it grew by only .82%.

Structural Adjustment

After international oil prices plummeted in the early 1980s, Nigeria was forced to turn to international organizations for help in managing its huge national debt. In 1985, the Babangida regime developed an **economic structural adjustment** program with the support of the World Bank and the International Monetary Fund. The program sought to restructure and diversify the Nigerian economy so that it could decrease its dependence on oil. The government also pledged to reduce government spending and to privatize its para-statals. This "shock treatment" has had mixed results, but generally timelines for debt repayment have been restructured because Nigeria could not keep up with its payments. Para-statals are still under state control, and the private economic sector has not grown significantly. The large national debt remains a major problem for Nigeria today, especially as oil prices plummeted in 2008. By 2011, with oil prices once again higher, the challenge of using the oil-created wealth to benefit the country was still unmet, and with the drop in oil prices in 2014, the problems deepened.

Recent reforms include a professionally managed sovereign-wealth fund to replace the current slush-fund that was used by the government to give away more than $10 billion in the run-up to the 2011 election. More Nigerians now have bank accounts, with more expected as mobile-phone banking becomes more common over the next few years. The main goal of most suggested reforms is to funnel oil revenues into a more efficient financial system that could provide capital to the private sector to build roads and power stations, and expand private enterprises, such as farming.

Reactions to the Global Economic Crisis of 2008

Nigeria's economy hasn't suffered as much as many others since the crisis of 2008, partly because the banking system improved significantly under an initiative during President Obasanjo's second term in office (2003-2007). As part of a policy to squeeze weak or failing banks out of business, in 2005 the Central Bank of Nigeria raised banks' capital requirements (money they must have on hand), so that the number of banks dropped from 89 to 24 by the end of the year. Another contributing factor to Nigeria's relatively stable economy was the fact that it had paid off sizeable debts under the structural adjustment program. However, the sharp decrease in the price of oil did a great deal of economic damage, including a devaluation of the currency, the naira. The Nigerian Stock Exchange also went into steep decline, housing prices dropped, and the small amount of international tourism that Nigeria attracted virtually disappeared.

Nigeria's inability to provide electric power has continued, with President Yar'Adua reversing Obasajanja's order to privatize power companies. President Jonathan made increasing electricity supply a priority, and he put forward a privatization plan that aims to raise $35 billion of investment over the next decade and stipulates that companies put money into electricity transmission. Under Jonathan's plan, grid transmission remained in government hands but was privately managed. The aim was to triple supply by 2013. However, the scandal that caused his power minister to resign derailed that goal since it discouraged investment.

"Federal Character"

Federalism is seen by most Nigerians as a positive, desirable characteristic for their country. Federalism appeals to many countries because it promises that power will be shared, and that all people in all parts of the country will be fairly represented. Federalism also allows citizens more contact points with government, so that true democratic rule can be more easily achieved. In Nigeria, the goal is to seek a "federal character" for the nation, a principle that recognizes people of all ethnicities, religions, and regions, and takes their needs into account. The Nigerian Constitution has put many provisions in place that support the goal of **"federal character."** For example, senators represent diverse states, representatives are elected from diverse districts, and the president must receive 25% of the vote in 2/3 of the regions in order to be elected. However, so far this ethnic balancing has not promoted unity or nationalism, but has only served to divide the country more.

One negative effect of federalism has been to bloat and promote corruption within the bureaucracy. Since all ethnicities must be represented, sometimes jobs have been created just to satisfy the demand. Once established within bureaucratic posts, these appointees see themselves as beholden to ethnic and regional interests. Another negative effect takes place within the legislative chambers. The 36 states vie for control of government resources, and see themselves in competition with other ethnic groups for political and economic benefits.

The "federal character" issue is based squarely on the fact that the "national question" in Nigeria remains unanswered. Do Nigerians have enough in common to remain together as a country?

Many southerners contend that true federalism will exist only when the central government devolves some of its power to the state and local levels. For example, Nigerians of the Niger Delta believe that regions should control their own resources. For them, that means that the federal government should not redistribute their region's oil revenues. Other southerners have suggested that police duties and personnel should be relegated to local and state levels as they are in the United States. Northerners generally don't support the **"true federalism" movement** because their regions historically have not had as many resources or as much revenue to share. Many northern states benefit more than southerners from nationally-sponsored redistribution programs.

Democratization

Some changes have occurred in Nigeria since the last military regime left in 1999. For example, some public enterprises have been privatized, opening the way for limitations on the economic control of the central government. Also, a scheme for alleviating poverty has been set forward. Public wages have increased in recent years, with the hope that well-paid public employees won't be as susceptible to bribery. Some of the money that General Abacha stashed in his foreign bank account has now been returned to the state treasury. Finally, Nigeria's financial reserves have grown, partly because oil prices have been rising over the past few years.

Despite all its problems, Nigeria shows some signs that democracy may be taking root in its presidential system, including these:

- **Some checks and balances between government branches** – The legislature rejected President Obasanjo's attempt to change the Constitution to allow him to run for a third term in 2007, despite a great deal of pressure from the political elite.

- **Some independent decisions in the courts** – President Obasanjo's attempt to keep his vice president, Atiku Abubakar, from running for president in 2007 were foiled by the courts after the president's allies used corruption charges to bar his candidacy. The Supreme Court ruled in Abubakar's favor, even though his name was not returned to the ballot until the last minute. The election tribunals set up to investigate allegations of electoral fraud were allowed to function under President Yar'Adua's new administration, and some officials were actually removed from office through court order.

- **Revival of civil society** – Nigeria's many civic and religious groups, driven underground by military rule, have reactivated and freely criticized the government's handling of the 2007 election. They pushed for reform for the elections that followed, with a fair degree of success

- **Independent media** – During the 2007 election the media sent countless correspondents across 36 states to bring back reports of stuffed ballot boxes, intimidated voters, and phony results. Internet and cell phone connections allowed poll observers, voters and political parties to freely communicate, making it much more difficult to hide election fraud. The media watched the 2011 and 2015 elections carefully and reported irregularities.

- **Peaceful succession of power** – For the first time in Nigeria's history, power passed between two civilians as President Olusegun Obasanjo stepped down in 2007, peacefully allowing Umaru Yar'Adua to take over. When Yar'Adua died in

2010, Goodluck Jonathan, his vice president, took over as acting president without any major problems. When Jonathan was defeated by Muhammadu Buhari in 2015, he conceded the election graciously, and Buhari took power without major resistance.

- **Improving Freedom House scores** – Freedom House, an organization that studies democracy around the world, ranks countries on a 1 to 7 freedom scale, with countries given a 1 being the most free and those given a 7 being the least free. In 2015 Freedom House gave Nigeria a "4.5", putting it squarely in the "partly free" category. Nigeria's score has improved over the years, along with those of many other countries in Africa. In 1976, the vast majority, 25 (including Nigeria) were "not free." Today the not-free category has shrunk to 14 states, with most falling into the "partly free" category (including Nigeria).

Are the recent reforms indications that Nigeria may finally be stabilizing as a nation? In many ways, Nigeria's massive economic and political troubles are intertwined in such a fashion that it is difficult to tell where to start in unraveling the issues. Economic problems are rooted in patron-clientelism, which in turn breeds corruption, which makes the economic problems more difficult to solve. Patron-clientelism also has encouraged ethnic discord, and has proved to be a major stumbling block to the development of a democracy.

One of the key characteristics of a true democracy is the existence of regular competitive elections in which citizens have real choices of leaders. Recent Nigerian elections may be interpreted to support either an optimistic or pessimistic view for Nigeria's future prospects. On the one hand, it is easy to criticize the Nigerian election process as a farce. After all, the election of 1993 was annulled, and the elections of 1999 and 2003 only put a former military general back in power. The elections of 1999, 2003, and 2007 were also characterized by ballot box theft and stuffing. Several candidates were assassinated, and ordinary people were killed in their efforts to vote. How can this be a democracy? On the other hand, three elections were held in a row without being suspended or annulled, and the elections of 2011 and 2015 were hailed by most observers as a big improvement over the previous ones. Some argue that the recent generation of presidential candidates consists of military men because they are the only ones with the experience necessary to govern. These hopeful ones point out that the two presidents of Nigeria before Buhari were not military men and predict that younger, nonmilitary leaders will emerge as political candidates in the near future. After all, the experience of democracy has deep roots in Nigerian political culture. Perhaps the best question is, "Was this election better than the last one?" If so, perhaps a new, more optimistic pattern is developing in Nigeria.

IMPORTANT TERMS AND CONCEPTS

Abacha, Sani
Abubakar, Atiku
ANC
Babangida, Ibrahim
Biafra
Buhari, Muhammudu
civil society
constitutionalism
corporatism
CPC
cultural diffusion
"federal character"
Hausa-Fulani
Ife
Igbo
indirect rule
informal economy
INEC
jihad
Jonathan, Goodluck
Kanuri
kinship-based politics
"loyalty pyramid"
"military in barracks"
"military in government"
National Assembly

"national question"
nongovernmental organizations
Obasanjo, Olusegun
Oyo
para-statals
patrimonialism
patron-client system (prebendalism)
PDP
plurality vote
rents, rent-seeking
revenue sharing
rule of law
Saro-Wiwa, Ken
sharia
Sokoto Caliphate
state corporatism
structural adjustment program
Transparency International
"true federalism" movement
Yar'Adua, Umaru
Yoruba

Nigeria Questions

1. Which of the following groups of countries have economies that are almost completely dependent on one product: oil?

A) Nigeria, Iran, and Mexico
B) China, Nigeria, and Iran
C) Russia, Britain, and Mexico
D) Britain, Nigeria, and Iran
E) Russia, China, and Mexico

"The trouble with Nigeria is simply and squarely a failure of leadership."

2. Chinua Achebe's statement above identfies the country's legitimacy crisis as one grounded in

A) lack of constitutionalism
B) competing sets of laws
C) the national question
D) corruption
E) oil dependency

3. In comparison to Britain and Russia, the literacy rates in Iran and Nigeria

A) are higher for men, but lower for women
B) show a larger gap between literacy rates for men and literacy rates for women
C) are higher for both men and women
D) show a smaller gap between literacy rates for men and literacy rates for women
E) are higher for women, but lower for men

4. The requirement that a president must receive at least 25% of all the votes cast in 2/3 of the states is intended to insure that

A) no candidate will win in the first round
B) the candidate of the elites will not automatically win
C) voting rates are relatively similar in all states
D) a purely regional candidate cannot win the presidency
E) the candidate with the most political experience will win

5. Between 1966 and 1999 all Nigerian presidents except for one were

A) democratically elected
B) assassinated
C) military dictators
D) northern Muslims
E) Southern Christians

6. Which of the following is a similarity in representation in the legislature in Iran and Nigeria?

A) Both countries select representatives through proporational representation.
B) Nigeria has a law that requires parties to run women candidates to the legeislature; Iran does not.
C) Women are seriously underrepresented in the legislatures of both countries.
D) In both countries, representatives are appointed by the president.
E) In both countries, representatives are selected through a system that combines both proportional representation and single-member districts.

7. One reason that a parliamentary-style government failed in Nigeria was that it was difficult to

A) identify a majority party
B) form interest groups
C) hold votes of no confidence
D) control corruption
E) control the military

Questions 8 and 9 refer to the map below:

8. The map above shows that one of the most important social cleavages in Nigeria is

A) religion
B) colonial/non-colonial areas
C) ethnicity
D) urban/rural differences
E) social class

9. The map provides evidence for which of the following statements?

A) Governments of religiously divided countries often must resort to force.

B) The political boundaries of states do not always coincide with boundaries of nations.

C) Colonialism shaped the development of most countries in Africa.

D) Northern Nigeria is much more densely populated than southern Nigeria.

E) Speaking a common language almost always serves as a centrifugal force within a country

10. Which of the following is an accurate comparison of the development of party systems in Nigeria and Mexico during the 20th century?

A) Neither country developed a coherent party system.

B) Both Mexico and Nigeria developed one-party systems that lasted until the last years of the century.

C) Whereas Mexico's one-party system contributed to political stability, Nigeria's extreme factionalism made it impossible to develop a coherent party system.

D) In Mexico, parties formed around powerful individuals, whereas in Nigeria parties formed based on ideological differences.

E) In both Mexico and Nigeria, so many parties formed that most were narrowly-based interest groups who ran candidates for public office.

11. The main goal of structural adjustment programs for Nigeria has been to

A) increase oil production and refinement

B) keep a steady flow of Nigerian oil going to North America and Europe

C) insure that the government keeps control of para-statals

D) reduce Nigeria's dependence on oil

E) use surpluses in the country's budget to help the poor

Questions 12 and 13 are based on the following chart:

CORRUPTION PERCEPTION INDEX 2017

COUNTRY	CPI SCORE*	RANK (178 COUNTRIES TOTAL)
China	41	77
Iran	30	130
Mexico	29	135**
Nigeria	27	148
Russia	29	135**
United Kingdom	82	8

12. Which of the following statements is supported by the information in the chart above?

A) All of the core countries except the United Kingdom have low literacy rates.
B) All of the core countries except the United Kingdom have high levels of economic inequality.
C) Russia, Nigeria, and Iran have high poverty rates.
D) Corruption is a problem for all of the core countries except for the United Kingdom.
E) Democratization has not taken hold in any of the core countries except the United Kingdom.

13. In China, Mexico, and Nigeria, the low CPI scores are almost certainly impacted by a history of

A) democratic centralism
B) statism
C) military dictatorships
D) patrimonialism
E) patron-clientelism

14. In comparison to the Iranian Constitution of 1979, the 1999 Nigerian Constitution

A) is a much less important source of political authority
B) has been amended less frequently
C) is based more solidly in sharia
D) provides for a president as head of government
E) gives the military much less policymaking power

15. Which of the following is a major societal problem for both Mexico and Nigeria?

A) conflict between Christians and Muslims
B) lack of natural resources
C) large gap between the rich and the poor
D) rates of HIV/AIDS higher than most other countries
E) below average literacy rates

16. The institution in the Nigerian government created to give equal representation to the states is

A) the Senate
B) the House of Representatives
C) the para-statal
D) the Supreme Court
E) the vice presidency

17. Prebendalism in Nigerian politics is a form of

A) interest group pluralism
B) statism
C) patrong-clientelism
D) structural adjustment
E) constitutionalism

18. In both Russia's civil war in Chechnya and Nigeria's Biafran
    Civil War, the conflicts were based on

A) ethnic differences
B) rural-urban differences
C) social class differences
D) competition among the elites
E) language differences

19. Which of the following is the most important social cleavage in
    modern Nigeria?

A) social class
B) urban v. rural
C) immigrant v. native
D) gender
E) ethnicity

20. The Mexican and Nigerian political systems both currently have

A) para-statals
B) military rule
C) electoral rules that include proportional representation
D) two-party systems
E) small bureaucracies

21. Which of the following characteristics is most problematic for
    answering Nigeria's "national question"?

A) lack of formal structures of government
B) lack of a colonial model for democratic government
C) reliance on *sharia*
D) lack of constitutionalism
E) adoption of the presidential style of government

22. Nigeria's move of their capital city from Lagos to Abuja was an attempt to

A) take power away from Muslim leaders
B) unify a multi-ethnic state
C) move control of its oil industry from the northern part of the country
D) encourage industrialization in the center of the country
E) create two major economic centers within the country

23. In China, Mexico, and Nigeria, patron-clientelism has almost always been accompanied by

A) fragmentation
B) federalism
C) religious conflict
D) rent seeking
E) corruption

24. Which of the following countries have formal federalist structures?

A) Britain, Mexico, and Nigeria
B) China, Russia, and Mexico
C) Nigeria, Iran, and Britain
D) China, Russia, and Iran
E) Nigeria, Russia, and Mexico

25. Which of the following is an accurate comparison of Mexico and Nigeria's south/north cleavages?

A) The south in both countries is poorer than the north.
B) The north in both countries is poorer than the south.
C) The cleavage between north and south in both countries is based on religion.
D) In Mexico, the north is poorer than the south; in Nigeria, the south is poorer than the north.
E) In Mexico, the south is poorer than the north; in Nigeria, the north is poorer than the south.

26. Which of the following correctly compares selection of representatives to the lower houses of the legislature in Nigeria and Russia?

A) Both countries use mixed systems with some representatives coming from single-member district elections and others elected by proportional representation.
B) Russia's deputies are elected from single-member districts; Nigeria's representatives are elected by proportional representation.
C) Nigeria's representatives are elected from single-member districts; Russia's deputies are elected by proportional representation.
D) Russia's deputies are appointed by the president; Nigeria's representatives are elected from single-member districts.
E) Both countries elect all of their representatives by proportional representation.

27. The relationship between the government and para-statals in Nigeria is an example of

A) neo-corporatism
B) interest group pluralism
C) rational-legal authority
D) fragmentation
E) state corporatism

28. Like Iran, Nigeria is a

A) federalist system
B) post-modernist society
C) military dictatorship
D) rentier state
E) unitary system

29. The impact of colonialism was different in Nigeria than in Iran because

A) Nigeria was never colonized; Iran was.
B) Iran was never colonized; Nigeria was.
C) both countries were colonized, but Nigeria's natural resources were exploited more completely.
D) both countries were colonizers, but Iran was more successful.
E) Iran had no natural resources that imperialist countries were interested in; Nigeria did.

30. The "national question" dilemma is whether or not Nigeria should

A) stay together as a nation
B) be Christian or Muslim
C) have a federal or a unitary government
D) allow the military to rule or not
E) have a parliamentary or presidential system

Country-Context Question (20 minutes):

Governments operate with different degrees of transparency.

(a) Define transparency.

(b) Identify a specific institution that would need to change to increase transparency in China, and explain how a change in that institution would increase transparency.

(c) Identify a specific institution that would need to change to increase transparency in Nigeria, and explain how a change in that institution would increase transparency.

PRACTICE EXAMINATION ONE

Part I – Multiple-choice Questions
55 Questions (45 minutes)
50% of the Exam

1. Which of the following is the best example of a regime change?

A) A successful coup d'état occurs in which one political leader replaces another as head of state.
B) A change occurs in a country's political institutions and practices, as from totalitarian to democratic rule.
C) One long-time ruler dies or retires, and is replaced by another, who in turn rules the country for a long period of time.
D) A country's political leader is replaced by a competitor, either by election or by military force.
E) An authoritarian ruler is defeated by military force, and a new leader emerges from the lower ranks of the military to replace him.

2. Deng Xiaoping Theory differed from Maoism, in that Deng Xiaoping Theory

A) denounced democratic centralism
B) allowed capitalism to function within the economy
C) deemphasized the importance of the military in the policy-making process
D) took political control from the Politburo
E) dismantled the parallel hierarchies

3. In contrast to the western value of equality of opportunity, Russian citizens tend to value

A) freedom of speech
B) wealth
C) national pride
D) equality of result
E) *perestroika*

4. Which of the following is a mismatch between country and ethnic minority group?

A) Iran/Azeri
B) China/Han
C) Russia/Chechen
D) Mexico/Amerindian
E) Britain/Pakistani

5. Russia probably came the closest to being a totalitarian regime under the leadership of

A) Alexander II
B) V. I. Lenin
C) Joseph Stalin
D) Mikhail Gorbachev
E) Boris Yeltsin

6. Which of the following is most likely to link the political attitudes of citizens to the government's policymaking process?

A) courts
B) political elites
C) political parties
D) bureaucracies
E) political culture

7. Which of the following was a common characteristic of the Russian, Chinese, and Mexican revolutions of the early 20th century?

A) All were ideological.
B) All resulted in the overthrow of a strong, authoritarian government.
C) All resulted eventually in a one-party state.
D) All put charismatic leaders strongly in control of the government.
E) All were focused on driving westerners from the country.

8. Interest group pluralism is best defined as

A) the existence of a high level of participation by citizens in a wide variety of interest groups

B) participation by ethnic and racial minorities in interest group politics

C) many interest groups competing to influence policy makers and the policy making process

D) participation by interest groups in decision making at local, regional, and national levels

E) successful lobbying efforts to influence policy making through an iron triangle network

9. Which of the following courts has used the power of judicial review most effectively?

A) the British Supreme Court

B) the Russian Constitutional Court

C) the Supreme Court in Mexico

D) the European Court of Justice

E) the People's Courts in China

10. Britain has a relatively high amount of social capital, which means that the country has

A) a high GDP per capita

B) a relatively narrow gap between the rich and the poor

C) a high Human Development Index (HDI) score, according to the United Nations

D) a mixed economy with a good bit of capitalism

E) reciprocity and trust among citizens and between citizens and the state

11. The presidents of both Mexico and Russia have the power to

A) appoint the prime minister.
B) dissolve the lower house of the legislature.
C) issue decrees.
D) appoint cabinet members.
E) write a new constitution.

12. Despite its authoritarian methods during the time it ruled Mexico, one of PRI's accomplishments was

A) establishing interest group pluralism.
B) gaining civilian control of the military.
C) developing an independent judiciary.
D) developing checks and balances between the executive and legislative branches.
E) weakening the patron-client system.

13. Political legitimacy is best defined as

A) the right to rule, as determined by a country's own citizens and recognized by other countries.
B) democratic rule by officials chosen in regularly scheduled elections.
C) the evolution of political traditions that shape the people's political beliefs so that they are uniform.
D) the collection of political beliefs, values, practices, and institutions that shape the nature of government and politics.
E) divisions within a country based on ethnic and racial groups, religions, and/or languages.

14. What common phenomenon that characterizes presidential systems is almost non-existent in parliamentary systems?

A) collective responsibility
B) arguments among major political parties
C) gridlock
D) majority rule
E) a strong bureaucracy

15. Which of the following countries is generally most tolerant of political protests and demonstrations against the government?

A) Britain
B) China
C) Mexico
D) Russia
E) Iran

16. Which of the following is the structure in Russia's government that is most comparable to the *Majles* in Iran?

A) the Duma
B) the Federation Council
C) the president's cabinet
D) the Constitutional Court
E) the Politburo

"A system in which a powerful boss or dominant party offers resources (such as land, jobs, and protection) in exchange for the support and services (such as labor or votes) of less powerful individuals"

17. The political system described above is

A) a representative democracy
B) *nomenklatura*
C) a matriarchy
D) protectionism
E) a patron-client system

18. A civil society is best defined as one that

A) emphasizes the importance of a strong government that provides for its citizens.
B) values privacy and freedom, and de-emphasizes the importance of having a strong government
C) accepts two areas of life: a public one defined by the government and a private one in which individuals have free choice.
D) is generally free of conflict and strife, and is characterized by a consensual political culture.
E) endorses considerate, cooperative behavior and punishes aggression and deviance.

19. A command economy is best defined as a system in which

A) key economic decisions are made by various private individuals and companies
B) the government has great control of the economy and competition and profit are prohibited or strongly restricted
C) the government owns basic industries, but citizens have some economic freedom
D) competition and profit are regulated by the government
E) the right of individuals to own private property is unlimited

20. Which of the following election systems is most likely to produce the largest number of competitive political parties?

A) plurality
B) first-past-the-post
C) proportional representation
D) two-round majority system
E) referendum-based system

21. "Slavophile vs. westernizer" is a basic issue in Russia's

A) coinciding cleavages
B) state corporatism
C) conflictual political culture
D) electoral system
E) separation of powers

22. A "mixed economy" is one that

A) is growing in some areas but shrinking in others
B) mixes elements of command and market economies
C) is market based but is heavily regulated by the government
D) experiences marketization but not privatization
E) combines both international and domestic trade

23. Political parties in Nigeria are characterized by all of the following EXCEPT:

A) fluidity and instability
B) ethnicity
C) domination by personalities
D) dependence of coalitions
E) corruption free

24. *Guanxi* in the Chinese political system is a variation of a(n)

A) political party system
B) electoral system
C) patron client system
D) military organization
E) state corporatist system

25. According to dependency theory, industrially developed countries

A) serve as models for less developed countries to follow
B) have very little influence on less developed countries
C) can best help less developed countries through allowing them to participate in international organizations
D) exploit less developed countries in order to enhance their own power
E) trade primarily among themselves, leaving the less developed countries outside the profits of world trade

26. Which of the following legislative houses consists of a number of seats that are based on heredity?

A) the Duma in Russia
B) the Senate in Nigeria
C) the House of Lords in Britain
D) the Senate in Mexico
E) the *Majles* in Iran

Questions 27 and 28 are based on the following quote:

"To bring political knowledge to the workers the Social Democrats [Bolsheviks] must go among all classes of the population; they must dispatch units of their army in all directions...For it is not enough to call ourselves the 'vanguard', the advanced contingent; we must act in such a way that all the other contingents recognise and are obliged to admit that we are marching in the vanguard."

27. The author of the quote is

A) V. I. Lenin
B) Karl Marx
C) Joseph Stalin
D) Nikita Khrushchev
E) Mikhail Gorbachev

28. The reasoning in the quote represents a significant revision in the theory of

A) conservatism
B) liberalism
C) fascism
D) Marxism
E) Mercantilism

29. A country is said to have an indirect democracy when

A) its executive branch is not directly elected by the people
B) decisions are made by the judicial branch
C) elected officials represent the people in government
D) the scope of government activity is limited
E) it allows citizens freedom but has identifiable political elites

30. The *maquiladora* district in Mexico developed in response to

A) joint U.S./Mexico policies to restrict immigration across mutual borders
B) demands of the Zapatistas for government action
C) pressures to decentralize the government
D) the NAFTA agreement
E) attempts to control drug trafficking

31. Which of the following countries all have a bicameral legislature?

A) Nigeria, China, and Russia
B) Britain, China, and Iran
C) Mexico, Russia, and Nigeria
D) Britain, Iran, and Mexico
E) Russia, China, and Iran

32. Which of the following is the BEST reason why Nigeria does not have as many women in their legislature as Mexico?

A) Nigeria is a more traditional society.
B) Nigeria does not have a law that requires parties to run female candidates for office.
C) Nigeria has not had an active women's rights movement.
D) Nigerian women are not allowed to vote.
E) Nigeria's middle class is much smaller in proportion to its total population.

33. Which of the following countries does NOT have a written constitution?

A) Britain
B) Russia
C) China
D) Iran
E) Nigeria

34. The legal system is based almost entirely on common law in

A) Britain
B) Russia
C) China
D) Iran
E) Nigeria

35. An opposite concept to devolution is

A) integration
B) fragmentation
C) sovereignty
D) succession
E) globalization

36. Britain's referendum in which voters supported Brexit reflected resistance to

A) nationalism
B) integration
C) fragmentation
D) marketization
E) privatization

37. Which of the following is the best description of the policymaking process in China?

A) The president and cabinet members make decisions that are presented to the legislature for rubber-stamp approval only.
B) The leader of the People's Liberation Army, the president, vice president, and premier make the decisions, but the legislature has the right to veto or amend the government's decisions.
C) Decisions are made by the members of the National People's Congress, but are formally announced by the politburo.
D) The general secretary of the party, who also is the president, has the final say over decisions made collectively by the Politburo.
E) The main decision making body is the Politburo, whose members' decisions are influenced heavily by *guanxi* connections and factions.

38. The political systems of Britain, Russia, and Mexico all have

A) more than two parties competing in popular elections
B) two political parties dominating the legislature
C) one party dominating the executive branch
D) parties of power that dominate both the executive and legislative branches
E) coalition parties forming a government

39. In China "parallel hierarchies" exist among the Communist Party, the state or government, and

A) interest groups
B) business leaders
C) the Russian Orthodox Church
D) ruling families
E) the military

40. Which of the following is the BEST description of China's criminal justice system?

A) China has no organized criminal justice system, since it was destroyed under Mao Zedong.
B) The Chinese criminal justice system has a high rate of conviction and often uses the death penalty as punishment.
C) The Chinese criminal justice system is highly decentralized and disconnected from the hierarchy of the Communist Party.
D) Since the reforms of Deng Xiaoping, the Chinese criminal justice system has been based on judicial review.
E) The Chinese criminal justice system is slow-moving and inefficient.

41. Which of the following principles/characteristics is relatively undeveloped in all six core countries?

A) democratic consolidation
B) transparency
C) common law
D) civil society
E) judicial review

42. Unlike the head of state in Britain, the head of state in Russia

A) is also the head of government
B) has much more actual policymaking power
C) only has ceremonial powers
D) is also a member of the upper house of the legislature
E) is an appointed official

43. Maoism contradicts Confucianism in that Maoism

A) emphasizes responsibility of the ruler to the people
B) does not rely on the teachings of one leader
C) does not support the idea of a political structure
D) emphasizes the importance of family
E) supports an egalitarian social structure

44. The most common type of political system in advanced
democracies is

A) parliamentary
B) presidential
C) semi-presidential
D) plurality
E) authoritarian

45. *Guanxi* and prebendalism are both based on

A) free market principles
B) democratic centralism
C) egalitarianism
D) patronage
E) parallel hierarchies

46. Which of the following countries has been MOST criticized in
recent years for holding fraudulant elections?

A) Russia
B) China
C) Mexico
D) Iran
E) Nigeria

47. If a study finds that a change in one variable is accompanied by a change in another, a researcher has proved the existence of

A) a causation
B) a correlation
C) empirical data
D) a dependent variable
E) normative influence

48. Which of the following types of organizations are MOST likely to directly foster the development of a global civil society?

A) unitary governments
B) federal governments
C) nongovernmental organizations
D) independent judiciaries
E) political parties with a broad appeal across many groups

49. Tatars, Ukrainians, Bashkir, and Chuvash are relatively large minority ethnic groups in

A) China
B) Iran
C) Nigeria
D) Russia
E) Britain

50. In a theocracy, political authority rests primarily with

A) elected officials
B) clerics
C) the bureaucracy
D) hereditary monarchs
E) the judiciary

51. Modern day China's regme type is BEST described as

A) a parliamentary democracy
B) an illiberal democracy
C) authoritarianism
D) a monarchy
E) a presidential democracy

52. As a general rule, cabinet members in Britain are

A) policy experts in their area of responsibility
B) politicians who rely on the expertise of high-level bureaucrats
C) usually a mix of leaders from both major political parties
D) relatively permanent in their positions
E) not held responsible for the decisions of the prime minister

53. Which of the following political bodies was (is) the center of
    policymaking in both the former Soviet Union and China?

A) the Central Committee
B) the Secretariat
C) the Council of Ministers
D) the National People's Congress
E) the Politburo

54. As an economic measure of comparison, Purchasing Power
    Parity (PPP) is different from Gross Domestic Product (GDP) per
    capita in that it takes into consideration

A) the Gini Index
B) adult literacy
C) life expectancy
D) educational enrollment
E) what people can buy in the local economy

55. Which country does NOT have a significant minority of Muslims?

A) Mexico
B) China
C) Russia
D) Nigeria
E) Britain

Section II – Free-Response Questions
Time – 1 hour and 40 minutes
50% of the Exam

Short-Answer Concepts: 5 questions (30 minutes)

1. Describe one advantage and one disadvantage of a federalist system. Identify one of the six countries in the AP Comparative Government and Politics course that has a federalist system.

2. Describe one defining characteristic of code law. Describe one defining characteristic of common law. Identify one country (of the six) that bases its political system on common law.

3. Describe a major difference between a parliamentary and a presidential system. Identify one country (of the six) that has a parliamentary system. Identify one country (of the six) that has a presidential system.

4. Explain the difference between a state and a nation. Explain two problems that this difference has caused for Nigeria's political system.

5. Define patron-clientelsim. Explain one benefit that patron-clientelism may have for a political system. Explain one problem that patron-clientelism may have for a political system.

Conceptual Analysis Question (30 minutes)

6. Corporatism exists in both authoritarian and democratic regimes.

(a) Define state corporatism, and explain why it usually occurs in authoritarian regimes.

(b) Explain one way that state corporatism is different from patron-clientelism.

(c) Define democratic corporatism, and explain one reason that it might encourage a democratic state to become more authoritarian.

(d) Explain one way that democratic corporatism is different from democratic pluralism.

Country Context Questions (40 minutes)

7. Both Nigeria and Britain have recently had problems with ethnic conflict.

(a) Describe one example of ethnic conflict in each country.

(b) Describe one reason for conflict that is common to both Nigeria and Britain.

(c) Describe one principal method used by the Nigerian government and one principal method used by the British government to resolve the conflict.

8. Political scientists use several measures to determine whether or not a country is a liberal democracy.

(a) Identify two measures, and explain why each indicates the existence of a liberal democracy.

(b) Using one of the measures you identified in (a) describe one way that Mexico may be described as a liberal democracy. Describe one way that Mexico cannot be described as a liberal democracy.

(c) Using the second measure you identified in (a), describe one way that Iran may be described as a liberal democracy. Describe one way that Iran cannot be described as a liberal democracy.

PRACTICE EXAMINATION TWO
Part I – Multiple-choice Questions
55 Questions (45 minutes)
50% of the Exam

1. An arrangement in which state-selected interest groups have the right to speak for the public is called

A) co-optation
B) state corporatism
C) neocorporatism
D) patron-clientelism
E) pluralism

2. The only international organization that has adopted a common currency is

A) NAFTA
B) the European Union
C) the United Nations
D) the World Trade Organization
E) the World Bank

3. Which of the following is the MOST significant source of legitimacy and authority for the Iranian political system?

A) The Constitution of 1979
B) *Qanun*
C) *Sharia*
D) Popular elections
E) *Velayat-e-faqih*

4. A unitary system of government is one that

A) rules in an autoritarian manner
B) has a weak central government
C) cooperates with other countries within the context of a supranational organization
D) has managed to tame strong centrifugal forces
E) concentrates policy-making powers in one central geographic place

5. Magna Carta, the Bill of Rights, and common law are basic to British

A) rational-legal authority
B) plurality electoral system
C) conflictual political culture
D) mixed economy
E) charismatic authority

6. A logical reaction by a government of a country with strong centrifugal forces is to institute a policy of

A) globalization
B) devolution
C) pluralism
D) checks and balances
E) conservatism

7. According to the Constitution of 1917, the Mexican political system is

A) presidential
B) parliamentary
C) semi-presidential
D) a theocracy
E) unitary

8. Which of the following institutions in the Iranian political system MOST directly reflects democratic principles?

A) the cabinet
B) the Guardian Council
C) the Expediency Council
D) the *Majles*
E) the Revolutionary Guards

9. Which of the following groups of countries is MOST affected when the price of oil goes up or down?

A) Britain, Russia, and China
B) Mexico, Iran, and Nigeria
C) China, Mexico, and Nigeria
D) Russia, China, and Iran
E) Britain, Mexico, and Nigerial

10. A cabinet coalition is most likely to form in a(n)

A) authoritarian state
B) country with a two-party system
C) illiberal democracy
D) country with a multi-party sytem
E) presidential system

11. Which of the following is an accurate comparison of political systems in Mexico and Iran?

A) Mexico has an elected president; Iran's president is appointed by the supreme leader.
B) Neither system makes use of a plurality electoral system.
C) In both systems, religious institutions play an active role in policymaking.
D) Both systems have bureaucracies that operate independently from the president.
E) Iran has a unicameral legislature; Mexico has a bicameral legislature.

12. International organizations have developed structural adjustment programs for Nigeria in order to help the country

A) boost profits from oil
B) pay down its debt
C) close the gap between the rich and the poor
D) compete with Latin American countries in the international market
E) develop a federal character

13. In comparison to the National People's Congress in China, the *Majles* in Iran

A) is not directly elected by the people
B) represents regions
C) selects the president
D) has real policymaking power
E) allows only clerics to be representatives

14. Two revolutions whose major goal was ideological purification were

A) China's Cultural Revolution and Iran's Cultural Revolution
B) Russia's Revolution of 1917 and Mexico's Revolution of 1910-1911
C) China's Cultural Revolution and Russia's Revolution of 1917
D) Iran's Cultural Revolution and Mexico's Revolution of 1910-1911
E) China's Revolution of 1911 and China's Cultural Revolution

15. According to the Constitution of 1917, the Mexican political system is

A) presidential
B) parliamentary
C) semi-presidential
D) a theocracy
E) unitary

16. Russian elections may be criticized as undemocratic because

A) very few people vote in presidential elections
B) no elections are held on the local level
C) they have become progressively less competitive
D) people can only vote for the president, and not for legislators or regional offices
E) the constitution does not provide for a referendum

17. Which of the following is an ideology that places a great deal of emphasis on individual political and economic freedom?

A) liberalism
B) communism
C) fascism
D) socialism
E) corporatism

18. Which British political party usually captures the most votes in urban and industrial areas?

A) Conservative Party
B) Labour Party
C) Liberal Democratic Party
D) UK Independence Party
E) National Union Party

19. Reactionaries are similar to conservatives in that they generally

A) support gradual reform
B) support revolutions
C) want to turn the clock back to an earlier era
D) advocate coups d'état
E) oppose both revolution and reform

20. In contrast to Mexico and Nigeria, in recent years the Iranian political system has been controlled by

A) a president
B) clerics
C) an ethnic minority
D) the legislature
E) the military

21. Asymmetric federalism describes the Russian political system because

A) the Duma has no real check on the president
B) the president is much more powerful than the prime minister
C) some regions are more autonomous than others
D) some areas are called republics and others are called autonomous regions
E) governors of states are appointed by the president

22. Which of the following types of organization generally exists within civil society?

A) legislatures
B) judiciaries
C) political parties
D) advocacy groups
E) government bureaucracies

23. In Mexico, both the Revolution of 1810 and the Revolution of 1911-1911 were attempts to

A) overthrow colonial rule
B) bring stability to the country
C) overthrow authoritarian rule
D) quiet populist demands
E) restore military rule

24. The ability of a state to carry out actions or policies within their borders independently from interference either from the inside or the outside is best defined as

A) power
B) sovereignty
C) authority
D) centralization
E) politicization

25. A group of people that is bound together by a common political identity is best defined as a(n)

A) state
B) regime
C) society
D) ethnicity
E) nation

26. A corporatist interest group system is usually characterized by

A) high levels of control of policymaking by populist groups
B) a relatively small number of interest groups having input into the policymaking process
C) a great deal of competition among interest groups for the government's attention
D) a lack of access to the government for business elites
E) almost no interest group activity in civil society

27. In contrast to proportional-representation systems, plurality electoral systems tend to encourage political party systems characterized by

A) large, broad-based, and fewer parties
B) more parties with extreme ideological views
C) large competitive regional parties
D) smaller, more ideological, and more parties
E) parties based on informal patron-client networks

28. Which of the following is an example of an organization that most clearly indicates the existence of a strong civil society in a country?

A) a bicameral legislature
B) an independent judiciary
C) an organization of local volunteers for the public schools
D) a competitive political party that regularly wins elections
E) a strong, well-organized agency for selecting bureaucrats

29. A major criticism of a pluralist interest group system is that it

A) creates confusion and inefficiency in the policymaking process
B) discourages interest group participation
C) gives the government too little power in the policymaking process
D) puts groups in an unequal partnership with government
E) allows interest groups to be controlled by the political parties

30. a coup d'état is LEAST likely to occur in a(n)

A) less developed country
B) developing country
C) authoritarian regime
D) totalitarian regime
E) liberal democracy

31. The presidents of Mexico and Russia are both

A) heads of majority parties in the lower house of the legislature
B) directly elected by the people
C) second in command to a prime minister
D) heads of unitary states
E) protected from impeachment by a constitution

32. A bureaucrat is most likely to have discretionary power in a(n)

A) authoritarian state
B) liberal democracy
C) country with a mixed economy
D) country that practices state corporatism
E) developing country

33. Which of the following is the BEST description of the geographic   distribution of power within states today?

A) Most states are federal systems.
B) Most states are unitary systems.
C) Most states are confederal systems.
D) States with federal systems are about equal in number to states
   with unitary systems.
E) States with confederal systems are about equal in number to states
   with unitary systems.

34. Gini coefficients tend to be higher in

A) more developed countries
B) communistand post-communist countries
C) countries of the Western Hemisphere
D) less developed countries
E) developing countries.

35. The European Parliament is the only directly elected body of the
    EU, and it is the weakest one. This fact may be used to argue
    that the EU

A) has not successfully formed a common market
B) can never replace national governments
C) will have problems integrating its newest members
D) does not have true separation of powers
E) has a democratic deficit

36. Which of the following political parties have formed a one-party system that controlled a country's government in recent years?

A) PRI in Mexico and CCP in China
B) People's Democratic Party in Nigeria and CCP of China
C) Communist Party in the Soviet Union and Labour Party in Britain
D) PRI in Mexico and People's Democratic Party in Nigeria
E) Communist Party in the Soviet Union and PAN in Mexico

37. *Sharia* law is commonly applied in the legal systems of

A) Iran and southern Nigeria
B) southern and northern Nigeria
C) Iran and northern Nigeria
D) Iran only
E) northern Nigeria only

38. Which of the following political parties has a history of domination by one man?

A) PRI in Mexico
B) Labour Party in Britain
C) People's Democratic Party in Nigeria
D) United Russia Party in Russia
E) Executives of Construction Party in Iran

39. Which of the following countries has had the MOST pronounced democratization movement in recent years?

A) Russia
B) Mexico
C) China
D) Nigeria
E) Iran

40. In recent years the most significant problems that the Chinese government has had in regard to ethnic minorities have been with

A) Tatars and Mongols
B) Uyghurs and Tibetans
C) Mongols and Uyghurs
D) Tibetans and Mongols
E) Tatars and Tibetans

41. Which of the following countries has created NO political structure for judicial review?

A) Nigeria and Iran
B) China and Russia
C) Mexico and Nigeria
D) Britain and Mexico
E) China and Britain

42. Which of the following is an accurate description of population issues in Russia?

(A) Currently there is a significant imbalance between the number of men and women.
(B) Currently, the population is growing more rapidly than the economy can comfortably accommodate.
(C) Life expectancy is significantly higher for men than for women.
(D) In recent years, Russia has suffered a dramatic drop in its overall population.
(E) Death rates in Russia are declining significantly, but so are birth rates.

43. Which of the following elected officials is limited by the country's constitution to only one term of office?

A) the Russian president
B) the British prime minister
C) the Nigerian president
D) the Mexican president
E) the Iranian president

44. Which of the following is the BEST description of the political system of Iran?

A) It is a unitary state, but has taken significant steps toward devolution.
B) It is a unitary state, with few signs of real authority granted to local officials.
C) It is a federalist state in name, but in reality is a unitary state.
D) It is a federalist state in name and in reality.
E) It is a confederal state, with little power granted to the central government.

45. Which of the following political parties have formed a one-party system that controlled a government in recent years?

A) PRI in Mexico and CCP in China
B) People's Democratic Party in Nigeria and CCP in China
C) PRI in Mexico and Executives of Construction in Iran
D) Communist Party in the Soviet Union and Labour Party in Britain
E) PAN in Mexico and Conservative Party in Britain

46. The gap in literacy rates between men and women is highest in

A) China and Iran
B) China and Russia
C) Iran and Nigeria
D) Nigeria and Mexico
E) Mexico and Russia

47. If a country has a low level of social capital, a likely result is that it will be

A) difficult to maintain economic health
B) more inclined to develop a conflictual political culture
C) difficult to establish reliable trade networks with other countries
D) more inclined toward authoritarian government
E) a parliamentary, rather than a presidential, system

48. Which of the following government officials would be most likely to have a considerable amount of discretionary power in political policymaking?

A) a cabinet member in a communist state
B) a patronage appointee in an authoritarian regime
C) a bureaucrat in a democratic regime
D) a technocrat
E) a military officer in a democratic regime

49. Which of the following national-level institutions in Iran has representatives that are directly elected by the people?

A) Assembly of Religious Experts and Guardian Council
B) Expediency Council and *Majles*
C) Guardian Council and *Majles*
D) Expediency Council and Guardian Council
E) Assembly of Religious Experts and *Majles*

50. The process of economic liberalization generally involves all of the following EXCEPT:

A) privatization
B) marketization
C) limiting the power of the state in the economy
D) lifting of quotas set by the government
E) centralized planning

51. The British House of Commons and the Russian Duma both have the power to

A) impeach the president
B) call for new elections to their respective upper houses
C) pass legislation
D) select a vice president
E) appoint judges to Constitutional Courts

52. Which of the following best explains why two parties have usually dominated the British House of Commons, even though several candidates compete in most races for seats in Commons?

A) Very often more than two candidates from the same party compete against one another.
B) Run-off elections almost always leave candidates from the major parties to compete in the second round.
C) No third party has ever garnered enough widespread support to gain seats in Commons.
D) Most challengers for seats in Commons are not affiliated with political parties.
E) The first-past-the-post (plurality) voting system strongly favors victory for large parties with widespread appeal.

53. The Russian tradition of statism has meant that citizens generally

A) mistrust the government
B) function more as subjects than as participants
C) believe in egalitarianism
D) experience conflict between Slavic and western values
E) support broad political and economic reforms

54. Which Russian tradition most directly opposes the development of a civil society in Russia today?

A) glasnost
B) statism
C) collectivization
D) conflict between Slavophiles and Westernizers
E) shock therapy

55. Which of the following is an incorrect match?

A) Nigeria/unitary state
B Britain/common law
C) Mexico/federal state
D) Mexico/code law
E) China/code law

Section II – Free-Response Questions
Time – 1 hour and 40 minutes
50% of the Exam

Short-Answer Concepts: 5 questions (30 minutes)

1. Define social cleavage. Describe one example of how a social cleavage has impacted the policy-making process in Russia. Describe one example of how a social cleavage has impacted the policy-making process in Mexico.

2. Describe one major difference between reform and revolution as types of change. Discuss one reform that has brought about political change in Great Britain since 1990. Discuss one economic change that revolution brought about in China during the 20th century.

3. Define civil society. Describe one indication that civil society is alive and well in Iran today. Describe one indication that civil society is undeveloped in Russia today.

4. Explain the difference between a state and a nation. Explain two problems that this difference has caused for Nigeria's political system.

5. Describe the main purpose of constitutional courts, and identify two countries in the AP Comparative Government and Politics course that have a constitutional court.

Conceptual Analysis Question (30 minutes)

6. Bureaucracies are a vital part of government in most countries.

(a) Describe two common characteristics of political bureaucracies.

(b) Explain one reason why bureaucrats often are a source of stability in a democratic regime.

(c) Explain two reasons why bureaucrats in authoritarian regimes usually do not have as much power as bureaucrats in democratic regimes do.

Country-Context Questions (40 minutes)

7. China and Russia have both experienced economic liberalization.

(a) Define economic liberalization.

(b) Describe two economic liberalization policies pursued in China since 1979.
(c) Describe two economic liberalization policies pursued in Russia since 1991.
(d) Compare one consequence of economic liberalization on China's political system with one consequence of economic liberalization on Russia's political system.

8. The representation of women in national parliaments varies from one country to another.

(a) Describe the level of women's participation in Iran's lower legislative house. Describe the level of women's participation in Mexico's lower legislative house.

(b) Explain one reason for the difference in the level of women's participation in Iran's lower legislative house and the level of women's participation in Mexico's lower legislative house.

(c) Describe one impact that Iran's level of women's participation in the lower legislative house might have on policy.

(d) Describe one impact that Mexico's level of women's participation in the lower legislative house might have on policy.

COMPARATIVE EXECUTIVES

"H.O.S." = Head of State, "H.O.G." = Head of Government

Country	Title(s)	How Chosen	Terms in Office	Powers
United Kingdom	Monarch (H.O.S)	Hereditary (Royal succession is approved by Parliament)	Life	Minimal: as symbolic H.O.S., she "approves" the election of the majority party and asks its leader (the future Prime Minister) to form "her Majesty's Government
	Prime Minister (H.O.G.)	Elected by a majority of the House of Commons	Five years; less, if a vote of "no confidence" requires new elections	
Russia	President (H.O.S.)	Elected by popular majority in a national election (a runoff election is required if no candidate wins over 50% of the vote)	Six years: with a consecutive two-term limit	Initiates domestic and foreign policies: submits legislation to the Duma for approval; may call a referendum
	Prime Minister (H.O.G.)	Appointed by President; must be approved by the Duma	Subject to removal by either the president or a vote of no confidence by the Duma	Manages legislation in the Duma; may initiate legislation; oversees cabinet and government departments
China	President and Vice President (H.O.S)	Top leaders of the Chinese Communist Party (CCP); formally elected by the National People's Congress	Five years, with a two term limit	All foreign and domestic policy
	Prime Minister (H.O.G)	Appointed by the President, confirmed by the NPC		Oversees government bureaus and the implementation of policies
Nigeria	President (H.O.S. and (H.O.G.) Vice President	Election by popular vote; a candidate must win a a minimum of 25% of votes in at least 2/3 of Nigeria's 36 states	Four years, with a two-term limit	Directs all foreign and domestic policy decision-making
Mexico	President (H.O.S. and H.O.G)	National popular election; there is no constitutional requirement that a candidate must win a majority of votes to win	Six years (*sexenio*) for one term only	--Foreign and domestic policy --cabinet appointments --appointment, with approval of the Senate, of judges of the the Supreme Court
Iran	Supreme Leader (H.O.S)	Chosen by the Assembly of Religious Experts. Must be a Shi'ite cleric (and thus always a male)	No fixed term. He may be replaced by the Assembly as well; the Assembly has never acted on this power.	Extensive powers include commander in chief of the armed forces, power to declare war; direct appointment of judges, nomination of half (6) of the Guardian Council, appointment of the Expediency Council, and dismissal of the president.
	President (H.O.G)	Popular election in a nationwide vote (all citizens 18 and over) Must be a Shi'ite Muslim.	four years, with a two-term limit	Manages the budget and economic policies, signs treaties, proposes legislation to the *Majles*. Appoints vice-presidents (no fixed number), cabinet officers, and most government officials, including governors

COMPARATIVE BUREAUCRACIES

The executive branch carries out ("executes") national policies and laws. Governments employ people as civil servants to do this work. This group is known collectively as the nation's bureaucracy.

UNITED KINGDOM

The party in power (known as "Her Majesty's Government") is led by the Prime Minister, who chooses a Cabinet, usually from among the Members of Parliament. Each Cabinet member is the head of an existing bureaucracy, and develops legislation in consultation its civil servants. Government employees in the United Kingdom are generally regarded as professionally trained and politically neutral.

RUSSIA

Since 1991 the Russian bureaucracy has remained large, as it was under the former Soviet regime. Civil servants can have great powers, especially when the Russian President decides to expand an agency or even to create a new one to carry out policies based on personal preferences. In practice, the Russian state bureaucracy has little separation or political independence from the President.

CHINA

An appointed State Council of appointed ministers directs the bureaucracy, which is very large (40 million is one estimate) and has extensive powers to manage all aspects of political, economic, and social life in China. Civil servants (called cadres) are often members of the Communist Party, but this is not a requirement. Recently the Chinese government has embarked on a program to reduce the overall size of the bureaucracy by eliminating many positions, especially at the local level.

NIGERIA

Nigeria's bureaucracy has grown in size for many years. Civil service positions are frequently treated as rewards and political favors, and used for personal benefit (in Nigeria this type of patron-client network is called prebendalism); in practice, the system diminishes the professionalism and political neutrality of Nigerian civil servants, and produces widespread corruption

MEXICO

Mexican Presidents appoint large numbers of upper-level civil servants as part of their party's patron-client system. Lower-level bureaucrats are unionized, and their positions are protected by civil service laws. The Mexican para-statal system also employs over a million Mexicans as well.

IRAN

Iran's bureaucracy is large, and has increased in size since the Revolution. Most senior positions are held by Shi'ite clerics, and policy decisions are consistently reviewed to make sure they are compatible with Islamic law.

(Charts compiled by Gray Pederson)

COMPARATIVE LEGISLATURES

UPPER HOUSE	LOWER HOUSE

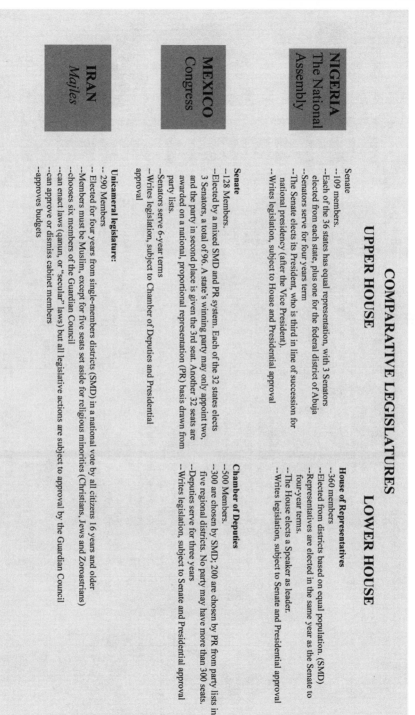

NIGERIA
The National
Assembly

Senate
--109 members.
--Each of the 36 states has equal representation, with 3 Senators elected from each state, plus one for the federal district of Abuja
--Senators serve for four years term
--The Senate elects its President, who is third in line of succession for national presidency (after the Vice President).
--Writes legislation, subject to House and Presidential approval

House of Representatives
--360 members
--Elected from districts based on equal population. (SMD)
--Representatives are elected in the same year as the Senate to four-year terms.
--The House elects a Speaker as leader.
--Writes legislation, subject to Senate and Presidential approval

MEXICO
Congress

Senate
--128 Members.
--Elected by a mixed SMD and PR system. Each of the 32 states elects 3 Senators, a total of 96. A state's winning party may only appoint two, and the party in second place is given the 3rd seat. Another 32 seats are awarded on a national, proportional representation (PR) basis drawn from party lists.
--Senators serve 6-year terms
--Writes legislation, subject to Chamber of Deputies and Presidential approval

Chamber of Deputies
--500 Members.
--300 are chosen by SMD; 200 are chosen by PR from party lists in five regional districts. No party may have more than 300 seats.
--Deputies serve for three years
--Writes legislation, subject to Senate and Presidential approval

IRAN
Majles

Unicameral legislature:
-- 290 Members
-- Elected for four years from single-members districts (SMD) in a national vote by all citizens 16 years and older
--Members must be Muslim, except for five seats set aside for religious minorities (Christians, Jews and Zoroastrians)
--chooses six members of the Guardian Council
--can enact laws (qanun, or "secular" laws) but all legislative actions are subject to approval by the Guardian Council
--can approve or dismiss cabinet members
--approves budgets

COMPARATIVE LEGISLATURES

Country	Upper House	Lower House
	(In a bicameral system, this term usually designates the chamber in which members are chosen by a *less directly representative* method. Also, the upper house often provides regional representation.)	(In a bicameral system, this term usually designates the chamber in which members are chosen by a *more representative* method.)
UNITED KINGDOM Parliament	**House of Lords** Approximately 720 members (this number can vary) —92 Hereditary Peers: hold their seats through inheritance —622 Life Lords: awarded seats by HM Government for an individual's lifetime only —Lords Spiritual: 26 Bishops of the Church of England —Lords has no power to initiate or veto legislation, but can delay bills originating in the House of Commons.	**House of Commons** —650 members (number can vary) ("MPs" elected in single-member-districts (SMD) —Hold office up to five years, unless an election is called sooner. —The majority party (or coalition) chooses its leading MP to be the Prime Minister (PM); PM chooses others MPs to be members of the Cabinet. —Speaker of the House presides, but does not vote unless there is a tie. —The Prime Minister and Cabinet initiate legislation, which must be approved by a majority of the House. The lack of majority on an important vote (called a "vote of no confidence") may result in the PM calling for a new election.
RUSSIA Federal Assembly	**Federation Council** —166 Seats, appointed by the executives and heads of legislatures in 83 sub-governments (republics, oblasts, and krais); each unit appoints two members —Members serve four year terms, but changes in term of office may occur because of changes in governorships —The Council may not propose legislation, but its approval is required for measures started by the Duma to become law. The Council may veto or delay passage of a bill.	**Duma** —450 seats, elected on a nationwide basis by proportional representation (PR). A party must receive 7% of the national vote to qualify for a seat. —The Duma may override, with a 2/3 vote, a veto by the Federation Council. —Russia's Prime Minister, who is appointed by the President, must be confirmed by a majority vote of the Duma. If, after three votes, the Duma does not approve the appointment, the President may call for the election of a new Duma. —Members elected for four-year terms, unless the President calls an election sooner.
CHINA National People's Congress	**The National People's Congress is a unicameral body.** -According to the 1982 Constitution, the Congress is highest political authority in the state. -Formal powers include approval of legislation and the appointment of the President, Vice-President, and Premier. -The Congress is composed of approximately 3,000 members who serve for five-year terms. -Election of members takes place through a multi-step process in which candidates run in competitive elections at the local level, then move up through further elections at city, county and provincial congresses. Except at the lowest level, candidates must be approved by the Communist Party. -The Congress meets for two-week sessions once a year. During the rest of the year the business of the Congress is carried on by the Standing Committee -Members of the Congress may carry on significant debate on some issues, but most policy decisions are made by the President and other executives, along with leaders of the Communist Party. Many observers, both inside and outside of China, believe the Congress has limited power to affect policy.	

ANSWER KEY
FOR
AP COMPARATIVE GOVERNMENT AND
POLITICS: AN ESSENTIAL COURSEBOOK
8TH EDITION

Ethel Wood

WoodYard Publications